Puebloan Societies

School for Advanced Research
Advanced Seminar Series
Michael F. Brown
General Editor

Since 1970 the School for Advanced Research (formerly the School of American Research) and SAR Press have published over one hundred volumes in the Advanced Seminar series. These volumes arise from seminars held on SAR's Santa Fe campus that bring together small groups of experts to explore a single issue. Participants assess recent innovations in theory and methods, appraise ongoing research, and share data relevant to problems of significance in anthropology and related disciplines. The resulting volumes reflect SAR's commitment to the development of new ideas and to scholarship of the highest caliber. The complete Advanced Seminar series can be found at www.sarweb.org.

Also available in the School for Advanced Research Advanced Seminar Series:

New Geospatial Approaches to the Anthropological Sciences edited by Robert L. Anemone and Glenn C. Conroy

Seduced and Betrayed: Exposing the Contemporary Microfinance Phenomenon edited by Milford Bateman and Kate Maclean

Fat Planet: Obesity, Culture, and Symbolic Body Capital edited by Eileen P. Anderson-Fye and Alexandra Brewis

Costly and Cute: Helpless Infants and Human Evolution edited by Wenda R. Trevathan and Karen R. Rosenberg

Why Forage?: Hunters and Gatherers in the Twenty-First Century edited by Brian F. Codding and Karen L. Kramer

Muslim Youth and the 9/11 Generation edited by Adeline Masquelier and Benjamin F. Soares

Childhood: Origins, Evolution, and Implications edited by Alyssa N. Crittenden and Courtney L. Meehan

Artisans and Advocacy in the Global Market: Walking the Heart Path edited by Jeanne Simonelli, Katherine O'Donnell, and June Nash

Disturbing Bodies: Perspectives on Forensic Anthropology edited by Rosemary A. Joyce and Zoë Crossland

Linking the Histories of Slavery: North America and Its Borderlands edited by Bonnie Martin and James F. Brooks

For additional titles in the School for Advanced Research Advanced Seminar Series, please visit unmpress.com.

Puebloan Societies

HOMOLOGY AND HETEROGENEITY IN TIME AND SPACE

Edited by Peter M. Whiteley

SCHOOL FOR ADVANCED RESEARCH PRESS • SANTA FE

UNIVERSITY OF NEW MEXICO PRESS • ALBUQUERQUE

© 2018 by the School for Advanced Research
All rights reserved. Published 2018
Printed in the United States of America

Library of Congress Cataloging-in-Publication Data
Names: Whiteley, Peter M., editor.
Title: Puebloan societies: homology and
    heterogeneity in time and space / edited by
    Peter M. Whiteley.
Description: Santa Fe: School for Advanced Research
    Press; Albuquerque: University of New Mexico
    Press, [2018] | Series: School for Advanced
    Research advanced seminar series |
    Includes bibliographical references and index.
Identifiers: LCCN 2018008530 (print) |
    LCCN 2018028010 (e-book) |
    ISBN 9780826360120 (e-book) |
    ISBN 9780826360113 (pbk.; alk. paper)
Subjects: LCSH: Pueblo Indians—Social life and
    customs. | Pueblo Indians—History. |
    Indians of North America—Southwest,
    New—Antiquities.
Classification: LCC E99.P9 (e-book) |
    LCC E99.P9 P94 2018 (print) |
    DDC 978.9004/974—dc23
LC record available at https://lccn.loc.gov/2018008530

Cover illustration: *Basket Dance,* by Quah Ah
(Tonita Peña, 1893–1949), San Ildefonso Pueblo.
North American Ethnographic Collection,
Division of Anthropology, American Museum of
Natural History. Catalog no. 50.2/4147. Donated by
Amelia E. White, 1937.
Composed in Minion Pro

To the memory of Alfonso Ortiz, Oku p'in

It is hardly necessary to make a general brief for the kind of interdependence that prevails in our Southwest, where extant cultures are historically related to cultures under archaeological research. There is no dispute that the living culture has light to throw upon the buried one. Theoretically no dispute; practically we are constantly surprised to find Southwestern archaeologists, even seasoned students, unfamiliar with the ethnological record and having to leave to the ethnologist interpretation of their data: plums for the ethnologist but a loss to the [wo]man who has been doing the work.

—Elsie Clews Parsons, "Relations between Ethnology
and Archaeology in the Southwest" (1940)

Ethnographic analogy, the use of comparative data from anthropology to inform reconstructions of past human societies, has a troubled history. Archaeologists often express concern about, or outright reject, the practice— and sometimes do so in problematically general terms. This is odd, as . . . the use of comparative data in archaeology is the same pattern of reasoning as the "comparative method" in biology, which is a well-developed and robust set of inferences which play a central role in discovering the biological past.

—Adrian Currie, "Ethnographic Analogy, the Comparative Method,
and Archaeological Special Pleading" (2016)

LIST OF ILLUSTRATIONS   ix

PREFACE   xi

CHAPTER ONE Introduction: Homology and Heterogeneity
  in Puebloan Social History   1
    Peter M. Whiteley

CHAPTER TWO *Ma:tu'in*: The Bridge between Kinship and
  "Clan" in the Tewa Pueblos of New Mexico   25
    Richard I. Ford

CHAPTER THREE The Historical Anthropology of Tewa
  Social Organization   51
    Scott G. Ortman

CHAPTER FOUR Taos Social History: A Rhizomatic Account   75
    Severin M. Fowles

CHAPTER FIVE From Keresan Bridge to Tewa Flyover:
  New Clues about Pueblo Social Formations   103
    Peter M. Whiteley

CHAPTER SIX The Historical Linguistics of Kin-Term
  Skewing in Puebloan Languages   133
    Jane H. Hill

CHAPTER SEVEN Archaeological Expressions of Ancestral
  Hopi Social Organization   157
    Kelley Hays-Gilpin and Dennis Gilpin

CHAPTER EIGHT A Diachronic Perspective on Household
  and Lineage Structure in a Western Pueblo Society   175
    Triloki Nath Pandey

CHAPTER NINE An Archaeological Perspective on Zuni
  Social History   187
    Barbara J. Mills and T. J. Ferguson

CHAPTER TEN From Mission to Mesa: Reconstructing Pueblo
   Social Networks during the Pueblo Revolt Period   207
      Robert W. Preucel and Joseph R. Aguilar

CHAPTER ELEVEN Dimensions and Dynamics of Pre-Hispanic Pueblo
   Organization and Authority: The Chaco Canyon Conundrum   237
      Stephen Plog

CHAPTER TWELVE Afterword: Reimagining Archaeology
   as Anthropology   261
      John A. Ware

NOTATIONS AND GLOSSARY   283
REFERENCES   291
CONTRIBUTORS   333
INDEX   335

FIGURES

1.1 Modern Eastern and Western Pueblos and their Native neighbors   5

2.1 Range of *Pinus edulis* and *Quercus gambelii* in the Greater Southwest   43

3.1 Waterflow Panel, northwestern New Mexico   59

3.2 Cuyamungue (LA38), a Tewa village   61

3.3 Equinox sunrise as viewed from Jackson's Castle   62

3.4 Virtual reconstruction of Goodman Point Pueblo   64

3.5 Distribution of corn-grinding complex sizes in Mesa Verde region unit pueblos   67

3.6 Scatterplot of the lengths and widths of individual complete manos   68

3.7 Tower at Painted Hand Pueblo   69

4.1 Schematic overview of the socioceremonial organization of Taos Pueblo   78

4.2 Taos kinship terminology during the 1930s   85

4.3 Evidence of early Plains–Pueblo networks at T'aitöna   97

4.4 Mixed ceramic traditions of the Developmental Period in Taos   98

5.1 Pueblo cultures and languages and their Native neighbors   108

5.2 Six basic kinship terminologies   111

5.3 Hopi kinship terminology   115

7.1 Map of Hopi and Hopi-ancestral sites   161

9.1 Greater Zuni or Cibola area   189

10.1 Tunyo (San Ildefonso mesa)   210

10.2 Northern Rio Grande settlement system   211

10.3 Old San Felipe Pueblo Mission church   214

10.4 Kotyiti, an ancestral Cochiti mesa village   215

10.5 Northern Rio Grande population movements during the Revolt Period   229

11.1 Geographic locations of some of the major great houses in Chaco Canyon   238

11.2 Plan view of Pueblo Bonito   240

11.3   Modeled distributions of AMS ^{14}C dates on Pueblo Bonito
       macaws   257

TABLES

2.1   Hodge's "Table Showing the Distribution of Pueblo Clans"   30
4.1   Languages Spoken by the Ancestors of the Taos Pueblo Community,
       as Related to Stevenson   91
5.1   Western versus Eastern Pueblo Social Organization   109
5.2   Exemplary Primordial Equations in N. J. Allen's Tetradic Model   116
5.3   Tewa *kiyu/ki'i*   122
5.4   Tewa *ka'je*   123
5.5   Tewa *ko'o*   123
5.6   Tewa *meme*   124
5.7   Tewa *tut'un/tu'unu/t'ono/tunu*   125
5.8   Tewa *tata* (*tada, tara*)   125
6.1   Serrano Kin-Terms   140
6.2   Hopi Kin-Terms   142
6.3   Towa Kin-Terms (Generations +1, 0, -1)   144
6.4   Proto-Kiowa-Tanoan "Woman's Brother's Son, Grandchild"   145
6.5   Zuni Kin-Terms, Blood Orientation (Generations +1, 0, -1)   146
6.6   Zuni Kin-Terms, Clan Orientation (Generations +1, 0, -1)   147
6.7   Acoma (Western Keresan) Kin-Terms   150
6.8   Laguna (Western Keresan) Kin-Terms   151
10.1   Rio Grande Mesa Village Room Counts, Population Estimates,
       and Date Ranges   212

This volume presents results of the School for Advanced Research Advanced Seminar "Puebloan Societies: New Perspectives across the Subfields," held in October 2015. The title alluded to two classic predecessors, "New Perspectives on the Pueblos," led by Alfonso Ortiz (1972), and "Reconstructing Prehistoric Pueblo Societies," led by William Longacre (1970). The immediate inspiration was another SAR volume, John Ware's *A Pueblo Social History* (2014), which has importantly reconnected Southwestern archaeology and ethnology. Seminar participants agreed it was high time to reengage some central questions on Pueblo social formations from deep history into the recent past, throughout the northern Southwest. For reasons that are neither sound nor valid scientifically, explanations in Puebloan anthropology have often been disjoint, especially between archaeology and ethnology, almost as if they occupy separate epistemological universes. Recent disaggregation of anthropological subfields in graduate programs and research practices explains this in part, although the divergence arose earlier and is more encompassing, as the volume epigraphs by Elsie Clews Parsons and Adrian Currie suggest.

While addressing a discrete cultural region, our inquiry is germane to central questions in anthropology, which rest on meaningful interconnections among the subdisciplines. Anthropology's strength lies in its unitary capacity to explain human social evolution and variation, via targeted foci on well-defined phenomena. Since the late nineteenth century, Puebloan societies, those of long ago and those of the present, have been both exemplars and explananda during all theoretical phases and paradigm shifts in anthropology. As the discipline begins to emerge from its postmodern slumber, reengagement with more rigorous analytical approaches offers much promise for enhanced explanation.

We here address Puebloan societies from comparative and specific perspectives, principally via archaeology and ethnology, but attendant also to linguistics and bioarchaeology, with the aim to reengage the subfields in analytical dialogue. Disjunction over the last few decades, we believe, is shortsighted. The problems and pitfalls of "ethnographic analogy" have been overstated, resulting in underinformed hypotheses that too often restrict rather than advance scientific explanation. Notwithstanding extensive changes—gradualist and punctuated, internally driven and externally imposed, environmental and sociological—there are palpable continuities in material practice, architecture, economy, and ritual symbolism between the Ancestral and modern Pueblos; the latter are better seen not as ethnographic analogies but as *ethnological homologies* that descend, with modification, from the former. The continuities extend also, this volume argues, to Pueblo social organization, though the seminar as a group diverged somewhat on how to read them, and the causes and consequences of their changing distributions in time and space. And as well as long-term homologies in sociocultural forms, there are substantive heterogeneities that represent serial and/or cumulative events and processes of ethnogenesis and multiple, sometimes intersecting lines of descent. These differences, as well as the similarities, require explaining: this is the task we set collectively for ourselves. Our divergent perspectives, as well as some clear convergences, make our volume's total trajectory particularly vibrant: while governed by thematic coherence, we do not seek uniformitarian consensus.

Accounting for patterns of similarity, difference, transformation, and continuity entails systematic comparison in time and space—culturally and regionally, specifically and generally. That requires the explanatory capabilities of all anthropological subfields, each with its own analytical strengths. These include kinship, ritual, and social organization from ethnology; site formation and succession and networks of connection over time from archaeology and ethnohistory; cross-language patterns and processes from linguistic anthropology; and demographic and genetic structures from biological anthropology. (Only intermittent allusions remain to the last, as its principal seminar representatives, John Crandall and Debra Martin, chose to publish their research elsewhere.) The seminar was one of the liveliest exchanges among a diverse array of scholars that I have experienced. It touched both on the deeply layered history of anthropological ideas (thanks especially to Triloki Pandey's extraordinary interventions) and on fine-grained empirical detail of Puebloan cases and sites, the specialties of individual participants. But the continuity and discontinuity of Ancestral and recent Pueblo social formations remained both the anchor and the guiding theme of all our conversations.

To what extent we have succeeded in casting new light will be judged by the reader, but the common sentiment among the seminar's participants was that the effort was very worthwhile, as well as deeply enjoyable. This was in no small part thanks to the support and hospitality of the School for Advanced Research. I would like especially to thank Michael Brown, Nicole Taylor, Cynthia Geoghegan, David Stuart, Sarah Soliz, and the late Douglas Schwartz for their multiple and varied contributions during, before, and after the seminar. My involvement with Puebloan societies goes back to the beginning of my work as a Southwestern anthropologist, which could not even have been imaginable without the guidance, influence, and encouragement of Alfonso Ortiz. As the volume's dedication (reproducing a collective sentiment voiced at the outset of seminar discussion) attests, Alfonso profoundly influenced the lives and ideas of many seminar participants in similar ways. John Ware's insights on Pueblo social history, his friendship, and his comprehensive engagement in this project have been consistently invaluable—even when we have disagreed! For support at the American Museum of Natural History, I would particularly like to thank Anthropology Chair Laurel Kendall, Provost Michael Novacek, Ward Wheeler (Invertebrate Zoology and Computational Sciences), and past and present Anthropology Division artists Jennifer Steffey and Kayla Younkin. The National Science Foundation under Program Officer Deborah Winslow supported earlier work (with colleague Ward Wheeler) on Crow-Omaha kinship systems that proved foundational to the seminar: specifically "Explaining Crow-Omaha Kinship Structures with Anthro-Informatics" (BCS-0925978) and "Workshop on Transitions in Human Social Organization" (BCS-0938505), the latter of which was presented as an Amerind Foundation Advanced Seminar, thanks also to John Ware's generous support.

Leigh Kuwanwisiwma (the Hopi Tribe), Thomas Trautmann (University of Michigan), Maurice Godelier (EHESS), Dwight Read (UCLA), David Kronenfeld (UC, Riverside), and Nick Allen (University of Oxford) have each influenced my own thinking on Pueblo kinship and social organization in more ways than they know. Although now ancient history, my nascent interest in social structure was forged in the early 1970s crucible of Cambridge anthropology, under the fortunate, often competing influence of Meyer Fortes, Jack Goody, and Edmund Leach; it is hard to imagine a sharper group of elders. That great good fortune expanded at the University of New Mexico through guidance by Harry Basehart. And, transcending all other influences, Jane Campbell continues to put up with me, for reasons I do not quite understand.

Peter M. Whiteley
American Museum of Natural History

CHAPTER ONE

Introduction

Homology and Heterogeneity in Puebloan Social History

PETER M. WHITELEY

Framing

This volume addresses core questions about Pueblo sociocultural formations of the past and present. Its overarching goal is to elucidate key patterns, revealed in specific times, places, and ethnolinguistic groups, via a series of focused inquiries, from deep history into the recent past. The volume results from an SAR Advanced Seminar addressing long-term continuities and discontinuities among Puebloan societies. We seek to identify points of genuine comparability over the long term, from Basketmaker times forward, as well as definitive distinctions. Drawing upon the insights of ethnology, archaeology, linguistics, and a little bioarchaeology, our collective aim is for a new benchmark of understanding. We examine structures of social history and social practice, including kinship groups, ritual sodalities, architectural forms, economic exchange, environmental adaptation, and political order, and their patterns of transmission over time and space. We suggest long-term persistences, as well as systemic differences: Pueblo social formations encode both homologies and heterogeneities. The result is a cumulative window upon how major Pueblo societies came to be and how they have transformed over time. Some chapters are more explicitly comparative and others attend to particular societies, sites, or time periods, but all speak to an overriding concern with the shapes and, broadly speaking, the "evolution" of Pueblo social forms. All told, the volume represents an interdisciplinary—or, at least, *intersubdisciplinary*—conjunction, bringing archaeology, ethnology, and linguistic anthropology into mutual dialogue.

The core analytical questions are vital to a genuinely comparative anthropology. What is a society? What are its building blocks, its moving parts? How are people woven together, e.g., by kinship and marriage, across households or other constituent elements? How does the whole operate collectively? What is its economy, its mode of adaptation to a particular ecosystem? Its principles of leadership, its governance, its division of labor? How does it produce and reproduce itself via structured relationships of gender and generation? What are its religious beliefs, ritual practices, worldview? What about boundaries, intersections, networks? How does a social formation perpetuate itself and arrange its relations—of both peace and war—with neighbors? Alternatively, how does it mutate, absorb, or amalgamate with others to produce novel rearrangements? And when "things fall apart," how does it respond—e.g., via migration and/or regrouping and reconstitution? Moreover, how does society imagine itself as the product of one history or several: how did present patterns come into being, and in what manners and measures do they represent a persistence of old forms and/or innovation, accretion, or change? For the analyst, these questions give rise to others, including how to calibrate relationships among successive societies over time or identify the most meaningful links between past and present—say, between the archaeological residue of long ago and living descendant communities.

Such questions used to be the staple diet of anthropology, binding together different strands among its subdisciplines with a common overall purpose. Willful abandonment of this epistemological core over the last few decades— often, it seems, for parts unknown and discourses tendentious—has enfeebled both scientific argument and anthropology's raison d'être as an objective investigation of the human condition. This volume seeks to demonstrate the value of substantive reengagement among ethnology, archaeology, and linguistics— which have too long languished in discrete silos—and to reconnect and reenergize diverse approaches to Puebloan sociocultural formations. We aim here for an analytical whole greater than the sum of its parts: to adumbrate a new synthesis in this fascinating region of human cultural history, which has provided a living "laboratory" for the development of global anthropology over the last century and a half.

Our purpose involves a deliberate double focus on past and present. Present and recent social formations are in effect the "downstream" result of past events, processes, and configurations. Explaining historical social phenomena is enhanced, we argue, by informed "upstreaming" from known ethnographic realities to structural and processual probabilities in the Puebloan past. But beyond material forms, how can known differences among the living

Pueblos—of language, kinship, polity, and ritual—meaningfully inform interpretations of earlier societies within, broadly speaking, the same overall tradition? How can ethnographic descriptions and oral traditions best enhance
explanations of the long-term archaeological record? And, turning the tele-
scope around, how did known societies such as the Hopi, Taos, Zuni, or Ohkay
Owingeh come to be? In what manners and measures do they descend from
Ancestral Pueblos of the last two thousand years, and how do they differ from
each other and from their own respective pasts, either as a result of precolonial
or colonial dislocations and reformations and/or historic and ongoing relations
with non-Puebloan peoples, both Native and non-Native? Moreover, what are
the explanatory implications of known differences among recent or present
Pueblo social structures? Do systems based, respectively, on matrilineal (the
Western Pueblos) or bilateral (the northern Rio Grande) kinship represent
distinct social formations over the long run, or variant transformations under
colonial rule? What about ritual moieties and sodalities—do these reflect,
oppose, or historically grow out of kinship-based organizations? The authors
of this volume may differ in their responses to these questions, but all believe
it is important to bring upstream and downstream perspectives into dialogue.
Past and present are a two-way street: our aim is to demonstrate how each may
illuminate the other.

Discovering the Pueblos

Puebloan societies have proved a fascination to outsiders ever since Alvar Nuñez
Cabeza de Vaca and Estevanico heard of fabled kingdoms to the north during
their trek from the Texas gulf coast to Sinaloa in 1536. Estevanico and Marcos
de Nizza's subsequent search for the Seven Cities of Gold ended tragically at
Zuni Kiakima in 1539. But de Nizza's fantastic reports prompted the Coronado
Expedition (1540–1542), resulting in the first ethnographic accounts of the
Pueblos. The newcomers discovered a culturally distinctive region "with storied
apartment-houses nucleated into towns . . . markedly different in their usages,
government, and political order from all the nations we have seen and discovered in these western regions" (Winship 1896, 454).[1] "All these towns," Pedro
de Castañeda reported, "have some rites and customs in common, although
each also has its own distinctive characteristics separate from the others" (Winship 1896, 451).[2] Compared to the Valley of Mexico, Pueblo populations were
small, Castañeda noted, comprising sixty-six to seventy-one towns in total, in

named clusters corresponding with Zuni, Hopi, Acoma, Southern Tiwas, Piros, Rio Grande Keresans, Galisteo Basin Tanos, Pecos, Jemez, Tewas, Taos, and Zia (Winship 1896, 524–25; Barrett 1997; Flint and Flint 2005). Puebloan commonality amid differences and collective distinction from other Native cultures were confirmed by later sixteenth- and early seventeenth-century chroniclers, including Chamuscado, Espejo, Castaño de Sosa, Oñate, Zárate Salmerón, and Benavides (Bandelier 1929–1930, Barrett 2002). Notwithstanding internal differences, the commonality moved Castañeda to infer a unified Pueblo migration to the Four Corners region "from that part of Greater India, the coast of which lies to the west of this country" (Winship 1896, 525).

The effects of Spanish, Mexican, and American dominion were incontestably considerable, but substantive continuities mark Pueblo societies and cultures from Coronado's time up to the present and stretch back noticeably into the Basketmaker period of Ancestral Pueblo culture (~200 BCE–750 CE). Variations both past and present should not be surprising given the overall linguistic and ecological diversity (fig. 1.1).

The nineteen current principal towns in New Mexico and twelve (the Hopi) in Arizona represent six languages: Tiwa, Tewa, and Towa, of the Kiowa-Tanoan family; Keresan and Zuni, both isolates; and Hopi, a Uto-Aztecan language. Since historic times, the Pueblos have dwelt on the southern Colorado Plateau or in the Rio Grande Valley (with a few cases on the Pecos River and in the Estancia Basin), with ecological distinctions that produced adaptive variations, and geographic distributions with internally variant trading patterns and interethnic relations (Ford 1983). Those adapted to the Rio Grande Valley depended on its relatively abundant water to irrigate their fields, and into the nineteenth century had a greater orientation to the Plains, for bison-hunting, for example, and also in terms of their relations with non-Pueblo Native peoples of several language groups (Kiowas, Utes, Jicarilla and Mescalero Apaches, Navajos, Comanches, et al.). Those near the southeastern edge of the plateau—Acoma, Laguna, Zuni—along upstream tributaries east and west of the Continental Divide (Rio San José, Zuni River)—had reliable water supplies but less capacity for irrigation. In historic times, apart from the other Pueblos, their nearest neighbors were Navajos and, west of the Divide, also Western Apaches and Yavapais. In the western portion of the plateau, upstream on the washes that drain into the Little Colorado River, the Hopi are the classic "dry farmers," dependent on snowmelt, rainfall, and floodwater to raise their crops, and with a greater orientation toward more variegated Great Basin–style foraging practices. Apart

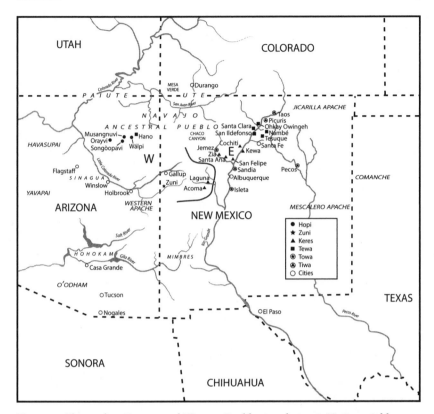

Figure 1.1. The modern Eastern and Western Pueblos in relation to Native neighbors in historic times, and locations of archaeological cultures. Base map drawn by Jennifer Steffey, expanded and revised by Kayla Younkin, AMNH Anthropology Division.

from Zunis and Navajos to the east, the Hopis' northern and western neighbors included primarily foraging or less agricultural Uto-Aztecans (Paiutes, Cheme-huevis, et al.) and Yumans (Havasupais, Walapais, Yavapais, et al.), and to the south and southwest riverine agricultural societies of both Yuman (Mohave, Halchidhoma, Quechan, et al.) and Uto-Aztecan (O'odham et al.) stocks.

Despite such differences in language, ecology, and intertribal relations, the Pueblos have much in common: ritual and cosmology, architecture, settlement patterns, and many features of material culture, as well as a shared sense of identity vis-à-vis their non-Pueblo Native neighbors. While some of this is undoubtedly the result of shared experiences and responses to colonial pres-sures and associated migrations and population intermixture, many common-alities appear to stretch deep into the past.

The Pueblo "Culture-Area" and the
Puebloan Societies Advanced Seminar

In 1540, Castañeda described what is in effect a "Pueblo culture-area" in ways that strikingly presage that concept in early twentieth-century anthropology (a concept that was later replaced by "Southwest" [Harris 1968, 374], but remained anchored to its Puebloan core). Castañeda's Pueblo region was distinguished by

- compact cellular settlements of multistory stone and adobe houses configured around plazas;
- towns of mostly a few hundred people;
- maize, beans, squash, and cotton horticulture;
- gendered architectural spaces, where women owned the houses and men the kivas;
- a division of labor by gender in house-building and crafts production;[3]
- noncentralized leadership by elders;
- common ritual symbols and ceremonial practices, such as the use of cornmeal and prayer feathers;
- a material culture that included feather robes, cotton blankets, decorated pottery, turquoise, and leather armor.

Coronado arrived roughly five hundred years after the florescence of Chaco and almost five hundred years before the present. That millennium, ca. 1000–2000 CE, brackets most concerns of the present volume, but with lines of inquiry also stretching back into the previous millennium. Both long-term similarities and differences within Puebloan culture from the Pueblo I period (750–950 CE) to the present are palpable, a cultural resilience amid linguistic diversity that contrasts with the situation of almost all other Native North American societies. Those patterns provided the impetus for the SAR Advanced Seminar "Puebloan Societies: New Perspectives across the Subfields" in October 2015, whose results are captured here. We are interested, broadly speaking, in what the great French historian Fernand Braudel referred to as structures of the *longue durée*, the long run: historical patterns that unite present Puebloan cultures with their antecedents at modest Pueblo I villages, Chacoan great houses, sixteenth-century towns at European contact, and seventeenth- to twentieth-century variations under the weight of colonial rule.

The Problematic

Much of Castañeda's description in 1540 resonates for anyone familiar with Pueblo life in the late twentieth or early twenty-first century, as it does for Puebloan archaeology. How to effectively engage two millennia of Puebloan sociocultural formations analytically has challenged successive anthropological paradigms since the discipline's inception in the late nineteenth century. The tendency of Cosmos Mindeleff, Jesse Walter Fewkes, Adolph Bandelier, and other early scholars to seek direct descent of the modern Pueblos via oral traditions and the archaeological record fell out of favor as indigenous oral histories were deemed by influential theorists such as Robert Lowie (1917) to be circular, mythological, or otherwise incommensurable with the objectivist modality coveted by the new science. The early dialogue between ethnography and archaeology deteriorated. Throughout the twentieth century, some scholars, including Florence Hawley Ellis and Edward Dozier, kept a foot in both camps. But a sharp turn away from "ethnographic analogy" by Southwestern archaeologists since the landmark SAR seminars "Reconstructing Prehistoric Pueblo Societies" (see Longacre 1970) and "New Perspectives on the Pueblos" (see Ortiz 1972b) has magnified the analytical estrangement, so that explanations of ethnological or archaeological type became epistemological ships passing in the night, especially after the diversions of postmodernism. In reestablishing that dialogue, we aim to demonstrate that a fuller comprehension must attend to both past and present, to the analytical perspectives of descendant communities, and to all available methodologies that help explain objective sociocultural phenomena.

The immediate catalyst for "Puebloan Societies" was John Ware's *A Pueblo Social History* (2014). Unlike many of his archaeological colleagues, Ware has been continuously concerned with sociocultural theory and Pueblo ethnography. Ware urges archaeologists to attend to nineteenth- and twentieth-century ethnography and to ethnohistory. Both he and I (Whiteley 2015) have argued that many modern Pueblo similarities with Ancestral Pueblo societies do not represent *ethnographic analogies* so much as *ethnological homologies* that descend, with modification, from them. These homologies coexist with substantive heterogeneities: language differences, variant social organization, and shifts in geographical distribution, population density, and settlement scale over time. At some especially epochal moments—for example, the rise and fall of Chaco, major fourteenth-century reorganizations following depopulation of the Colorado Plateau, the seventeenth-century Mission period, and the Pueblo Revolt—striking changes occurred: communities fractured and/or consolidated, population diminished or rose (sometimes markedly), migrations and community intermingling were extensive. Colonial pressures to assimilate were forceful in both the Spanish and Anglo-American periods. A precipitous decline after European colonization saw forty-six pueblos in 1679 (one year before the Pueblo Revolt), with a total population of seventeen thousand—down by perhaps 75 percent since the late sixteenth century—thanks to epidemics, warfare, and other imperial effects such as forced consolidation or *reducción* (Schroeder 1979, 254).[4] In 1900, a total of twenty-six Pueblo towns existed in New Mexico and Arizona, a major decline since the sixteenth century, when there were some 93 to 102 occupied pueblos (Piro, Southern Tiwa, Keresan, Tompiro, Tano, Towa, Tewa, Northern Tiwa) east of the Continental Divide (Barrett 1997, 2) and fourteen (Zuni and Hopi) west of it (Winship 1896, 524). In the seventeenth and eighteenth centuries, equestrian Native raiders and traders (especially Navajo, Apache, and Comanche) provided additional forms of influence, alliance, and exchange, as well as intermittent conflict; over time, most Eastern Pueblos allied themselves in part to the Spanish regime, supplying auxiliaries for anti-insurgent campaigns. Into the American period, waves of Old World diseases such as smallpox, influenza, and measles continued to wreak havoc: Pueblo population reached its likely nadir in the early 1860s, with 9,050 people in twenty-six towns. By the 1930s, population had rebounded, but expropriations of Pueblo lands under the new regime and continuing punitive efforts by both church and state to eliminate Pueblo cultures and languages left their mark (Simmons 1979b, 220–21).

Against this background, any notion that we could expect a complete identity of sociocultural patterns from the present back to the Pueblo I period is a chimera. Still, the evident patterns of sociocultural persistence across time periods and regions demand, we believe, explanatory engagement attentive to salient ethnological homologies.

The Chapters of This Volume

The Advanced Seminar brought together scholars from all four subfields, representing expertise on different regions and time periods from the "ethnographic present" to the Basketmaker period and points in between. Primary foci included Tewa and Northern Tiwa origins and social organization (Richard Ford, Severin Fowles, Scott Ortman), Zuni society archaeologically (Barbara Mills and T. J. Ferguson) and ethnographically (Triloki Pandey), Hopi social systems archaeologically (Kelley Hays-Gilpin and Dennis Gilpin), Hopi and Tewa kinship (Peter Whiteley), the linguistics of kinship system differences across and beyond the Pueblos (Jane Hill), post–Pueblo Revolt reorganizations (Robert Preucel and Joseph Aguilar), institutionalized violence in the pre-Hispanic past (John J. Crandall and Debra L. Martin), and Chaco social formations (Stephen Plog). Our biological anthropologists, Crandall and Martin, elected to pursue the ideas of their paper, "When Spider Woman Remade the World from War and Bone: An Interpretive Bioarchaeology of Pueblo Violence," in other contexts. So the present volume reaches across three of anthropology's four subfields. (Bioarchaeological elements persist in some chapters.) Neither seminar nor volume can claim that its coverage is, or could ever be, complete. But our total representation remains reasonably comprehensive across both subfields and the Puebloan world in time and space.

Notwithstanding moderate disagreements in lively seminar discussions, all participants—most significantly for the influence of his work, Ware—agree that the absence of Pueblo ethnography from archaeological explanations represents the warrantless abandonment of a vital methodology. The chapters of this volume revise the papers as presented, in response to the dynamic interchange of the seminar. They are arranged to reflect regional and topical concentrations.

RIO GRANDE TEWA AND NORTHERN TIWA SOCIAL FORMATIONS

Chapter 2, Richard Ford's "*Ma:tu'in*: The Bridge between Kinship and 'Clan' in the Tewa Pueblos of New Mexico," critiques views of Tewa social organization dependent on a "clan" model imported from the Western Pueblo Hopi. Assumed as the *ur* form at one point, the clan model foregrounds unilineal descent as the key principle of all Pueblo social organization. Instead, Ford argues that Tewa *ma:tu'in*, extended bilateral households, are the essential kinship units of Tewa society, variously engaging with ritual moieties (Winter and Summer) and initiated sodalities. Ford's interpretation derives from Tewa ethnosociological analyses learned over his five decades of ethnographic experience with Tewa people. Tewa *ma:tu'in* are a type of bilateral kindred that contrasts markedly with the matrilineal descent groups of the Western Pueblos. Ford clarifies Tewa kinship groups in crucial ways for cross-Pueblo comparisons, urging us to consider the explanatory value of Lévi-Strauss's "house societies" model, insofar as it matches Tewa social forms.

In chapter 3, Scott Ortman examines "The Historical Anthropology of Tewa Social Organization" as a means to disclose the processes of Tewa ethnogenesis: how the Tewa as an ethnolinguistic entity originally came into being, especially via descent and migration from communities at Mesa Verde. Drawing upon Tewa oral histories, Ortman argues for the replacement of kin-group forms of social organization among the pre-Hispanic Tewa by ritual-sodality organization following migration into the northern Rio Grande. Using evidence from archaeology, linguistics, and ethnography, he asserts that oral traditions may be read as encoding historical Tewa social principles, and seeks upstream signs of moieties, sodalities, and households back to Mesa Verde, and to early postmigration Tewa presence in the northern Rio Grande. Ortman's perspective examines processes of transmission and transformation of homologous social elements from pre-Columbian to contemporary Tewa social structures.

Severin Fowles's "Taos Social History: A Rhizomatic Account" (chapter 4) develops a fresh understanding of Taos social organization and emphasizes the value of an ethnogenetic network model rather than a dendritic (tree) model of vertical transmission. Fowles draws especially upon two sources previously little considered by scholars: Taos oral history and the unpublished fieldnotes of Matilda Coxe Stevenson. Standard depictions show Taos's social history as a branchlike growth from the Tanoan tree; instead, Fowles shows that much influence, even a majority of Taos's historical population, came from groups of Apaches incorporated and amalgamated into Taos society. Using Stevenson's notes, Fowles shows that Taos moieties were not epiphenomenal, as often argued, but fundamental. Moreover, he demonstrates (from George Trager's linguistic fieldnotes) a presence of classificatory kinship and infers patrilineal kin groups within Taos social structure (against the received view). Fowles thus emphasizes a complex interweaving of Taos social origins over time and heuristically complicates monolithic notions of social history. There are some obvious contrasts here with Ortman's approach in chapter 2, and some similarities with approaches to Hopi, Zuni, and Rio Grande Tanoan and Keresan social history in chapters 7, 9, and 10.

KINSHIP AND SOCIALITY ALONG, ACROSS,
AND BEYOND THE KERESAN BRIDGE

The next two chapters address the underlying principles of Pueblo social organization via a concentration on kinship, especially kin-terminologies. Kinterms classify individuals into social positions vis-à-vis each other, producing an overall structure of relationships that articulates the formation of social groups. Insofar as kin-terminologies specify principles of grouping — especially via correlated rules regulating descent and marriage — they offer a window upon the organizational architecture of a social system. The received division of Western and Eastern Pueblo social organization opposes systems based on kinship groups to those based on ritual sodalities: in the East, ritual moieties and sodalities take the place of weakly articulating kinship of "Eskimo" type, whereas in the West social organization is geared to strongly articulating kinship of "Crow" type. (See below and the glossary for brief explanations of these terms.)

In "From Keresan Bridge to Tewa Flyover: New Clues about Pueblo Social Formations" (chapter 5), I focus on the West kinship vs. East ritual division, represented by the Crow-matrilineal Hopi and the Eskimo-bilateral Rio Grande Tewa. I contend there are previously undetected commonalities in Hopi and Tewa kinship indicative of an underlying structural dualism of "Iroquois" type. Contravening the formal Crow rules, Hopi marriages show repeated exchanges between paired clan-sets, somewhat like societies with exogamous moieties based on Iroquois kinship. Kinship dualism is detectable in Arizona (Hano) and Rio Grande Tewa kin-terms too, with Hano (a Crow system like that of their Hopi neighbors) representing an older Tewa pattern, in my view. Both kinship theory (notably, N. J. Allen's "tetradic" evolutionary model) and the ethnohistorical record suggest that Eskimo-bilateral kin-terminologies of the Rio Grande were influenced by colonialism, rather than representing a precolonial Tewa form. (Opposing views are argued in chapters 2, 3, and 12.) The ethnographic record shows elements of crossness and lineal skewing in Rio Grande Tewa kin-terms to be clearly present. I thus argue that Hano terminology is more likely to reflect a preexisting Rio Grande pattern brought over to Hopi after the Pueblo Revolt. I conclude that ritual moieties on the Rio Grande probably developed in the colonial period out of an earlier system of exogamous moieties articulated by Iroquois kin structures (cf. Murdock 1949, Fox 1967), and that bilateral kinship patterns only fledged fully after the Pueblo Revolt. If both Hopi and Tewa kinship rest on the same deep-structural Iroquois dualism, the standard East–West division is not so stark after all.

In "The Historical Linguistics of Kin-Term Skewing in Puebloan Languages" (chapter 6), Jane Hill addresses kin-terms from a linguistic perspective, offering a much-needed strict comparison of Pueblo kin-terminologies. Crow-matrilineal kinship (i.e., with "skewing"—see below) has been regarded as an ancient Pueblo form (Eggan 1950). Hill shows there is considerable variation in Crow-type patterns at Hopi, Zuni, Acoma, Laguna, and Jemez. And if Crow skewing was ever present (beyond Jemez) in Rio Grande Tanoan terminologies, it appears to have been historically eliminated or "neutralized," along with correlated marriage rules. Hill also focuses on another common feature of Rio Grande terminologies that equates members of alternate generations terminologically, such that, for example, Ego uses the same kin-term for his/her parent's parent as for his/her child's child. In tetradic theory (see also chapter 5), both patterns—neutralization of key distinctions and presence of intergenerational equations—carry important implications for the evolution of social systems. Moreover, Hill shows that Hopi is the only Uto-Aztecan society with Crow-type kin-terms. This may suggest that the Hopi did not acquire Crow terminology until their ancestors "became Pueblo," so to speak. Hill's analysis affirms the likelihood that there were greater commonalities among Pueblo kinship systems—and thus forms of social organization—in the past.

ARCHAEOLOGY AND ETHNOLOGY OF HOPI
AND ZUNI SOCIAL SYSTEMS

The next three chapters go to the western edge of the modern Pueblo world to examine Hopi and Zuni continuities in archaeological and ethnological time. In chapter 7, Kelley Hays-Gilpin and Dennis Gilpin's "Archaeological Expressions of Ancestral Hopi Social Organization" explains how Hopi ethnogenesis involved a combination of homologous practices inherited over the long term and heterogeneous introductions from diverse in-migrating groups at different junctures. After long neglect (Bernardini [e.g., 2005a] provides the major exception), Hays-Gilpin and Gilpin draw upon Hopi clan migration narratives to examine "Hopification," or how in-migrating groups were successively absorbed into the Hopi ecumene. They address long-term architectural traditions (e.g., multistoried house-blocks, kivas, plazas), ritual paraphernalia, and iconography. Historic Hopi villages were formed from diverse population sources, some with different languages and traditions, during post-Chaco as well as post-Columbian times, who migrated from all directions of the compass into the contemporary Hopi heartland. Exact continuities between some precise ritual-sodality markers (notably Ridge Ruin's "Ancient Magician"), identified in similar detail by independent groups of Hopis (and also Zunis—see chapter 9), argue for substantive homologies between ethnographically known practices and sociocultural antecedents over an eight-hundred-year span. Matrilocal households, migrating clans, kivas, sodalities, and suprahousehold groups all feature as major social elements aggregating and reaggregating to form the modern Hopi community. Hays-Gilpin and Gilpin thus argue for the conceptual value of both homology and heterogeneity in their upstream-downstream lens on Hopi ethnogenesis.

In chapter 8, "A Diachronic Perspective on Household and Lineage Structure in a Western Pueblo Society," Triloki Pandey critiques received models of Zuni social organization driven by overdetermining theory. Pandey shows how matrilocal households, recognized theoretically as primary, alternate with patrilocal groups, depending on types of economic activity. In activities oriented toward animal husbandry, for example, sheep camps, Zuni households are constituted patrilocally. Matrilocal households structured most other economic activity, but that pattern was transformed by systematic decline of agricultural practices through the twentieth century. So the economic underpinnings of Zuni household groups have shifted, notably via transformations due to the market economy, in the cottage industry of silverwork, pottery, and other forms of artisanry. Pandey concludes that, as contrasted with households, Zuni lineages (i.e., matrilineal descent groups) operate ideologically within the Zuni hierarchical system of ritual sodalities, but do not organize everyday activity. In other words, lineages do not form corporate social groups with joint estates in material property (cf. Whiteley 1985, 1986 on Hopi). Pandey also highlights perspectival differences in individual Zuni analyses of their social system (including the patrilocal vs. matrilocal household orientation) that complicate reductive models inherited especially from Eggan's (1950) classic structural-functionalist analysis of Western Pueblo social organization.

Chapter 9, "An Archaeological Perspective on Zuni Social History" by Barbara J. Mills and T. J. Ferguson, reconstructs the evolution of Zuni social organization using a combination of archaeology, ethnography, and oral tradition. Zuni society is unusually complex for its scale of population, interweaving diverse kinship groups, sodalities, residence patterns, and exchange structures.

Mills and Ferguson argue this owes to cumulative in-migration and absorption of multiple groups by an emergent Zuni polity over the course of a millennium. Relying especially on architecture, they examine regional archaeological history through successive phases since Pueblo I to determine "how Zuni society became what it is today." Zuni narratives describe migration by ritual sodalities rather than matrilineal clans (the Hopi case). Informed by Ware (2014), Mills and Ferguson see early-emerging sodalities as providing a network of sociality that knitted diverse kin groups together and was the foundation for later (fifteenth-century) incorporation of the Kachina religion as a tribal sodality. Zuni social history, they observe, represents an "accumulation of social institutions" with substantive heterogeneity and persistent homologies in architecture, ritual, and artifact assemblages.

THE ARCHAEOLOGY OF PUEBLO HISTORY

Chapters 10 and 11 focus on two critical moments of Puebloan history: the Pueblo Revolt and the rise of the Chaco phenomenon. In "From Mission to Mesa: Reconstructing Pueblo Social Networks during the Pueblo Revolt Period" (chapter 10), Robert W. Preucel and Joseph R. Aguilar take a "microhistorical" approach to social networks evidenced by community re-formations and alliance structures after the Pueblo Revolt, especially among Rio Grande Keresans and Tanoans. This epochal moment in Pueblo history rearranged and reconstituted social forms vis-à-vis the reconquest efforts of Don Diego de Vargas (1692–1696). Mesatop refuge villages constructed after the Revolt facilitated the restructuring of Pueblo society within a moral landscape structured by reciprocal relationships of obligation that drew strength from ancestral traditions. The mesa villages stood in counterpoint to the mission villages where the Spanish focused their reconquest efforts, and formed new nodes for alliance networks. Some alliances were encompassing and enduring, others more fleeting and contingent upon perceived needs of resistance to and/or coalition with Spanish forces. War captains were agents of alliance across Pueblos, suggesting an undergirding role of ritual sodalities in interpueblo alliance networks. Architectural evidence of moiety plazas and kivas in the mesa villages suggests a resurgence of primary social patterns against colonially imposed models. Combining archaeology and ethnohistory, Preucel and Aguilar cast new light on post-Revolt processes and networks of Pueblo sociality and their constituent agents and structures.

Stephen Plog's "Dimensions and Dynamics of Pre-Hispanic Pueblo Organization and Authority: The Chaco Canyon Conundrum" (chapter 11) reappraises Chacoan sociopolitical organization and social history, especially in light of recent work demonstrating the early presence of hierarchy and long-distance trade networks. Chaco is the eight-hundred-pound gorilla of Puebloan social history, an apogee of complexity; although far removed in time from the historic Pueblos, its signs refract through many subsequent Pueblo sociocultural elements and structures. Plog argues for a long-established population in the canyon as opposed to a major episode of in-migration. He contends Chaco became "a central node for a broad swath of the Pueblo Southwest . . . having a significant impact on ritual and cosmology over a large area," but disputes the notion of an encompassing "Chaco system" or polity. Architecturally and organizationally, Chacoan great houses were unique, with "no subsequent parallel among the historic Pueblos, East or West." Plog investigates evidence of matrilineal descent (supported by recent mitochondrial DNA research), ritual sodalities, kivas, and dual organization by moieties. He favors a Lévi-Straussian "house" model of Chaco social organization, with social groups probably based on a matrilineal core but including affines and some non-kin. There are clear homologous Pueblo elements in Chacoan sociocultural structures—matriliny, moieties, kivas, "houses," ritual hierarchy, and long-distance trade networks— which evolved and transformed in multiple ways after population reorganizations and social re-formations beginning in the twelfth century.

AFTERWORD: REIMAGINING ARCHAEOLOGY AS ANTHROPOLOGY

John Ware (chapter 12) provides a critical analysis of the overall arc of the volume's chapters. It seems especially appropriate to let him have the "last word," as he both inspired the "Puebloan Societies" SAR seminar and, in the day-to-day to-and-fro in Santa Fe, alternated with me in leading the discussions. Ware's chapter highlights the opposition between kinship and ritual organization, as alternative or historically successive social structures, also a primary theme in his influential *A Pueblo Social History*. The foundations and historical evolution of ritual sodalities and moieties are key questions, especially vis-à-vis descent groups. Ware considers how forces of kinship, religion, ethnicity, and identity refract through the different chapters, noticing how unusual it is in a volume dominated by archaeological and historical studies that kinship should play such a major role. Ware's fine synthesis of the volume's intentions and results calls us to ponder the future of anthropological interpretations of Puebloan homologies and heterogeneities as informed by a synthesis of ethnology, linguistics, archaeology, ethnohistory, and bioarchaeology.

The Historical Background of Anthropological Argument

This book draws on a rich SAR tradition, including the two early Advanced Seminars mentioned previously. "Reconstructing Prehistoric Pueblo Societies" was couched in the deductivist emphasis of Lewis Binford's "new archaeology," which had begun to emerge in the early 1960s. But that seminar too included a significant dialogue between archaeologists and ethnologists, especially Edward Dozier and David Aberle. The archaeologists who tried to model social organization for prehistoric Puebloan sites, notably Gwinn Vivian, depended upon Eggan's (1950) analysis of Pueblo social forms, which was couched in the framework of Radcliffe-Brownian structural-functionalism. Eggan was a prominent "descent theorist," so it is perhaps not surprising that the seminar's contributors altogether omitted alliance theory, by then a major concern in European social anthropology thanks to Claude Lévi-Strauss (1949, 1969). This omission evidently represented a deliberate theoretical decision, as Eggan, still at the height of his influence in North American anthropology, had recently (1964) repudiated an alliance model for Pueblo social organization.

"New Perspectives on the Pueblos" produced a benchmark volume (Ortiz 1972b) that is still turned to by scholars and students nearly half a century later. With the exception of Robin Fox's "Some Unsolved Problems of Pueblo Social Organization," however, it omitted presentations on kinship and social organization specifically because of the ongoing dominance of Eggan's synthesis and Fox's own recent work (1967) on Keresan kinship. But while Ortiz was explicit about the volume's downplaying of that approach, he was also clear that "if there is a center of gravity in social and cultural anthropology it is in the study of kinship and social organization" (xvii).

Kinship studies declined after 1972, especially after Schneider's (1984) critique. There has been something of a renaissance recently (e.g., Jones and Milicic 2011, Godelier 2011, Trautmann and Whiteley 2012c, Sahlins 2013, Read and El Guindi 2016). But with the exception of Bradley Ensor's work (e.g., 2013), John Ware's *A Pueblo Social History* (2014) is the principal exception to the rule that kinship studies have not been much taken up in Puebloan archaeology. Ware's approach has renewed the central role of kinship structures in seeking to understand the foundations of Pueblo society, especially vis-à-vis their distinction from ritual sodalities, and the differential implications of these two social forms for understanding social organization in the past and present. A related issue is that in response to archaeology's critique of Pueblo ethnographic analogy in the 1980s, familiarity with Pueblo ethnography among Southwestern archaeologists diminished. While there may be gestures toward classics by Eggan (1950), Ortiz (1969), and Dozier (1970), other major ethnographic works—by, among others, Ruth Bunzel (1932) on Zuni, Leslie White on the Keresan Pueblos (e.g., 1942), Robert Lowie on Hopi (1929a), Elsie Parsons among all the Pueblos (e.g., 1923, 1929, 1933, 1939), and Florence Hawley Ellis among both Tanoans and Keresans (e.g., Hawley 1950, Ellis 1964)—is now largely unknown, and certainly not discussed in print. Instead, archaeologists still feel compelled to rehearse old concerns about projecting the present into the past, even if their ethnographic knowledge is so slender that the danger is negligible. In short, this background—especially the two landmark SAR volumes that provide the last major comparative treatments of Puebloan social formations over time and space, and Ware's recent book renewing that rigorous comparativism—provides the epistemological foundation for *Puebloan Societies.*

In his preface to *New Perspectives*, Ortiz remarked on four previous benchmarks in Puebloan studies:

1. Elsie Clews Parsons's "monumental" *Pueblo Indian Religion* (1939), which integrated an enormous amount of post-1880s ethnographic data;

2. Fred Eggan's *Social Organization of the Western Pueblos* (1950), the first systematic comparison of Puebloan social systems;

3. Robin Fox's *The Keresan Bridge* (1967), on social organization of Cochiti, highlighting a "Keresan bridge" between Eastern Pueblo ritual patrimoieties and Western Pueblo matrilineal clans;

4. Edward Dozier's survey *The Pueblo Indians of North America* (1970), a state-of-the-art synthesis of archaeological, historical, and ethnographic features.

Eggan's work is one of the most cogent and systematic ethnological surveys of any global region of related societies, and remains important for some themes in this volume. Indeed, the "Puebloan Societies" seminar could not have pursued many of its arguments without Eggan, not least because Ware (2014) significantly relies upon that work. Yet Pandey (chapter 8), citing his own eulogy for Eggan at the University of Chicago, reminds us playfully that *Social Organization* was not founded so much upon Eggan's ethnography as on his a priori theoretical convictions: "That much Eggan himself admits when he says that 'the analysis of the kinship system . . . was developed in part before fieldwork was carried out among the Hopi'" (Eggan 1950, 178).

I have critiqued Eggan's descent-theory approach to Hopi society (Whiteley 1985, 1986, 1988), and suggested that a "house society" model attendant to marriage alliance is more effective, both for the Hopi social system and for inferring systematic patterns in the Ancestral Pueblo past (Whiteley 2008, 2015). Notwithstanding Eggan's (1964) rejection of alliance theory, Lévi-Strauss's major contribution was to restore Lewis Henry Morgan's coordinate emphasis on *marriage practices* with kinship terminologies and descent-reckoning (see, e.g., Trautmann and Whiteley 2012a). Descent—whether unilineal or bilateral—is clearly important for ascertaining how social groups such as Hopi and Zuni matrilineal clans, Tewa *ma:tu'in*, Taos "people groups," or Chacoan "houses" are constituted in Pueblo social formations. However, alliance theory is an indispensable component in the analyst's toolbox to enable understanding of how such groups operate through time, from one generation to the next, to reproduce themselves via systematic exchange patterns and processes (Whiteley 2012).

Kinship and Social Organization: Key Principles

Over recent decades, anthropology has tended to squander its insights, consign rigorous arguments to the scrap heap, and casually celebrate conceptual obsolescence. Kinship is the poster child for this statement. Albeit the *fons et origo* of comparative sociocultural anthropology and its long-term theoretical core (Morgan 1871), kinship has been sidelined, indeed almost erased from our discipline's concerns. Kinship is no longer taught in most anthropology departments, and the old basic training that would make specialists of one kind or another conversant with the general principles of the other subfields has declined. So, to contextualize arguments in the chapters that follow, let me here, in simplified fashion, outline some conceptual principles that may not be as well-known as they once were (see also the glossary and, for further details, Whiteley 2016).

Until its recent decline, kinship was seen as the basic scheme for organizing social life in nonstate societies. Whether it was at a "level of sociocultural integration" (to use Julian Steward's language) of bands, tribes, or chiefdoms—all contested terms, to be sure—kinship relationships were held to provide the "idiom" in which all meaningful social relations were cast. Learning a society's "kinship system" was the first charge to the field ethnographer, without which s/he could not hope to understand its structural forms and dynamic processes. Basic aspects of social production and reproduction—the economy, political leadership, religious organization—were deemed geared to underlying kinship structures. Knowing the particular form a kinship system took was not peripheral but utterly foundational to understanding a social formation.

Kinship comprises four key, interrelated axes: terminology, descent, marriage rules, and postmarital residence. The degree to which these axes are interrelated or independent, and which are "causes" and which "effects," are the subject of more than a century of argument. While there are variations, kinship terminologies comprise six basic types, defined by the ways they group cousins, and named after eponymous cultures where they were classically described: "Eskimo," Iroquois, Hawaiian, Sudanese, Crow, and Omaha. The main types of interest here are Eskimo, Iroquois, and Crow: all three are found among the Pueblos, as described by ethnographers since the late nineteenth century. Most readers are familiar with Eskimo type from their own experience: Ego calls his/her cousins on both mother's and father's sides by the same terms, but distinguishes them from his/her siblings. Iroquois instead groups *parallel* cousins (i.e., those linked to Ego by same-sex relatives) with siblings: the persons Ego calls "siblings" (brother [B] or sister [Z]) are not just nuclear-family siblings, but also Ego's mother's sister's children (MZCh) and father's brother's children (FBCh). The only "cousin" category in an Iroquois system is a *cross*-cousin, i.e., those linked to Ego by opposite-sex relatives: mother's brother's children (MBCh) and father's sister's children (FZCh). Crow terminology is constructed upon this basic pattern of Iroquois "crossness," but "skews" father's side cross-cousins down a matriline: e.g., father's sister's daughter (FZD) is equated with (i.e., has the same kin-term as) father's sister (FZ) and father's sister's daughter's daughter (FZDD). Generational skewing is the diagnostic Crow feature, and seems to represent the strengthening of a matrilineal descent principle (see Trautmann and Whiteley 2012c).

Iroquois terminology correlates with unilineal descent of either matrilineal or patrilineal form (and residence of either matrilocal or patrilocal form), and frequently co-occurs with clans and lineages, i.e., *descent groups* arranged on unilineal lines. A clan system predicates that the important people in your community for forming social action groups *descend* through a particular line: patrilineal descent is through a line of males (father–son–son's son, etc.), matrilineal through a line of females (mother–daughter–daughter's daughter, etc.). These patrilines or matrilines provide axes of relationship through which active social groups are formed. Crow terminology typically correlates with matrilineal descent and matrilocal residence—and is the type that characterizes the Western Pueblos, and historically Rio Grande Keresans and Jemez. Eskimo terminology forms bilateral groups, technically "kindreds" rather than "descent groups," by drawing on both sides of Ego's family, involving both lineal and collateral kin; postmarital residence rules are more flexible than in a unilineal system. Bilateral kindreds with Eskimo terminology are typical of the Rio Grande Tanoans (except Jemez).

Importantly for some arguments in this volume, Iroquois and Crow belong to Morgan's (1871) grand category of "classificatory" systems, while Eskimo is in the opposite category, "descriptive." Classificatory systems group multiple genealogical relatives into the same term: at Hopi, while you have a single actual "mother," there are many in the community you refer to by the "mother" kinterm—all senior female members of your own matrilineal clan, for example. "Descriptive" terminologies, on the other hand, tend to individuate relatives: explaining how you are related to a particular person requires that you "describe" all the links between the two of you ("I call Joe 'cousin' because he is my mother's brother's son").[5] Moving from the Western Pueblos to the Rio Grande Tewa, therefore, engages a transition from *classificatory* to *descriptive* kinship systems.

Marriage systems or "alliance structures" take three basic forms in Lévi-Strauss's (1969) taxonomy: elementary, complex, and semicomplex. Elementary systems *prescribe* marriage with a particular social group (e.g., the opposite moiety). Complex systems only *proscribe* (prohibit) marriage with close kin: they do not *prescribe* any group one must marry into. Semicomplex systems are a mixture of the two: they *proscribe* a large group of people (for Hopi, own clan-set, father's clan-set, and mother's father's clan-set—or one-third of the clans in a typical village), leaving a limited number of social segments available for marriage (roughly two-thirds of all the clans in the same village).[6] That limitation is thus quasi-*prescriptive*: the large portion that is off limits means, in effect, you are *prescribed* to marry within the remaining portions. The three alliance structures are coordinate with the three terminologies and associated descent and residence systems we have been considering: elementary with Iroquois, complex with Eskimo, and semicomplex with Crow. These associated types present contrastive possibilities for social organization, for fundamental structures of social exchange, and for how a system is reproduced from one generation to the next. As noted above, a major hypothesis is that Crow/matrilineal/matrilocal/semicomplex is the underlying Puebloan social form from which others have developed, arguably in association with the rise of ritual sodalities to replace kinship structures as the key organizational principle.

Worldwide, Iroquois/elementary systems often correlate with exogamous moieties. In your own generation, your own moiety (A) contains your siblings and parallel cousins, Moiety B your cross-cousins. As a member of Moiety A, you must marry Moiety B (and vice versa)—i.e., a cross-cousin. Rio Grande Tewa and Keresan moieties have patrilineal tendencies (with a substrate Iroquois terminology [Fox 1967]), but they are not exogamous: i.e., a Winter/Turquoise person is not prescribed to marry a Summer/Squash person or vice versa. And Tewa moieties coexist with a descriptive (bilateral Eskimo) system of kin-terminology that is logically antithetical to moieties based on kinship. Rio Grande "ritual moieties," or "tribal sodalities" in Ware's terms, thus depart from the standard cross-cultural moiety pattern, and demand explanation of a different sort, attempted by various arguments hitherto (notably Ortiz 1969, Ware 2014) and in the present volume.

In twentieth-century social anthropology, kinship theory was marked by prevailing tendencies of one sort or another. The "British" school highlighted *descent* as the key principle of a kinship system—not terminology, and not marriage. "Descent theory" provided the analytical architecture for the classic ethnographies of African societies such as the Nuer and the Tallensi, but also of North American societies (e.g., Eggan 1937b). Eggan's *Social Organization* (1950) is the exemplar of "descent theory" in Americanist anthropology. As influential as it has been, this means that most ethnologists or archaeologists who have looked at Pueblo social organization since Eggan are constrained to see the ethnography through a descent-theory lens. Descent theory focuses on how primary social entities (clans or lineages) are constituted and how they operate as jural units deemed to own joint estates in property such as agricultural land or livestock or perhaps ritual practices. But in common with other problems of structural-functionalism, descent theory, concentrating on social structure at a particular moment (i.e., "synchronically") suffers from an inability to analyze processes over time ("diachronically"). Partly in response to this, Lévi-Strauss's magnum opus on kinship and marriage (1949) gave us "alliance theory," which focuses on how social groups *exchange* with each other: gifts, goods, labor, and people (in marriage). As noted, Eggan (1964), defending descent theory against all comers, specifically rejected alliance theory for the Pueblos. My own arguments (e.g., 2008) embrace alliance theory partly in opposition to the received view of Pueblo societies as governed by descent theory, while Ware (2014) continues to value the heuristics of descent theory for interpreting Pueblo social structures (see chapter 12). In that regard, some arguments in the present volume revisit old descent vs. alliance debates on the operation of social formations.

Summary Thoughts

Taken together, the chapters of this volume address key issues reflecting larger patterns of homology and heterogeneity in Puebloan social formations. While there are overlaps and intersections beyond those listed below, the following are issues addressed by multiple chapters:

- appropriate descriptive units for Pueblo social forms, in terms of kinship, ritual, or both—clans, lineages, kindreds, moieties, "houses," sodalities, etc. (chapters 2, 3, 4, 7, 8, 9, 10, 11, 12);
- continuity and discontinuity from Ancestral Pueblo social formations to both Eastern and Western Pueblo late prehistoric and historical forms (chapters 2, 3, 4, 5, 8, 9, 10, 11, 12);
- the role of kinship and ritual organization in social systems, both comparatively—e.g., Eastern vs. Western Pueblos—and specifically—e.g., among Tewas and prehistoric Tanoans (chapters 2, 3, 4, 5, 6, 7, 9, 10, 11, 12);
- whether and, if so, how language groups correlate with sociocultural formations, and whether these imply correspondence between ethnolinguistic groups and archaeological sites (chapters 2, 3, 5, 6);
- whether there is a meaningful continuum from Eastern to Western Pueblos, perhaps pivoting on a "Keresan bridge" that combines Eastern-type moiety organizations with Western-type multiple matrilineal descent groups (chapters 2, 5, 6, 9, 12);

- the relative roles of vertical vs. horizontal transmission, or phylogenetic trees and ethnogenetic networks, in the development of prehistoric and historic Puebloan sociocultural formations (chapters 4, 7, 9, 10);
- the historical processes via which ethnographically known Pueblo societies—Hopi, Zuni, Rio Grande Tewa, Taos—came to be (chapters 2, 3, 4, 7, 8, 9, 10);
- the effects of colonial power on Pueblo polities, societies, and alliance networks, notably at the late seventeenth-century Pueblo Revolt (chapters 5, 10);
- the inheritance of social-organizational forms—e.g., ritual moieties for Tanoans, plural sodalities for Zunis, matrilineal descent groups for Hopis—from the pre-Hispanic past to the present, as shown both linguistically and ethnologically (chapters 2, 3, 4, 7, 8, 9, 10, 12);
- the "Chaco phenomenon" in Pueblo social history, including its antecedents, rise, fall, and radiating effects on protohistoric and historic pueblos (chapters 7, 9, 11, 12).

While only one Native author (Joseph Aguilar) has contributed to this volume, it should be apparent that many of the contributions are deeply informed by internal Pueblo analytical views. Anthropologists of all stripes, especially since the passage of the Native American Graves Protection and Repatriation Act (NAGPRA), have come to attend to Native perspectives not as those of *informants*, but of thinkers in their own right: analysts with deeply informed conceptual schemes for explaining past and present social life. These are configured under different interpretive imperatives than formal anthropology, and are often embedded in cultural principles that are more encompassing than mere social explanation. It will be the conjunction of these analytical perspectives with the best techniques and ideas of formal anthropology, it seems to me, that represents the bright future of Puebloan historiography, ethnology, and archaeology: a hybrid analysis that draws on the best of all possible sources to illuminate the understanding of this fascinating sociocultural world region.

Acknowledgments

I am most grateful to John Ware and Loki Pandey for their comments on this chapter.

Notes

1. "Casas de altos en pueblos congregados . . . tan diferençiados en trato gouierno
    y poliçia de todas las naçiones que se an bisto y descubierto en estas partes
    de poniente" (Winship 1896, 454). In my view, existing translations do not
    approximate Castañeda's full ethnographic voice, so those in the text are my
    own, except where I quote Winship's translation (which begins on his page
    500). For *casos de altos*, my "storied apartment-houses" follows the descriptions
    earlier in Castañeda's account. For *trato*, my "usages" covers the general sense of
    "intercourse," "dealings," and "relationships" I infer Castañeda is thinking about
    here; "culture" might not be a bad alternative, but that would overdetermine the
    meaning from our contemporary perspective. Translating *poliçia* as "politi-
    cal order" follows this term's usage in early colonial Mexico (Lechner 1989;
    Martínez 2000, 15–16).

2. "Todos estos pueblos en general tienen unos ritos y costumbres aunque tienen
    algunas cosas en particulares que no las tienen los otros" (Winship 1896, 451).
    Winship's translation of *ritos* as "habits" both misconstrues and blurs Casta-
    ñeda's intent here.

3. For example, "the men spin and weave. The women bring up the children and
    prepare the food"/"los hombres hilan y texen las mugeres crian los hijos y gui-
    san de comer" (Winship 1896, 521, 452).

4. Contact period estimates vary extensively. (See, e.g., Ubelaker 2006.)

5. European terms, such as the English "cousin" and "aunt," have "classificatory"
    aspects in that they encompass different kin-types. It was for such reasons that
    Kroeber (1909) rejected Morgan's (1871) classificatory-descriptive dichotomy,
    but it has retained value as a broader lens on structurally lineal versus bilateral
    systems.

6. Lévi-Strauss (1969) based much of his argument for "semicomplex alliance" on
    Eggan's (1950) description of Hopi marriage rules.

CHAPTER TWO

Ma:tu'in

The Bridge between Kinship and "Clan"
in the Tewa Pueblos of New Mexico

RICHARD I. FORD

Dedication

I gratefully acknowledge Oku pi'n, the Tewa name for Professor Alfonso Ortiz. Oku, as we affectionately called him, is responsible for any original contributions this chapter makes to understanding Tewa social relations. In 1962, he taught me how to do ethnological fieldwork and introduced me to the importance of kinship in anthropology, lessons reflected, I hope, below. His influence and intellectual leadership inspired the topics and any insights developed here.

Introduction

This chapter addresses a central problem in Pueblo kinship and social organization regarding the Rio Grande Tewa, with implications for interpreting Ancestral Pueblo systems. The Tewa exemplify the eastern pole in a continuum of Pueblo social organization, with the Hopi at its opposite, western end (see also chapters 5 and 12). Hopi society articulates upon matrilineal descent: primary social units are "descent groups," especially "clans" and "lineages," which descend through the female line. By contrast, Tewa kinship-reckoning is "bilateral," like non-Native North American kinship systems: you identify with significant relatives on *both sides* of your extended family, producing a "kindred," structured very differently than a descent group. Bilateral kinship is the basis for a primary Tewa social group, the *ma:tu'i* (pl. *ma:tu'in*), an extended named household that presents a version of Pueblo social forms distinct from those based on unilineal descent. My primary concern here is to show how ma:tu'in differ from clans, how they are imagined in Tewa social thought and their cultural history, and how they operate in practice.

Whither the Tewa Clan

The pioneering anthropologists who researched the Tewa Pueblos in the late nineteenth and early twentieth centuries did two disservices to the Tewa and to subsequent anthropology. First, after suffering their probing questions and ceremonial disruptions, the Tewa appreciated their departure. Unfortunately, the early ethnologists' minimal knowledge of the culture, including multiple meanings of words and metaphors, led to misinterpretations. Second, they introduced the idea of the "clan," apparently from studies of the then better-known Hopi; the ethnologists expected to find the same social units among the Rio Grande Tewa. In fact, there is virtually no similarity between Hopi clans and Eastern Tewa social organization. Hopi clans are composed of one or more matrilineal lineages. Clan emblems are totemic, i.e., named for some aspect of nature, often an animal. Most Hopi clans have an apical lineage that owns a community ritual (e.g., the Snake clan owns the Snake ceremony), presided over by a senior male or female member. A Hopi clan has a clanhouse (and often a kiva) and a senior female leader. Anthropologists' frequent use of "clan" devoid of a definition infected Tewa usage in English. For several generations, "clan" has been applied by the Tewa to their social segments with little or no appreciation of its established anthropological meaning. Today the term is applied by many Tewa to moieties (e.g., "I am in the Winter clan"), ceremonial sodalities (e.g., "I am in the Clown clan"), or named ma:tu'in (e.g., "I am in the Badger clan"). This lack of linguistic and cultural clarity has misled anthropologists and confused Tewa-speakers. I will question the appropriateness of using "clan" at all for the Eastern Tewa, either historically or at present.

Tewa villages, since the Pueblo Revolt, have consisted of three basic features: the community, the sodalities (non-kinship groups organized for ritual and other purposes), and the system of households. The community (*owingeh*) functions for the physical protection of the inhabitants and provides access to wild food resources, arable land, and water from irrigation canals. Sodalities cut across the community and its households, involving about 20 percent of adult men and a handful of women, in eight initiated ritual sodalities: Women's, Scalp/War, Hunt, Kossa (Warm Clown), Kwirana (Cold Clown), Bear Medicine, Summer, and Winter (the last two, select groups from within the moieties of the same names). Collectively, the sodalities constitute the "Made people" (*pa:t'owa*), the highest of three general social ranks; the others being "Dry Food" (*seh t'a*) people, who account for most of the population ("commoners," we might say), and the *Towa é* ("outside chiefs" or village guardians), a mediating category between Dry Food and Made people (Ortiz 1969). The whole community is arranged into two named moieties (a division of society into halves), Winter and Summer. The moieties provide for the spiritual well-being of the people and keep natural forces in balance through monthly rituals; from one perspective, they belong to the sodality system, and are considered by Ware (2014, 59–74) as in themselves "dual tribal sodalities." Unlike classic cases in anthropology, however, Tewa moieties are "agamous," i.e., they play no role in arranging marriages. The third basic feature of a Tewa community, and my main concern here, is the extended household, or ma:tu'i.

Tewa descent and inheritance are bilateral, with individuals acknowledging both the mother's and father's relatives; postmarital residence is ambilocal, i.e., with the mother's side or father's side, contrasting with the Hopi rule of matrilocality (where a husband must move into his wife's matrilineal household). For the Tewa, both father's side and mother's side constitute separate ma:tu'in, and everyone with two Tewa parents has two ma:tu'in. One, however, is more prominent in the individual's life cycle, as determined at initiation (see below). Each ma:tu'i is named, often with the name of an animal or other natural phenomenon—hence the confusion with totemic clans of the Hopi type—and has many responsibilities to nurture the life of a relative. A person can inherit land or a house from either ma:tu'i.

In anthropological usage, "clan" and "lineage" only came to exclusively denote unilineal descent groups in the middle years of the twentieth century, following several decades of debate. Earlier, reflecting vernacular usage (e.g., for Scottish "clans") anthropological usage was poorly defined. It is in those historical circumstances that the term "clan" was applied by the first ethnologists to Tewa social groups, some of which were based on kinship and others (the moieties and sodalities) not. The more precise anthropological usage established in the mid-twentieth century is exampled by George Peter Murdock in his classic *Social Structure* (1949); Murdock defined a clan by a unilineal rule of descent, with clans and lineages (a clan's constituent units) comprising "descent groups." That view became standard, and persists in contemporary social theory, in which a lineage is defined as "a group of people who can trace their descent back to a single known, and in most cases, named human ancestor" (Dousset 2011, 67). A *descent group* comprises people who consider themselves to be identical in some respects because they are descendants from one real or mythological individual. Likewise, a clan "is a group of people, or a number of lineages, whose members claim to be descendants of a distant ancestor who is usually mythological" (Dousset 2011, 67). Such definitions do not characterize Tewa social groups.

My approach here is ethnographic, based on interviews, observation, and attending household ceremonies. I have long appreciated the revisionist anthropologists who questioned the research conclusions of our anthropological ancestors. It is too easy to accept earlier publications uncritically without evaluating their implications. This is particularly true when an anthropologist from one subdiscipline draws generalizations from another. Peter Whiteley (e.g., 1985, 1986) has not shied away from criticizing Southwestern archaeologists who do this with Hopi ethnography, in his critique of the "descent-theory" model[1] of Hopi clans deriving from earlier anthropologists (Eggan 1950). Whiteley opposed a static view of Hopi clans as estate or landholding social units that control agriculture, at least corn production, and animal husbandry. He continued (1987) by showing there is hierarchy within and among clans based on unequal access to ceremonial knowledge. And Hopi clan and lineage unity is extensively crosscut by patrilateral (father's side) ties in actual social behavior (Whiteley 1986). My analysis of nonexistent clans among the Eastern Tewa I hope will be as equally revisionist as Whiteley's analyses of Hopi clans.

The first anthropologists were anxious to find clans in the Rio Grande Tewa Pueblos. Frederick W. Hodge (1896, 345) indicated: "In the study of the Pueblo tribes of New Mexico and Arizona there is no subject of greater importance and interest than the clanship system of that people." Hodge never defined what a "clan" was, but he knew about "clan" names in most pueblos, and emphasized that Pueblo cultural history could not be reconstructed without first knowing the clans. Thus began a quest that would last another half century.

Hodge drew on several predecessors. Albert S. Gatschet, an exceptional European-trained linguist, came to the Southwest as part of the Wheeler survey, recording many Native vocabularies (Gatschet 1879). Gatschet was the first to list Tewa clan names recorded from men of San Juan Pueblo (Ohkay Owingeh), but he did not define clan functions or social roles. In the early 1880s, after brief visits, Adolph Bandelier reported San Juan possessed fourteen "gentes"[2] or clans (Bandelier 1890, 273), and, even more misleadingly, that "marriage is still strictly exogamous; the children belong to the gens or clan of the mother, consequently the clan is, in reality, the unit of pueblo society" (272).

John G. Bourke, Bandelier's contemporary, recorded Tewa social relations and lifeways independently in 1881, focusing on "clans" in intricate detail

(Bloom 1937). In every house visited (in San Juan, Santa Clara, San Ildefonso, Nambé, and Pojoaque), Bourke recorded the residents' "clans" by name. He expected to find clans, so he did, but information about clans was never reconfirmed (Bourke 1881). Hodge's (1896) summary "Table Showing the Distribution of Pueblo Clans" included nineteen clans for San Juan and twenty-nine for San Ildefonso. Although misleading, Hodge's table (table 2.1) helps support an argument I will soon make: that of the thirty named Tewa clans, only two (Gopher and Willow) are not found in Keresan pueblos, which have true clans.

Later students of Tewa social organization followed the lead of these prior scholars, though the analytical categories were beginning to crack. John Peabody Harrington, an exceptional linguist and usually a critical ethnologist, simply reiterated the view that "clans at the Tewa villages are quite numerous." While he accepted Hodge's list of clans, he noted, contradicting Bandelier and Bourke, "Tewa children belong to the clan of the father" (Harrington 1912, 475). Harrington also described Tewa "clans" as localized, i.e., that clan members resided in a common location in a pueblo. (This is true of each ma:tu'i, another point of confusion.) Herbert J. Spinden came periodically to research in the Tewa Pueblos, mainly Nambé, between 1909 and 1913. He learned Tewa and was an exceptional translator (see, e.g., Spinden 1933). However, Spinden too assigned clans to the Tewa: "The Tewa villages are all divided into two groups of clans, one commonly known as the Summer People and the other as the Winter People" (Spinden 1933, 122). The two groups were, of course, the ceremonial moieties later so effectively explained by Alfonso Ortiz (1969). In Spinden's unpublished notes, we learn, "The clan system prevails among these Indians (Tewa) but it is now fast dying out and the information available is not always trustworthy. Clan names are used in the native christening and on ceremonial occasions by priests and medicine men when addressing an individual. It is often possible to confuse a clan name with a personal name" (Spinden 1913, 1). Following Bandelier and Hodge, Spinden collected clan names and attempted to correct the consolidated list. It does appear, however, that he was suspicious of the importance of Tewa clans and their origin. After a brief review of kin-terminology, he concluded that, contrary to expectations, "the relationship terms throw practically no new light on the development of the clan system, so far as I have been able to observe" (Spinden 1913, 2).

Edward S. Curtis worked sporadically for over twenty years in the Tewa pueblos, collecting many clan names but few details about how they functioned. Contrary to Bandelier and Bourke but in common with Harrington,

Table 2.I. Hodge's "Table Showing the Distribution of Pueblo Clans"

"B, signifies that the clan name is given by Bandelier; ex, signifies that the clan is extinct; 1, almost extinct; 2, probably extinct; 3, probably identical with the Gopher clan; 4, see also Tree; 5, see also Firewood or Timber" (Hodge 1896). The bird referred to as a piñon-eater is a Clark's nutcracker, today classified as *Nucifraga Columbiana*. "Turkois" is an obsolete spelling of "turquoise." The designation 4 was not included in the published chart.

Clans

TANOAN

	S.Jn	S.Ca	S.Ild	Nbe	Tsqe	Hano
Ant				*		
Antelope			*			
Arrow						
Axe						
Badger	*	*	*			
Bear	*			*		*
Bluebird			*			
Buffalo			*			
Calabash	*	*	*	*	ex	
Chaparral Cock						
Cloud	*	*	*	*	*	*
Coral	*	*	*		ex	
Corn	*	*				*
Corn (black)			*			
Corn (blue)			*			
Corn (brown)						
Corn (red)			*			
Corn (sweet)			*			
Corn (white)			*			
Corn (yellow)			*			
Cottonwood	*	*	*			
Coyote	*		*		ex	
Crane or Heron						ex
Crow						
Dance-kilt						
Deer		*	*			
Dove						
Duck						
Eagle	B	*	*	*	ex	
Eagle (painted)	*					
Earth	*	*		*	ex	*
Feather						
Fire			*	*		
Firewood or Timber	*	*	*			ex
Flower (red and white)						
Flower (genus Dandelion)						
Frog or Toad						

Taos	Islta	Jemz	Pecs	Lgna	Acma	Sia	S.F.	S.A.	Ccht	Zuni
								KERESAN		ZUNIAN
			ex		ex	ex	*			
	*			*	*	*	*		ex	
						ex	ex			
B										
		*	ex	*		*				*
			ex	*	*	*1	*		*	*
			ex		ex	ex				
		*	ex		*	*1	*		*	
				*	*	*	ex			*
		*?	ex			ex				
							*			
		*	ex			*	*	*	*	*
	*				ex					
					ex					
	*			*	*					
	*				ex					
	*			*	*					
									*	
		*	ex	*		*	*	*	*	*
						ex				*
		*	ex			ex	ex			
							ex		*	
	*		ex			*	ex			*
						ex	*	*		
							*			
	*	*	ex	*	*	*1	*	*	ex	*
	*	*	ex	ex			ex			
B										
			ex		ex	*	*	*	*	
							*1			
		B								
							*			*

Table 2.I. (*continued*)

Clans

	S.Jn	S.Ca	S.Ild	Nbe	Tsqe	Hano
Goose						
Gopher	*	*	*		*	
Grass	*			*	ex	ex
Hawk			*			
Herb (sp. incog.)						ex
Humming-bird						
Ivy						
Knife						
Lizard	*		*			
Marten	B[3]					
Mole						
Moon	B					
Mountain lion	*		*	*		
Oak		*				
Parrot						
Pegwood? (*Chánatya*)						
Pine						*
Piñon						
Piñon-eater (*Picicorvus Columbinus*)						
Reindeer						
Sacred dancer						*
Sage (Mexican)						
Salt						
Shell (pink conch)						ex
Shell bead			*			
Shrub (red top)						
Sky						
Snake (rattle)						
Snake (water)						
Star						
Stone	*		*			ex
Sun	*	*	*	ex	*	*
Swallow						
Tobacco				*		*
Tree (mountain: probably birch[5])				*		
Tree (mountain: probably spruce)			*			
Turkey						
Turkois	*	*	*		*	ex
Water	*		*			
Water pebble (bowlder)						
Willow		*				
Wolf						
Yellow-wood						

Pueblos

				KERESAN						ZUNIAN
Taos	*Islta*	*Jemz*	*Pecs*	*Lgna*	*Acma*	*Sia*	*S.F.*	*S.A.*	*Ccht*	*Zuni*
	*									
						ex				
							*1			
					B	ex	B¹		B	
B										
				*		ex				
	*									
						ex	ex			
	*		ex	*2		ex	ex		*	
			ex	*	*	ex	*		*	
	*			*	*	*	*	*		*
						ex				
		*	ex							
					B	ex				
									ex	
									B	
						ex	ex			
B						ex				
										*
					*					
				*	*	*			ex	*
				*						
						ex				
						ex				
B	*	*?	ex	*	*	*	*		*	*
							*1			
						*	*			*
			ex	*	*	*	*	*	ex	*
	*	*	ex	*		ex	ex		*	
B				*	*	*	*		*1	
	*									
	*			*						
										*

Curtis (1926) maintained that Tewa clans were patrilineal and exogamous. He was surprised at how numerous clan names were, considering population size. He reported San Juan had twenty-one clans in a population of 445, and that San Ildefonso's population of ninety-seven was divided into twenty-five families with seventeen clans. Curtis usefully noted, "clans are like family names." He further grouped clans by either moiety, but absent any explanation, these "clan" names could just as easily have been the ma:tu'in names (see below) of the members.

By the 1920s, the contradictory accounts and superficiality of analysis produced a substantive ethnological critique. Elsie Clews Parsons (1924, 1929) wrote the most definitive works about Tewa kinship and social organization, including clans, prior to 1940. Parsons tried to confirm the names found by her predecessors, but recorded a greatly shortened list. She also tried to match clans to moieties and house ownership, ultimately concluding that Tewa clans were "very feeble," while the moieties were strong, and houses were owned by both men and women (Parsons 1924, 339). Although she did not report a word for clan, following Harrington (1912, 474) she reported that *t'owa* could refer to clans and more specifically *nabii t'owa* to "my people" (cf. Whiteley and Snow 2015, 562–63). However, Parsons did us an enormous favor by uncovering the term matu'i [*sic*], which she translated as "my relations" (Parsons 1929, 83). She thus gave us a Tewa concept for kinship groups without any implication that these were "clans," and she rejected earlier ethnologists' contentions about purported clan structure and functions: "Among the Tewa, clanship is still more insignificant, functioning not even as an exogamous institution, and as far as I could learn, devoid of ceremonial associations. It is merely a question of a name, which, to the younger people at least, may be even unknown" (82).

Finally, two noted Tewa scholars who were fluent in their languages and cultures offered transforming insights on this question. Edward Dozier, from Santa Clara, was the first ethnologist to attack directly the existence of Tewa clans: "The Tewa clan names have nothing to do with clans. These names are inherited variously from the mother or father. As with other property, a clan name seems to be the possession of the bilateral kin group." He concluded emphatically, "There is no evidence of a former lineage or clan system" (Dozier 1970, 165). While rejecting Tewa clans or any secular or ceremonial function for them, he still had to account for the names, arguing for their diffusion from the Keresan Pueblos: "We suggest that Tewa clan names are an imperfect and undigested diffusion of the clan concept from Keresan neighbors" (166). Alfonso Ortiz, of

Ohkay Owingeh (San Juan), also dismissed clans, and saw Tewa social organization as built instead on the Winter-Summer dual division of moieties in
each Tewa village (following Parsons 1924, Eggan 1950, and Dozier 1970). Ortiz
(1969, 53) elevated the social importance of close relatives, the ma:tu'in, noting,
for example, that this group assembles for the releasing rite of a deceased relative. Furthermore, he emphasized that in Tewa creation stories only the moieties
and ritual sodalities are ever named, not clans or family names. Ortiz concluded
there is nothing fundamental about clans in Tewa society.

In view of this ethnographic history, with its contrasts, contradictions, and
outright rejection by more knowledgeable scholars that Tewa clans were unilineal descent groups, we must conclude that it is at least uncertain whether
the Tewa ever had clans (Ware 2014, 61). It is theoretically possible that, centuries ago, the Eastern Tewa had unilineal descent groups, but they did not
when the early anthropologists, using a then ill-defined term, reported on Tewa
"clans." At the time of their inquiries, Hodge, Bourke, Bandelier, and Curtis felt
the so-called clans they recorded were declining. Harrington (1912) thought he
found a lapsed system of patrilineal clans in Santa Clara, and Murdock (1949,
351) used this tidbit to view Tewa clans and moieties as extinct patrilineal organizations. However, Parsons (1924) found that Tewa clan names at Santa Clara
were matrilineally inherited, while moiety membership was primarily patrilineal (with changes of natal moiety possible at marriage if marrying a person of
the opposite moiety), but that did not lead her to infer true clans there or anywhere else among the Tewa. So, although the earliest anthropologists thought
they had discovered Tewa clans, they did not. Why not?

What They Were Seeing: *Ma:tu'in* (Next of Kin)

Ma:tu'in certainly are not clans; they are closer to the idea of kindreds (*sensu*
Nadel 1947), with many functions in a Tewa pueblo.[3] Most are related to an individual's life cycle, from birth to death. On a day-to-day basis, ma:tu'in relatives
provide assistance and labor when needed. The ma:tu'i is an important kinship
unit that can rapidly accomplish much for members that the moiety and even
the sodalities cannot in a village with a large population. Ma:tu'in names serve
no purpose within the pueblo or moieties, but they are inherited for external
functions—to facilitate trade and hospitality when visiting other pueblos.

It is within the ma:tu'in that kinship terms are used. Membership in a
ma:tu'i is bilateral. Ma:tu'in are complex households comprising mainly but

not entirely biological relatives; adoption and distant kindred affiliations add members. Marriage is a source of new members through an adoption ritual similar to the initiation of youths. If a woman of the Summer moiety marries into the ma:tu'i of a man of the Winter moiety, she joins his ma:tu'i and transfers her moiety membership to his; people say of her that, in this transfer, she "loses her petals." Conversely, when a Winter woman marries into the ma:tu'i of a man of the Summer moiety, she "loses her icicles." Each ma:tu'i comprises several nuclear and extended, multigenerational families. The ma:tu'i is traditionally exogamous, a rule enforced by the exhortations of the elders. The sense of ma:tu'i solidarity is emphasized in how some Tewa individuals state the order of their allegiances: first to kin (ma:tu'in), then to sodality, then moiety, and finally to the pueblo. The most vulnerable Tewa social unit is the village, which can fracture into the smaller social units when natural disasters occur, when attacked, or when epidemics strike.

The ma:tu'in names, as Hodge discovered, are found in the Keresan pueblos and Jemez, all with true clans (Eggan 1950). Ma:tu'in names duplicated elsewhere as clan names include Ant, Antelope, Badger, Bear, Cloud, Corn, Coyote, Deer, Eagle, Fire, Pumpkin, Sun, Tobacco, Turquoise, and Water. Ma:tu'in names appear to have been borrowed from pueblos with clans because of trade contacts. Tewas were traditionally long-distance traders. For success, trade had three mutually reinforcing requirements: protection, facilitation, and personal association. The "peace of trade" that guarantees protection when you enter a foreign village allows for trade to transpire and reciprocity to function. In other words, you will be safe and your goods protected when you enter a distant village to trade with fictive relatives of the same "family" name (clan or ma:tu'i), and the same protections are afforded to that village's traders when they enter your pueblo. The facilitator of trade might be a relative married into another village or a specific trade partner that you visit often. The third requirement, personal association, takes the form of a fictive kinship relationship, in which the ma:tu'i name duplicates another pueblo's clan name. Hypothetically, if you visit a distant village, you will introduce yourself by your ma:tu'i name, e.g., "I am Badger." You can then ask where the Badgers live in that village, and, once contacted, they will offer you a meal and probably a place to sleep and serve as a go-between to help announce your trade goods.

Ma:tu'in in Social and Ceremonial Contexts

In the life cycle, people do not choose which of their two ma:tu'in to formally affiliate with until they are initiated. As children, there are frequent visits to all their relatives' homes. Because of their parents' visitation pattern, they may favor one grandparent over another. At the time of initiation, they are already learning about the status of adults in the village and now they may select the most respected senior relative and associate with his/her ma:tu'i. The intention is to learn the rudiments of the pueblo's history and cultural traditions from that relative. With further maturity, the criteria for selecting one ma:tu'i over another are the leader's status, knowledge, and "wisdom." Wealth or land do not enter the equation. The favored relative can be male or female.

Most leadership roles and ceremonial offices in the Tewa Pueblos are filled by kinship affiliation. However, leadership of the ma:tu'i is more comprehensive. You must be an esteemed elder, male or female, in the extended kinship group, well versed in kinship ceremonial knowledge, and know the necessary rite-of-passage prayers. Ma:tu'i leadership is defined by numerous ritual expectations throughout the year and at times of familial crises. It is an achieved position of high regard and respect but not one that is sought. An elder's knowledge and status leads to informal selection by senior kinsmen. W. W. Hill defined people with "esteemed status," an honorific position at Santa Clara, as those with acquired "wisdom" from extensive ceremonial activities for the benefit of the pueblo. Only three men and a couple of women were accorded this status in the 1930s (Hill in Lange 1982, 168–70). However, if Hill had discovered ma:tu'in in Santa Clara, I am certain he would have recognized more elders regarded this way. In the other Eastern Tewa pueblos where this kinship category is acknowledged, most of the elderly heads of ma:tu'in are accorded this status. A ma:tu'i leader may change several times following the death of the previous incumbent and can alternate from male to female. In starting my close relationship with the Badger ma:tu'i in Ohkay Owingeh, I have witnessed the leadership go from one religious leader (male) to another prominent ritual leader (male) to the current leader with no ritual affiliation but who is a highly respected Tewa-speaker and traditionalist (female). Such rotations are typical, given that seniority, knowledge, and achievement are the criteria that determine succession.

Tewa rites of passage are *wowatsi*, or the "milestones of life." Based on biology and age, the basic rites are birth, marriage, and death. At birth, some female members of the family's ma:tu'i will assist the midwife if asked, and care for the new mother. Within the first four days they will mainly care for the new infant, aid the mother, and give assistance to young children in the family. During preparations for a marriage, negotiations between the prospective groom's and bride's immediate families turn quickly to a council of ma:tu'in elders from each side. Four elders customarily appear: two for the groom and two for the bride. A celebration and feasting soon turn serious when the groom's family's preferred ma:tu'i elders address the couple, advising them of a marriage's expectations, the importance of children for the ma:tu'i, and how to care for, comfort, and protect all members of the new family. Similarly, at the death of a member the ma:tu'i relatives gather several times over a four-day period culminating with the burial and soul-releasing ritual. At death, if the deceased was not a Made Person (*pa:t'owa*), the family members handle much of the ritual: the ma:tu'i women wash, dress, and prepare the body for burial, and during this period ma:tu'i adults care for the family, protect the children, and feed the extended family (see Ortiz 1969, 50–57).

Calendrical rituals, including ceremonial dances, ditch cleaning, esoteric private ceremonies, or the all-important initiations, are determined by the movement of the sun, and are generally held at the same month of the year. Moreover, at the time of the moiety's "water pouring" initiation for teenagers or adults changing moiety because of marriage (see Ortiz 1969, 30–43), the adult ma:tu'i females have an important role to prepare the children being initiated, to relax them in this time of heightened anxiety, and to feed all the participants a menu of traditional foods. Modern-day activities added to the pueblo calendar include Catholic baptism, First Communion, and school graduations: all engage ma:tu'i members. A particularly important annual ceremony for the whole ma:tu'i is on All Souls Eve, November 1. This is a special releasing rite modified from an individual's death rite and extended to all generalized ancestors. Now the members gather in the home of the focal elder and each family brings food to share with all present, with leftovers later distributed to those physically unable to attend. The door is left open so that the spirits of the ancestors can attend and portions of all food are placed in bowls for them. The relatives in attendance can be quite numerous because the ma:tu'i is multigenerational; generally at least thirty are present. In place of sadness at the funeral, there is a degree of festiveness (Ortiz 1969, 55).

Even though All Souls is the Catholic "Day of the Dead," it is special to all the Eastern Pueblos and accommodates the preservation of Pueblo beliefs; indeed, it is understood as a basically Pueblo ceremony, not an orthodox Catholic ritual.

The ritual accentuates past family practices. Blankets are spread on the floor for children and younger adult relatives. Behind them, elders sit on low benches to eat. The food for the ancestors, representing what they would have known and liked, is placed in the center of the room with all seated around it. It ranges from very old-recipe paper bead (*buwa*), corn stew (*chicos*), chile, fish, and venison to more recent *horno*-baked leavened bread and bread pudding (*sopa*) to packaged food and store-prepared chicken wings and pizza. Familiar Pueblo feast-day foods are always accoutrements. At the conclusion, any remaining food is brought to the missing relatives and divided by all present to take home for future consumption. The commensality reinforces ma:tu'i solidarity. The conversations are about the food, which items deceased relatives liked, and how much they would enjoy this meal. For all present, memories of the ma:tu'i relatives are recalled and the importance of living relatives is reinforced.

When a relative is preparing for initiation into a sodality, his/her fellow ma:tu'i members assist in collecting the items needed to pay the sodality members for membership. These can be very numerous (e.g., several thousand parrot feathers) and expensive (e.g., dozens of baskets of ground cornmeal). Some ma:tu'i members may belong to different sodalities. Once a member is initiated, he or she is eligible to receive food products that community members gave for the ceremony as "gifts" to the spirits. These are divided afterward among the fully initiated members to take home for the family or, if there is a surplus, to the head of the ma:tu'i to further share with its members. When a sodality decides to "take out a dance," if a ma:tu'i member wants to participate, he or she may not have a complete costume at home. The head of the ma:tu'i will help assemble the proper costume for the ceremony. The kinsmen, in turn, do not want to be embarrassed by the members not performing in the proper traditional attire, so they willingly lend dance apparel.

The ma:tu'in have family rituals and shrines (*kaye*) shared by all members but known best to seniors who have memorized the prayers. If there is no dedicated shrine, the ma:tu'i might use a sodality shrine familiar to one of its members and that is regarded as especially powerful. Here, special prayers are recited by the focal elder for the well-being of the members, their prosperity, and successful crop production. The shrines are often found in shared field areas or in ancestral areas where the families once farmed. One Santa Clara ma:tu'i has its shrine in a field area near Puje (the archaeological site more commonly called Puye) where ma:tu'i ancestors once farmed and where some male members still pray and make offerings for bountiful harvests and successful hunting. These are rituals unique to the ma:tu'i and performed in secret for the benefit of its members but not for the whole pueblo.

Today, as in the recent past, male ma:tu'in elders and sodality heads conduct pilgrimages to ancestral sites or shrines with younger relatives or members, respectively. These reinforce culture history by recapitulating ancient migrations to "living sites" where the *p'oe-wha-hah* (breath of life) of the ancestors is always present (Swentzell 2001). This is linguistically supported in that *-uinge*, referring to a house area or village, applies to both a current dwelling and an ancestral home. The suffix *-keyi* in the derived term *-onwinkeyi* means "my ancestors live here." The living essence of the ancestors still inhabits the named ruins. In 1962, I accompanied a focal male elder of an Ohkay Owingeh ma:tu'i and his son to get firewood in Comanche Canyon north of Ojo Caliente. Along the way we stopped at several Tewa archaeological sites (Ponsipa-akeri, Posi, Hunpobi, and Howiri), all called *-onwinkeyi*, to introduce the boy to them, to recite stories about them, and to make cornmeal offerings at village *p'oe kwan* (shrines). Prayer sticks may also be placed here on these family pilgrimages, just as they were fifty years later when I brought Ohkay elders to Ponsipa-akeri.

The ma:tu'in are vital economic units to assure adequate farm produce for their members and labor for construction projects. We can only guess at the pre-Hispanic land tenure system. The prehistoric settlement pattern in the upper Rio Grande suggests that there was some type of extended kinship-based landholding and irrigation group. When the Spanish arrived, they made grants of land that the Pueblos already owned back to them and imposed a council of Spanish-style government officials for the Indians to assume (Ortiz 1969, 156–58). This council now allocated land. However, it appears that the ma:tu'i maintained usufruct rights to land its members were already farming and constituted a parallel land-distributing unit following a member's death. When a person dies and does not name an heir, his or her land reverts to the ma:tu'i. Ma:tu'i elders may parcel out portions for house sites and new farmland, especially for new families. As a family grows, the ma:tu'i has land to distribute to those desiring more. Members of the ma:tu'i may provide labor when requested to help construct a house, repair lateral irrigation ditches, assist with the harvest, build a corral, stack hay, and assist during cattle and sheep birthing or with herding to and from distant pastures. In return, they are given surplus food.

Historically, Tewa pueblos are defensive in design. Their location accommodates the need for domestic water and irrigation water for home, crops, and stock. At the same time, they once suffered threats from nomadic mounted raiders that necessitated architecture to defend the people and property against raids. Ma:tu'i members assisted the War Society to protect the village, but they also helped members to respond to these threats. In households without resident men, male ma:tu'i members had to protect these relatives.

I began this research by trying to understand the history of Tewa migrations. As I asked more questions, I discovered the view that in the distant past, members of ma:tu'in usually moved together, weakly coordinated with other named groups via members' sodality memberships. The Pueblo Revolt (1680–1694) successfully brought the desired religious freedom, but as fissures developed in the grand trans-Pueblo alliance, warfare commenced both internally and with mounted nomads living on the eastern Plains. Drought and crop losses imposed additional stresses. Groups of Tewa began to vacate pueblos for security before Diego de Vargas returned (1692), but his presence led to more groups seeking refuge in mountainous redoubts. Most Tewa Pueblos have oral stories about how they handled the tumultuous years following the Revolt (see chapter 10). Ohkay Owingeh talks about individual ma:tu'in moving to Mesa Prieta (Black Mesa), up the Ojo Caliente, Rio del Oso (Pesede), and Rio Chama (Poshu and Tsama). Santa Clara groups moved to several mountainous locations, including with families from other pueblos. One ma:tu'i had members in the Scalp Society (War sodality) and late in the Reconquest it joined co-members from San Ildefonso and other Tewa families on top of Black Mesa (*Ton-ya*) preparing to fight Vargas and his troops. San Ildefonso families were also living simultaneously above Pojoaque and back at their ancestral sites on the Pajarito Plateau, including Nake'muu, Navawi, and perhaps cavates within modern Bandelier National Monument. Whole villages did not move together; some fragmented social groups were led by sodality members, but most departed as ma:tu'in. This variability is suggestive of an ancient migration pattern.

The ma:tu'in probably formed the migrating population units. How they moved is unknown, and where they stopped en route awaits archaeological discovery. At the end of their movements they coalesced, built their domestic portion of the newly constructed pueblo, and contributed to building kivas once the sodalities reassembled. Sometimes a community had to respond to crop failures, internal social friction, or external aggression. The unit that responded the quickest was, and is, the ma:tu'i. A second form of short-term household movement is to a summer field house. Such houses are close to the ma:tu'i's agricultural fields and shrine. The initial move is in the late spring and return in the fall when the crops are brought to the pueblo for storage before the Second

Harvest Dance. Ma:tu'i members might be requested to assist with the move and to return the harvest to a home in the village in exchange for surplus food.

In the Beginning . . .

Without further research, we cannot say how or whether ma:tu'in-type extended households coexisted with emerging unilineal social groups. My hypothesis is that they came in after full development of the dual organization represented by Tewa bilateral social relations. In all events, I believe we should seek to address such questions in the archaeological record.

The Archaic in the Southwest was a long period of hunting and gathering subsistence and nomadic living. The people were proto-Tanoan-speakers who moved in kinship bands from one food resource area to another throughout the year. These linguistically undifferentiated Tanoan bands probably consisted of natal relatives and women who married into the group (Steward 1937). Not many families could depend annually upon the limited seasonal food supply. Leadership was probably by a resourceful senior male relative as the band leader, who may have been a shaman as well (a typical pattern in band societies; see Service 1962).

Geographically, proto-Kiowa-Tanoan bands covered an area from north of the Colorado River, the states of Utah and Colorado, the short-grass prairie lands from the foothills of the Rockies through eastern New Mexico to the Rio Grande, the Jemez Mountains, and the San Juan back to the Colorado. The ecological basis of these preagricultural bands was dependence upon unreliable seasonal edible resources and foods that were ephemeral in quantity. The inferred Kiowa-Tanoan language area corresponded with the pinyon (*Pinus edulis*) and acorn (*Quercus gambelii*) growth areas; both are very nutritious but unreliable food plants. The total resource assemblage in these areas (including aquatic plants and game) would rarely have permitted a gathering of more than a few families. In other words, the subsistence life of Kiowa-Tanoan ancestors was problematic and did not allow large gatherings of families or bands most years. Population assemblages were infrequent, there was no social complexity, and survival required maximal dispersal of families.

Following the introduction of agriculture, the archaeology of the San Juan Basin shows a transition from the Archaic to semisedentary Basketmaker periods, with shifts in technology, corn based agriculture, and changing social organization, with the emergence of proto-Puebloan social forms and physical

Figure 2.1. Range of *Pinus edulis* and *Quercus gambelii* in the Greater Southwest. AMNH Anthropology Division.

isolation leading to new Tanoan language groups. These nascent communities may have consisted of merged kinship bands now coalescing into multifamily villages but with each former family band maintaining a separate identity. Perhaps these residential groups were the beginning of our ma:tu'in. If linguistic divisions began at this point, Kiowa-Tanoan social and economic patterns lacked the nutritional stability for permanent social institutions predicating community life until the arrival and development of maize horticulture. Maize was introduced in the Archaic from Mexico into southern Arizona and soon after into New Mexico west of the Rio Grande. The Archaic farmers selected maize to increase their yield and by 1000 BCE it proved ample to support bands' sedentism, at least during the growing season. Genetic selection yielded a more productive and easier-to-grind flour maize, which became the basis for the Late Archaic "Neolithic Revolution" for Tanoan bands in the San Juan Basin, enabling an increase in human populations and stored food for part of the year.

The succeeding Basketmaker periods saw enhanced corn and squash agriculture production, an emphasis on food storage, periods of permanent residence, and the possible beginning of intervillage conflict over arable land and water. There was a foundation for possible sodality shaman groups in the Late Archaic, shown in rock art imagery depicting weather control, animal and plant reproduction, and curing. The early Basketmaker people in the Rio Grande Valley, with their stored corn surplus, were vulnerable to predation by marauding bands of Caddoan-speakers from the eastern Plains. For defense, armed men would protect both stores and people. We do not know when raiding began, but it certainly was present after the introduction of the bow and arrow by 600 CE, and these defensive male associations may have started war societies.

Ware (2014, 69–70) has suggested an outline of Ancestral Pueblo community patterns starting with Basketmaker III, the genesis of the first matrilocal kin groups, and by the 700s matrilineal villages, with women owning land and houses, and mobile, sometimes absent, men providing leadership roles and protecting the estate of agricultural land. Ware envisions great kivas as the archaeological evidence for tribal sodalities. By this time recognizable social forms were evolving. Small villages began to coalesce and corporate descent groups were emerging. Sodalities now had small kivas to perpetuate their secret ceremonial life free from the inquisitive eyes of non-sodality members. By this time in the San Juan Basin male associations of shamans that served important functions for the protection and survival of the growing villages were evolving into ritual sodalities. The advantages of sodalities were soon recognized because they were borrowed or duplicated quickly elsewhere to serve other communities. They continue up to the present (Ware 2014, 92–97).

The origin of Pueblo moieties per Eggan (1950) and Dozier (1970), following Wittfogel and Goldfrank (1943), was the organization of irrigation. Large-scale irrigation required authoritative political decision-making, centralized leadership, facilitated, they argued, by the moiety social structure of the Eastern Pueblos. Unfortunately, this ignores the history of irrigation in the Eastern Pueblos as a technique and social institution, which developed as two sequential methods. First came indigenous *ditch diversion irrigation*. Water was diverted by a minimal head gate from a secondary but permanently running stream, mainly a tributary of a major river such as the Rio Grande or Colorado. The water ran within a single village and only to water the fields of a single farmer or his close relatives with adjoining farmland. It was created and maintained by a single lineage or household—or possibly a ma:tu'i. The ditches were narrow, shallow, and usually no more than a quarter of a mile in length. This form of irrigation was used with other water-controlled farming methods (sometimes erroneously called dry farming) and not all the farmers in a community practiced it (Ford and Swentzell 2015, 347–49). This system began on a small scale about 700 CE and continued into the 1700s, but did not require a dual organization or authoritarian caciques to function. Eggan and Dozier did not acknowledge this early form of irrigation.

The second type, *Iberian irrigation*, was introduced by the Spanish, with the first ditch dug at San Gabriel under Juan de Oñate's direction in August 1598 (Ford and Swentzell 2015, 352). These large, complex ditches connected multiple unrelated farmers, even communities, and were several miles in length with numerous lateral side ditches (Ford 1977). The first ditch in New Spain connected Spanish-speaking Chamita and Tewa-speaking San Gabriel. Two Tewa ceremonies performed by alternating Summer and Winter caciques opened and closed the ditches, respectively. All the able men in the villages were required to maintain them (just as Wittfogel and Goldfrank [1943] argued). This type of productive irrigation spread quickly throughout the Eastern Pueblo riverine world and Spanish settlements. It had nothing to do with the origin of dual organization or moieties, but the labor requirements may have strengthened the caciques' authority. It was this sixteenth-century irrigation system, introduced by the Spanish, that was the basis of the Eggan-Dozier social theory distinguishing the Eastern from the Western Pueblos.

Ware (2014) delineates several other theories to account for the origin of Pueblo moieties. Ortiz (1969) thought they were ancient because of how pervasive binary oppositions are in Tewa culture and philosophical reasoning. The most widespread explanation is diffusion. Dozier (1970, 175–76) argued that the Rio Grande Keresans borrowed Tewa moieties and Jemez borrowed them from the Keresans. This chain of duplication is very possible but does not account for the much earlier origin of Tewa moieties. Ortman (2012) explained this by having dual organization originate in the San Juan in the 1100s and then be brought to the Rio Grande by Tewa migrants. Heitman and Plog (2005) found evidence of dualism in their study of the burial crypts in Pueblo Bonito in Chaco Canyon. But dualism did not originate there and must have been part of the cultural philosophy brought during the migration southward from the San Juan Basin. Ware (2014, 70) also invokes the possibility of amalgamation's occurring in the early Pueblo period when two independent groups merged and their leaders negotiated ritual responsibilities to be complementary and noncompetitive. By this means, all would benefit spiritually from their mutual coordinated ritual leadership.

Based on Tewa binary oppositions in the culture and architecture, I suspect we are dealing with a very old concept that evolved into the social order of ritual moieties. Tewa origin legends claim that an originally unitary group divided and accepted complementary leadership responsibilities to benefit the society (Ortiz 1969, 13). The legend tells how all the Tewa were living under Sandy Place

Lake in the southern San Luis basin in Colorado. Following the instructions of the Corn Mothers, they emerged to start their migration southward to a new home, but they had to return to the lake several times because the earth was not passable or wild animals threatened them. The people started as a unified group, but during the migration, the Hunt Chief was instructed to divide them into two groups, each to follow the lead of two respected chiefs—Winter eating meat along the eastern mountains (Sangre de Cristo) and Summer eating plants along the western mountains (Jemez)—with each now moving down opposite sides of the Rio Grande. After a passage of time and living in several pueblos, the groups joined again at Posi-Owingeh (Ojo Caliente), where they split into today's villages with members of both moieties and all sodalities going to the new pueblos. These stories vary depending upon which moiety the narrator belonged to or in which pueblo he lived.

Kindreds, "Houses," and Ma:tu'in

Lévi-Strauss (1982) created a new social form to account for certain phenomena he termed "*sociétés à maison*" or "house societies." He defines a house as "a corporate body holding an estate made up of both material and immaterial wealth, which perpetuates itself through the transmission of its name, its goods and its titles down a real or imaginary line considered legitimate as long as this continuity can express itself in the language of kinship or of affinity and, most often, of both" (194). Beyond medieval Europe with its royal estates or hierarchical Southeast Asian societies, Lévi-Strauss found houses in North America among the *Kwakwaka'wakw* (Kwakiutl) on the Northwest Coast and Yurok in California. As examples have grown, the house society concept has been expanded and found greater relevancy for social interpretation (Carsten and Hugh-Jones 1995). Because it applied to European societies, archaeologists quickly adopted it and made modifications to fit their evidence (González-Ruibal 2007). New World archaeologists have found this a productive concept as well (Joyce and Gillespie 2000 in Mesoamerica, Beck 2007 in the Southeast, Heitman and Plog 2005 in Chaco Canyon). The house is central to Whiteley's (2008) reanalysis of Hopi social structure, which questions the purported unity and solidarity of clans as corporate descent groups. At the Orayvi split, it was bilateral households, the core principles of houses, that moved as units to form new villages, in no instance whole clans. In Whiteley's analysis, the house framework inclines understanding of Hopi social structure away from descent toward alliance theory, focusing on households united or "allied" by patterns of marriage exchange. The house concept may also be applied to the Tewa, insofar as Lévi-Strauss's definition fits ma:tu'in quite well. (My perspective here was specifically enhanced by discussions at the SAR seminar.)

In the Tewa case, the physical embodiment of the house is not elaborate, being consistent with the Tewa ethos of equality, the traditional physical non-differentiation of houses, and a failure to invest conspicuously in the structure. The socioreligious activities and the relatives inside distinguish it as a Lévi-Straussian-type house. One of the best descriptions of the Tewa as a house society (without any anthropological jargon) is a series of papers by the Tewa architectural historian Rina Swentzell (2001, 2006, and Naranjo and Swentzell 1989). For the Tewa, there may be a physical structure, a dwelling, where the most esteemed elder lives. This building is used for corporate rituals where all the members of a ma:tu'i congregate (as for All Souls, described above). This has been called "an occasional kinship group" where the members meet for calendrical or crisis events but not on a regular basis. The physical houses are real, sacred, and symbolic among the Tewa and there are beliefs about the "life of the house." It needs to be fed with cornmeal, blessed with prayers, and the life cycle of deterioration it experiences through time acknowledged and appreciated (Swentzell 2001). The pueblo is built around a shrine (*nansipu*) in the plaza (*bu-ping-geh*), which makes all village space sacred (Naranjo 1995). The house gains ritual importance as the owners' achieved status is acknowledged. The ma:tu'in are not in competition the way noble houses are elsewhere. By preserving their bilateral character, they have a steady recruitment of members by birth (although adoption is possible), a productive land base, and names in the social structure to accommodate external trade. In fact, the named ma:tu'in are undoubtedly a stimulus to intertribal economic exchanges. The Tewa have a house society to the degree that the ma:tu'i is multidimensional in its many obligations, noncompetitive, dynamic in behavior and social relations, and highly ritualistic. More traditional functional and economic family obligations also apply but are not foremost.

Seen through the lens of the "house," aspects of Tewa and Hopi social organization may not be so far apart after all. In this regard, at least, the old opposition between Western and Eastern Pueblo social and kinship systems (the latter defined as unilineal clans vs. kindreds) to some extent begins to dissolve.

What Have We Learned?

Social organization of the Eastern Pueblos has undergone numerous examinations and dramatic explanations by anthropologists. Some were short-lived but left erroneous lasting impressions. One produced Tewa "clans." John Ware has convinced me (in discussions at the SAR seminar) that at some point in precontact history the Tewa had clans for a short period before they were totally replaced, in part by sodalities and in part possibly by bilateral kindreds, ma:tu'in, and their correlation with the "house society" form, which deserves to be further developed for the Tewa and possibly other Eastern Pueblos. Can ma:tu'in be found in the archaeological record? Do they date before Spanish contact? How important were ma:tu'in in the Tewa past? These are questions that remain to be investigated, but I doubt that ma:tu'in existed before the evolution of a sophisticated dual organization and a highly developed maize horticulture. Ma:tu'in are important social units today in some of the Eastern Tewa pueblos (Ohkay Owingeh, Santa Clara, San Ildefonso, and Tesuque), but in others they have been partially lost (Pojoaque, Nambé). Those that have them recognize their importance for sustaining the family and keeping it adaptable to meet new economic and social challenges.

I apologize to Robin Fox for bastardizing his title *The Keresan Bridge* to form a similar metaphor to understand Tewa kinship (see also chapter 5). Ma:tu'i is one of the most important social-organizational categories in the Tewa Pueblos, but it has been neglected or ignored owing to confused and contradictory applications of "clan." The ma:tu'in have been confused with clans for over a century and still are. Early Southwestern anthropologists spent an exasperating amount of time obtaining clan names for no known purpose other than to suggest a parallel to Hopi. Once this nonsense ceased, a more productive approach to kinship and social organization began with Parsons learning about ma:tu'in, Dozier emphasizing their distinctive kinship functions, and Ortiz using them to explain family social behavior at times of personal stress and crises (Ortiz 1969, 53). Ma:tu'in function to give aid and material and spiritual support to their members by responding to emergencies and crises more quickly than can any other social unit in a pueblo. They were and still are indispensable for the smooth functioning of the entire pueblo.

Kin groups are encapsulated structurally in the term ma:tu'i. It is full of cultural substance and Tewa linguistic meaning and certainly provides a vital social linkage. But defense of nonexistent clans in these Tewa pueblos is a bridge to nowhere.

Acknowledgments

I want to thank many friends in San Ildefonso, Santa Clara, and Ohkay Owingeh for discussing this term and its cultural significance with me. We spoke in English, leading me to miss the subtle meanings of the words and the metaphors that characterize Tewa speech. I tried to learn, to comprehend, and to respect what my teachers were telling me. I thank all of them. However, I am solely responsible for mistakes and misunderstandings incorporated into this chapter. Someday I will get it!

Peter Whiteley organized an inspired Advanced Seminar under the auspices of the School for Advanced Research. I learned a great deal from all the participants. I want to express appreciation to Peter and to John Ware for discovering logical discrepancies and omissions in my paper and contributing to my thinking about Lévi-Strauss's "house society" model.

Notes

1. Descent theory classically derives from the work of the leading structural-functionalist, A. R. Radcliffe-Brown, and others of the British school. Fred Eggan, the most influential scholar of Pueblo social organization, was a student of Radcliffe-Brown and a strong proponent of his views (Whiteley 1985).

2. "Gens" (pl. "gentes") was used interchangeably with "clan" during this period. "Clan" eventually prevailed.

3. Like that of "clan," the meaning of "kindred" evolved in anthropological usage, but its specific distinction from clan and lineage (as unilineal descent groups) is the important point here. Although Freeman (1961) dismissed the idea that kindred may include affines (in-laws) as well as biological and adoptive kin, Nadel's expanded sense captures the Tewa concept of *ma:tu'i* quite well. He states that kindred means "the ramifications of the biological family. The kindred thus embrace both lines of descent, with all the agnatic and collateral links. We also include in-law relationships in this term" (Nadel 1947, 12).

CHAPTER THREE

The Historical Anthropology of Tewa Social Organization

SCOTT G. ORTMAN

In this chapter, I examine the "homologies and heterogeneities" in Tewa social history using multiple lines of evidence, including archaeology, linguistics, ethno-toponymy, oral tradition, and ethnography. I use the term "social organization" to refer to society overall, while recognizing that it is helpful to distinguish *community* organization from *household* organization in certain situations. My basic model (Ortman 2012) is that the Tewa *language*, and most of the Ancestral Tewa *population*, originated in the Mesa Verde (hereafter "MV") region, but Tewa *culture* and *identity* took shape as a large portion of this population entered the Northern Rio Grande and interacted with existing inhabitants of the Tewa Basin in the thirteenth century CE. This model is based on analyses of population histories of the source and destination areas; biodistance of osteometric traits; phonological and etymological patterns in Kiowa-Tanoan languages; oral traditions, place names, and place lore; connections between MV material culture and "semantic fossils" in the Tewa language; and archaeological patterns from the source and destination areas.

Archaeologists have long debated the relationship between Ancestral Tewa society and the earlier MV society (Boyer et al. 2010; Dutton 1964; Duwe and Anschuetz 2013; Habicht-Mauche 1993; Kidder 1924; Lakatos 2007; Lipe 2010; Mera 1935; Wendorf and Reed 1955; Wilson 2013). The framework adopted here postulates that Tewa culture and identity originated in the thirteenth-century Northern Rio Grande, but also recognizes that most of the people who formed and formulated this society were migrants from the MV region; and that the language of this new society, which we know today as the Tewa language, was introduced to the Northern Rio Grande via these migrants.

Although I here draw several links between MV region archaeology and Tewa oral tradition and language, these should not be taken as evidence for a one-to-one relationship between MV archaeology and contemporary Tewa people. It remains possible, even likely, that additional languages were once spoken in the MV region, and that MV people migrated to a variety of destinations during the late 1200s. Also, people were clearly already living in the areas that would become the Tewa homeland prior to this time. It is reasonable to ask how these people contributed to an emergent Tewa society. Still, my purpose is not to provide a comparative analysis, but to focus on historical developments along specific paths that tie contemporary Tewa communities back to MV. In focusing on this particular thread, I do not mean to suggest that the characteristics of Tewa culture and tradition I discuss are unique to Tewa communities. Many are in fact widely shared across the Pueblo world. I also beg readers to resist the temptation to generalize from this specific case — the view of Tewa ethnogenesis that emerges from this discussion looks the way it does because that is what the evidence suggests. Whether this process applies to the emergence of any other Pueblo group is an empirical question, and there is no a priori reason to assume that it does.

My framework concerning Tewa origins leads to several possible scenarios regarding the history of Tewa social organization. Given that the Tewa language and most of the Ancestral Tewa population derived from the MV region, many elements of ethnographically described Tewa social organization could have originated in MV and been carried over into Ancestral Tewa society. On the other hand, several elements of Coalition Period (1200–1350 CE) material culture in the Tewa Basin derive from earlier Developmental Period (900–1200 CE) traditions, and many elements of MV material culture were effectively "lost in transit" to the Rio Grande (Lakatos 2007; Lipe 2010; Wilson 2013). So it is also possible that the elements of Tewa social organization were invented in Developmental communities, among MV migrants as they moved, or in the context of interethnic interaction following migration. I will address each of these scenarios and conclude that all three processes were involved.

Tewa Oral Tradition as History

In the early days of American archaeology, researchers paid close attention to Native oral traditions and interpreted them as relatively straightforward reflections of tribal histories (Cushing 1888; Fewkes 1900; Jeançon 1925; Mooney 1898a). Lowie (1915b, 598) questioned this approach, noting that "we cannot know [oral traditions] to be true except on the basis of extraneous evidence, and in that case they are superfluous since the linguistic, ethnological, or archaeological data suffice to establish the conclusions in question." This critique led to decades of neglect of oral traditions as historical evidence, but from today's post-NAGPRA perspective, Lowie's view has two shortcomings. First, it overlooks the role of oral tradition for narrowing the range of hypotheses to be tested; and second, it presumes that the interpretation of linguistic, ethnological, and archaeological data is more straightforward than it actually is. Today, researchers acknowledge that interpretations of every line of evidence depend on evolving theoretical paradigms, and that with proper care, oral tradition can provide evidence that stands on its own (e.g., Vansina 1961). As a result, there has been renewed interest in the integration of archaeology and oral tradition (Beekman and Christenson 2003; Bernardini 2005a; Echo-Hawk 2000; Fowles 2004; Schmidt 2006). The following analysis continues this trend and makes the case that Tewa origin narratives, in the words of one Santa Clara elder, "contain the historical knowledge of how we came to be and how we now live our simultaneous realities of past and present" (Naranjo 2008, 258). While I acknowledge that Pueblo origin narratives also support the central values, ideas, and institutions of Pueblo culture (Ortiz 1969), I suggest this structural dimension is grounded in actual past events, as it is this connection with reality that ultimately gives oral traditions their moral authority.

Several versions of the Tewa origin narrative have appeared in print (Naranjo 2006; Ortiz 1969; Parsons 1929, 1994[1926]; Yava 1978). The most detailed are those of Parsons and Ortiz, both of which derive from Ohkay Owingeh. The elements common to both are as follows:

1. The people were living in *Sip'op^{h}ene* beneath *^{7}Ok^{h}angep'ok^{w}inge* "Sandy Lake Place" in the distant north. Supernaturals, humans, and animals all lived together in this place, including the first mothers of the Tewa, "Blue Corn Close to Summer" and "White Corn Close to Winter."

2. The corn mothers asked one of the men to go out and explore the way by which the people might leave the lake. This man went out to the north, west, south, and east, but each time returned, reporting that the world above was still *ochu,* "unripe."

3. Then the corn mothers asked this man to go to the above. There, he was attacked by all of the predatory animals and then magically healed and given a bow and arrow, buckskin clothes, and a headdress of feathers

from carrion birds. He returned to the lake as "mountain-lion man," or the Hunt Chief.

4. The Hunt Chief then gave an ear of white corn to a man and told him to lead and care for the people during the summer, and a second ear of white corn to another man, telling him to lead and care for the people during the winter. Thus the dual chieftainship of the Summer and Winter moieties came into being, and the moiety chiefs joined the Hunt Chief as *pa:t'owa* or "Made People."

5. The Made People then told six pairs of brothers, the *Towa'e*, to go out to each of the directions and scout the way for the people to leave the lake. Each pair shot arrows to determine the orientation of the directions. The blue brothers went to the north; the red brothers to the west; the yellow to the south; and the white to the east, and all reported seeing a mountain on the horizon, and they slung mud toward each of these, creating the *tsin* or cardinal flat-topped hills. The black-colored brothers then went to the above and saw the morning star on the horizon, indicating that the dawn was near, and the all-colored brothers went to the below and saw a rainbow in the distance against the hardening ground. Following this, the Towa'e were added to the ranks of the Made People.

6. Based on these reports, the people prepared to leave the lake. Summer Chief went out first, but his feet sank into the mud, so Winter Chief led the way, freezing the ground before him so the people could walk. Soon some of the people began to get ill, so the Made People concluded the group was not yet complete; they needed something else before they could leave the lake. Accordingly, they returned to the lake and the Hunt Chief created the first leader of the medicine society.

7. The people then attempted to leave the lake three additional times, but each time they discovered they were still not complete. Upon a second return to the lake, the *K'ósa* or "Clown" Society was established; upon the third, the Scalp Society; and upon the fourth, the Women's Society. The leaders of all these societies were added to the ranks of the Made People.

8. Finally, the people were ready to leave, and they proceeded southward in two groups. The first group followed the Winter Chief down the east side of the Rio Grande and subsisted by means of hunting. The second

group followed the Summer Chief down the west side of the river, subsisting by means of farming. After proceeding southward in twelve steps, they came back together and formed a village containing both groups.

In the accounts summarized above, the primordial, preemergence home of the Tewa is referred to as Sip'op^{h}ene, which lies beneath a brackish lake called ʾOkhągep'o:kwinge "Sandy Lake Place." Harrington (1916, 567) associated these names with Sierra Blanca Lake, in the San Luis Valley of Colorado, some 150 miles north of the present-day Tewa villages and in an area where Ancestral Pueblo settlements do not occur. Thus, a key issue that arises with respect to historical interpretation of Tewa origin narratives is how to interpret references to this point of origin. I suggest the solution rests on three points.

First, in other contexts Tewa people often reference the MV region, located northwest of the Tewa Basin, as a prior homeland. For example, Aniceto Swaso, a Tewa from Santa Clara Pueblo, specifically named Mesa Verde as a place Tewa ancestors dwelled in the past (Jeançon 1923, 75–76). Harrington (1916, 564) also recorded a Tewa name for the Montezuma Valley (*Phaa p'innae'ahkongeh* "Plain of the Yucca Mountain"), adding: "It is said that in ancient times when the Tewa were journeying south from *Sip'op^{h}ene* the *K'ósa*, a mythic person who founded the *K'ósa* society of the Tewa, first appeared to the people while they were sojourning in this valley." Note that this statement refers to Sip'op^{h}ene as having been north of the Montezuma Valley as opposed to beneath Sandy Lake Place itself. This transposability suggests that Tewa people often conceive of the emergence place as being in the distant north from wherever the community happens to be, as opposed to being an absolute geographic location. Finally, Spanish documents, maps, and ethnographic sources suggest that Tewa people do maintain social memories of an ancestral homeland in Southwest Colorado and refer to this place as *Tewayó* (Ortman 2012, chapter 8). So it is clear that Tewa people have retained awareness of the MV region as an ancestral homeland despite its absence from published origin narratives.[1]

Second, the placement of Sip'op^{h}ene in the San Luis Valley is appropriate given contemporary Tewa (and general Pueblo) cosmology. All traditional Tewa ceremonies are performed four times, following a ritual circuit that begins in the north, then proceeds to the west, the south, and finally east, as reflected in the activities of the Towa'e in origin narratives (Kurath and Garcia 1970; Laski

1959; Ortiz 1969). Naranjo (2006) explains that Tewa people today conceive of the world as having nested layers of lakes corresponding to the cardinal directions of the ritual circuit, at the far edges of the world, on the tops of the cardinal mountains, within the cardinal hills, beneath the directional village shrines, and in the center of the village itself. Importantly, the underworld waters of the emergence place can be accessed at any number of places, including at *P'osí'p'o:pí*, the hot springs adjacent to *P'osí'ówîngeh*, the northernmost ancestral Tewa village (Richard Ford, personal communication, 2009). This suggests that geographic referents in Tewa origin narratives are not intended to index locations where events actually occurred, but rather places in the current tribal landscape that reinforce the primary purposes of these narratives (Basso 1996; Ortiz 1969; Ortman 2008a).[2]

Third, the ultimate significance of the lake in Tewa origin narratives is spiritual. Tewa people today explain that the ancestral spirit world is the mirror image of this one and can be seen as the reflection on a still body of water. A range of bodily experiences, from the reflection one sees in a still body of water, to one's shadow on the rocks, to the movement of sunbeams in a kiva, all reinforce this conceptualization of the spirit world in terms of mirror-image reflection. From this perspective, then, to say that Tewa ancestors lived beneath the surface of a lake is to emphasize that they lived in a world that was the mirror image of the present world. This provides deep insight into the nature of Tewa origins — namely, that it involved the creation of a society that was viewed as the mirror image of the one from which it derived.

These points suggest it is best to think of Sip'op^h^ene and Sandy Lake Place as metaphors for the more general concept that Tewa ancestors dwelled in the distant north, in a world that was very different from the present one. Given this, an appropriate follow-up question is whether other episodes of Tewa origin narratives echo the history reconstructed from archaeological, bioarchaeological, and linguistic data. The answer here is clearly "yes." The narrative refers to the ancestors of Tewa people as having lived in the distant north, in another land, where they gradually developed the core institutions of Tewa social organization and obtained knowledge of the new land they would eventually occupy. Then, when all was ready, the people left this ancestral homeland in two waves, with the Winter People leading the way along the east side of the Rio Grande, the Summer People settling the west side somewhat later, and the two groups eventually coming together in the Tewa Basin. These elements are consistent with the evidence presented in my previous work, and may even suggest a more detailed association of the Winter People with Tiwa-speaking immigrants from the Upper San Juan during the tenth century (Ortman 2012, 333, note 10), and the Summer People with Tewa-speaking immigrants from the MV region in the thirteenth.[3] If so, Tewa origin narratives may enshrine social memories of the processes by which MV and previous immigrants forged a new society in the Rio Grande, in addition to the MV migration itself (Duwe and Anschuetz 2013; Ortman 2012).

Tewa Institutions in Oral Tradition and Archaeology

Given that Tewa oral tradition emphasizes the historical relationship between contemporary Tewa people and the MV component of their ancestry, the origin narratives outlined above lead to the hypothesis that many core institutions of Tewa social organization were established prior to, or coincident with, the migration of MV people to the Northern Rio Grande. In the order of their creation, these institutions are: 1) the hunt chieftainship; 2) moieties; 3) the directional scouts; 4) the medicine or curing society; 5) the K'ósa society; 6) the Scalp Society; and 7) the Women's Society. Below, I discuss evidence related to a possible MV origin of each of these.

THE HUNT CHIEF

Traditional Tewa communities maintained a hunt society with a permanent head whose responsibilities included the organization of communal hunts (Parsons 1939, 126–27). It is reasonable to propose that the earliest leadership institutions emerged in the domain of hunting, as game animals represent one of the most important common-pool resources of early agricultural societies, and collective action would have been needed to maintain a secure, long-term supply of essential animal products. Tewa origin narratives also emphasize the association of the Hunt Chief with carnivores, raptors, and carrion birds, and the traditional attire of this person also involves parts of such animals. In traditional Tewa culture, the Hunt Chief is appointed for life, so one would expect the items used by such a person to be associated with their residence and with locations in which political leadership is exercised. Thus, one might expect archaeological correlates of a Hunt Chief to include an association of carnivores, raptors, and carrion birds with architectural spaces where leaders lived or worked.

These associations are apparent in two different aspects of MV region archaeology. Several studies have noted the association of faunal remains of carnivores and birds (not turkeys) with pit structures or kivas that were both the homes of political leaders and locations where important meetings of small groups took place. This pattern has been identified for the D-shaped building at Sand Canyon Pueblo, a thirteenth-century village (Muir 1999), and an oversized pit structure in the center of a U-shaped roomblock at McPhee Pueblo, a ninth-century village (Potter 1997). These patterns suggest an association between hunting imagery and political leadership from at least the ninth through thirteenth centuries.

Rock art imagery also suggests an association of hunting with leadership. For example, a procession panel dating from the tenth century depicts a procession of animals and humans to a rectilinear structure that is guarded by mountain lions (fig. 3.1). Wilshusen, Ortman, and Phillips (2012) interpret this scene as a reflection of Early Pueblo social organization in which mountain lions were icons for leaders, as is reflected in Tewa origin narratives. Although none of this evidence is conclusive, it at least suggests that the association between hunting and political leadership has significant time depth.

SUMMER CHIEF AND WINTER CHIEF

Today, Tewa villages are governed by earthly representatives of the primordial chiefs, with the Summer Chief presiding over the entire community during the summer and the Winter Chief during the winter. Tewa communities are also divided into moieties known as the Summer People and the Winter People, each headed by its respective chief. Membership in a moiety is initially inherited through the father's line, but a person's moiety membership can change upon marriage to a person from the other moiety, or for a variety of other reasons. In some Tewa communities, each moiety has its own kiva; in others, the moieties have separate meeting rooms but share a single kiva.[4] Maps of historic Tewa communities also suggest that moiety members tended to cluster on opposite sides of central plaza areas (Parsons 1929).

Although the Summer Chief is in charge for more of the year today, in the early twentieth century the equinox was viewed as the triggering event for the change of seasons and thus, of leadership (Curtis 1926; Harrington 1916; Hill 1982, 203). Thus, archaeological correlates of Tewa-style moiety organization would appear to include: 1) localization of houses in two distinct groupings and 2) public marking of the equinoxes. There is evidence for both of these in

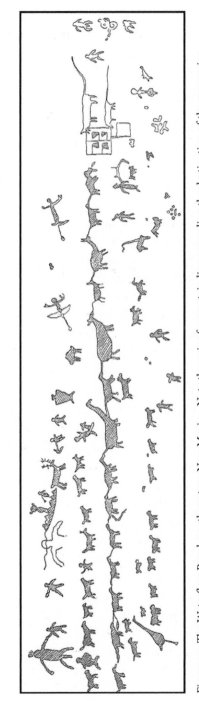

Figure 3.1. The Waterflow Panel, northwestern New Mexico. Note the pair of mountain lions guarding the destination of the procession. Created by the author; modified from Wilshusen, Ortman, and Phillips 2012, figure 11.6.

northern Rio Grande sites dating from the Late Coalition period. Bilocalization of house groups is apparent where Late Coalition communities comprise
paired villages that merged into one during the Classic period (see figure 3.2
for an example). And evidence that the equinoxes were publicly marked via
architecture-landform interactions is apparent at Lamy Junction Ruin, a Late
Coalition site in the Galisteo Basin (1250–1315 CE, from ceramic dating). At this
site on the morning of the equinox, the sun rises in the exact center of Cerro
Colorado, in alignment with the kiva on the most prominent mound (Bernhart
and Ortman 2014, figure 2). Due to the vertical angle from the house mound to
the top of Cerro Colorado, this sunrise does not occur at 90 degrees, so direct
observation of the shadows cast across the site from the hill that morning is the
only way this orientation could have been established.

Both patterns—bilocalization of house groups and public marking of equinoxes—are also apparent in thirteenth-century MV communities. Several
writers have commented on the apparent division of MV region villages into
two complementary parts via a central wall, a central avenue, or a natural drainage, as in the case of MV cliff dwellings (Nordby 1999), canyon-rim villages
(Lipe and Ortman 2000), and Early Pueblo villages of the Dolores area (Ware
2013). In all cases, these divisions have been interpreted as evidence of moiety
organization. In addition, the same relationship between a village, a prominent
hill, and the equinox sunrise observed at Lamy Junction is apparent at Jackson's
Castle, a thirteenth-century MV region village (Bernhart and Ortman 2014).
That this relationship was not coincidental is reinforced by the alignment of
the flat face of a D-shaped stone masonry tower with the hilltop (fig. 3.3), and
the placement of a stone circle shrine on the crest of the hill itself. Thus, there is
good archaeological support for the contention of origin narratives that Tewa
moiety organization originated in the MV region.

DIRECTIONAL SCOUTS

The conceptual structure of the Tewa world (see Ortiz 1969, 18–25) places the
village in the center, around which is a series of cardinal mountains, low hills,
and shrines radiating inward toward the center. Ortiz further notes that an earth
navel shrine (*nansipu*) consisting of a keyhole-shaped arrangement of stones
with the opening facing toward the village adorns each cardinal mountaintop.
These earth navels are spiritual power conduits that gather blessings from the
four directions and channel them back to the village through the opening. In an

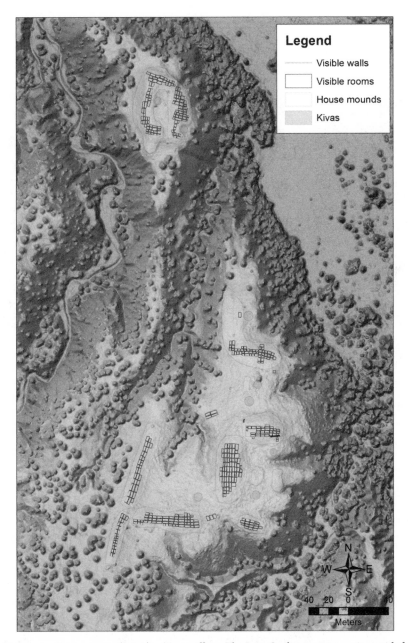

Figure 3.2. Cuyamungue (LA38), a Tewa village. The Late Coalition community resided in the northernmost roomblock on the southern mesa, and on the adjacent mesita to the north. During the Classic Period the community coalesced into a single village on the southern mesa (see Ortman 2014 for details). Created by the author.

Figure 3.3. The equinox sunrise as viewed from the D-shaped building at Jackson's Castle, southwest Colorado. Photo by Robert L. Bernhart, reproduced with permission.

unpublished manuscript Ortiz (n.d., 8) indicates that Tewa people also construct directional shrines on the cardinal hills closer to specific villages. Archaeological evidence indicates that this practice has been going on for many centuries. The best-documented example is the system of four directional shrines identified on hills surrounding *Poshú'owîngeh*, a fifteenth-century Tewa village in the Chama river valley (Jeançon 1923, 70–73).

According to Tewa origin narratives, these directional shrines reflect the activities of the Towa'e. When the people left the lake, each pair of Towa'e went back to the cardinal hill that they had visited when scouting out the world. These primordial beings are said to still inhabit these cardinal hills, standing guard over the community in the middle place. These narratives thus suggest that two purposes of directional shrines on the hills surrounding ancestral Tewa villages were to demarcate the community's territory and to mark the locations where the Towa'e first beheld the distant landforms that define the edge of the world.

Dry-laid stone shrines are widespread in Pueblo ethnographic accounts (e.g., Fewkes 1906; Snead and Preucel 1999) and in the archaeological record (Fowles 2009). However, Tewa shrine *systems* are distinctive in terms of their locations in the four directions surrounding a village, openings that face inward (Duwe and Anschuetz 2013), and their explicit association with the Towa'e in oral tradition. Just such a system has been identified surrounding Castle Rock Pueblo, a thirteenth-century village in the MV region (Ortman 2008a). The placement and characteristics of the directional shrines in this system are nearly identical to those of ancestral Tewa shrines surrounding Poshú'owîngeh. In addition, three of the directional shrines at Castle Rock are close to prominent defensive towers on the edge of the local settlement cluster that appear to demarcate community territory. All of this suggests that institutions similar in conception and function to present-day Towa'e existed in at least some thirteenth-century MV communities.

There are also possible archaeological indications of scouting activity during the period of migration from the MV region. Arakawa et al. (2011) have shown that projectile points were imported to MV sites at increasing rates during the 1200s, and that most were made of obsidian from the Pajarito Plateau, the area that received the largest numbers of MV migrants late in the century. It is well-known that scouting and return migration are important parts of population movement as a social process (Anthony 1990; Duff 1998). Such activities are resonant with the described activities of the Towa'e, who shot arrows to determine the directions in which to scout out the land to be inhabited after leaving the lake. Perhaps these activities are reflected in the obsidian data and are enshrined in Tewa traditions surrounding the directional scouts.

THE K'ÓSA SOCIETY

Ritual clown associations exist in most Pueblo communities (Hieb 1972). In Tewa communities, there are two such societies: K'ósa and Kʷirana. These clowns, along with the other Made People, are tepíngéh, "of the middle of the house," meaning that they occupy a liminal position between the moieties and mediate in ceremonial (and thus political) contexts. This role is marked by their black-and-white striped skin: black is associated with summer and white with winter. During public dances, the clowns typically meander among the dancers, straightening their costumes, pantomiming their motions, and singing out of time. They also walk around the community telling jokes about community members who have not been behaving properly in an attempt to shame the subjects into better behavior. Tewa clowns are thus important enforcers of social cohesion.

Several statements by Tewa people suggest that one group of these clowns,

Figure 3.4. Virtual reconstruction of Goodman Point Pueblo. Note the open plaza spaces within the village. Image © Dennis Holloway, used with permission. Aerial photo by Adriel Heisey and Crow Canyon Archaeological Center.

the K'ósa, is associated with MV ancestors. For example, in the early twentieth century, Curtis (1926, 18) was told that "the *K'ósa* 'come from the north,' that is, the society was instituted in the ancient home of the Tewa." Harrington (1916, 564) independently recorded that the K'ósa first appeared to Tewa ancestors when they lived in the Montezuma Valley. This suggests the K'ósa society was initially adopted by Tewa ancestors living in the MV region.[5]

Direct archaeological evidence for the K'ósa society at MV is lacking. However, given the central role of the K'ósa in plaza ceremonies today, it may be reasonable to associate clown societies with plazas, which began to appear in the MV region and other areas in the thirteenth century (fig. 3.4). Such features appear to date no earlier than the middle 1200s, coincident with a transformation of great kivas from roofed to unroofed forms (Glowacki 2011; Glowacki and Ortman 2012). Perhaps the K'ósa society was adopted as these new public ceremonial spaces developed.

SCALP AND WOMEN'S SOCIETIES

All historic pueblos maintained organized war and women's societies (Ellis 1951). Tewa origin narratives indicate that these were established or adopted prior to the migration of Tewa ancestors from the lake of emergence, the former so as to ensure success in warfare and the latter to care for the scalps taken. The traditional activities of these societies are only vaguely understood, but it is reasonable to assume that they provided leadership and organization for war. As with the clowns, there is no specific evidence these institutions were part of MV society. However, direct evidence of warfare, including scalp-taking, is documented on human skeletal remains from thirteenth-century MV sites (Kuckelman 2010; Kuckelman et al. 2002). Further, defensive architecture became much more common during the final decades of Ancestral Pueblo occupation (Kuckelman 2002; Kuckelman, Lightfoot, and Martin 2000). Osteo-logical and other physical evidence indicates interpersonal violence increased significantly during the mid-thirteenth century (Cole 2012). In addition, artifact assemblages throughout the northern Southwest show that mid-1200s Central MV sites contain much higher densities of projectile points, and much lower densities of artiodactyl bones, than elsewhere (Arakawa, Nicholson, and Rasic 2013). This suggests an emphasis on the use of projectiles in war as opposed to hunting. Finally, evidence from villages inhabited at the time of the final depopulation, including Sand Canyon and Castle Rock Pueblos, indicates that organized war parties were responsible for particular attacks (Kuckelman 2002, 2010; Kuckelman, Lightfoot, and Martin 2002; Kuckelman and Martin 2007). All of this implies that warrior organizations were part of MV society prior to the final depopulation of the region.

SUMMARY

The evidence reviewed above suggests that several core institutions of Tewa community organization were at least nascent in MV society. There is also a rough correspondence between the archaeological record and sequences in Tewa origin narratives: the association of hunting with leadership and villages with divided layouts (hunt and moiety chiefs) dates from the Early Pueblo period (800–1000 CE), whereas directional shrine systems and central plazas (scouts and clowns) date from the mid-1200s, and the best evidence for orga-nized warfare (war societies) to the final decades of occupation. This corre-spondence suggests that Tewa oral traditions commemorate the historical development of Tewa institutions in addition to providing a social charter for contemporary Tewa communities.

This analysis also generally supports Ware's (2013) contention that sodality organizations began to develop long before the thirteenth century, and that sev-eral were introduced to the Rio Grande via migrants from the San Juan drain-age. Yet the archaeological evidence reviewed here also suggests that some of these institutions—including scouts, clowns, and war societies—could have been invented or adopted during the middle 1200s, by all accounts a period of rapid social change in the MV region itself (Glowacki 2010, 2015; Lipe 1995; Varien 2010).

Transformations: Archaeological and Linguistic Evidence

Despite evidence of continuity between late MV and ancestral Tewa sodality organizations, other evidence suggests that household and kinship organization changed substantially as Tewa society formed. The clearest archaeological traces of this transformation are architectural. The basic building blocks of MV region communities were "unit pueblos" consisting of a small aboveground block of four to six living and storage rooms, a circular subterranean kiva of about twelve square meters in floor area, and a trash midden (Lipe 1989). During most periods, unit pueblos were dispersed across the landscape, on or adjacent to prime agricultural land, and thus were the primary units of agricultural production (Coffey 2010; Varien 1999). There is also direct evidence of pottery production in most unit pueblos (Bernardini 2000; Till and Ortman 2007). The only significant thermal feature was the kiva hearth, the ashes from which are typically rich in food remains (Adams and Bowyer 2002; Kuckelman 2000). Thus small kivas were the central spaces of houses, almost certainly descended from the pit houses that had characterized domestic architecture since the seventh century. Each unit pueblo also contained a corn-grinding area in a specialized mealing-room, an area of the kiva, or a living room (Hegmon et al. 1999; Mobley-Tanaka 1997; Ortman 1998). The number of adjacent bins in these areas is a measure of the number of adult women who ground corn together, and thus a rough proxy for overall household size (Ortman 1998). Distribution of mealing-area "sizes" (fig. 3.5, top), demonstrates that most unit-pueblo residences housed multiple adult women, presumably members of the same matrilineage. This in turn suggests that unit pueblos were often home to extended three-generational families, perhaps similar to the present-day *ma:tu'in* discussed by Ford (chapter 2, this volume).

In the mid-1200s, every unit-pueblo residence included a kiva. Although the form and decoration of these structures does vary, the prototypical MV kiva presents the family home as a microcosm of a world consisting of an earth bowl below, a sky basket above (Ortman 2008b), and a sipapu (Tewa *nansipu*, "earth navel") in the floor genealogically connecting the household group with the spirit world. Walls of aboveground rooms were finely constructed of pecked-block

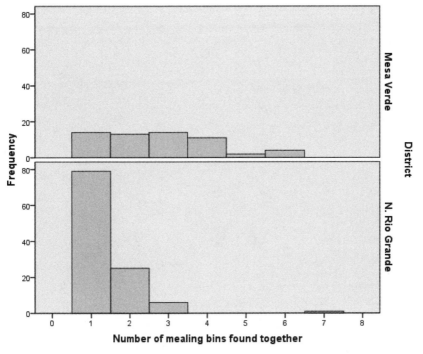

Figure 3.5. Distribution of corn grinding complex sizes in Mesa Verde region unit pueblos dating from 1020–1280 CE and northern Rio Grande sites dating after 1300 CE. Created by the author; data from Ortman (1998).

stone masonry, the exterior surfaces of which resembled the manos used to grind corn inside the house (fig. 3.6). Moreover, these stones were shaped with the same techniques as grinding stones—correspondences that echo the common Pueblo metaphor of people as corn (see, e.g., Black 1984). This is also reflected in the Tewa term for adults initiated into a moiety as *sǫ́tá:towa*, "dry-food people" (Ortiz 1969), or, more literally, "ground and stewed people." The unit-pueblo kiva was where cornmeal was cooked, the above-grade rooms where corn was stored and ground. In the same way, the kiva was the realm of the elder "ground and stewed people" in the family, and above-grade rooms that of the younger members, who were only partly transformed (fig. 3.7).[6]

However, early Tewa houses were very different from MV unit pueblos. While the latter were always built individually, even when they shared walls, early Tewa houses were often apartment-style blocks, with adjacent homes built simultaneously (Creamer 1993; Peckham 1996). Also, whereas unit-pueblo residences apparently housed extended families, corn-grinding areas in Northern

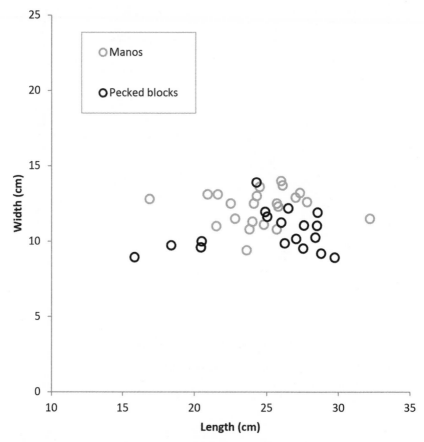

Figure 3.6. Scatterplot of the lengths and widths of individual complete manos from Castle Rock and Woods Canyon Pueblos, and mean lengths and widths of the faces of in situ masonry stones on the external faces of walls at the Hedley Main Ruin. Created by the author.

Rio Grande sites almost always contain a single mealing-bin (see figure 3.5, below), and many were in public view under ramadas or on rooftops (Ortman 1998). Finally, while MV unit-pueblo kivas were architecturally elaborate, early Tewa village kivas were much simpler, and similar to others in the Northern Rio Grande (Lakatos 2007). Moreover, kivas became much rarer in early Tewa villages than they had been in MV: by the early fourteenth century a central single kiva in a plaza surrounded by roomblocks was typical (Adler and Wilshusen 1990; Kohler and Root 2004; Ruscavage-Barz and Bagwell 2006; Windes and McKenna 2006).

These architectural changes betray a pronounced shift in household organization, from extended-family households in MV to nuclear-family households in Tewa society.[7] They also suggest a comparable shift in community organization, away from a system of competing corporate lineages to a more communal form in which sodalities were much more prominent and lineages were deemphasized. This suggests that, even if the important social institutions of contemporary Tewa society first emerged in MV society, they became much more central in early Tewa society.

Figure 3.7. The tower at Painted Hand Pueblo, Canyons of the Ancients National Monument, Colorado. Note the correspondence between the faces of the stone blocks and the surfaces of manos and between the overall shape of the tower and an ear of corn. Photograph by the author.

Images of Community

Etymological evidence suggests that migration to the Rio Grande was also associated with changes in political discourses that deemphasized lineage and emphasized community. One of the Tewa terms for village is *bú:ʔú*, which is related to *bé:ʔe~bú:ʔú*, "small~large low roundish place," and *be* "pottery bowl," both of which are reflexes of Proto-Tanoan **búlu* "pottery (bowl)" (Ortman 2012, appendix A, no. 36). However, the more commonly used term for "village" is *ówînge*, literally "there-standing-at" from the verb *wįnú* "to stand." Wįnú is also applied to growing corn plants and female dancers in the plaza. Thus 'ówînge appears to reflect a conceptualization of the village as a garden, not as a pottery vessel. Ówînge has no known cognates in other Tanoan languages and was thus probably coined after Tewa became distinct, but it was also probably coined prior to 1350 CE because the oldest Tewa sites labeled *ówînkeyi* "village ruin" date from the Late Coalition period (Ortman 2012, chapter 8).

The implied change in the imagining of community (Anderson 1983) embedded in these terms maps nicely onto the changes in community plan that took place as MV society was transformed into ancestral Tewa society. The older term, bú:ʔú, evokes the roundish, concave canyon-rim villages that enclosed natural springs in thirteenth-century MV society (Glowacki and Ortman 2012).[8] In contrast, the newer term, 'ówînge, evokes a garden full of growing corn plants and the plaza full of male and female dancers (Ortman 2011, 2012).

Kiowa-Tanoan Kin-Terms

Finally, comparative linguistic evidence suggests the same scenario reflected in these architectural and semantic changes. Patrick Cruz and I have compiled and analyzed a database of kinship terms for Kiowa-Tanoan languages (2016). Based on these data, it appears that the Tanoan-speaking ancestors of Tewa people had an Iroquois-type kinship system, in which parallel cousins were referred to as siblings and parallel aunts and uncles as mothers and fathers (Trautman and Whiteley 2012a; Whiteley 2015). It also appears from the fact that maternal kin-terminology is more highly developed and exhibits more cognates across the languages that early Tanoan kinship was matrilineal, and thus probably matrilocal. (For a broader discussion of kin-terminologies, see Hill, chapter 6, this volume.) These findings suggest that Tanoan-speaking peoples were originally organized around matrilineal exogamous moieties, as opposed to the nonexogamous moieties of contemporary Tewa communities (see Whiteley, chapter 5, this volume). Proto-Tanoan was probably spoken until the mid-eighth century (Ortman 2012, chapter 7), and thus a matrilineal, exogamous moiety system may have been part of the "San Juan Pattern" of unit-pueblo organization that emerged in Early Pueblo communities (Lipe 2006). Indeed, an ancestral social organization involving exogamous matrilineal moieties maps nicely onto the pattern of unit pueblos, mealing rooms, and divided villages that characterized the MV region.

However, at some point in Tewa history, the uses of kin-terms changed dramatically. The relative ages of siblings continued to be distinguished but not their gender; a number of basic kin-terms came to be mapped onto relations across the community. For example, in both Tewa Village (at Hopi since 1700 CE) and Santa Clara Pueblo, any person of one's grandparents' generation is called "mother" or "father"; anyone of one's parents' generation is called "aunt" or "uncle," using terms that were reserved only for *maternal* aunts and uncles in earlier times. Changes in the treatment of cousins are also interesting, with older cousins coming to be referred to as "maternal aunt" or "maternal uncle," cousins of similar age as "siblings," and younger cousins as "maternal uncle's child" or "maternal aunt's child" (Dozier 1955). These changes mark the extension of family relations to the entire community, and I suspect they occurred during the period of Tewa ethnogenesis along with the architectural changes discussed above.

Conclusions

The basic findings of this study are as follows. First, there is abundant evidence that Tewa origin narratives encode significant historical information concerning the process of Tewa ethnogenesis. When combined with other lines of evidence, these narratives suggest that it is best to think of the process as one where the initial settlers of the Tewa Basin, who did not speak Tewa (but may have spoken Tiwa), were later joined by a much larger group of Tewa-speaking migrants from the MV region. The result was the social and cultural merging of these two groups to form the single society we know today as Tewa society. Second, there is good evidence from archaeology and oral tradition that the key social institutions of historic Tewa society—the hunt chief, moieties, directional scouts, clowns, and warrior societies—were present in MV society prior to the migrations of the late 1200s. This finding is consistent with Ware's (2013) hypothesis that important institutions of Rio Grande Pueblo social organization developed in the San Juan drainage between 600 and 1300 CE. However, several institutions that ended up being central to Tewa social organization may have been adopted in the decades immediately preceding migration. Third, there is clear evidence for a transformation in other aspects of social organization as MV society became early Tewa society, including a change in household (but not necessarily kinship) organization from extended to nuclear families, the reorientation of kinship as an organizing principle for social action, and the extension of familial relatedness to all members of the community. These changes are also largely consistent with Ware's (2013) ideas.

Several lines of evidence adduced in this study support Ware's view that unit-pueblo organization was matrilineal in nature and that Pueblo sodality institutions came about in response to social problems arising from unilineal kinship organizations. MV unit pueblos appear to have been home to unilineal kin groups that varied substantially in size and likely competed for resources and status; traces of Iroquois kinship in Tanoan kin-terms suggest that Tewa moieties as dual tribal sodalities are generalizations from earlier kin-based moieties. The big-picture pattern of Tewa social history that emerges from this analysis is one where non-kin-based organizations were first invented in a society organized around unilineal kin groups, and that these non-kin-based sodality organizations gradually supplanted lineage-based organizations.

Finally, it is important to emphasize that traditional Tewa social organization is not a straightforward descendant of *either* MV *or* Developmental Rio Grande society. Tewa social organization took shape through the process of Tewa ethnogenesis, in which the norms and institutions of both societies were combined in novel ways, in accordance with a discourse of creating a new society that was the mirror image of the old MV society. The result was an innovative type of social organization that reverberated across the Pueblo world and created a remarkably resilient society that continues to thrive in the present.

Notes

1. Of course, this conclusion does not necessarily imply that other Pueblo people do not also trace their origins to the North or to MV in particular.

2. This also provides an explanation for the association of the initial Tewa village at *P'osí'ówîngeh* in the Ortiz version of the narrative.

3. This interpretation of Tewa traditions is also consistent with Taos traditions regarding the origins of Northern Tiwa society as discussed by Fowles (2004). In Taos tradition, the initial settlers of the Taos Valley were the Winter People, who spoke Tiwa. The Summer People, who spoke a different language (Tewa) entered the area by following the Rio Grande northward from the Tewa Basin. In the end, the Tiwa language of the Winter People became the language of the amalgamated Northern Tiwa community, whereas in the Tewa Basin, the Tewa language of the Summer People prevailed. For further discussion, see Fowles, chapter 4.

4. Ware (2013) emphasizes that Tewa moieties are not true moieties because they do not regulate marriage, and should therefore be considered dual tribal sodalities.

5. Whether this society was actually invented by Tewa-speaking people or simply adopted by them prior to migration is less clear.

6. The correspondence between thirteenth-century unit-pueblo architecture and *sǫ́įá:* appears to be another example of a Tewa concept that is materially explicit in MV material culture (see Ortman 2012, chapter 10).

7. This does not necessarily mean that extended groups of relatives did not cooperate on a variety of tasks, only that domestic architecture suggests the basic ideal unit of residence shrank from an extended to a nuclear family.

8. I also note that these villages provide additional context for the concept of *sǫ́įá:*, "ground and stewed people," discussed earlier with respect to unit-pueblo architecture.

CHAPTER FOUR

Taos Social History

A Rhizomatic Account

SEVERIN M. FOWLES

How does society imagine itself as the product of one history or several . . . ?
—Peter M. Whiteley (chapter 1, this volume)

Taos is a Tanoan pueblo whose traditional language is a dialect of Tiwa, and this simple fact strongly governs the way anthropologists and archaeologists have positioned the community within the larger sweep of Southwest history. As Tiwa-speakers, they are often portrayed as isolated Rio Grande autochthons living on the margins of Pueblo history—a conservative branch, little diverged from its Tanoan trunk. The village is ceremonially divided into north and south halves, but this is considered a very weak dual division when compared with the complex moiety arrangements of the neighboring Tewa pueblos to the south. Most anthropologists assume that moieties were principally a Tewa innovation and that the Northern Tiwa simply adopted a veneer of dualism when the Tewa immigrated to the Rio Grande during the thirteenth century. So too with other Pueblo traditions such as katsina ceremonialism. Taos katsina beliefs have been portrayed as superficial, their lack of masked katsina dances serving as evidence that the Ancestral Taos community never quite developed this otherwise pan-Pueblo tradition. Parsons (1936) envisioned two possible scenarios: that Taos either represents a holdover from the old proto-katsina beliefs of the deep past or reflects the recent diffusion of merely rudimentary katsina concepts onto the Pueblo frontier.

Such characterizations have always been problematic, in part because anthropological knowledge of Taos rests on the shakiest of foundations. Parsons was the only ethnographer to publish a descriptive monograph, and her brief and disjointed account repeatedly emphasized both the pueblo's unwillingness to share their knowledge and her own lack of confidence in what little data she did collect. Indeed, Taos continues to be among the most secretive of all the pueblos. This ethnographic problem is compounded by the fact that our understanding of the traditional social organization of Picuris Pueblo—the other Northern Tiwa–speaking community—is even more limited than that of Taos. Picuris would presumably provide an important comparative case, but it suffered mightily during the Spanish colonial period and was reduced to a tiny population by the time anthropologists arrived. There is no synthetic treatment of traditional Picuris social organization or beliefs, no clear understanding of its traditional architectural layout, and almost no documentation of the tribe's own account of the past. Hence, anyone who offers a straightforward and confident characterization of "traditional Northern Tiwa society"—for example, that it lacked the katsina religion or medicine sodalities, or that it was organized by kivas rather than named lineages—has not looked very deeply into the subject.

The presumed provincialism of Taos Pueblo also flies in the face of evidence from the Spanish colonial period. The first sixteenth-century references to Taos describe it as the most populous of all the pueblos in the Southwest (Winship 1896, 575). During the seventeenth century, Taos was an important base of operations for the pan-Pueblo Revolt. And throughout the eighteenth and early nineteenth centuries, it was home to the region's largest trade fair. An economic linchpin, Taos was a cosmopolitan destination for travelers far and wide. It was, in short, anything but marginal and hardly naïve to regional events. And yet, in the hands of most twentieth-century anthropologists, the community comes out looking like an end-of-the-line offshoot. I can only conclude that it was Taos's very success at marginalizing ethnographers and limiting outsiders' access to tribal knowledge that led those same ethnographers to portray the village as marginal to Pueblo history. Somewhere along the way, Southwest anthropologists mistook secrecy for historical conservatism in their accounts of the pueblo.

Things might have developed differently had Matilda Coxe Stevenson, the first serious ethnographer to work at Taos, not been so disrespectful to her Native hosts. Stevenson visited the pueblo between 1906 and 1910, and her aggressive prying did much to mobilize the community against future research. Moreover, her detailed notes were never published. Had they been, a number of new questions regarding Taos social organization would have opened up, and the position of the community within Southwest historical anthropology would today be quite different. Elsewhere I have dusted off Stevenson's notes in an effort to belatedly offer a synthetic model of Taos social organization, circa 1906

(Fowles 2004, 2013).[1] I will not review that model in detail here. Summarily, however, the community appears to have been (1) divided into two ceremonial moieties, which were (2) divided into three kivas each, which were (3) internally divided into various "peoples" (*tai'na* in Northern Tiwa) who had certain ceremonial responsibilities and who (4) participated in a range of crosscutting ritual sodalities (fig. 4.1).

In the present chapter, I focus instead on the contingent pathways that resulted in this specific social organization. My central argument is that an adequate account of Taos social history will be achieved only once we abandon the linguistically derived assumption that the contemporary Northern Tiwa-speaking pueblos evolved out of a more generalized Ancestral Tiwa society that, in turn, evolved from an imagined Tanoan root. Purified histories of this sort—in which a subsequent diversity is preceded by a prior unity—seduce us with their simplicity, but they rarely offer realistic accounts of the past. As the Taos case will amply illustrate, history is always messy, and society's ancestral roots are more often than not a rhizomatic multiplicity. In response to Peter Whiteley's question in the epigraph, then, this chapter explores how we—no less than those we study—might imagine a history that is several. This is to say that, in addition to advancing a number of specific claims regarding Taos's past, my aim is to tackle a broader methodological problem in historical anthropology.

Ethnographic Preliminaries

To lay the groundwork for these inquiries, three ethnographic matters demand our immediate consideration, each of which has been the source of no little confusion in the study of Taos social history.

THE PRESUMED INSIGNIFICANCE OF TAOS MOIETIES

As I have noted, most commentators regard the division of the community into north and south halves as a superficial overlay of dualism that diffused out of the Tewa tradition onto the Northern Tiwa frontier at some point in late precolonial times. As among the Tewa, the Taos moieties are ceremonial divisions with no direct connection to kinship or marriage patterns. But whereas Tewa moiety organization exerts a foundational influence on leadership, group identity, and seasonal ceremonies, it is the kivas that are thought to have always served these basic functions at Taos. We should not ignore this important

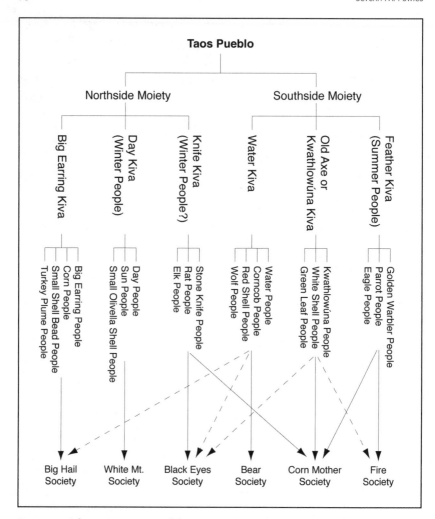

Figure 4.1. Schematic overview of the socioceremonial organization of Taos Pueblo, circa 1906. Arrows indicate kiva contributions to various societies. Solid arrows represent leadership or significant membership; dashed arrows represent minor membership. Created by the author.

Tiwa–Tewa contrast. However, past scholarship has, by my reading, underestimated the role played by the Taos moieties.

Material expressions of dualism at Taos are especially strong: the community is famously divided by Red Willow Creek, establishing a symmetrical north–south opposition between major residential blocks, kiva groups, and ash piles. Stevenson's (1906–1910, file 3.1) research also demonstrated that the kiva clusters had named leaders—the Big Earring Man of the north side and the Water Man of the south—who were the major players in community decision-making, who curated sacred bundles, and whose kivas assumed leadership of the important Blue Lake ceremonies in alternate years. Moreover, the moieties had seasonal and subsistence associations: the north-side kivas were in charge of most ceremonial obligations associated with winter and hunting, while the south-side kivas were similarly associated with summer and agriculture. We can, then, identify a seasonal alternation in leadership comparable to that of the neighboring Tewa.

From a historical perspective, there is no a priori reason to conclude that moiety organization at Taos was either a late or a superficial addition. Indeed, as I have argued elsewhere, the material expression of dualism has even deeper roots in the Northern Tiwa region than in the Tewa region (Fowles 2005). Nor is there any a priori reason to assume that moiety organization at Taos was either ascendant, stable, or in decline during the period of early twentieth-century ethnography.

THE PRESUMED SIGNIFICANCE OF TAOS KIVAS

The traditional view is that kivas, rather than moieties, were the key social institutions at Taos. Certainly kivas were (and are) architecturally prominent in the village, and kiva affiliation was (and is) sometimes expressed to outsiders in the same way that clan affiliation is expressed at Hopi. For men, a strong identification with one's kiva began in adolescence during the period of kiva seclusion and its associated initiation rites. But the more pressing question surrounds the degree to which kivas functioned as corporate actors in Taos society.

Kiva membership was not directly determined by kinship, and Taos kivas were not, strictly speaking, lineage or clan houses. Rather, children were dedicated to particular kivas at birth and, in some cases, were drawn into new kiva affiliations by marriage or a curing ceremony. In this way, kiva relationships tended to crosscut kin relationships. Kiva representatives also played major roles in community decision-making. Consider the case of the Big Earring Kiva and its leader, Big Earring Man. He served as chief of not just his kiva, but all the north-side kivas. Parsons (1936, 77–78) described him as "Chief of the Houses, i.e., Town Chief and Council Chief," adding that his position came with a sacred bundle that was kept especially secret. As such, Big Earring Man's kiva would seem to have been a strongly incorporated body within the Taos political system. Of course, the prominence of this position may have been historically variable, depending on the charisma of the particular individual holding it. Stevenson's notes make it clear, for instance, that the power of Venturo Romero—who was Big Earring Man in 1906—derived from his own personal abilities and strong leadership style. Nevertheless, the Big Earring Man was still a *kiva* leader. Hence, Romero's influence while holding this position would appear to point both to the importance of the kiva system and to the victory of ritual sodalities within what Ware (2014) discusses as the enduring struggle against kinship organizations in Eastern Pueblo history.

But the devil is in the details. Venturo Romero had been trained by his maternal great-grandfather, who personally selected him as his successor (Stevenson 1906–1910, file 2.18). He, in turn, apprenticed his son Tomás to be his own successor. Tomás was only twenty years old when Venturo passed away; despite his youth, he inherited the Big Earring Man position from his father and took a seat among the most powerful *łułina* ("old men" or "grandfathers") in the village. Leadership of the Big Earring Kiva, then, did not draw from across the community's kin groups. Rather, the kiva provided an institutional umbrella within which particular family lines could establish long-term influence in community affairs through the monopolization of ceremonial positions, filled by apprentices who obtained the requisite ceremonial knowledge as a personal gift from parents and grandparents. Far from undercutting the power of kin groups—which for the Romero family appears to have been reckoned bilaterally—kivas were the very means by which kin groups solidified their power and influence.

The situation becomes even more complex when we consider the fact that the Big Earring Kiva, like all kivas at Taos, comprised a number of different "people" groups, each of which was composed primarily of a cluster of patrilineally related kin. These people groups seem to have controlled the most important ceremonies and leadership positions. In this sense, the kivas come out looking less like institutions and more like collective facilities serving alliances of corporate kin groups, each conceptually distinct from the kiva that housed it. The Big Earring Kiva, to continue this example, may have contained two ceremonial flutes, but it would be misleading to describe these important objects as the property of the kiva as a collective institution. There were four distinct peoples in the Big Earring Kiva: the "Abalone Shell" people, the "Turkey Plume of Kwathlowúna" people, the "Corn" people, and the "Small White Shell Bead" people. The first two peoples owned one ceremonial flute each; the latter two were fluteless. A similar situation occurred in the Day, Water, and Feather kivas.

As Stevenson observed, "these flutes are regarded as among the most sacred possessions of the Taos and are kept closely in the possession of the fathers of the gentes" (1906–1910, file 4.15) — not, mind you, in the possession of the kivas.

Nearly all of the major ceremonial objects appear to have been owned by individual peoples at Taos. This becomes more significant when combined with the fact that a single people group often had members from multiple kivas. Those Stevenson spoke with were explicit on this point. The Abalone Shell people may have been the leading people in the Big Earring Kiva, with twenty affiliated men in 1906, but "others of the same gens have allied themselves, or their fathers did so for them, to other gens [*sic*] in other estufas [kivas]" (Stevenson 1906–1910, file 3.24). The Golden Warbler People provide another case in point. Stevenson learned that they had "21 men and a number of women. The men all belong as a body to [the Feather Kiva] but others are allied to other kivas. For example, Juan's youngest son joined the kiva of the gens of his mother, [the Sun Kiva], through his mother's gens, the [Day People]. And in like manner, different gentes[2] are scattered among the main bodies of gentes in the different kivas" (1906–1910, file 3.9).

There are serious grounds, then, for questioning the common assumption that kivas were the dominant organizational units at Taos. Kivas may have provided institutional spaces for multiplicities of unrelated families, but there is little evidence that the kiva system actually took social power away from kin groups. Rather, kivas — literally "gathering houses" in Northern Tiwa (Trager 1935–1937) — seem to have been the stages on which the many Taos peoples jockeyed for influence.

THE PRESUMED LACK OF CORPORATE KIN GROUPS

Anthropological accounts of Taos social organization continue to be influenced by Parsons, whose limited access to the community nevertheless led her to strongly assert that Taos altogether lacked corporate kin groups. What prior visitors had mistakenly referred to as "clans" or "gentes," argued Parsons, were simply ritual societies, fully unrelated to kinship. Her comments are worth quoting at length:

> After recording a list of kinship terms . . . the next step was, as usual,
> enquiry into clanship. Indirect questions on collective terms for mother's
> people or father's people or on exogamous rules being inconclusive, I put

a direct question, using the term clan. My informant looked startled. "Are you going to ask questions about religion?" he asked. If so, he was determined not to answer further questions, furthermore no explanation I could offer succeeded in breaking the association in his mind, frightened as he was, between the term clan and religion, any explicit reference to clans was an approach to religion, and implicit references led nowhere. In talk with other Taos townspeople, formal or informal, the outcome was identical. They had no conception, I found, of any matronymic or patronymic exogamous group, and yet the term clan was part of their English vocabulary, and as I came to learn, it denoted a ceremonial group, that is, a clan meant a society. Curiously enough, this misconception due presumably to some visiting ethnologist, has never been corrected by subsequent White visitors, scientist or otherwise (Parsons 1936, 38–39).

Thus did Taos come to provide Southwest anthropology with a clear Eastern Pueblo contrast to the dominance of clanship among the better-known Western Pueblos.

Parsons's information on the major socioreligious groups at Taos was incomplete and inconsistent. Nevertheless, she made three interrelated claims that have come to define Taos's position within comparative Pueblo studies: that (1) the Taos clans were really ritual societies, (2) Taos ritual societies were really kiva societies, and (3) kivas had nothing to do with kinship. This tidy conclusion left Parsons with a fair number of named groups in her own data that could not be explained, and it also contradicted the extensive list of named (kin) groups that Hodge (1912, 690) had obtained from Stevenson and previously published. But Parsons (1936, 39) had a ready answer for at least the latter discrepancy: "That the . . . names in her [Stevenson's] list were given her for the entertainment of her informant, I can but surmise [*sic*]," she wrote.

In retrospect, it was Parsons who was more naïve. Stevenson, in fact, received detailed information on a complex world of Taos social and ceremonial organization that Parsons's data only hint at. As we have seen, Stevenson documented the conceptual autonomy of kivas from the various named people groups housed within them. Each kiva was led by a dominant people group, but each kiva also included members of additional peoples who took part in the kiva's doings without enjoying the same potential for leadership. Moreover, people groups did not have exclusive relationships with particular kivas. The memberships of some were split between multiple kivas. A few people groups even seemed to lack kiva affiliations altogether (Stevenson 1906–1910, file 3.24). Moreover, Stevenson's informants distinguished between what I have been referring to as people groups, on the one hand, and purely ritual societies, on the other. While the names of ritual societies typically also ended in *tai'na* (people), they did not have the same foundation in kinship and were instead defined around particular ceremonies or community obligations.

What were the Taos peoples, then? Were they corporate kin groups? Were they named lineages in possession of traditional privileges, objects, and bodies of knowledge in a way that mirrored the clan systems of the Western Pueblos? Did they once operate like dispersed clans, laying the social groundwork for interpueblo alliances, trade, or the movement of individuals from one community to another?

No one at Taos has ever claimed that formal rules of exogamy accompanied one's membership in, say, the Water People or Abalone Shell People. This, for Parsons, was enough to altogether dismiss the community's repeated reference to these groups as "clans." The more anthropologically nuanced approach, however, would have been to explore more deeply what a clan is (or was) *for Taos*, and how this might have differed from the understanding of clans elsewhere. Such a task remains to be attempted.

The existing evidence at least suggests that one's membership in a Taos people group was usually a matter of patrilineal inheritance. Various affiliations with people groups other than one's father's might develop as well. After marriage, a woman typically built connections with and responsibilities toward her husband's people, for instance. And a child might be promised to a kiva where he would be hosted by his mother's father's people, as in the following scenario narrated to Stevenson by one of her consultants:

> My wife desired that our younger son should join the kiva of her father who belongs to the Ice People. I sent for a member of the *Harl tai'na* [the Ice People of the Day Kiva], this being the name of the kiva to which my wife's father belonged, and made known my wish that my youngest son should become allied with his kiva. My son accompanied the man to his house and ate with him. He afterwards told the boy when in the kiva of the *Harl tai'na* that though he belonged to the *Tocholimofia tai'na* gens [the Golden Warbler People], he also belonged to the *Harl tai'na* by adoption. The children of my boy will belong to the *Tocholimofia tai'na*, because this is his real gens (Stevenson 1906–1910, file 3.11).

Stevenson summarized the situation as follows:

> While certain gens as a body are associated each with some particular
> estufa there is a great mixture of gentes in the different estufas, the child
> becoming ~~associated~~ allied with an estufa chosen by his parents. Involun-
> tary joining of the estufa is done the day of birth. While it is customary
> for the parents to enter the child in the father's estufa it is common for the
> parents to choose another than the father's estufa, and while the boy is
> ceremonially known as belonging to the ~~clan~~ gens of that to which his par-
> ents allied him, this gens plays no part in his family, his children belong-
> ing to his gens by descent, which is through the paternal side (Stevenson
> 1906–1910, file 3.4, corrections in original).[3]

In short, the distinction between an individual's "real" people (his patrilineal
kin-group, by descent) and his other affiliations (his ceremonial/fictive kin-
groups, by parental dedication and often following matrilineal patterns) was
clearly articulated at the start of the twentieth century.

Strictly speaking, Taos kinship adheres to a bilateral Eskimo system with
loose patrilineal tendencies that manifest primarily in ceremonial contexts.
Indeed, when anthropologists began to record kin-terms at Taos during the
first half of the twentieth century, they found that all maternal and paternal
cousins were referred to using the same kin designations, suggesting that mates
were not prescribed and that marriage was instead organized around a simple
prohibition on unions between close blood relations. But in dutifully making
their lists of kin-terms, the anthropologists also documented hints that Taos
kinship organization was more complex in the past (fig. 4.2). In the course of
his linguistic studies during the 1930s, for instance, George Trager (1935–1937,
1943; cf. Curtis 1926; Parsons 1936) encountered a series of distinct maternal
and paternal kin-terms: mother's brother (MB) was linguistically distinguished
from father's brother (FB), as was mother's sister (MZ) from father's sister (FZ),
mother's mother (MM) from father's mother (FM), and so on. Moreover, Taos
kinship organization contained clear instances of skewing insofar as particular
terms were used to refer to related individuals in multiple generations (e.g., one
referred to mother's sister [MZ] using the same term as mother's mother's sister
[MMZ]). Put simply, such terminological complexity was unnecessary for the
operation of a simple Eskimo system.[4]

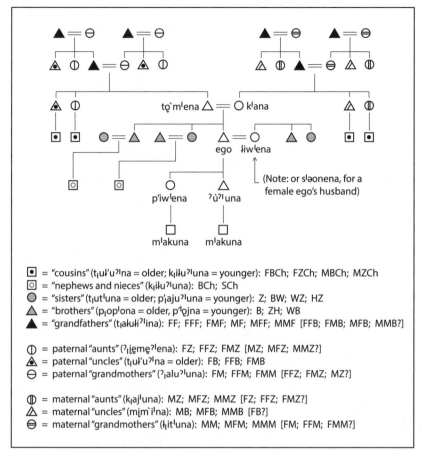

Figure 4.2. Taos kinship terminology during the 1930s, based on Trager (1935–1937, 1943). Brackets include the secondary and presumably more recent extensions of kin terms to wider sets of kin relations. Created by the author.

This evidence strengthens the possibility that at least part of the Ancestral Taos population was once organized around more sharply defined lineages with corporate identities. Beyond the possible traces of this in twentieth-century kinship terms, the patrilineal tai'na or people groups themselves might be regarded as carryovers from earlier times, kept alive in the kiva due to their persistent ceremonial obligations as well as the leadership opportunities they continued to offer. Again, such patterns also demand that we question the common assumption that kinship had been fully supplanted by kivas in the organization of Taos. Named patrilineal groups, as we have seen, continued to be important reservoirs of social and ceremonial power, even if they did little or nothing to regulate marriage.

"A Great Mixture of Gentes": Taos's Tangled Past

Let us now consider the deeper history behind Taos social organization. Most anthropologists have approached this question guided by dendritic models, broadly conceived. They have assumed, for instance, that both Taos and Picuris descend from a shared proto–Northern Tiwa society, from which each has diverged to a greater or lesser degree. Thus, when excavations began in the 1950s at the large Coalition Period village of T'aitöna ("People House" in Tiwa, also known as "Pot Creek Pueblo"), the site naturally came to serve as the model of this common ancestor. It didn't hurt that T'aitöna is located directly in between Taos and Picuris, that it is claimed as a cultural heritage site by both, and that oral histories report that T'aitöna met its end due to a factional dispute (see Fowles 2013). The image of a branching tree diagram arose very easily, in other words. Indeed, we often simply assume that this is how history works: an original unity (e.g., proto–Northern Tiwa society at T'aitöna) diversifies over time into a subsequent plurality (e.g., modern Northern Tiwa societies at Taos and Picuris).

Moving deeper into the past, a dendritic logic continues to govern dominant accounts. Northern Tiwa is linguistically related to the Southern Tiwa language spoken historically in the Albuquerque area, and so it has been assumed that something like a proto-Tiwa society must also have existed as a distant common ancestor to both Taos and Picuris pueblos in the north and Sandia and Isleta pueblos in the south. Most archaeologists think that proto-Tiwa was probably spoken up and down the Rio Grande valley by the region's original agricultural occupants during the Developmental period (600–1150 CE). How proto-Tiwa split into proto–Southern Tiwa and proto–Northern Tiwa is a matter of ongoing debate (Ortman 2012, chapter 3). Some maintain that the original Tiwa society was pushed apart when populations of Tewa- and Keresan-speakers migrated into the Rio Grande valley a few centuries before the Spanish arrived. Others suggest that the Northern Tiwa represent a splinter group that moved north, away from the Ancestral Tiwa homeland in the middle Rio Grande valley. Either way, all accept the basic reality of a sociolinguistic "proto-Tiwa" entity that branched and diversified over time (Boyer et al. 2010, Duwe 2011, Ford et al. 1972, Fowles 2004, Ortman 2012, Wendorf and Reed 1955).

The pattern continues as we move more deeply into remote antiquity. Linguistic affinities between Tiwa and Tewa have prompted hazy visions of a proto-Tiwa-Tewa society that perhaps occupied an expansive region during the first millennium CE. And if we go back far enough, it is assumed that many more groups (not just the Tiwa and Tewa but also the Towa, Kiowa, Piro, and perhaps others) share a common ancestral population that spoke proto-Kiowa-Tanoan and was universally structured by simple principles of matrilineality or some other equally trunklike form of social organization. The adventuresome sometimes squint and search for an even deeper—and perhaps, by this point, Paleo-indian—ancestor that would draw the ancestral Kiowa-Tanoan and ancestral Uto-Aztecan traditions into a single sociolinguistic collectivity.

As should be abundantly clear, such reconstructions depend not just upon a peculiar understanding of how societies evolve—namely, through branching and diversification—but also upon a basic equation of language and society that is usually indefensible. Suffice it to say that (1) languages have their own histories that can be quite distinct from the social and biological histories of language-speakers; (2) language shifts occur for a variety of reasons, not just in colonial contexts but in precolonial ones as well; (3) languages diverge over time, but they can also converge; and (4) the ethnographic record—diverse though it is—is of little use as we attempt to take into account the many languages and language groups that surely died out prior to the colonial era. And yet, these complications rarely prevent us from mapping reconstructed language trees directly onto the social history of a region, such that proto-languages come to assume the position of proto-societies. Thus have archaeologists repeatedly posited the presence of, say, Ancestral Tewas in the Mesa Verde region during the Pueblo II period, or of an original Tanoan population that once extended over much of the Eastern Pueblo world. All such models are governed by a dendritic imaginary in which historical branches necessarily sprout from more generalized ancestral trunks.

There are good historiographical reasons for bracketing off language trees and instead pursuing social accounts of the past that are more attentive to contingent processes of hybridization, creative opposition, selective borrowing, hegemonic emulation, cultural revolution, conquest, alliance, and the like—processes that often involve language change, of course, but that the methodologies of historical linguistics frequently obscure. In the case of Taos, however, there is a special reason for seeking out more complex historical models.

The "people" groups, as we have just seen, were almost certainly the principal corporate actors in the pueblo at the start of the twentieth century. Stevenson's informants offered the names of thirty-four peoples: eight were extinct, six were active but minor players without a strong foothold in the kiva system, and the remaining twenty comprised the core of the community. These were not just structural elements of early twentieth-century Taos society; they were also linked to elaborate narratives detailing individual group migrations over time. Migration histories of this sort are best known among the Hopi, who recount stories of past clan movements that crisscrossed the continent before finally arriving at the Hopi Mesas. Indeed, Hopi historiography could be said to present us with the inverse of anthropological models derived from historical linguistics, insofar as the former emphasizes themes of social *convergence* (i.e., the gathering of the clans) whereas the latter cannot help but see the past as a process of social *divergence* (i.e., the branching of language families). True, the Hopi are often thought to be extreme in this regard. The Tewa, by contrast, recount a somewhat different origin story in which a formative social unity diverged into Summer and Winter Peoples at the time of emergence, only to converge again at the end of an extended period of migrations. This, then, provides a teleological justification for the necessity of Tewa dualism as a balance between interdependent moieties. Despite the linguistic affinities between the Tewa and Northern Tiwa–speaking pueblos and their shared tradition of moiety organization, however, Taos historiography conforms more closely to the "convergence model" of the Hopi.

Consider the ancestral migrations of the Water People, who roamed widely in the Rio Grande valley prior to their arrival at Taos. In one Taos man's words:

> They journeyed slowly, stopping often and building houses as they proceeded to *Kiä chiuthlu biän'ta* (Galisteo). There they lived a short time, and then went to *Towulu tun'ta* (Sage Mountain), a low mountain, where they lived a short time. Then [they] traveled to *Hal ba biän'ta* (Santa Fe Mountain) where they lived a short time. Then [they] traveled to *Poäta biän'ta*, a mountain near Picurís, where they lived a short time. Then they traveled to *Toni chäli sän'ba*, where they lived a short time . . . While here, they were joined by a small number of the Summer People of the different gentes . . .

After leaving *Toni chäli sän'ba*, the Water People journeyed a short distance to *Napä go'na* which . . . is located in Taos canyon. Here they lived a short time and then traveled to *A'täl pa'chiba* and then on to *Whän pa'na*, a valley in the mountains very near to the present pueblo at Taos. They left here and came to *Namulu tu't läda*. After remaining at this place for a short time, the Water People came to *Muluta*, where they lived a short time, then came to the Pueblo of Taos (in Stevenson 1906–1910, file 2.19).

Diverse migration histories of this sort stand behind all the Taos people groups. The more important point, perhaps, is that these narratives present us with a set of ancestral connections that extend not just up and down the Rio Grande valley but also across the Colorado Plateau, into the Rocky Mountains, and out onto the Plains (Fowles 2004).

To engage such indigenous knowledge seriously is to set aside archaeological desires to understand Taos history in the singular as the genealogical outgrowth of a local proto-Tanoan trunk. Here again, we might look to Hopi for more appropriate models. Mindeleff (1900, 645) once portrayed Hopi migrations as "trickling stream[s] of humanity . . . like little rivulets after a rain storm, moving here and there . . . sometimes combining, then separating, but finally collecting to form the pueblo groups as we now know them." Rivulets wandering across the plane of history produce different sorts of historical patterns than trees rising up out of the ground. But we might also draw our models from Taos oral history itself. "The Taos people," Stevenson was told, "were . . . much scattered over a large area. But they finally concentrated at Taos Pueblo, many of the people flocking in at the command of Kwathlowúna like so many birds." This image of pueblo communities as changeable formations of birds, flocking together and then—prior to the reservation system, at least—dispersing again, is even better suited to Taos social history. As we have seen, the Taos peoples did not blend like water but aggregated like birds, keeping their distinctions even while temporarily flying in formation alongside each other.

Some of these distinctions were maintained by people groups through kiva doings such as the narration of origin stories or the use of ancestral languages in prayers and songs. The latter detail is of special importance insofar as it helps us understand why Stevenson's informants were able to offer specific claims about the diverse linguistic heritage of the various people groups before their arrival at Taos. And this brings us to what is perhaps the most historically significant discovery buried within Stevenson's ethnographic notes: most of the precolonial ancestors of Taos—ostensibly a "Northern Tiwa" pueblo—do not appear to have spoken Northern Tiwa at all. Most, in fact, did not even speak a Tanoan language!

Table 4.1 re-creates Stevenson's list of the twenty major Taos peoples, their primary kiva affiliations, and the language each was reported to have spoken at the time of emergence. Note that only six of the twenty spoke the Taos variant of Northern Tiwa prior to joining the pueblo. In fact, the most common ancestral language—previously spoken by nearly half the community—was Apache. Just as surprising is the fact that Stevenson's informants included no Ancestral Tewa–speakers, despite the close linguistic relationship between Tiwa and Tewa; all the remaining peoples are instead reported to have spoken a Santo Domingo dialect of Keresan. This could not possibly represent the full extent of the linguistic and cultural diversity of those who joined Taos over the centuries. During the colonial period alone, we know that various Tewa, Navajo, Ute, Comanche, Kiowa, Spanish, and Anglo individuals, as well as many with "mixed" heritage, found their way into Taos society as well, whether through marriage, adoption, asylum, captive-taking, or some other such process. But table 4.1 at least suggests that Stevenson's informants were attempting to summarize a meaningful chunk of their ancestors' cultural diversity prior to their arrival at Taos and their adoption of Northern Tiwa as a lingua franca.

Note that the summary does not lack nuance. Whereas the Sun People once spoke Jicarilla Apache, the Elk People are said to have spoken Jicarilla Apache "with a slight difference," and the White Shell People are said to have spoken a language that was "only a very, very little like the Jicarilla Apache." An effort, then, was made to distinguish subtle dialectal variations. I see no reason not to trust the historical accuracy of all this. Let me emphasize again that descendant groups continued to speak their ancestral languages in ceremonial contexts. Many historical details would have been accurately remembered for this reason alone.

What, then, are we to make of this information, which is clearly relevant to any historical reconstruction of Taos society but quite at odds with traditional archaeological accounts of the pueblo's past as a purely Tanoan story of descent with modification? What, in particular, are we to make of the indigenous suggestion that the linguistic and cultural ancestry of Taos is instead a hybridic mixture of various Athapaskan and Pueblo traditions?

The individuals Stevenson spoke with had their own answer to this question. They related an elaborate series of oral histories focused on migrations,

Table 4.I. Languages Spoken by the Ancestors of the Taos Pueblo Community, as Related to Stevenson (1906–1910, file 3.1)

Kiva	People name	Language spoken at emergence
Big Earring	Abalone Shell	Keresan (Santo Domingo dialect)?
Big Earring	Corn	Keresan (Santo Domingo dialect)
Big Earring	Small White Shell Bead	Keresan (Santo Domingo dialect)
Big Earring	Turkey Plume of Kwathlowúna	Keresan (Santo Domingo dialect)
Day	Day	Jicarilla Apache
Day	Sun	Jicarilla Apache
Day	Very Small Olivella Shell	Jicarilla Apache
Feather	Eagle	Tiwa (Taos variant)
Feather	Golden Warbler	Tiwa (Taos variant)
Feather	Macaw or Parrot	Tiwa (Taos variant)
Knife	Elk	Jicarilla Apache "with a slight difference"
Knife	Rat-Like Animal	Tiwa (Taos variant)
Knife	Stone Knife	Jicarilla Apache "with a slight difference"
Old Axe	Green Leaf	Apache "but . . . only a very, very little like the Jicarilla Apache"
Old Axe	"Named for the Creator"	Apache "but . . . only a very, very little like the Jicarilla Apache"
Old Axe	White Shell	Apache "but . . . only a very, very little like the Jicarilla Apache"
Water	Corn Cob	Tiwa (Taos variant)
Water	Red Shell	Apache
Water	Water	Tiwa (Taos variant)
Water	Wolf	Tiwa (Taos variant)

conflicts, and the eventual alliance of two broad cultural communities: the Apache-speaking Winter or Ice People of the north and the Tiwa-speaking Summer People of the south. The Winter People were a mixture of the ancestors of the Day, Sun, and Very Small Olivella Shell peoples, whose traditional homeland lay in the snow-covered mountains of Colorado. The Summer People were a mixture of the ancestors of the Golden Warbler, Macaw, and Eagle peoples; their traditional homeland was to the south near "Ojo Caliente" — possibly a reference to the region by that name in the Chama watershed. Taos stories recount the first encounter between these groups as well as the protracted battle that ensued, out of which the Summer People eventually emerged victorious. Once peace was made, a village community composed of both Summer and Winter Peoples was established, to which were added other peoples during subsequent periods of immigration (see Fowles 2004, 2005). From an indigenous perspective, then, Taos society clearly arose through the interweaving of formerly divergent threads of cultural development.

This indigenous narrative differs from dominant non-Native models in a number of respects. Anthropologists have tended to see Eastern Pueblo moieties either in functionalist terms, as a strategy of internal bifurcation designed to manage a growing population (e.g., Dozier 1970; Eggan 1950, 315–17; Hawley 1937; Wittfogel and Goldfrank 1943), or, more recently, in genealogical terms as the long-term inheritance of a basic germ of dual organization that arose during Chacoan times and descended with modification during the post-Chacoan migrations. Proponents of the latter model debate whether this dualistic germ involved actual exogamous moieties or something more similar to the ceremonial moieties of recent times (Ware 2014; Whiteley 2015). Be that as it may, the anthropological account, unlike its indigenous equivalent, remains consistent with the dendritic understanding of historical change discussed above.

The Taos account also differs from dominant anthropological models in its willingness to place Athapaskan groups in a historically foundational position. In fact, most Taos origin narratives state that it was the Apache who first explored and settled the present world at the time of emergence:

Kwathlowúna [a Creator deity of sorts in the Taos tradition] then gave to the Apache a quantity of the hair of the buffalo, deer and other large game mixed together, [as well as] one grain of yellow corn and a little medicine . . . He told the Apache to deposit a small quantity of the mixture in the beautiful springs and rivers of the east, north, west, and south that the game would be plentiful in the four regions of the earth . . . The Pueblos remained with Kwathlowúna for some time after the nomads ascended to the outer world (in Stevenson 1906–1910, file 2.19).

In the fragmentary version related to Parsons (1939, 938), the ancestors of Taos were led from the underworld by Red Person, a figure probably related to the "Red Boy" of Jicarilla Apache mythology (see Opler 1994, 12–13, passim). Curtis (1926, 28–29) also learned that at least some of the Taos ancestors were led by a character known as *Tai'faína* (or "person red-that"), "who is now the recipient of supplication." Tai'faína took his people on wide-ranging migrations: "In groups corresponding to the present ceremonial societies they [the Taos ancestors] traveled in an easterly direction to the plains, where they turned southward to a large river which the present traditionalists believe to have been near Arkansas. They long roamed the plains before recrossing the mountains to become a sedentary tribe in their present habitat" (Curtis 1926, 29). This account, we might imagine, was part of the traditional knowledge passed down among one of the nine peoples at Taos with an Apachean heritage.

Anthropologists have long commented on the close connection between Taos Pueblo and the Apache. Parsons went so far as to report the following:

> In Taos culture there are many Apache-Plains traits or characters . . . :
> Bilateral descent and clanlessness; exclusion of women from the ceremonial life; marked separations of women from warriors; comparatively simple ceremonialism; comparatively indifferent craftsmanship; buffalo hunting; details in dress and headdress of men and women; aggressive, self-assertive, comparatively individualistic temper or character. In physical characteristics also Taos people are said to approximate Plains type. Indeed, except for their houses, Taos people might well pass for Indians of the Plains (Parsons 1939, 3).

The inclusion of both biological and cultural characteristics in Parsons's Taos–Apache comparison should give us pause (see also Curtis 1926)—as should her suggestion that (beyond their Tanoan language, presumably), it is really only Taos's iconic architecture that has led us to label them a "Pueblo" rather than a "Plains" population. But while anthropologists have readily acknowledged this mix of Pueblo and Apache traits, they have largely ignored its social and historical implications. Taos continues to be regarded as an essentially Puebloan community; the Apache are treated merely as an outside influence; the Northern Tiwa are repeatedly reduced to one branch in a diversifying Tanoan tree. We continue, in other words, to search for certain core elements of social organization that have evolved in a quasi-biological manner via descent with modification.

I have been guilty of this tendency to read the Northern Tiwa past in purely Puebloan terms as well. In my own consideration of the confrontation between the Summer and Winter People in Taos oral history, I once proposed that we treat the Apachean identity of the various Winter Peoples as more metaphoric than real. "Apache," I suggested, may have been a narrative stand-in for the earlier, hunting adaptation of the Winter People, who nevertheless were still "Ancestral Pueblo" at heart (Fowles 2013). Notions of a cosmic balance between summer/winter, agriculture/hunting, female/male, and so on are very common across the Pueblo world, particularly up and down the Rio Grande valley; my prior proposition, then, was that the Northern Tiwa simply reconstituted an ancient and decidedly Pueblo tradition of dualism using local social categories following their arrival in the Taos region.

I now see two problems with this position. First, it tends to encourage an understanding of Taos oral history as a fundamentally mythological discourse in which the overriding symbolic structure is taken as more meaningful than the many historical details. To be sure, all Pueblo oral histories invoke cosmological themes and draw upon stock narrative conventions of one sort or another, but this is not to say that they lack a robust engagement with the "real" history of contingent events. Second, the treatment of "Apache" as a kind of floating signifier rather than a set of specific historical actors once again draws us away from grappling seriously with the pluralism of the Taos peoples and their varied pasts.

The alternative is to approach Taos social history from a rhizomatic perspective. Indeed, if we are to escape the successive reduction of Taos's genealogy to a purified Tanoan trunk, then we must begin by taking the pluralism that is already documented within indigenous oral history seriously—which is to say, literally. Might it be the case that what we now know as "Taos Pueblo" actually did emerge through the interweaving of diverse peoples, including many with Athapaskan backgrounds? Might the past be *more* complex, in this sense, than the present? In short: might history take the form, not of a trunk diversifying into branches, but of roots gathering together into a trunk?

Thinking Rhizomatically

Space does not allow a thorough consideration of such questions. But we can open a small door by briefly considering the evidence in support of Taos's claim that many of its people groups did indeed have Athapaskan ancestry and that the community itself grew as a marriage between Apache and Pueblo groups.

Certainly there is nothing in the documentary record of the Spanish colonial period that would contradict this central proposition. Various Apache-speaking bands were already well established throughout the territories surrounding Taos in the earliest Spanish reports. Presumably the ancestors of the Jicarilla Apache had even begun to develop, by this point, their distinctive understanding of Taos as "the middle of the earth" and as the storied landscape where White Bead Woman and her children dwelt (see Mooney 1898b). Moreover, it is well-known that during the seventeenth and early eighteenth centuries, when the colonial yoke became oppressive, both Taos and Picuris readily left their pueblos to join the Apache on the Plains. The close connection between the Northern Tiwa and Apache during the Spanish period went both ways, of course. The Apache not only wintered regularly at Taos and Picuris, but when Comanche incursions on the Plains became severe in the eighteenth century, many Jicarilla Apache fell back to the Taos region permanently, where they quickly integrated themselves into local economic and political life (see Eiselt 2012).

It comes as little surprise, then, that the colonial era material cultures of Taos and the Apache reveal a great many similarities. I have already noted Parsons's early opinion that "except for their houses, Taos people might well pass for Indians of the Plains." Here I might add that, ironically, many Apache sites just east of the Sangre de Cristo Mountains might pass equally well as Puebloan — but for certain subtle details of their pottery. In his seminal early summary of Apache archaeology in northeastern New Mexico, for instance, Gunnerson (1969) reported on the Glasscock Site, a classic "unit pueblo" settlement that was more or less identical to those of thirteenth-century Taos in morphology and orientation. However, the Glasscock Site was built around 1700 CE, is dominated by micaceous pottery, and was presumably occupied by one of the various semisedentary Apache bands whom the Spanish found living in scattered farming rancherías. In fact, even the presence of micaceous pottery does little to distinguish these sorts of sites from the Northern Tiwa pueblos, for a shared tradition of micaceous pottery production seems to have simultaneously come to dominate *both* the Jicarilla bands and Taos and Picuris during the seventeeth century (Dick et al. 1999, 92–94; Eiselt and Ford 2007; Woosely and Olinger 1990). Suffice it to say that a complex back-and-forth between "Apache" and "Pueblo" worlds was central to the lived experience of most Native groups in the greater Taos region as far back as we have written records on the subject.

The traditional interpretation of such interethnic connections is that they lack significant time depth: the Apache are thought to have arrived in New Mexico only circa 1500 CE, and their alliance with certain pueblos — Taos, in particular — is assumed to have simply been a strategic component of the wider Plains–Pueblo macroeconomy, which emerged during the sixteenth century and was greatly amplified by equestrianism in the seventeenth and eighteenth centuries. As such, there has been no archaeological effort to envision a pre-colonial Apachean presence in Taos. Northern Tiwa "prehistory" still tends to be regarded as an exclusively Ancestral Pueblo affair.

However, a spate of new research is now pushing back our estimates of Athapaskan entry into the Southwest. Gilmore and Larmore (2012) provide a good sense of this: "The early dates associated with Athapaskan sites along Colorado's Front Range," they argue, "support a pre-AD 1400 entry of the proto-Apache into eastern Colorado and the Southern Plains and provide tantalizing evidence for a much earlier, perhaps fourteenth-century (or earlier) entry of Athapaskan people into the traditional Southern Athapaskan homelands" (67). Located at the base of the southern Rocky Mountains, Taos would have been among the very first "Pueblo" areas to grapple with the Athapaskan arrival. Indeed, in the Cimarron region — just over the mountains from Taos — plausibly Apache tipi hearths have produced radiocarbon dates in the fourteenth century (Winter 1988, 60).

Provocative hints of an early Apache presence have been found within the core Taos region itself. At the thirteenth- and early fourteenth-century site of T'aitöna, for instance, excavations have produced an array of Plains artifacts fashioned from nonlocal materials. Beveled "diamond knives," "turkey tail" bifaces, large snub-nosed scrapers, serrated-edge bone fleshers, bison humerus-head abraders, a red stone elbow pipe (fig. 4.3) — all these objects point to a transfer of technologies from Upper Republican and/or Panhandle cultures into the Taos region some time around 1300 CE.

In fact, there is no point in the past millennium when Taos archaeology does not reflect the creative entwining of different peoples and traditions. The earliest part-time farmers of the Developmental Period (locally, 950–1200 CE), for instance, produced small numbers of Kwahe'e black-on-white jars that look

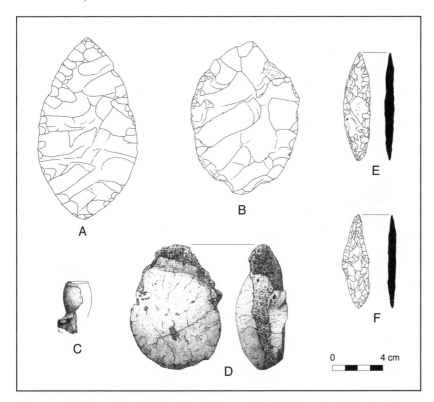

Figure 4.3. Evidence of early Plains–Pueblo networks at T'aitöna. A and B = "turkey tail" bifaces fashioned out of fine-grained banded quartzite and exotic brown chert, respectively. C = a red stone elbow pipe. D = a bison humerus-head abrader. E and F = "diamond" knives fashioned out of exotic chert. Created by the author.

similar to contemporaneous Chacoan vessels; but they also produced plenty of unpainted jars with incised herringbone motifs and neck-banding that have no Puebloan antecedents and instead link early Taos pottery to that of Cimarron and Trinidad, if not also to Southern Plains ceramic traditions more generally (fig. 4.4). Strong Pueblo influences from the south and west—including the brief introduction of katsina iconography, specialized corn-grinding rooms, the great kiva, and the D-shaped kiva (Fowles 2013)—appear during the Coalition Period (1200–1325 CE); as we have just seen, so too do new material influences from the Plains. Osteological studies have even demonstrated the cohabitation of two morphologically distinct populations of women at T'aitöna during the Coalition period: one with the skeletal markers of a life spent grinding corn and another without such markers (Whitley 2009).

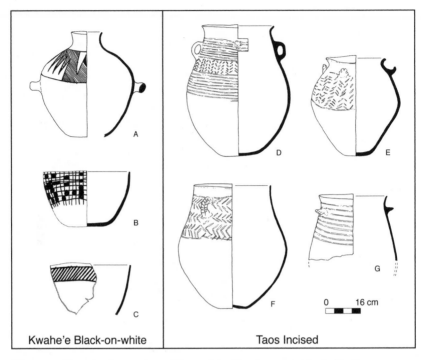

Figure 4.4. The mixed ceramic traditions of the Developmental Period in Taos (Provenience: A = LA 260. B = LA 102063. C = LA 102062. D and E = Cerrita Site. F and G = LA 102062.). Created by the author.

Whether or not these hints of an early Apache presence in the region are amplified by future research, I submit that the emphasis on ethnic admixture in Taos oral history better accounts for the empirical record than the traditional archaeological understanding of Taos as a Tanoan offshoot. In this sense, the fact that Northern Tiwa eventually emerged as the indigenous lingua franca at both Taos and Picuris should not be prioritized any more than the fact that English has more recently become linguistically hegemonic among all Native groups in the region. Here I am reminded of an old Jicarilla story:

> When a small group broke off from the main body the children would begin playing games. The children of one group would say, "Let's play we are Pueblo people." The grownups paid no attention at first, but the children kept on using this strange language and carrying on in these strange ways. Soon everyone began to know this manner of talking and these ways, and before long this was the way everybody talked and acted . . . This is

how the different groups originated and the different languages and customs came to be (Opler 1994, 47).

Conclusions

Taos social history, as I hope to have made clear, cannot be viewed simply as a branch of a Tanoan tree that grew outward from a singular trunk. Nor can it be reconstructed through a search for proto-versions of successively simpler and more generalized Pueblo societies. Taos should instead be viewed as the fertile ground in which a plurality of histories came together and grew into one another, resulting in the complicated mix of institutions, kinship patterns, ceremonial commitments, and material styles that twentieth-century ethnographers spent so much time trying to sort out.

Some cultural elements were likely inherited from long-standing Pueblo traditions. The moiety division established at each of the major villages in the Taos region, for instance, may have roots that extend back to Mesa Verde and Chaco; at least, the formal architectural division of settlements into complementary halves seems to be a regular occurrence in the San Juan Basin and Four Corners area beginning in the eleventh century. As I have suggested, however, the historical encounters between Tiwa-speaking and Apache-speaking peoples in the Taos region during the past millennium appear to have served as their own wellspring of dualistic understandings, reconfiguring local notions of moiety organization in the process. Other cultural elements, such as patrilineality, almost certainly derive from a Plains source. Still others may have sprung from the process of immigration itself; the tradition of clustering kin-based people groups into kiva collectives at Taos Pueblo, in particular, is perhaps best understood as a pragmatic means of structurally incorporating strangers and ensuring that their divergent traditions are kept in check. In fact, the very corporateness of the people groups may have arisen as immigrants joined the community and suddenly found themselves occupying newly marked social categories vis-à-vis the locals. Thus might a series of families from, say, the Rocky Mountains or the Plains or the Mesa Verde region have abruptly come to see themselves as a common "people" precisely because the languages, customs, kinship patterns, and even biology of their hosts stood in sharp contrast to their own.

We must also leave open the possibility that some cultural elements introduced into Taos society met with resistance and were curtailed accordingly. Katsina iconography was present in the region early on at the start of the fourteenth century, for instance, but all indications from the fifteenth and later centuries suggest that Taos and Picuris came to purposefully restrict their engagement with katsina practices, and with masking in particular (Fowles 2013). So, too, might the division of Taos society into (Tiwa-speaking) "Summer People" and (Apache-speaking) "Winter People" have once held a greater ceremonial significance, akin to the role such divisions now play among the Tewa. By the time of Stevenson's research, however, these named macro-groups appeared as mere vestiges, still commemorated in historical narratives, but without the social impact they perhaps once had.

This, then, is what I mean by a rhizomatic account of Pueblo social history. Dendritic models must be turned on their heads, such that branching genealogies leading to common ancestors are instead viewed as complex root systems spreading far and wide as one investigates deeper into the past. We need look no further than to the name of the Taos community itself to visualize this shift in perspective. Collectively, the various groups at Taos are known as the "Red Willow People." The metaphorical reference in this case seems not to be the surface appearance of the red willow tree, which grows along the banks of Red Willow Creek, but rather the vast and famously complicated root structure that red willows build just beneath the ground, of which the visible shoots are merely the latest outgrowth. Our challenge, then, is to find new ways of writing the history of this subterranean tangle.

Notes

1. I am interested in a social history that resulted in an ethnographic pattern that existed at the start of the twentieth century—hence, my frequent use of the past tense. Contemporary Taos Pueblo is a vibrant community that both respects its traditions and continues to change with the times, but I make no effort to portray the community as it exists today.

2. What exactly Stevenson meant by "gentes" in her Taos notes is opaque. Peter Whiteley (personal communication, 2016) observed that early usage, in the decades after Morgan, was equivocal, but that by the early twentieth century most anthropologists had come to equate "gentes" with patrilines. Stevenson seems to follow in this tradition, but offers no explicit clarification. Nevertheless, her notes do hint at a marked difference between "gens" and "clan" (see note 3), the latter of which may have had matrilineal associations that rendered it a poor fit with Taos society. Stevenson also repeatedly emphasized the structural importance of the "fathers" of the gentes, and whereas she offered specific

counts of the number of men in each gens she frequently offered only general assessments of the number of women.

3. Two words in this passage were initially typed and then crossed out by Stevenson. Both editorial corrections are significant. Rather than describing a child as becoming "associated" with a kiva group when dedicated by his parents, Stevenson found it more appropriate to describe the infant as becoming "allied" with the group. Here she seems to be underscoring the role of kiva dedication as a mode of alliance-building within the pueblo. Stevenson's second correction involves the replacement of "clan" with "gens." Here, too, the change is significant. She appears to be acknowledging the existence of kin-based groups at Taos that differ significantly from the clan system of the Western Pueblos.

4. Other examples of seemingly unnecessary complexity in Taos kinship organization might be noted, such as (1) the conflation of cousin and paternal uncle terms or (2) the conflation of terms for paternal grandfather and maternal grandfather but *not* for paternal grandmother and maternal grandmother. Be that as it may, Trager's (1935–1937, 1943) research suggests that by the 1930s, some of these patterns were already beginning to blur as lineally specific kin-terms were cut free and applied more generally. The brackets in Figure 4.2 provide a sense of this; they include the relational extensions of kin-terms that—while absent from Curtis's (1926) earlier study of Taos kinship—were noted as secondary uses by Trager's informants a generation later.

CHAPTER FIVE

From Keresan Bridge to Tewa Flyover

New Clues about Pueblo Social Formations

PETER M. WHITELEY

Introduction

This chapter addresses the underlying frameworks of Puebloan social systems via their patterns of kinship and marriage, as evidenced in the ethnographic record and as supported by selected aspects of kinship theory. As outlined in chapter 1, kinship systems are fundamental to social organization in nonstate societies (indeed, in many state societies, too), and thus should be important for all attempts to reconstruct Puebloan social histories from Basketmaker times forward. A received contrast, especially since Eggan (1950), between Western and Eastern Pueblo social organization hinges upon differences in their kinship systems. In the West, Crow-type kinship is the articulating force, producing matrilineal clans and lineages as the key units, grounded in matrilocal residence, and "semicomplex" marriage practices. Even Hopi ritual sodalities, while a source of social integration that cuts across clans and lineages at one level, are also governed by them at another. Rio Grande Tewa social structure lacks these features: its kinship system is Eskimo-bilateral, postmarital residence is ambilocal (with either husband's or wife's kin), and its marriage rules, insofar as these are known, are "complex," in Lévi-Strauss's sense: i.e., with only a negative rule that proscribes certain kin categories as marital choices, but not (positively) prescribing others. Tewa kinship structures thus appear weakly articulating by comparison with the Hopi. The contrast between Western and Eastern Pueblo kinship also conforms to Lewis Henry Morgan's classical opposition between "classificatory" vs. "descriptive" systems. For the Rio Grande Tewa, rather than kinship, it is ritual sodalities, notably the Winter-Summer moieties and the eight Made People societies (see Ford, chapter 2) that provide the primary articulation of society. According to Ware (2014), Eastern systems shifted, in an evolutionary transition, from a kinship-based social system to one by ritual sodalities during the Chaco era. Focusing on some aspects of Hopi, Hano, and Rio Grande Tewa kinship systems, this chapter argues for previously unnoticed similarities in their underlying kinship systems, concluding that the differences have been overdrawn and result from later historical changes in Rio Grande Tanoan kinship practices.

Kinship vs. Ritual in Puebloan Social History

Recent analyses in Puebloan archaeology have emphasized the importance of religious belief and ritual organization for interpreting social formations (see, e.g., Glowacki and Van Keuren 2011, Ware 2014, Mills 2015). This emphasis contrasts with the focus on *kinship* as the primary analytic for nonstate social systems in much twentieth-century anthropology. In that regard, the new emphasis in sociocultural anthropology of the 1960s through 1980s reflects a movement away from kinship toward ritual and symbolism. In Puebloan studies, that shift is bookended by two works: Fred Eggan's *Social Organization of the Western Pueblos* (1950) and Alfonso Ortiz's *The Tewa World* (1969). For Eggan, Western Pueblo social structure

> is characterized by a kinship system of "Crow" type organized in terms of the lineage principle; a household organization on the basis of the matrilineal extended family; a formal organization based on the lineage and clan and, in some cases, the phratry group; an associational structure organized around the ceremony and its symbols, with relationships to the lineage, clan, and household; and a theocratic system of social control. . . . The basic feature of western Pueblo social structure is the kinship system (Eggan 1950, 291).

Moreover, for Eggan, matrilineal descent groups—as households, lineages, clans, and phratries—were the foundation of *all* Pueblo social organization: those societies historically lacking them, he held, represented a departure from aboriginal conditions. For the Tewa, "the key group in any reconstruction of eastern Pueblo social organization" (Eggan 1950, 315), he attributed that departure to: 1) a fourteenth-century CE migration from the San Juan region into the northern Rio Grande (see also Ortman, chapter 3, this volume); and 2) after 1600, assimilation of Spanish colonial social norms. The current Tewa system of dual organization into Summer and Winter moieties, Eggan argued, had replaced a preexisting matrilineal clan system:

> The clan system would be reduced in importance by . . . [the fourteenth-century migration] but would be further affected by the extensive period of Spanish acculturation. Catholic regulation of marriage practices would take away the last remaining functions of the clan system, and intimate contacts with Spanish (and later Spanish-American) settlements would give a patrilineal tinge to the remnants. . . . These same influences would tend toward the development of a kinship system on a bilateral, non-classificatory basis and a family system on the Spanish model (Eggan 1950, 316).

Yet while losing their clan system, Eggan argued (156–57), the Rio Grande Tewa had retained their aboriginal kin-terminology, in contrast to Hano, the post–Pueblo Revolt community of Tewa migrants to Hopi, whose kin-terms had changed meanings to coincide with the Hopi kinship system.

In contrast to Eggan, Ortiz's approach to Tewa social organization focused on ritual rather than kinship:

> I have . . . asked here the same grand questions that students of kinship and marriage ask: What are the relevant groups in the society? How do they recruit their members? How do they achieve continuity? What is the total framework of integration for the society? Consequently, while this work has had less to do with kinship and marriage—and, therefore, with social structure, insofar as it is defined in these terms—than with religious ideas and practices, it is because *ritual shapes social relations to such a tremendous extent.* Thus, we have not descent but ritual, not exogamy but ritual again (Ortiz 1969, 130, emphasis added).

Ortiz's analytic is directly ancestral to the "rituality" in recent Puebloan archaeology, i.e., a system governed primarily by ritual institutions (e.g., Yoffee 2001, Mills 2012). Ortiz did not displace Eggan's analysis so much as give it a new dimension. The West–East opposition was no longer between types of kinship systems, but between social structures articulated by kinship vs. those articulated by ritual.

In his important interpretation of Puebloan social history, John Ware (2014) has refocused the kinship–ritual, West–East polarity. Ware suggests that the ritual moieties of Rio Grande Pueblos such as the Tewa are "tribal sodalities" and represent an evolutionary transition in social organization. The key questions for Pueblo social history, he holds, should thus be "How and when did independent sodalities first emerge, when did they take over community leadership in the east, and why did kin-based institutions prevail in the west?" (Ware 2014, 186). Ritual sodalities independent of kinship structures, he asserts, go back to Basketmaker III (500–600 CE), coinciding with the emergence of great kivas (69–70). Toward the end of the Chaco phenomenon (ca. eleventh century CE), Tewa-type ritual moieties first emerged (exemplified by binarily opposed architectural forms in Chacoan sites), combining independent tribal sodalities into a dual division, thus much earlier than Eggan had suggested. Ware concludes, "Eastern Pueblo sodality-based polities are probably very old and . . . Chaco may have been where they first sprouted" (186). He thus argues for the antiquity of the divide between Eastern and Western Pueblo social organization. Largely accepting Eggan, Ware argues that Western systems are structured by corporate matrilineal descent groups, to which (Western) ritual sodalities remain subordinate. The West–East, kinship-vs.-ritual contrast thus rests on an evolutionary transition: once ritual sodalities arose in the East, kinship receded, becoming largely irrelevant to social structuration.

I am in great sympathy with Ware's overall mission to rejoin Southwestern archaeology and ethnology: it has been hugely important in Puebloan studies. While we agree on most matters of this overdue reengagement, I demur in the area of kinship systems, particularly with regard to: 1) how these operate among the Western Pueblos; 2) how different kinship systems are related to each other; and 3) how they evolve. I thus here offer an alternative take on the East–West divide. I have long rejected Eggan's arguments for corporate descent groups with joint estates as an effective model of Hopi social structure (e.g., Whiteley 1985, 1988, 2008). Kinship and clanship are unquestionably major features of social organization in the Western Pueblos, though so too are ritual sodalities and kivas, in which matrilineal descent is often transcended by associations more reflective of a "house" model, i.e., via marriage and locality as well as (cognatic) kinship (Whiteley 2008). The main difference, it seems to me, between Western and Eastern systems described in the ethnographic record is the relative emphasis on pluralism vs. dualism, and, as I will show below, this is better treated as a continuum than a genuine dichotomy for both kinship and ritual. The Hopi social system, while exhibiting clear plural features, is also marked by fundamentally dualist patterns (e.g., Whiteley 2008, 2012, 2015). Aspects of an earlier kinship dualism are also evident, I believe, in Tewa kin-terminologies. In that my perspective on both Hopi and Tewa dualism departs from conventional wisdom, it requires demonstrating both ethnographically and theoretically, especially with regard to kinship systems.

Explaining Pueblo Social Systems

Pueblo social systems are notoriously complex for their population size, interweaving kinship groups with layered ritual sodalities (e.g., Hawley 1937, Dozier 1961, Eggan 1979). With one thousand people in 1900, Hopi Orayvi had some twenty-eight matrilineal clans grouped in nine exogamous sets ("phratries"), sixteen initiated ritual sodalities, and fourteen kiva groups (Whiteley 2008). Western Pueblo kinship is basically Crow in type (see below). Eastern Pueblo integration is similarly intricate. For example, at Jemez, with a population in 1900 of less than five hundred (Sando 1979, 423), Ellis (1964, 15) described twenty-one ritual sodalities, configured in relation to dual Turquoise and Squash kivas and to several other structural elements. (Sando [1979, 425] scores the sodalities at twenty-three.)[1] The Tewa towns had fewer sodalities (eight), but were similarly geared to ritual moieties and a hierarchy of ritual authority. To be sure, some complexities reflect historical consolidation of formerly discrete villages, but the basic pattern of interwoven groups with interdigitating, calendrically sequenced rituals, is similar in both West and East. Eastern Keresan and Towa kinship includes Crow and some Iroquois terminology, and matrilineal clans, while Tewa and Northern Tiwa descent, at least as this is prevailingly described, is bilateral with a "normal Eskimo" terminology (Murdock 1949, 343–44).

Central ritual structures among both Tanoans and eastern Keresans are non-exogamous patrimoieties aligned in some cases with dual kivas: Turquoise and Squash moieties and kivas (Keresans and Towa Jemez), Winter and Summer moieties (Tewa), Eagle and Arrow sodalities (Towa Jemez), Red Eyes and Black Eyes moieties (Tiwa Isleta), and North and South moieties (Tiwa Taos). Weak, noncorporate patriclans among the Tewa feature naming practices that echo matrilineal conventions further west (Parsons 1924, though see Ford, chapter 2, this volume). Winter and Summer moieties are especially significant among the Tewa, with one moiety and its chief, or *cacique*, presiding over village affairs for half of the year, then switching the presiding moiety at the equinoxes (e.g., Dozier 1961, 1970).

Analytically, Pueblo social systems have thus been arrayed along a continuum (table 5.1), with Crow kinship and matrilineal descent the core features in the west and dual organization by ritual moieties in the east. In between, the "Keresan bridge" (Eggan 1950, Fox 1967) contains elements of both.

Importantly, though largely neglected for its analytical value, there is also a Tewa bridge, or perhaps "flyover" is more appropriate, from the northern Rio Grande to Hano, the refugee Tewa community formed ca. 1700 on the Hopi First Mesa. Tewa remains actively spoken at Hano, where there is a dual kiva system, but plural matriclans, Crow skewing in kin-terminology but some differences in kin classification from their Hopi neighbors, and some ritual distinctions too. Differences in kin-term usage between eastern Tewa and Hano have been described by several ethnographers (Freire-Marreco 1914, 1915; Harrington 1912; Parsons 1932; Dozier 1954, 1955). Interpretations fall starkly into opposing camps. Freire-Marreco, who investigated both Hano and Rio Grande Tewa, argued that Hano represents the older Tewa pattern. Kroeber (1917, 85) agreed, noting that the Rio Grande Tewa "have very likely simplified their system from its original form to accord with the Castilian one." On the question of matrilineal clans, Eggan agreed. On the other hand, Harrington

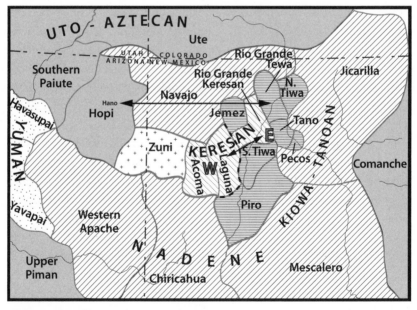

Figure 5.1. Pueblo cultures and languages and their Native neighbors, showing the East-West Pueblo divide, "Keresan bridge" transecting it, and Tewa "flyover." AMNH Anthropology Division.

Table 5.I. Western versus Eastern Pueblo Social Organization

Western		Eastern
Hopi, Zuni, W. Keresans	E. Keresans, Towa in part	Tewa, Tiwa
Exogamous matriclans	Exogamous matriclans	(weak, notional) Patriclans
(weak, diffuse) Ritual moieties	Ritual patrimoieties	Ritual patrimoieties
Multiple kivas	Dual kivas	Kivas coordinate with moieties
Crow kinship	Crow and Iroquois kinship	Eskimo kinship

(1912), depending heavily on Freire-Marreco's data, saw the eastern system as purer, with Hano having assimilated its kin-terms and behavior to the Hopi model. Here Eggan agreed, stating that the Rio Grande Tewa had retained their kinship terminology intact, notwithstanding the loss of their matrilineal clan system. For theoretical reasons, he treated kin-terminology and descent as independent variables (arguing against Kroeber and Parsons in this regard). But this evidently led him into a paradox, with important implications for the whole framing of the West–East polarity: that historical events, both pre-Hispanic and colonial, had eliminated one key aspect of the kinship system—matrilineal clans—but had virtually no effect on another key aspect, the kin-terminology. Dozier (1954, 1955), a Santa Clara native and fluent Tewa-speaker who conducted ethnographic fieldwork at Hano, agreed with Eggan that Rio Grande Tewa kin-terminology was aboriginal, from which Hano had diverged. My own view is that Eggan's and Dozier's depiction misconceives how kinship systems operate, particularly as regards the separation of kin-terminology from descent, and also from marriage alliance.

Kinship Orientation

Kinship systems (see also chapter 1)[2] comprise three intersecting axes— terminology, descent, and marriage—that typically determine a fourth, of particular interest for archaeology: postmarital residence. Kin-terms classify individuals into pairs of reciprocal relationships: sister–brother, mother– daughter, etc. The total kinship system provides a logical scheme to arrange individuals into corporate social groups, especially in small-scale societies.

Insofar as kin-terminologies specify principles of grouping—especially via correlated rules regulating descent and marriage—they open a window upon the architecture of a social system. Linked to residence rules, that window may extend to the physical architecture of archaeological sites. Kinship systems are often the central articulators of political and economic institutions, as well as of biological reproduction, hence kinship should be of vital importance to the explanation of all nonstate social formations, including those only known through the archaeological record. Theorists (still) disagree about whether terminologies should be treated independently of descent and marriage (see Whiteley 2012). Eggan, as noted, thought terminology was separable from descent, and he later (1964) rejected the significance of marriage practices to explain Pueblo social systems, faithfully adhering to his descent-theory credo. (For descent theory, see chapter 1.) For heuristic purposes, I treat the four axes of kinship as coordinate. There are, of course, empirical exceptions, like "disharmonic regimes" that, for example, feature matrilineal descent with patrilocal residence. However, kin-terminology, descent, residence, and marriage rules correlate significantly in most cases. Pueblo social organization may be more effectively explained if we begin from that premise.

Whole kinship systems are generally named for their terminologies, with six basic types: Eskimo, Hawaiian, Sudanese, Iroquois, Crow, and Omaha. Apart from Eskimo and Sudanese ("descriptive"), the other four are "classificatory," in Morgan's (1871) terms. Classificatory systems group lineal (e.g., my mother) and collateral (e.g., my mother's sister) relatives into *classes* with single kin-terms applied to several (genealogical) kin-types. Thus, in the Hopi case, all male members of my generation in my clan (and clan-set) are classed as my "brothers" (elder or younger); all female members of my father's clan (and clan-set)—no matter their generation—are my "aunts." In a classificatory system, kin-terms encompass all members of society, often dovetailing with a clan system: at Hopi, if my mother's father is of the Bear clan, I call all males of that clan—and of its clan-set mates, Spider and Bluebird—"grandfather." Crow systems are prevailingly associated with matrilineal descent and matrilocal residence, just as their counterpart Omaha systems are typically patrilineal and patrilocal (e.g., Dyen and Aberle 1974, 75–77; Trautmann and Whiteley 2012c). Conversely, a "descriptive" system of Eskimo type aligns with bilateral descent and ambilocal or neolocal residence. Descriptive terminologies require naming the links to Ego by primary kin-terms: "I call Jane my 'cousin' because she is my father's sister's child." Such strings of primary terms needed to define a

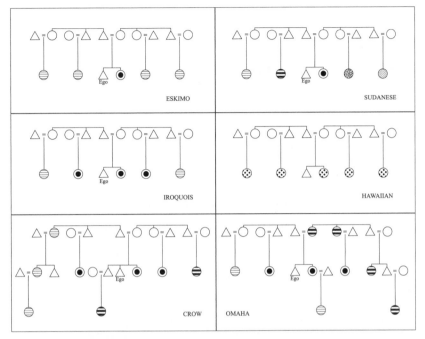

Figure 5.2. The six basic kinship terminologies, represented by groupings and distinctions of cousin terms used by Ego-male for his female relatives. AMNH Anthropology Division.

particular person ("father's sister's child") are what define "descriptive" systems as such.

The six basic terminologies may be specified formally by a series of equations and distinctions among kin-types (fig. 5.2). Formal statements are just that, of course, and subject to extensive empirical deviations, but they provide important clues to the logic of a social system (Lounsbury 1965, 147). Definitive cousin-term equations and distinctions for the six basic systems are shown below, for simplicity, just taking Ego-male's terms for his same-generation female kin. The same patterns hold if we were to take Ego-female's terms for her same-generation male kin, or Ego-neutral's terms for same-generation kin of both genders. (Notation: F father; M mother; P parent; B brother; Z sister; S son; D daughter; Ch child; E spouse; e elder; y younger. Strings are possessive: e.g., MZD means "mother's sister's daughter.")

ESKIMO

Z≠MZD=FBD=FZD=MBD (sister is distinguished from female cousins, but no distinctions between parallel and cross-cousins).

SUDANESE

Z≠MZD≠FBD≠FZD≠MBD (sister and each female cousin have distinctive terms).

HAWAIIAN (GENERATIONAL)

Z=MZD=FBD=FZD=MBD (no distinctions in terms for sister and all female cousins).

IROQUOIS

Z=MZD=FBD≠FZD=MBD ("sister" term also used for female parallel cousins; a separate term for female cross-cousins, applied equally to those on father's and mother's sides).

CROW

Z=MZD=FBD≠FZD=FZ≠MBD=D (some shared equations with Iroquois; but cross-cousins on father's side are distinguished from those on mother's side, and both exhibit intergenerational skewing: i.e., the term for a father's sister's daughter is the same as for father's sister, that for a mother's brother's daughter the same as for own daughter).

OMAHA

Z=MZD=FBD≠FZD=ZD≠MBD=MZ (some shared equations with Iroquois, but cross-cousins on father's side are distinguished from those on mother's side, and both exhibit intergenerational skewing: i.e., the term for a father's sister's daughter is the same as for sister's daughter and that for a mother's brother's daughter is the same as for mother's sister).

Iroquois is the essential "classificatory" system, with its distinction of parallel from cross-relatives, or "crossness."[3] Iroquois, Crow, and Omaha are the systems with crossness. As is evident from their diagnostic formal patterns, Crow and Omaha are mirror variants: indeed, actual Crow and Omaha systems often co-occur in the same regional environments (e.g., Trautmann and Whiteley 2012c, passim) or Omaha elements appear in Crow structures, and vice versa. Crow-Omaha systems are defined by generational *skewing* of some kin-types, primarily down the father's matriline (Crow) or the mother's patriline (Omaha). The basic crossness equations, *from which all systems with crossness flow* (Trautmann and Whiteley 2012a), occur not in Ego's own generation (G°) but in the generation above (G^{+1}):

F=FB≠MB; M=MZ≠FZ (father and father's brother are equated, but are distinguished from mother's brother; mother and mother's sister are equated, but are distinguished from father's sister).

Basic Iroquois crossness inheres in both Crow and Omaha terminologies (seen, for example, in their common classification of parallel cousins with siblings: see figure 5.2). In effect, these are surface-structure variations on an Iroquois base (Trautmann and Whiteley 2012b).

Viveiros de Castro (1998, 354), echoing Lowie (1915a) and Dumont (1953), emphasizes that crossness appears always associated with *marriage* rules or practices: parallel relatives, "kin," are prohibited as spouses; cross-relatives, "affines," are prescribed as spouses or stipulated as in-laws. This discovery critically reorients understanding of kinship systems marked by crossness: *the terminologies with crossness in and of themselves predicate marriageable/nonmarriageable categories.* In other words, the kin-terms—together with the kin-types they signify, equate, and distinguish—are not (*contra* some theorists) free-floating signifiers in a social vacuum. Like chess pieces, each kin-term has a position vis-à-vis others, each has rules for moving in alignment or opposition to others, and some conjunctures result in structural realignments. But while the mathematical properties of kin-terms are palpable (e.g., Gould 2000, Read 2001), social context, in my view, is all-determining: kin-terms are grounded in and reflective of a society's rules of marriage, residence, and descent, which together structure social and biological reproduction. The association between crossness and marriage is seen most clearly in Dravidian, a variant of Iroquois, where the terms for cross-cousins simultaneously *mean* "spouse"/"sibling-in-law": MBCh=FZCh=E/sibling-in-law (i.e., cross-cousins *are* spouses/siblings-in-law). It took until Lévi-Strauss's seminal alliance theory (1949) for marriage and kin-terminology to be fully restored to the partnership Morgan (1871) had first demonstrated. However, descent theory (which focused on descent groups to the neglect of marriage practices—see chapter 1), continued to prevail in Puebloan ethnology, owing in large part to Eggan's influence and hostility to alliance theory (1950, 1964), entailing a fundamental analytical lacuna.

To Iroquois crossness, Crow and Omaha systems add intergenerational "skewing." The "gender" of skewing is female for Crow (i.e., skewing operates down a matriline) and male for Omaha (skewing operates down a patriline); hence, Crow and Omaha terminologies typically correlate with matrilineal and patrilineal descent rules, respectively. For example, the Hopi system (fig. 5.3) is archetypally Crow, including the basic *crossness* equations and distinctions in G^{+1}: F=FB≠MB; M=MZ≠FZ; and *skewing* down the father's matriline: FZD=FZ=FZDD ('*kya*'); FZS=F=FB=FZDS ('*na*').

N. J. Allen's (e.g., 2004) tetradic model of kinship system evolution—one of the most theoretically interesting to emerge in recent years—argues for an original (hypothetical) human kinship system, comprising three sorts of "primordial" equations among kin-types: classificatory, prescriptive (i.e., pertaining to marriage), and between alternate generations in opposition to the intervening generation (table 5.2).

Allen's thesis is that from this putatively original condition, all kinship systems have evolved and/or historically transformed via the progressive erosion or breaking of such equations. Sometimes new equations such as skewing may be introduced, but always the evolutionary trend is toward terminologies with fewer classificatory and prescriptive patterns and more "descriptive" terms. Moreover, once lost via progressive breaking, primordial equations cannot be restored: thus the evolutionary aspect of the model. Prescriptive equations of the cross-cousin=affine sort (Dravidian-type) were the first to be lost, resulting in a broadly Iroquois type. Only after that transition, in this hypothetical ordering, might there be a subsequent transformation toward Omaha or Crow terminologies (cf., Kryukov 1998, Godelier 2011, Allen 2012).

Allen's tetradic model is particularly instructive, I believe, for the Hopi vs. Tewa contrast.

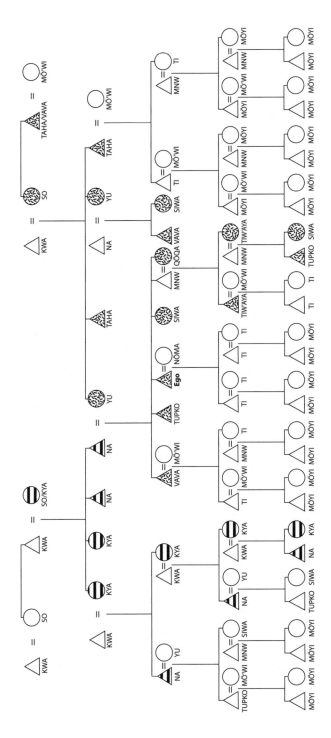

MNW abbreviation for Mö'nangw

Ego's matrilineal relatives (own clan)

Ego's patrilateral relatives (father's clan) - all skewed

Figure 5.3. Hopi kinship terminology. AMNH Anthropology Division.

Table 5.2. Exemplary Primordial Equations in N. J. Allen's Tetradic Model

Classificatory	F=FB; S=BS; W=WZ
Prescriptive	W=MBD=FZD; MB=FZH=WF
Intergenerational	MM=DD≠M=MMM=DDD; FF=SS≠F=FFF=SSS

Puebloan Alliance

As Lévi-Strauss demonstrated, marriage is not only a domestic condition, but the archetypal form of social exchange and engine of social structuration, especially in societies of small and middle scale:

> Exogamy should be recognized as an important element—doubtless by far the most important element—in that solemn collection of manifestations, which, continually or periodically, ensures the integration of partial units within the total group, and demands the collaboration of outside groups. Such are the banquets, feasts and ceremonies of various kinds which form the web of social life. But exogamy is not merely one manifestation among many others. The feasts and ceremonies are periodic, and for the most part have limited functions. The law of exogamy, by contrast, is omnipresent, acting permanently and continually. . . . It is no exaggeration, then, to say that *exogamy is the archetype of all other manifestations based upon reciprocity, and that it provides the fundamental and immutable rule ensuring the existence of the group as a group* (Lévi-Strauss 1969, 480–81, emphasis added).

While banquets, feasts, and ceremonies have loomed large in recent Puebloan archaeology (e.g., Potter 2000, Mills 2004b, Cameron 2009), marriage, more important than all these in Lévi-Strauss's estimation, has been ignored. He argued (1949, 1969) that kinship systems are fundamentally *about* marriage alliances between groups and postulated two major types of alliance: "elementary" and "complex." Elementary alliance *prescribes* which category of person one must marry—typically a classificatory cross-cousin. "Complex" alliance (as in Western society) has only a negative rule, *proscribing* close kin, but otherwise silent as to marriageable categories. Elementary alliance often coincides with a social system organized by kinship moieties: Moiety A gives its people as spouses to Moiety B, which reciprocates (A↔B). Such "symmetric-prescriptive" exchange dovetails with Dravidian and Iroquois terminologies.

There are many types of social dualism worldwide (e.g., Maybury-Lewis and Almagor 1989). However, the frequent presence in small-scale societies of exogamous moieties coordinate with kinship systems marked by crossness suggests—especially if exogamy is the archetypal exchange—that kinship moieties are the *ur* form of social dualism. Other types, such as ritual moieties lacking a basis in marriage exchange, are thus likely to derive, in an evolutionary sense, from kinship moieties, especially if seen via Allen's model. The key point here is that if Rio Grande Tanoan ritual moieties were once exogamous kinship moieties, lingering traces of crossness and perhaps also skewing may be discernible in their kin-terminologies. If so, the strong differentiation between Western and Eastern Pueblo social systems diminishes, as does the idea that non-kinship ritualities are a sufficient model to explain the Eastern variety.

First, on the opposite end of the Keresan bridge, is there evidence of kinship moieties among the *Western* Pueblos? Crow and Omaha terminology aligns with a third type of marriage alliance, "semicomplex" (Lévi-Strauss 1966, 1969), which disperses marriage through a more diverse social field than elementary exchange of A↔B type. Semicomplex systems combine proscriptive (complex) and prescriptive (elementary) rules: within a relatively small endogamous community, *proscribing* a substantial sector of the population has the effect of *prescribing* marriage from within the remainder. So for the Hopi, Lévi-Strauss's exemplar of semicomplex alliance, formal rules proscribe Ego's marriage within own clan-set, father's clan-set, and mother's father's clan-set. In a village (such as Orayvi) with nine clan-sets in total, proscription of three clan-sets means Ego must choose his or her partner from the remaining six. However, in practice, Orayvi marriages show extensive violations, over several generations, of the rule against marriage with the father's clan-set. Such repeat marriages between paired clan-sets (formally, "patrilateral cross-cousin marriage") suggest the shadow presence of kinship moieties. My analysis of Bear and Spider clan marriages (Whiteley 2012, 102–7) echoed Titiev (1938) in stating that patrilateral cross-cousin marriage had once been the Hopi marriage rule, but disputed that this was a thing of the past. If the focus is shifted toward *classificatory* cross-cousins (i.e., to include all members of the father's clan-set who stand terminologically in a "cross-cousin" relationship to Ego), rather than just genealogical cross-cousins (Titiev's angle), such marriages remain pervasive in the recent historical data. However, the total marriage data show that a dual, quasi-moiety[4] pattern at Orayvi coexisted with another, involving marriages within the community but beyond exchanging clan-set pairs, thus producing the plural element diagnostic of semicomplex alliance (cf. Whiteley 2012, 2016). The presence in Orayvi marriages of both dual and plural tendencies confirms McKinley (1971, 424) that Crow (and Omaha) systems feature competing social imperatives "to retain old marriage alliances while at the same time creating as many new ones as possible."

These Hopi marriages are consistent with the view that Crow-matrilineal kinship is an overlay on an Iroquois base (cf. Trautmann and Whiteley 2012b, Fox 1994). Felicitously, this coincides with Fox's (1967) analysis of Eastern Keresan kinship and marriage patterns. (Ware reports that Fox has changed his view in this regard: see chapter 12, this volume.) Fox originally asserted that Keresan moieties were once exogamous, with prescriptive cross-cousin marriage (i.e., classic kinship moieties), noting that Cochiti favored a form of elementary exchange marriage. At Laguna and Zuni, also with Crow terminology (see also Hill, chapter 6, this volume), Parsons identified a preference for (classificatory) cross-cousin marriage. Particularly notable is her remark, "At Laguna I was told explicitly that to use the reciprocal of father's sister's daughter or mother's brother's son was tantamount to using a wife-husband term"—i.e., suggesting an Iroquois/Dravidian equation and patrilateral cross-cousin marriage (Parsons 1932, 384). Combined with my analysis of Orayvi, these accounts of Cochiti, Laguna, and Zuni marriage alliance suggest a shared Pueblo pattern from the Rio Grande Keresans all the way west to the Hopi.

As to ritual dualism—supposedly a distinctive feature of Eastern systems—that is also present in the Western Pueblos, including paired sodalities (e.g., Hopi Snake and Antelope) and seasonal alternations, as when "the dual interplay of *Soyalangw* [Winter Solstice] and *Leenangw* [Flute] echoes the Rio Grande Tewa Summer and Winter moieties that provide alternating village leadership by a Winter Chief and Summer Chief" (Whiteley 2008, 27). At the Orayvi split, two rival Kikmongwis, Tawakwaptiwa (Bear, Friendly, Soyalangw) and Lomahongiwma (Spider, Hostile, Flute), divided the village along lines that echo the Winter/Turquoise–Summer/Squash moieties of the Rio Grande Pueblos. The Bear clan remained in Orayvi with its Winter ceremony while the Spider clan departed for Hotvela and Paaqavi with its Summer ceremonies (Blue Flute and Antelope): "as structural principles, seasonally alternating socio-ritual pairing and dualism (on an axis including both ritual associations and kinship ties) were clearly expressed in the overall pattern of Orayvi's fission" (Whiteley 2008, 826). In this regard, the Orayvi split produced a structurally similar result to (Tewa) San Ildefonso, where early twentieth-century factionalism led to the complete demise of the Winter moiety (Edelman 1979).

For the Orayvi case, at least, the interplay of kinship dualism with ritual dualism is shown also by the marriage alliances of these leading two clans (for which, see Whiteley 2012). Comparable data for Tanoan marriages are undeveloped, so inferring the underlying logic of Tanoan kinship structures is largely restricted to kin-terminologies and descent practices.

Puebloan Kin-Terminology

For kin-terminology, the key West–East opposition among the Pueblos appears to be between systems *with* crossness and skewing—such as Hopi, Zuni, the Keresans, and Jemez—and those *without*, especially Rio Grande Tewa and Tiwa. The former involve Crow terminologies, matrilineal descent groups, and matrilocal residence; the latter Eskimo terminologies, bilateral kindreds, and bilocal residence (Dozier 1961, 103–7). In Allen's theory (2012), skewing of Crow-matrilineal type emerges as a later development upon crossness, while bilateral-descriptive kin-terms emerge after the erosion of primordial equations.

From the first systematic study of Pueblo kinship, Kroeber concluded that, "in essentials, a single system of clan organization pervades all of the Pueblos, from Oraibi to Taos" (Kroeber 1917, 135—Ford, in chapter 2 of this volume, takes issue with this view). Translated into our present terms, Kroeber thus identified *lineality* (clans) *underlain by crossness*, and perhaps also *skewing* (as noted, crossness correlates strongly with unilineal descent; skewing enhances unilineal descent, but is not prerequisite to it). Like Eggan later and Freire-Marreco earlier, he argued that Spanish influence on the Rio Grande Pueblos may have caused the "decadence of the clan and a corresponding exaltation of the [patrilineal] moiety as an institution at the expense of the clan" (143). Notwithstanding her awareness of bilateral Tewa *ma:tu'in* kindreds (see Ford, chapter 2, this volume), Parsons (1932) agreed with Kroeber that Pueblo kin-terminologies were all based on Iroquois crossness (see below).

Dozier (e.g., 1955) argued that Rio Grande Tewa kin-terms are almost perfectly bilateral—thus lacking in crossness—as well as generational, i.e., grouping siblings and cousins together in G°. Like Eggan, he asserted (1955) that Rio Grande kin-terminology was an old pattern, marked by conservatism, while

Hano's system had shifted to converge with Hopi. From a descriptive bilateral system, Hano was thus held to have moved to a classificatory system, adding *both Iroquois crossness and Crow skewing* to its terminology, and either keeping or restoring matrilineal clans, depending on the historical alternatives floated by Eggan. But with the putative *addition* of crossness (primordial equations), Hano would have reversed the universal trend of kinship system evolution identified by Allen—a problem to which we will return. Freire-Marreco (1914) took the opposite position: Hano represented an earlier, "purer" form of Tewa kinship from which the Rio Grande system had devolved. Dozier, a native Tewa-speaker from Santa Clara, had an insider's perspective on cultural categories, but in this instance it may have clouded his comparison. His position (e.g., 1961) is clearly more in line with the "rituality" model of Eastern Pueblo systems.

Freire-Marreco's comparison of Hano and Rio Grande Tewa kinship emphasized a diminution of matrilineal descent and kin-terms in the latter:

Tewa kinship terms belong to a clan system.[5] At Hano, where the matrilinear clan system is in full force, the Tewa kinship terms express the facts of social life and are used consistently; in the Tewa pueblos of New Mexico, where clanship is now reckoned almost entirely by paternal descent and the clans have lost their importance, while the father-mother-and-child family has become the primary unit of social life, the same kinship terms are used inconsistently, with many local variations, and "descriptive" compound terms are being introduced to remedy the confusion (Freire-Marreco 1914, 269–70).

As Harrington (1912) concluded, "No other set of relationship terms of Southwestern Indians has been studied in which the classificatory system is so little developed as in Tewa. The writer believes that in the common talk of the Tewa Indians more descriptive terms denoting relationship are used than even in our highly analytic English system" (472).

In general, descriptive kin-terminologies are rare in the indigenous Americas (e.g., Driver and Massey 1957, map 161), and apart from the Tewa and Tiwa are absent in the Southwest or neighboring Plains. Here Freire-Marreco's argument that Rio Grande Tewa kin-terminology had assimilated Spanish norms is particularly noteworthy: while Eggan and Dozier asserted that Spanish influence was limited to descent, Freire-Marreco clearly saw descent and kin-terminology as covariant.

Tewa Kin-Terms: Hano vs. Rio Grande

Hano and Rio Grande Tewa kin-terms[6] display some signal differences (e.g., Harrington 1912; Freire-Marreco 1914; Parsons 1924, 1929, 1932; Dozier 1954, 1955). Hano kin-terms strongly feature Crow skewing (e.g., the term *kiyu* equates FZ and FZD: see table 5.3; see also Hill, chapter 6, this volume). In general, Hano kinship does seem to have converged with Hopi, no doubt partly via extensive intermarriages.[7] But in light of Allen's argument for evolutionary irreversibility, a hypothesis that Hano-Tewas preserved crossness, and perhaps also skewing, from their premigration Rio Grande ancestors seems worth investigating. And if that proves out, the full-fledged bilateralism and descriptivism of Eastern Tewa kin-terms likely postdates the Pueblo Revolt.

Some Spanish features are clearly present in Rio Grande Tewa and Tiwa kin-terminologies (de Angulo 1925, Trager 1943), and it is historically clear that the Franciscan church had a major impact on kinship, marriage, and domestic ritual (e.g., Dozier 1961, Gutiérrez 1991). Notwithstanding the changes, the key question here concerns whether there is evidence of underlying crossness. Like Harrington and Freire-Marreco, Parsons avowed crossness was characteristic of *all* Pueblo kinship, writing, "Throughout [all] the [Pueblo] tribes, direct and collateral kin are classified together, and maternal and paternal lines are distinguished; to use Lowie's term, we have the forked merging [i.e., bifurcate-merging or Iroquois] type of classification which is associated with clanship" (Parsons 1932, 79).

As pointed out above, the criterial equations and distinctions for crossness occur in the generation above Ego (G^{+1}): F=FB≠MB; M=MZ≠FZ, and of these it is the FB≠MB and MZ≠FZ that provide the key. Parsons notes some exceptions, but the *only* cases she records as not distinguishing maternal and paternal uncles (Keresan Cochiti and Tiwa Taos) are *partial* exceptions. While not all parallel uncles are assimilated to fathers, the essential form of crossness (F=FB≠MB) is thus hinted at here. Even at Taos, the most apparently Eskimo system of all, lacking in unilineality, "there is the same term for father's sister and for mother's sister, *although the aunt term appears to be applied more distinctively to father's sister*" (Parsons 1932, 381, emphasis added). This again suggests a trace of crossness (M=MZ≠FZ).

Dozier (1954) argued that while Hano and Rio Grande Tewa kin-terms are the same words, they are attached to different kinship "structures": "Hopi-Tewa kinship terms are the same or obviously cognate with those of the Rio Grande

Table 5.3. Tewa *kiyu/ki'i*

Hano	Kin-types	Implications
Dozier (1955)	FZ and all women except FM (*kuukuh*) in F's matrilineage	crossness, suggested skewing
Freire-Marreco (1914)	FZ=FZD=FMZ=F's clanswoman irrespective of generation	crossness, clear Crow skewing
Rio Grande Tewa		
Parsons (1929, 70, 74; 1932) *ki'i*	FZ=FZD; MFZ, FFZD, FMZD	crossness, Crow skewing; but some lateral neutralization
Towa (cognate *chi'i*)		
Parsons (1925, 10–22) — Jemez	FZ=FZD=FMZ=FZDD	crossness, clear Crow skewing

Tewa . . . In spite of these similarities to the Rio Grande Tewa kinship system, Hopi-Tewa kinship structure differs hardly at all from the Hopi. The system, like that of the Hopi, is organized on a lineage principle, quite different from the bilateral, generational type of the Rio Grande Tewa" (309). Yet if kin-terms are inherently relational and reciprocal, the "lineage principle" (derived by Dozier from Eggan; see also Pandey, chapter 8, this volume) *entails* a structure of crossness (and perhaps skewing). It is thus difficult to imagine the same kin-terms as capable sui generis of expressing a bilateral — non-crossed, non-skewed — form. Here again, Dozier's (and Eggan's and Harrington's) position that a kin-terminology can stand alone from descent, alliance, and residence is problematic. Freire-Marreco's perspective differed: while Dozier's characterization of Hano kin-terms does not call attention to Crow-matrilineal skewing, Freire-Marreco's consistently does. (Given that the discussion of Tewa kin-terms here is somewhat complicated, the same information is also set out in tables 5.3–5.8.)

Two kin-terms, *kiyu/ki'i* (primarily FZ) and *meme* (primarily MB), are particularly significant to my inquiry. At Hano, *kiyu* (table 5.3), as the term for FZ, contrasts with *ka'je*, MeZ, and *ko'o*, MyZ — tables 5.4–5.5 (Dozier 1954, 309, 316–17). In Rio Grande Tewa terminology, *kiyu*'s cognate *ki'i* (Parsons's orthography) exhibits the same contrast with *ka'je* and *ko'o* (Parsons 1929, 70, 74; 1932,

Table 5.4. Tewa *ka'je*

Hano	Kin-types	Implications
Dozier (1955)	MeZ	crossness, no evident skewing
Freire-Marreco (1914)	MeZ	crossness, no evident skewing
Rio Grande Tewa		
Parsons (1932)	MeZ	crossness, no skewing

Table 5.5. Tewa *ko'o*

Hano	Kin-types	Implications
Dozier (1955)	MyZ	crossness
Freire-Marreco (1914)	MZ, MZD senior to speaker, and MMZDD senior to speaker	crossness, lineal skewing
Rio Grande Tewa		
Parsons (1932, 1929, 73)	MyZ; MyZ=MZD	crossness, hinted skewing, but several non-lineal kin-type applications also
Harrington (1912)	FZ, MZ; PPZ; female first cousin; "aunt second removed"	no crossness, some non-lineal skewing

table 1). This contrast, present in both Hano and Rio Grande Tewa kin-terms, thus represents the criterial crossness distinction: FZ≠MZ.

At Hano, *kiyu* is also skewed, especially in Freire-Marreco's depiction. Dozier defines *kiyu* as FZ and all women except FM (*kuukuh*) in F's matrilineage, whereas Freire-Marreco's (1914, 278) definition foregrounds the Crow-matrilineal equations: FZ=FZD=FMZ=F's clanswoman irrespective of generation. Very significantly for the present inquiry, Parsons (1929, 70, 74) also defines the Rio Grande cognate *ki'i* as a Crow-skewed term: FZ=FZD. She includes some extensions of *ki'i* to include MFZ, FFZD, and FMZD. Only the last entails a Crow-matrilineal equation, but the first indicates extension into G^{+2}; unfortunately, Parsons does not discuss a kin-term for FMZ, which might have extended the Crow equation to a third generation (i.e., including G^{+2}, as

Table 5.6. Tewa *meme*

Hano	Kin-types	Implications
Dozier (1955)	MB and all "senior males of the lineage," except MMB and MMMB	crossness, suggested skewing
Freire-Marreco (1914)	"MB, MZS senior to the speaker, elder clansman"	crossness, Crow skewing
Rio Grande Tewa		
Harrington (1912)	Bilateral male first cousin; "uncle second removed"	no crossness, non-lineal skewing
Parsons (1924, 333; 1929, 70, 74)	MB, MBS, FZS; FZH/ FZDH (Ohkay Owingeh)	crossness, elementary prescriptive alliance, Omaha skewing, but also erosion of classificatory distinctions
Tiwa cognate *mimi* (Trager 1943)		
Taos	"uncle"	
Picuris	"cousin"	variance with Taos and S. Tiwa suggests latent skewing
Isleta	"uncle"	
Sandia	"uncle"	

well as G^{+1} and G^{o}). However, at Jemez, Towa *chi'i* (cognate with Tewa *ki'i* [Parsons 1932, table 1]) exhibits very clear Crow skewing over four generations, including FMZ: FZ=FMZ=FZD=FZDD (Parsons 1925, 10–22). While Jemez society was influenced historically by Hopi and Keres (e.g., Ellis 1964), in this case Towa *chi'i* may authentically illustrate a fuller depth of earlier lineal skewing applications for Tewa *ki'i* than appears in the ethnographic record. As a general matter, Parsons (1924, 333) indicated that for "cross-cousins," Rio Grande Tewa "use the uncle-aunt terms" (see Parsons 1932, table 1) evidently referring to *ki'i* and *meme* (below), i.e., the *cross* uncle and aunt terms, again showing these are lineally skewed (FZ=FZD; MB=MBS) in Rio Grande usage.[8]

While identically indicative of crossness in their contrast with *kiyu*, the Hano MZ terms *ka'je* and *ko'o* differ in skewing tendencies (Freire-Marreco 1914, 275),

Table 5.7. Tewa *tut'un/tu'unu/t'ono/tunu*

Hano	Kin-types	Implications
Dozier (1955)	FB, extended to all men (except F [*tata*]) in F's matriclan	crossness, suggested skewing
Freire-Marreco (1914)	FB, extended to all men (except F [*tata*]) in F's matriclan	crossness, suggested skewing
Rio Grande Tewa		
Harrington (1912) *tu'unu*	FB, MB, and PPB	no crossness, bilateral skewing
Parsons (1929, 70, 74; 1932) *t'ono/tunu*	FB=FBS	crossness, patrilateral skewing

Table 5.8. Tewa *tata (tada, tara)*

Hano	Kin-types	Implications
Freire-Marreco (1914)	F, FB, F's clansman	crossness, suggested skewing
Rio Grande Tewa		
Harrington (1912)	F, FB, eB, "other relatives older than self"	apparent crossness, possible skewing, not specified as lineal

with only *ko'o* subject to these (table 5.5). Dozier (1954, 305) defined Hano *ko'o* primarily as MyZ (mother's younger sister). Again in contrast, Freire-Marreco (1914, 275) gives *ko'o* as MZ, MZD senior to speaker, and MMZDD senior to speaker: both crossness and matrilineal skewing are thus clear in her account here too.

Harrington's (1912) list of Rio Grande kin-terms does not include *ka'je* or *ki'i*, with *ko'o* the only "aunt" term shown (488). He reports *ko'o* as FZ as well as MZ for Rio Grande Tewa, a sign of neutralized crossness or a shift toward bilateralism; but he also lists PPZ, "female 1st cousin" and "aunt second removed," which altogether imply some skewing down three generations, evidently of a bilateral or not clearly lineal nature. The reliability of Harrington's ethnographic interpretations is questionable here, however. Parsons (1929, 73) is much clearer on

Rio Grande Tewa *ko'o*, foregrounding the same MZ=MZD equation recorded by Freire-Marreco at Hano (as well as including Rio Grande Tewa *ka'je* and *ki'i*), though she lists several subsidiary nonlineal kin-type meanings for *ko'o* also.

Like *kiyu/ki'i*, and forming a pair with it, *meme* is particularly significant for the present inquiry. At Hano, *meme* (table 5.6) as MB forms a primary crossness distinction with *tut'un*, FB. Hano *tut'un* (table 5.7) is applied to all men in the father's matrilineage (except father [*tata*]) (Dozier 1954, 309; Freire-Marreco's definition here agrees). Thus Hano *meme≠tut'un* represents a classic Morganian crossness equation and evidently includes some matrilineal skewing. Dozier (1954, 305–9) lists Hano *meme* as MB and all "senior males of the lineage" except MMB and MMMB; Freire-Marreco (1914, 274) defines *meme* as "MB, MZS senior to the speaker, elder clansman," thus foregrounding a matrilineal skewing equation (MB=MZS). For Rio Grande Tewa, by contrast, according to Harrington, *meme* (*mæ'ᵆmæ* in his orthography, simplified) designates both a bilateral male first cousin and an "uncle second removed" (Harrington 1912, 488). But this is vague, and Parsons (1924, 333; 1929, 70) defines Rio Grande Tewa *meme* more precisely, primarily as MB, though with some extensions. The Rio Grande cognate for Hano *tut'un* is *tu'unu*, "uncle," defined by Harrington (1912, 487) as FB, MB, and PPB. Again Parsons is more precise, defining this term (her rendering is *t'ono/tunu*) particularly for Ohkay Owingeh (San Juan pueblo)—the Tewas' "Mother Village" (Ortiz 1969)—as "father's brother, father's brother's son" (Parsons 1929, 70, 74; Parsons 1932, table 1). Thus while crossness appears absent from Rio Grande Tewa *meme* and *tu'unu* in Harrington's depiction, it is clearly present in Parsons's prioritizing of MB in her definition of *meme* (see below) and FB=FBS in her definition of *t'ono*—which latter also contains a patrilineal skewing equation.

In a passage noted above in the discussion of *kiyu/ki'i*, Parsons indicates Rio Grande Tewa *meme* is also skewed: that "in the speaker's generation parallel cousins may be addressed by the brother-sister terms. Cross-cousins use the uncle-aunt terms" (Parsons 1924, 333; see also Parsons 1932, table 1). Further, for Ohkay Owingeh, Parsons (1929, 70) lists *meme* as "mother's brother, husband of *ki'i*." The latter application, indicating *meme* and *ki'i* (the Crow-skewed kin-term FZ=FZD) *are spouses to each other*, signals a classic Dravidian/Iroquois equation, associated with elementary alliance of classificatory cross-cousins typical of societies with kinship moieties. Parsons's report that *meme* may also mean cross-cousin, contrasted to parallel cousins who are referred

to by brother-sister terms—i.e., basic Iroquois crossness in Ego's own generation—strengthens that inference. As to specific applications of *meme* to male
cross-cousins, her discussion of actual Tewa genealogies *shows only MBS* (Parsons 1929, 74, Genealogy III), with no examples of FZS. This appears significant.
Whether her earlier statement (1924, 333) was correct to imply that FZS (i.e.,
as the other male cross-cousin) may also be referred to as *meme* is doubtful
too insofar as it violates a basic kin vs. affine distinction (if *meme* could apply
to both FZS—the patrilateral male cross-cousin—and FZDH—the patrilateral
female cross-cousin's husband [i.e., the "husband of *ki'i*" definition]). It seems
more likely, given her prioritizing of the MB kin-type to define the term and
her actual genealogical examples, that the principal cross-cousin equation is
with MBS; any equation with FZS, if this is in fact ethnographically correct,
would then reflect the general erosion of classificatory distinctions apparent in
much Rio Grande kin-terminology and a shift to bilateralism. The proliferation
of kin-type applications of *meme* in practice (Parsons 1929, 73–74), though evidently, from her discussion, subsidiary to the primary meanings, further exem-
plifies that erosion. Cognate Northern Tiwa *mimi* at Taos means MB primarily
(see also Fowles, chapter 4, this volume), with more general applications to
bilateral "uncle" and "mother's uncle" (with similar "uncle" meaning at southern Tiwa Isleta and Sandia), but "cousin" at Picuris (Trager 1943, 561–69). Both
Rio Grande Tewa and Northern Tiwa usage suggests underlying generational
(not necessarily lineal) skewing, as for *ko'o*. In the Northern Tiwa case, a skewed
term thus "fissioned" between kin-types (uncle vs. cousin) in Taos and Picuris, respectively: differential adaptations to the influence of Spanish kin-terms
here seems a likely cause. Crow-matrilineal skewing in Hano *meme* contrasts
with Omaha-patrilineal skewing in Rio Grande *meme*, but these are simple
kinship-logic (Crow-Omaha) alternatives upon Iroquois crossness, and as Fox
(1967) argued, Omaha elements occur frequently in Crow structures, including at Cochiti. Notwithstanding that variation, the crucial equation here indicates both crossness and prescriptive alliance: *meme*'s distinction from *tu'unu*
and marital pairing with *ki'i* (MB=FZH) at Ohkay Owingeh represents one of
Allen's major prescriptive primordial equations (table 5.2), suggestive of elementary dual exchange by kinship moieties.

Harrington (1912, 479) considered *tata* (table 5.8) a Spanish loanword into
Tewa, though he noted that the Tewa do not consider it such. The primary
kin-type this term identifies is "father," used as an alternative to *tara*, which

Harrington treats as autochthonously Tewa; Freire-Marreco, Parsons, and Dozier treated the two variants as basically identical. Again, this represents the fundamental crossness equation F=FB. *Tata*, Harrington notes, is also "applied loosely to father, elder brother, father's brother, or other relatives older than self. According to Miss B. Freire-Marreco a child at Santa Clara applied tatà to its mother's brother, *but this was considered to be a child's mistake*" (Harrington 1912, 479, emphasis added).

The correction, we may infer, was to *meme*. In this corrected mistake lies another clear trace of crossness in the generation above Ego: for Santa Clara Tewas, it was perfectly acceptable to refer to father and father's brother and other male relatives as *tata*, but *not* mother's brother. Together with *tu'unu*, *tata* thus forms an opposition to *meme*, configuring the basic crossness equation and distinction F=FB≠MB. Freire-Marreco (1914, 277) defines Hano *tada* (equated to both Rio Grande Tewa *tata* and *tara*) as F, FB, F's clansman. Combined with the FZ≠MZ contrast of *kiyu/ki'i* with *ko'o* and *ka'je*, Tewa kin-terms, both at Hano and on the Rio Grande, thus exhibit the classic equations definitive of crossness in G^{+1}, from which all others in an Iroquois, Dravidian, Crow, Omaha, or Cheyenne (see below) system flow.[9]

From the above information, Tewa crossness and skewing equations may be summarized as follows:

> Crossness (both Hano and Rio Grande Tewa):
> *tata=tut'un/tu'unu≠meme*: F=FB≠MB
> *kiyu/ki'i≠ka'je/ko'o*: FZ≠MZ
> Also (Ohkway Owingeh):
> *meme*: FZH
> *ki'i*: MBH
> Skewing (Hano—all Crow-matrilineal):
> *meme*: MB=MZS
> *kiyu*: FZ=FZD
> *ko'o*: MZ=MZD
> *tata*: FB=FZS
> *tut'un*: FB=FZS

(Rio Grande Tewa has some similar Crow equations as Hano, most notably *kiyu/ki'i* [FZ=FZD]. It adds Omaha skewing for *meme* [MB=MBS] and some bilateral skewing extensions too.)

Further Comparisons: Kiowa, Tiwa, Keresan

It is also instructive to compare Tanoans with the Kiowa, the only non-Pueblo representative of the Kiowa-Tanoan language-family, who lived in some geographic proximity to the northern Pueblos. The Kiowa have a "Cheyenne" kin-terminology (see also Hill, chapter 6, this volume), where cross-parallel distinctions are explicit in the parents' (and children's) generations (i.e., F=FB≠MB, M=MZ≠FZ), but "neutralized" in one's own (Lowie 1923, 279): i.e., all siblings and cousins in the same generation get the same terms. The Kiowa term for F and FB, *to* or *to'i*, may be cognate with Tewa *tut'un*. The term for MB (also ZCh and FZH), *seqyai'* or *not'ei*, is not evidently cognate with a Tewa term, although several others appear so (notably *tsayu'i*, FZ, probably cognate with Tewa *kiyu*). Even more telling in this regard are the Kiowa equations FZ=MBW and MB=FZH, i.e., Dravidian with a cross-cousin marriage rule, just like the *meme-ki'i* pairing at Ohkay Owingeh. While intergenerational equations are not necessarily indicative of social practices per se, note that at Taos a man's term for wife is also applied to his MM, suggesting the possibility of exogamous kinship moieties in the past.[10] Supporting this interpretation, other Taos equations include: PF=B-i-L (de Angulo 1925), PF=H (Trager 1943), and ChS=F-i-L, ChD=M-i-L (de Angulo 1925, 483).

The former presence of crossness in Rio Grande Tewa kin-terms may also be indicated by Keresan borrowings of such terms. Tewa *meme* is borrowed in some Keresan usages, appearing as *nyenye* at Santo Domingo (Kewa), San Felipe, and Cochiti, where it means MB (Hawley 1950, 503, 509). Variable neutralization of crossness (see Hill, chapter 6, this volume) is also reported for some Keresan kin-terms: "Usage of the term for sister to cover parallel cousins is constant . . . and in Santa Ana, Cochiti, and Acoma [*but not Laguna or Zia*] it covers cross-cousins as well" (Hawley 1950, 503). Florence Hawley Ellis regarded the correlated classification of FZ=M=MZ and MB=F=FB at Cochiti, Santa Ana, and Santo Domingo, but not evidently at Zia or the other Keresan pueblos, as indicative of the "breaking down of old categories," resonant with Allen's "breaking of primordial equations." Similarly, variant patterns of usage among Keresan individuals and the inner logic of reciprocal kin-terms were pointed out by Leslie White (1942) for Santa Ana: "If an informant gave 'uncle' for mother's brother, he always gave 'son' or 'daughter' for his children [a Crow equation], never 'brother' or 'sister.' If the informant gave 'father' for mother's brother, he always gave 'brother' and 'sister' for his children, never 'son' and

'daughter'" (150, quoted in Hawley ibid.). This suggests an emergent neutralization of crossness and skewing introduced by generational, bilateral categories.

Conclusion

Overall, clear hints of latent crossness and skewing among Rio Grande Tewa
and Tiwa, combined with dual-exchange marriage patterns among the Hopi
and reported for both Western and Eastern Keresans and Zuni, suggest how
Pueblo social structures may not be so mutually divergent after all (cf. Fox 1972,
1994). The idea that a dual, Dravidianate deep structure underlies both Iroquois and Crow-Omaha systems gains support from both ethnographic and
comparative perspectives. That such a system could evolve into a ritual moiety
structure seems more likely than that ritual moieties are an autonomous evolutionary development or historical amalgamation (e.g., Fowles 2005) with no
correspondence to kinship and marriage structures.

On whether the Tewa-Tiwa transition from kinship dualism to ritual dualism was pre-Columbian or occurred in colonial times, I affirm Freire-Marreco's
and Kroeber's contention that Eastern Tewa kinship systems, both in terms of
descent (with which Eggan and Dozier concurred) and kin-terminology (with
which they did not), were significantly changed by Spanish impositions. (Ware
2014 and chapter 12, this volume, offer a contrastive view.) Like Freire-Marreco
and Lévi-Strauss, I contend that scientifically adequate explanation of empirical kinship systems cannot sustainably separate descent from terminology (and
also residence and marriage alliance, though that was not Freire-Marreco's concern). It seems probable also, both from global ethnography and Allen's tetradic
theory, that the highly descriptive elements in Rio Grande Tewa terminologies
derive from Spanish and Anglo-American influence. Why Eastern Keresan systems were better able to resist that influence requires further research, though
it is clear from twentieth-century ethnographies that both within-generation
neutralization of crossness and a drift toward bilateral application of terms that
were formerly lineal were already underway. Greater Keresan distance than the
Tewas from the center of Spanish settlement and power in Santa Fe, especially
after the 1692 reconquest, may be significant. The continuous (and contiguous)
Keresan bridge across the East–West divide, as opposed to the discontinuous
Tewa flyover, is probably important too.

The generational neutralization of differences—of both crossness and gender—in Rio Grande Tewa kin-terminology would also suggest the demise of

a more differentiated classificatory system in the past, especially by comparison with Hano. This conforms with the inferences of earlier anthropologists—Harrington, Freire-Marreco, Kroeber, and Parsons—that all Pueblo kinship systems were fundamentally classificatory. To be sure, pre-Hispanic Pueblo systems varied, but I suggest there were fundamental similarities in an underlying classificatory crossness in their terminologies and dualism in their exchange structures, and that these remain evident in attenuated form even in the least "bifurcate-merging" cases among the Rio Grande Tewa and at Taos. Iroquois crossness and elementary alliance, I infer, go far back into the Puebloan past. From these, the suite of Crow terminology, matrilineal descent, matrilocal residence, and semicomplex alliance emerged and crystallized at certain times and in certain places, very probably reinforced by intermarriage among ethnolinguistic groups. As I have suggested elsewhere (Whiteley 2015), full-fledged Crow kinship among the Pueblos likely emerged from and receded to its base in Iroquois dualism depending on cyclical historical forces of an environmental, demographic, or social nature, or all three.

Finally, I conclude—differing from Ware (2014, and chapter 12, this volume) in this regard—Pueblo ritual moieties evolved from kinship moieties only under colonial influence, for two reasons. First, there are clear signs of crossness and primarily lineal skewing even in the most apparently bilateral-descriptive Rio Grande kin-terminologies. Second, classificatory cross-cousin marriage of the kinship-moiety type appears to be a normative preference from the Rio Grande Keresans on west to Hopi and is implicit in some Rio Grande Tewa and Tiwa kin-term pairings (especially Tewa *meme-ki'i*).

Acknowledgments

I am most grateful to Jane Hill and John Ware for their thoughtful comments on this chapter and its earlier version, presented at the SAR seminar. Thanks also to Joseph Aguilar for pointing out the similarities between the Orayvi and San Ildefonso factional splits.

Notes

1. The East–West dividing line has varied somewhat. Earlier, Hawley (1937) treated Jemez as Western, while for Eggan (1950) it belongs in the Eastern division.

2. For a fuller discussion, see Whiteley 2012, 2015, 2016.

3. "Crossness" corresponds with Lowie's "bifurcate-merging" terminology.

4. "Quasi-moieties" because there is more than just one pair. In the focal case analyzed (Whiteley 2012), the "moiety" involves clan-sets II and VI; others occur, notably between clan-sets I and VII, but that analysis requires further development.

5. In Freire-Marreco's terminology (1914, 269), "clan system" corresponds with Morgan's "classificatory system," while "father-mother-and-child family" corresponds with Morgan's "descriptive system."

6. The following discussion gives simplified versions of Tewa kin-terms. Orthographic renderings—among Harrington, Freire-Marreco, Parsons, and Dozier—vary, but exhibit clear correspondences.

7. The exact extent is uncertain. Spuhler (1980, 66) accepts Fewkes's (1894, 165) reading of Stephen's 1893 census that just "less than half of Hano adults [117] were 'pure Tewa.'" Spuhler (1980, 66, 96–97) infers a century-long prohibition against Hopi-Hano intermarriage from 1700 to 1800, though evidence cited is slight. Fewkes's representation of Stephen's census in 1894 differs, however, with his remark five years later, discussing the same census, that "only six persons of pure Tanoan ancestry are now living at Hano" (Fewkes 1899, 253). Either way, extensive intermarriage had occured, though whether it affected ~50 percent of Hano individuals or ~95 percent is not clear from Fewkes's discrepant representations.

8. FZ=FZD is a Crow, MB=MBS an Omaha skewing equation. The co-presence of Crow and Omaha patterns in Pueblo kinship and more generally is discussed by Fox (1967, 1994; see also Whiteley 2012, 96–99).

9. The only missing equation is M=MZ; all accounts indicate both Hopi-Tewa and Rio Grande Tewa have distinctive terms for these two categories, but this is not of great significance in view of the FZ≠MZ contrast and the identification of parallel cousins with siblings.

10. In other words, the marital exchange pattern (between two lineages) sees a Moiety A lineage woman marrying a Moiety B lineage man in generation 1. In generation 2, for proper reciprocation, the gender flow is reversed. But in generation 3, the correct reciprocal balance requires repeating the flow in generation 1. Thus a man calling his MM by the same term he calls his wife is consistent with such intergenerational marriage flows between exogamous kinship moieties. Such patterns intriguingly echo Ortiz's (1969) discussion of leadership in Tewa Made People sodalities alternating successively between Winter and Summer incumbents.

CHAPTER SIX

The Historical Linguistics of Kin-Term Skewing in Puebloan Languages

JANE H. HILL

Introduction

As Peter Whiteley points out in his introduction to this volume, Crow kinship terminology has been seen, not least by Eggan (1950), as the ancestral form of Puebloan terminologies. Because Crow-type terminologies are associated with matrilineality, if this view is correct, it has important implications for the historical evolution of Puebloan social organization. A defining feature of Crow terminologies is skewing—the terminological collapse of generationally distinct kin. If we are to work out in detail the transformations of kinship for the last thousand years of Puebloan history, a thorough understanding of skewing, and how it might be diversely embedded in Puebloan terminological usages that are not obviously Crow, must be a central concern. In this chapter, I attempt progress toward such an understanding, exploring Crow-type skewing in the several Puebloan languages with two goals: 1) using historical linguistic methods to understand how kin-terms evolve to express skewed meanings; and 2) asking what kinds of diversity in the skewing equations and their usage appear in these languages.

Crow-type skewing exhibits terminological equations that cross generations within a matrilineal descent line. We introduce skewing with Hopi and Arizona Tewa terminologies with well-developed skewing equations. The Hopi equations for the father's matriline appear in (1). The Arizona Tewa equations are in (2).[1]

1. FZD=FZ
   FZS=F

2. FZ=FM
FZD=FZ
FZS=F (or FB)

The two sets of equations differ slightly. Arizona Tewa has a kin-term *kiyû* 'FZ, FM.' Hopi kin-term usage does not express this equation explicitly. There are, however, other equations in the Hopi system that presuppose the equation. For instance, consider the equation in (3):

3. FZH=FMH

Lowie (1929b, 383) observes that this equation is the natural consequence of the second equation in (1): if FZS=F, then FZH is a grandfather, FMH. But the equation also presupposes that FZ=FM, and Lowie reports that the Hopi grandmother term, *so*, can be applied to the eldest FZ.

The presupposition that FZ=FM is also reflected in the Hopi equation in (4), expressed terminologically by *mööyi* '♀BCh, ChCh.'

4. ♀BCh=ChCh

Although Arizona Tewa has terminological FZ=FM, its term for BCh, expressing the equation in (5), does not develop this consequence; unlike Hopi, Arizona Tewa ♀BCh is not a ChCh.[2]

5. BCh=MBCh

While Crow skewing equations on the father's side, as in (1) and (2), are "raising," including terms for grandparents and parents, those on the mother's side are "lowering," including terms for kin in junior generations. Another example of this type, along with (4) and (5), is the Hopi skewing equation in (6).

6. MBCh=Ch

In Hopi and Arizona Tewa, the Crow-type skewing equations can be used for all appropriate relatives in all contexts. But in Zuni and some Keresan pueblos, skewing equations are an "overlay" (Kronenfeld 2012). I do not use this term to label skewing as a historical elaboration of terminologies with crossness as do Trautmann and Whiteley (2012a, b), but to describe a discourse of kinship used alongside another such discourse, according to speaker's stance.

Eggan (1950, 291) understood skewing as expressive of "the solidarity and unity of the lineage group." But skewing also expresses preference and proscription in alliance. In the cross-parallel distinctions in the Iroquois systems that are precursors of Crow systems (Trautmann and Whiteley 2012a, b), FZCh and MBCh are potential spouses of Ego.[3] Crow skewing, however, equates these cross-cousins with nonmarriageable kin in adjacent senior and junior generations, although there are extensive exceptions to the formal rule against classificatory patrilateral cross-cousin marriage in Hopi practice (Whiteley 2012). This proscription of bilateral cross-cousin marriage yields a "semicomplex" pattern of alliance, opening up the field of potential affines (Whiteley 2008, 2012). In Puebloan history, this provides a mechanism for integrating newcomers into endogamous villages and connecting lineages within them through complex networks of affinal linkage.

The Crow terminologies of the Western pueblos are often contrasted with the Eskimo-type systems of the Rio Grande, which exhibit "generational" equations that collapse groups of kin in the same generation, thereby losing "crossness." In G° this makes both cross and parallel cousins "cousins" (in the Tanoan languages) or "siblings" (in the Cheyenne-type Keresan kin-terminologies). (Cheyenne terminologies neutralize cross-parallel distinctions in G° while retaining them in G^{+1} and G^{-1}.) Alliance theory suggests that the difference in affordances between intergenerational skewing and generational equations may be subtle. Dousset (2012) argues that generational equations in G° accomplish "horizontal skewing." Like "vertical skewing" in Crow and Omaha, horizontal skewing cuts out cross-cousins as potential mates by equating them with siblings, with the effect of pushing alliances out to a greater social distance, thereby facilitating flexible responses to demographic and environmental challenges (see also Ives 1998). In Puebloan terms, both Western vertical and Eastern horizontal skewing, by opening up marriage systems, permit the incorporation of newcomers during episodes of in-gathering to large endogamous pueblos and yield complex networks of marriage alliance within them.

The literature on Puebloan terminologies has neglected a second type of equation, found in almost all Puebloan kin-terminologies between generations G^{+2} and G^{-2} and, less commonly, G^{+1} and G^{-1}. The Western Keresan systems have a third equation, PPP=P, or $G^{+3}=G^{+1}$. Arizona Tewa intergenerational equations in (7) illustrate these. The junior terms are marked with the diminutive suffix in Arizona Tewa, but in many languages the paired terms are identical.

7. FF=♂SCh

MM=♀DCh

FM=♀SCh

MB=♂ZCh

MZ=♀ZCh; FB=♂BCh

Allen (1989, 177) calls these "alternate generation equations." Alliance between adjacent generations is typically incestuous, but Allen's tetradic theory, with generationally defined cycles of alliance, predicts that alternate-generation alliances are possible and alternate-generation equations make these generations terminologically "the same." Combined with the "classificatory equations" of crossness that equate same-sex siblings in G^{+1} and have, as a consequence, the distinction between parallel cousins who are the same as siblings and cross-cousins who are not, alternate-generation equations yield the intersections of generation and descent line called "sections." No Puebloan language recognizes such sections as named units, even though they are implied by terminologies with alternate-generation equations and crossness. These alternate-generation equations do not appear in Hopi or the Tanoan language Towa, suggesting that the section principle has been completely lost there. However, they are not incompatible with Crow skewing and semicomplex alliance systems, as they are present alongside skewing in Arizona Tewa, Zuni, and Western Keresan. Notably, in these languages the Crow skewing equations do not include G^{+2} and G^{-2} kin.

Hopi Kin-Terminology: A Northern Uto-Aztecan Perspective

The Hopi language is a branch of Northern Uto-Aztecan (NUA). No other NUA system has a Crow-type kin-terminology. While Numic groups of the Great Basin are the closest NUA speakers to the Hopi geographically, the more likely precursors of the Hopi system, both in terms of the evolutionary theory advanced by Trautmann and Whiteley (2012a, b) and in terms of specific histories of semantic change, are seen in the terminologies of the Takic groups in southern California.

Numic kinship terminologies are all very similar. Many of them have "prescriptive equations" (Allen 1989)—"prescriptive" in that they appear to prescribe certain marriage alliances. Examples appear in (8), for Duck Valley Shoshone (Crum and Dayley 1993). Such equations are typical of Dravidian-type terminological systems.[4] The Numic array, with WF=MB and WM=FZ, has been taken to index sister-exchange marriage (Hage et al. 2004).

8. FBW=MZ
FZH=MB
MBW=FZ
WF=MB
WM=FZ

Many Numic languages have horizontal skewing, with the "sibling" terms applied equally to all kin in Ego's generation. For Australia, McConvell (2001, 2012) and Dousset (2012) suggest that horizontal skewing was a terminological strategy appropriate to "upstream expansions," moves into relatively unoccupied territory whose demographic and environmental challenges could be mitigated by far-flung marriage alliances. Numic prehistory almost certainly involved such an expansion. Hage et al. (2004) assert that this and many other features of Numic terminologies are innovative responses to circumstances specific to Numic history. They do not represent some ancient Uto-Aztecan type from which Hopi and other systems are descended.

While Hopi shares only two kin-terms with Numic languages, eight of the fifteen core consanguineal Hopi kin-terms have cognates in Proto-Takic (PT). All of these reconstruct also to Proto-Uto-Aztecan (PUA). These appear in (9).[5]

9. Hopi *kwa* 'PF,' PT (Proto-Takic) *kwa 'PF'
Hopi *so* 'PM,' PT *su 'MM'
Hopi *na* 'F,' PT *na 'F'
Hopi *yu* 'M,' PT *yɨ 'M'
Hopi *taha* 'MB,' PT *taha 'MB'
Hopi *paava* 'eB,' PT *pahas 'eB'
Hopi *tupko* (from /*tu-poko*/) 'yB,' PT *po'ok 'yB'
Hopi *qööqa* 'eZ,' PT *qos 'eZ'

Takic groups had named patriclans that held corporate property of several types. Senior clans that held sacred bundles and ceremonial houses were distinguished from "commoner" clans that did not. Strong (1929) reports clan-sets or "parties," where several commoner clans supported a senior clan in carrying out ceremonies. As Strong (1927) points out, this Takic "house-priest-fetish" complex resembled that of the Western Pueblos.

The consanguineal kin-terms of Serrano, spoken in the western Mojave Desert, can exemplify Takic systems. They appear in table 6.1. I include the in-law terms for the parent's generation, because these show prescriptive equations like those in (7), but without WF=MB and WM=FZ. Hage et al. (2004) point out that equations of the Serrano type are associated with cross-cousin marriage, as opposed to sister exchange.

Takic systems lack some Dravidian features. Same-sex siblings' children are called "niece" and "nephew" rather than "child." Terminological crossness in G^{+1} is lost in favor of marking seniority by distinguishing parents' older and younger siblings with special terms. But since crossness appears in G^{0}, with siblings and parallel cousins equated and cross-cousins distinguished from these, crossness in the G^{+1} generation is presupposed.

Takic languages all have the $G^{+2}=G^{-2}$ and some $G^{+1}=G^{-1}$ alternate-generation equations (although again, as in the Puebloan languages, there are no named sections). Serrano has all the $G^{+2}=G^{-2}$ equations seen in (6), but the only $G^{+1}=G^{-1}$ equations are FeB=♂yBS and MeZ=♀yZCh.

Hopi kin-terms appear in table 6.2. No trace survives of the alternate-generation equations. Instead of potential "sections," Hopi terminology defines only exogamous matrilineal descent lines. There is crossness in every generation, although the skewing equations interrupt this for ♀BCh, who are equated with a woman's ChCh.

Hopi has no prescriptive equations. The logic of crossness equates the spouses of parents' same-sex siblings with parents, interrupted by the skewing equation FZH=FMH.

Table 6.2 shows the terminological expression of the skewing equations introduced in (1), (4), and (6). The equations as given there list only the primary kin-types, but in fact all the women in the father's matrilineage (and clan, and clan-set) except father's mother are called *kya* 'FZ,' regardless of generation, and all the men are called *na* 'F' (including father's mother's brother). Any son of a man in *kya's* clan or clan-set is *mööyi* 'grandchild.' Whiteley (2012, 101) describes the *kya-mööyi* relationship as "the hinge on which Hopi structure articulates." Notoriously, *kya* and *mööyi* exchange bawdy sexual jokes and teasing, hinting at what Whiteley calls "affinal tension." Furthermore, Lowie (1929b, 384–85) reports vigorous teasing between ♀BCh and FZH, hinting at a sort of rivalry for a potential bride.

Hopi kin-terms include no loan words or morphologically complex neologisms. Instead, Hopi has retained PUA kin-terms, adapting these to the classificatory principles of the Crow system. The kinds of meaning changes that must have taken place can be exemplified by the "linchpin" terms *kya* and *mööyi*. Hopi *mööyi* '♀BCh, ChCh' is unusual in that it is the only ChCh word; other NUA languages have three or four, these being the reciprocals of the grandparent terms in the alternate generation $G^{+2}=G^{-2}$ equations that are missing in Hopi. The word has only one UA cognate, Upper Piman *moos* '♀DCh,' both from PUA *moci (Stubbs 2011, #1793). This is the only Upper Piman grandchild term that is not part of an alternate-generation equation. The reciprocal of *moos* is *kaak* 'FM' or *hu'ul* 'MM.' Men use diminutive forms of FF and MF for ♂ChCh, realizing $G^{+2}=G^{-2}$ equations. Because Upper Piman is a Southern UA (SUA) language, and Hopi is NUA, this suggests that a special treatment of ♀ChCh, as opposed to a full set of $G^{+2}=G^{-2}$ equations, may reflect ancient contact, or even predate the SUA-NUA split.

Hopi *kya* 'FZ' is most probably an irregular reflex of PUA *ka (Stubbs 2011, #1050a). SUA has *ka 'FM'—the Upper Piman reflex, *kaak* 'FM,' was mentioned above—while the NUA languages except for Hopi all have *qa 'FP.' The logic of the Hopi system, where FZH=FMH and ♀BS=ChCh, suggests that it makes sense to trace *kya* 'FZ' to a word that, like PNUA *qa, included FM in its range of meanings. Another line of evidence is a set of changes in the Hopi PP terms. Hopi *kwa*, from PUA *kwa'a 'MF' (Stubbs 2011, #1047), uniquely among the UA languages also means 'FF.' This change probably reflects a semantic "chain shift": as *qa*, adapting to Crow-type skewing, shifted its meaning from FP to FM, FZ, a new term was needed for FF. Similarly, PUA *su'u 'MM' (Stubbs 2011, #1051) was extended to FM, again uniquely in Hopi among the NUA languages, as *qa* further specialized to mean only FZ instead of FM, FZ. These changes left Hopi with only two grandparent terms instead of three or four as in other NUA languages.

All Hopi kin-terms except *kya* 'FZ' exhibit regular sound correspondences with words in other UA languages, but we do not find the expected /qa/ for FZ. Instead, only in this word, NUA *q is realized irregularly as /ky/. This change is probably a "Puebloanization" of the word. In both Zuni and the Tanoan language Towa, [ky] is a regular allophone of /k/ before /i, a, e/ (Newman 1965, Yumitani 1998), with no sound-symbolic meaning as far as I know. In Hopi, the sequence /ky/ is not a regular allophone of /q/. Instead, it appears only before /a/

Table 6.1. Serrano Kin-Terms

	Male				Female			
	Male		**Female**		**Male**		**Female**	
+2	FF	*-ka'*			FM	*-ka'*		
	MF	*-kwa:r(i)*			MM	*-ču:r(i)*		
+1	F	*-na'*	M	*-iy'*	WF	*-kwa'* (before child)	WM	*-či:č* (before child)
	FB	*-ku:mu* (e) *-maq* (y)	MZ	*-nym* (e) *-iyr* (y)	MB	*-ta:r*	FZ	*-pah*
	MZH	*-ku:mu* (e) *-maq* (y)	FBW	*-nym* (e) *-iyr* (e)	FZH	*-ta:r*	MBW	*-pah*
0	B	*-pa:r* (e) *-pö:t* (y) *-hamut* (♂)	Z	*-qö:r* (e) *-pi:t* (y) *-hamut* (♀)				
	FBS	*-pa:r* (e) *-pö:t* (y)	FBD	*-pi:t* (y) *-qö:r* (e)	MBS	*-puju'* (♂) *-nuku'* (♀)	MBD	*-jyr* (♂) *-nuku'* (♀)
	MZS	*-pa:r* (e) *-pö:t* (y)	MZD	*-pi:t* (y) *-qö:r* (e)	FZS	*-puju'* (♂) *-nuku'* (♀)	FZD	*-jyr* (♂) *-nuku'* (♀)

Gen	Kin	Term	Kin	Term
	Male			
-1	S	-mair	D	-pulin (♀) / -šung (♂)
	BS	-àqàʔ(-nam) (e, ♂) / -ku:mu (y, ♂) / -àmšt (♀)	BD	-a:hir (♂) / -àmšt (♀)
	MBSCh	-àqàʔ(-nam) (e, ♂) / -àmšt (♀)	MBDch	-à:hir (♂) / -àmšt (♀)
-2	SS	-kaʔ	DS	-kwa:r(i) (♂) / -ču:r(i) (♀)
	Female			
-1	ZS	-mašt (e, ♀) / -nym (y, ♀) / -à:hir (♂)	ZD	-a:hir (♂) / -nym (y, ♀)
	FZSch	-à:hir (♂) / -mašt (♀)	FZDch	-à:hir (♂) / -mašt (♀)
-2	SD	-kaʔ	DD	-kwa:r(i) (♂) / -ču:r(i) (♀)

Source: Gifford (1922, 54), orthography following K. Hill (2012).

Table 6.2. Hopi Kin-Terms

	Male				Female		
+2	FF	*kwa*	MMB	*taaha~ paava*	FM	*so*	FFZ	*so*
	FFB	*kwa*	FMB	*na*	MM	*so*		
	MF	*kwa*			MMZ	*so*		

	Male		Female		Male		Female	
+1	F	*na*	M	*yu, -ngu*	WF	*na*	WM	*yu*
	FB	*na*	MZ	*yu, -ngu*	MB	*taha*	FZ	*kya*
	MZH	*na*	FBW	*yu, -ngu*	FZH	*kwa*	MBW	*mö'wi*
0	B	*paava* (e) *tupko* (y)	Z	*qööqa* (e) *siwa* (y)	H	*koongya*	W	*nööma, wùuti*
	FBS	*paava* (e) *tupko* (y)	FBD	*qööqa* (e) *siwa* (y)	MBS	*ti*	MBD	*ti*
	MZS	*paava* (e) *tupko* (y)	MZD	*qööqa* (e) *siwa* (y)	FZS	*na*	FZD	*kya*
					ZH	*möönangw*	BW	*mö'wi*
-1	S	*ti ~ tiyo*	D	*ti ~ maana*				
	BS	*ti* (♂) *mööyi* (♀)	BD	*ti* (♂) *mööyi* (♀)	ZS	*-tiw'aya* (♂) *ti* (♀)	ZD	*-tiw'aya* (♂) *ti* (♀)
					DH	*möönangw*	SW	*mö'wi*

	Male		Female	
-2	SS	*mööyi*	SD	*mööyi*
	DS	*mööyi*	DD	*mööyi*

Source: Titiev (1944); orthography from the Hopi Dictionary Project (1998).

and /e/, and in only a few roots. While a few perfectly ordinary forms (including particles and affixes) begin with *kya-* and *kye-*, /ky/ most commonly appears in ritually charged items. These include a very productive prefix *kyaa-* 'awesome, intensively, extremely (both good and bad), inspiring awe or interest,' as in the first element in *Kyaa-muy* 'the month of the Solstice.' Other examples of *kya* appear in *kyaaro* 'parrot,' *kyalmoki* 'rattlesnake venom sac,' *kyaptsi* 'respect,' and *kyasimuya* 'back tablet of certain kachinas.' I am not arguing that *kya* 'FZ' is the same morpheme as the *kya* in the words above, but simply that it shares with them the sound /ky/ that is one mark of Hopi high language, and that links the sound of some Hopi words to characteristic sounds in nearby Puebloan languages. This phonological transformation is evidence in favor of a Puebloan *Sprachbund* (e.g., Bereznak 1995; Whiteley and Snow 2015).

Hopi *kya* 'FZ' replaces one of the most stable of all Uto-Aztecan etyma: PUA *pah(w)a 'FZ' (Stubbs 2011, #88). The only UA languages other than Hopi that lack reflexes of this etymon are Cora and Huichol. It seems likely that this unusual replacement occurred due to the formation of the Crow terminology, with this FZ word replaced by the FM word.

In summary, the move to Crow-type skewing in Hopi kin-terms involved losing PUA *-pah(w)a 'FZ' and replacing it with *qa, originally 'FF, FM.' The skewing equation FM=FZ required *qa 'FF' to be replaced by *kwa* 'MF.' When the equation FM=FZ was lost, *qa* 'FM' was replaced by *so*, originally only 'MM,' leaving Hopi with a reduced set of PP terms. But the grandparental reference of *-qa must have remained long enough for the rest of the skewing equations shown in (1), (3), and (4) to fall into place. At some point, phonological modification of expected *qa* to *kya* 'FZ' expressed the importance and ritual loading of that term (Nagata n.d.).

Notes on Skewing in the Tanoan Languages

Among the Tanoan languages, Arizona Tewa has Crow skewing equations (see [2] and [5]), and Towa has the odd, partly skewing equations in (10). The other Tewa varieties and Tiwa lack such equations. However, there are historical linguistic hints that Crow skewing may have a deep Tanoan history. These hints challenge the claim by Eggan (1950, 153) and Dozier (1955, 248) that skewing in Arizona Tewa derives entirely from contact with Hopi. Because Whiteley (chapter 5, this volume) discusses this issue, I restrict attention here to two bits of historical linguistic evidence for Tanoan skewing.

Unlike the probable history of Hopi *kya* 'FZ' sketched above, there is no evidence that Arizona Tewa *kiyû·* 'FZ, FM' comes from a Proto-Tanoan (PT) or Proto-Kiowa-Tanoan (PKT) word for 'FM.' Instead, Arizona Tewa's equation FZ=FM is an innovation. This raises the interesting possibility that when *kiyû·* came to label FM as well as FZ,[6] this change was modeled on a Hopi system in which the ancestral form of *kya* 'FZ' was still used for FM.

The poorly documented core kin-terms for Towa, the Tanoan language of matrilineally organized Jemez Pueblo, appear in table 6.3. Towa has crossness in every generation and, like Hopi, has a single ChCh term rather than inter-generational equations in the G^{+2}-G^{-2} reciprocal forms.

Towa kin-terms, consistent with the matrilineal descent documented for Jemez Pueblo, include some Crow skewing equations. The equations on the cross-relative side as recorded by Parsons (1932) are shown in (10).

10. MB=MBS=FZS=ZS=ZD (*tǫ́mų́*)
FZ=FZD=MBD (*chíyu*)

The equations in (10) include the classic Crow skewing equations MB=MBS and FZ=FZD, but add relatives from the opposite matriline, in a shift toward a generational system like those in Rio Grande Tewa and Tiwa.

Towa *chíyu* is probably cognate to Arizona Tewa *kiyû* 'FZ, FM.' Because Towa is a separate branch of Tanoan from Tiwa-Tewa (Ortman 2012), this hints that skewing for this etymon could date to Proto-Tanoan. Evidence for ancient skewing appears as well in the Tiwa languages. Tiwa terminologies lack the G^{+2}=G^{-2} alternate-generation equations and instead have a single term for "grandchild." Because G^{+2}=G^{-2} equations are common features of Dravidian and

Table 6.3. Towa Kin-Terms (Generations +1, 0, -1)

	Male		Female		Male		Female	
+1	F	*tǫ́ǫ́'e* (*tǽtǽ* "dad")	M	*zé'e*				
	FB	*tǫ́ǫ́'e*	MZ	*zé'e*	MB	*tǫ́mų́**	FZ	*chíyu*
0	B	*pǽpú* (e) *pétú* (y)	Z	*khôo* (e) *p'ǽǽ'e* (y)				
	FBS	*pǽpú* (e) *pétú* (y)	FBD	*khôo* (e) *p'ǽǽ'e* (y)	MBS	*tǫ́mų́*	MBD	*chíyu*
	MZS	—	MZD	—	FZS	*tǫ́mų́*	FZD	*chíyu*
−1	S	*kį́*	D	*kį́*				
	BS	*kį́* ?	BD	*kį́*	ZS	*tǫ́mų́*	ZD	*tǫ́mų́*

Source: Parsons (1932) (roman type), Yumitani (1998) (italics), Sprott (1992) (bold italics).
**tǫ́mų́* is the diminutive of "father" (Trager 1943).

Table 6.4. Proto-Kiowa-Tanoan "Woman's Brother's Son, Grandchild"

	Kiowa	RG Tewa	Arizona Tewa	Taos	Picuris	Southern Tiwa	Towa	PKT
ChCh	mə́gi ♀BS	mą:tu "relative" (?)	—	mə̨kuna	mą̨koʼone	mą̨kude	[meku] loan	*mą̨qwi

Source: Sutton (2014, 512).

Iroquoian systems, the probable ancestors of the Tanoan systems (Whiteley, chapter 5, this volume), the single "grandchild" word is likely to be an innovation in Tiwa, consistent with the tendency toward generational terminology in the Tanoan languages.

Sutton (2014, 512) proposed the Kiowa-Tanoan cognate set and reconstruction shown in table 6.4. The Kiowa and Tiwa words exhibit regular correspondences for vowels and consonants that are supported by other Kiowa-Tanoan cognate sets. The very similar Towa word for "grandchild," shown in brackets, does not have the expected Towa vowels (the predicted cognate would be /mį̨:ko/). Thus the Towa word is probably a loan from Tiwa, perhaps motivated by the loss of the $G^{+2}=G^{-2}$ equations in Towa.

The comparative linguistics of this "grandchild" term suggests that its history may include a Crow-type equation like the Hopi equation in (4), repeated in (11).

11. ♀BCh=ChCh

If Kiowa mə́gi '♀BS' reflects the original meaning of the word, as seems likely, it shifted to the more general meaning "grandchild" in Tiwa and was then loaned into Towa. The skewing equation in (11), a corollary of the skewing equation FZ=FM, would motivate precisely this semantic change. This cognate set thus suggests that the Tiwa languages may at one time have had the skewing equation in (11), and later replaced the term for BS with a general "nibling" (nephew/niece) term as G^{-1} shifted to Eskimo type.

Zuni Kinship Terminology: Crow Overlay on Cheyenne

Zuni skewing departs from the logic that equates FZ with FM. Instead, Zuni skewing equations express parent-child reciprocity. Furthermore, Zuni speakers

Table 6.5. Zuni Kin-Terms, Blood Orientation (Generations +1, 0, -1)

	Male		Female		Male		Female	
+1	F	*taččʼu*	M	*citta*	MB	*kaka*	FZ	*kuku*
	FB	*taččʼu*	MZ	*citta*	FZH	*taččʼu**	MBW	*cilu*
0	B	*papa* (e) *suwe* (y, ♂)	Z	*kawu* (e) *ikina* (y, ♂) *hanni* (y, ♀)				
	FBS	*papa* (e) *suwe* (y, ♂) *hanni* (y, ♀)	FBD	*kawu* (e) *ikina* (y, ♂) *hanni* (y, ♀)	MBS	*papa* (e) *suwe* (y, ♂) *hanni* (y, ♀)	MBD	*kawu* (e) *ikina* (y, ♂) *hanni* (y, ♀)
	MZS	*papa* (e) *suwe* (y, ♂) *hanni* (y, ♀)	MZD	*kawu* (e) *ikina* (y, ♂) *hanni* (y, ♀)	FZS	*papa* (e) *suwe* (y, ♂) *hanni* (y, ♀)	FZD	*kawu* (e) *ikina* (y, ♂) *hanni* (y, ♀)
-1	S	*čaʼle*	D	*čaʼle*				
	BS	*čaʼle* (♂) *tale* (♀)	BD	*čaʼle* (♂) *eyye* (♀)	ZS	*kʼašše* (♂) *čaʼle* (♀)	ZD	*kʼašše* (♂) *čaʼle* (♀)

Source: Ladd (1979).
*Schneider and Roberts (1956).

use Crow-type skewing equations primarily in contexts where clan membership is highlighted and to categorize a relative as distant rather than close blood kin. In everyday usage with close relatives, Zuni uses terminological equations of Cheyenne type, where all cousins in G° are Ego's siblings.

Zuni overlay was first recognized by Schneider and Roberts (1956), in an analysis that largely resolved the contradictions in reports by Kroeber (1917) and Parsons (1932) discussed by Eggan (1950). Schneider and Roberts showed that Zuni-speakers used two different terminologies, which they labeled "role designating" (the unskewed system) and "classifying/ordering" (the skewed system). Ladd (1979), who referred to the two systems as "blood" (unskewed) and "clan" (skewed), states that the choice of terms depends "on how close the speaker wishes to bring the person into the circle of kin—blood or clan" (484). Consultants for Schneider and Roberts (1956, 11–12) suggested that skewed terms were "more respectful" and more likely to be used in reference than in direct address.

The core-generation Zuni terms of the non-skewed system, in table 6.5, are those Ladd (1979, 484) states are used for "true blood kin." This system is of Cheyenne type, with crossness in the parental and child generations, but leveling to a single set of sibling terms in Ego's generation. In this system FZH=FB,

Table 6.6. Zuni Kin-Terms, Clan Orientation (Generations +I, 0, -I)

	Male		Female		Male		Female	
+1	F	*tačču*	M	*citta*				
	FB	*tačču*	MZ	*citta*	MB	*kaka*	FZ	*kuku*
					FZH*	*nana*		
0	B	*papa* (e)	Z	*kawu* (e)				
		suwe (y, ♂)		*ikina* (y, ♂)				
		hanni (y, ♀)		*hanni* (y, ♀)				
					MBS	*ča'le*	MBD	*ča'le*
	FBS	*papa* (e)	FBD	*kawu* (e)				
		suwe (y, ♂)		*ikina* (y, ♀)				
		hanni (y, ♀)		*hanni* (y, ♀)	FZS	*tačču*	FZD	*kuku*
	MZS	*papa* (e)	MZD	*kawu* (e)				
		suwe (y, ♂)		*ikina* (y, ♂)				
		hanni (y, ♀)		*hanni* (y, ♀)	FZDH	*nana**		
−1	S	*ča'le*	D	*ča'le*	ZS	*k'ašše* (♂)	ZD	*k'ašše* (♂)
	BS	*ča'le*	BD	*ča'le*		*ča'le* (♀)		*ča'le* (♀)

Source: Ladd (1979).
*Schneider and Roberts 1956.

yielding a single 'uncle' term *tačču*, although FZ and MBW are distinguished from one another. Not shown are G^{+2} and G^{-2} terms. In both blood and clan orientations these exhibit the section-defining alternate-generation equation $G^{+2}=G^{-2}$.

The "clan" orientation terms in table 6.6 have crossness not only in G^{+1}, but also in Ego's generation, and also have Crow-type skewing.

Equations for the father's matriline and its affines appear in (12). Here FZH is not equated with FB, as in blood orientation, but with PF, *nana*.

12. FZD=FZ
FZS=F
FZH=PF
FZDH=FZH

The skewing equation for males in the mother's matriline and those linked through them appears in (13).

13. MBCh=Ch

The equations in (12), as in Hopi, presuppose that FZ=FM, since the term *nana* equates FZH and FZDH with PF. But members of the father's matriline, including FZ, call Ego *ča'le* 'child,' not 'grandchild' (for which there are three terms, linked by intergenerational equation to the three grandparent terms). So Zuni skewing is different from that of Hopi, which uses 'grandchild' for ♀BS, and from Arizona Tewa as well, where we find a special term *'è·sèŋ*, 'man child,' which can be understood as a diminutive of the word for "husband." However, in spite of the fact that no affinal tension would appear to inhere in a term meaning "child," Zuni has the same kind of joking relationship between FZ and ♀BS seen in Hopi and Arizona Tewa.

While the two Zuni terminologies are quite different, they express a similar logic from the point of view of alliance theory. The Cheyenne equations that unite all "close" relatives in Ego's generation under the sibling terms can be understood as horizontal skewing, expressing proscriptions against marriage with close cousins. But the Crow system has important consequences for alliance as well, proscribing marriage between cross-cousins and thereby yielding a "semicomplex" alliance system. Ladd (1979) believed that the skewing terminology emphasizes the descent line, hence his label "clan orientation." Detailed observation of naturally occurring usage will be required in order to untangle the functions of the two orientations.

Zuni has no known genealogical relatives, so we cannot use comparative linguistic methods. However, areal-linguistic methods are relevant to this case. Unlike Hopi, Zuni probably has loan vocabulary among its kin-terms. Zuni *kuku* 'FZ' may be from Keresan **k'u:* 'woman' (Miller and Davis 1963, 323); Arizona Tewa *kúkú* 'umbilical-cord cutter, ritually confirmed father's mother' may also be from the Keresan word. If Keresan was indeed a regional sacred language during Puebloan prehistory, as argued by Shaul (2014), then its word for "woman" may have conveyed what Nagata (n.d.) has suggested is the ritual potency of the FZ in a matrilineal society.

Parsons (1932, 387) considered Western Keres *nána* '♂PF' to be "obviously" a loan from Zuni *nana* 'PF.' But such a loan would be opposite to the direction predicted by Shaul (2014), and I believe that Parsons's case is weak. Keresan has /na/ in other words for male kin: **náwé* 'mother's brother, sister's son' (Miller and Davis 1963, 324) and *n'a'isdʸíy'a* 'father, father's brother.' (This is the Acoma word; closely resemblant forms appear in all Keresan varieties.) Zuni has the syllable /na/ only in *nana* 'grandfather.' Thus the possibility of a Keresan-to-Zuni loan should not be dismissed. And chance resemblance cannot be ruled out.

Western Keresan Kin-Terminology: Crow Overlay on Cheyenne?

Eastern and Western Keresan languages share most terms and structures (Parsons 1923, 1932; Hawley 1950). All have $G^{+2}=G^{-2}$ equations and crossness in the parental generation. Male speakers distinguish ZCh from BCh, but female speakers call all G^{-1} relatives son or daughter. All varieties but Laguna permit cross-parallel neutralization in G^0, with all cousins labeled with sibling terms, yielding a horizontally skewed Cheyenne-type system.

As is obvious in table 6.7, for Acoma, the documentation of Keresan terminologies is plagued by conflicting accounts. Parsons (1923, 170) observed that, rather than indicating "looseness" of usage, these conflicts reflected "freedom of choice among various fixed principles." I follow this suggestion: that these conflicts reflect, not transition or breakdown, but diverse stances, like those identified for Zuni. As in Zuni, it seems likely that in Keresan we encounter Crow skewing overlaid on a Cheyenne-type terminology. Fox (1967, 160) confirmed this point for Cochiti Pueblo. When Cochiti clans act as formal units, as during weddings, men address males in their father's clan as "father" and all female members as "mother."

The core-generation terms for the Western Keresan pueblos, Acoma and Laguna, appear in tables 6.7 and 6.8. These terminologies extend equations between alternate-generation kin to the great-grand level, as seen in (14). Grand-kin-terms are not included in the tables, but they exhibit $G^{+2}=G^{-2}$ equations, and $G^{+1}=G^{-1}$ for cross-kin. Acoma and Laguna share the alternate-generation equation PPP=P, found in no other Puebloan language. In contrast, Eastern Keresan equates great-grandparents and grandparents, and the other Puebloan languages have special terms for great grandrelatives (Parsons 1932).

14. PPP=P

ChChCh=Ch

PP=ChCh

Two Western Keresan alternate-generation $G^{+1}=G^{-1}$ equations, shown in (15), are used only by men. Women call ZS and ZD "son" and "daughter."

15. MB=♂ZS

FZ=♂ZD (Acoma -*n'à·ya* ~ Laguna -*naaya*)

Table 6.7. Acoma (Western Keresan) Kin-Terms

		Male		Female		Male		Female
+1	F	-nꞌaꞌisdʸíyꞌa	M	-nâ·ya	MB	-ꞌá·náwé (♂) -mə́·tʸi (♀)	FZ	-kʼú·yá (†) -nâ·ya (*, ‡, Mr)
	FB	-nꞌaꞌisdʸíyꞌa	MZ	-nâ·ya			MBW	-bî·yꞌa ~ -máꞌakə
	FBW	-nâ·ya	MZH	-nꞌaꞌisdʸíyꞌa	FZH	-nꞌaꞌisdʸíyꞌa		
0	B	-dʸúmꞌə (♂) -waçə (♀)	Z	-kûiça (♂) -ꞌáu (♀)				
	FBS	-dʸúmꞌə (♂) -waçə (♀)	FBD	-kûiça (♂) -ꞌáu (♀)	MBS	-mə́·tʸi (♂) -dʸúmꞌə (♂*) -waçə (♀*)	MBD	-máꞌakə (♂) -kûiça (♂*) -ꞌáu (♀*)
	MZS	-dʸúmꞌə (♂) -waçə (♀)	MZD	-kûiça (♂) -ꞌáu (♀)	FZS	-dʸúmꞌə (♂) -waçə (♀) -nꞌaꞌisdʸíyꞌa (†, Mr)	FZD	-kûiça (♂) (*, ‡, Mr) -ꞌáu (♀) (-nâ·ya †)
−1	S	-mə́·tʸi	D	-máꞌakə				
	BS	-mə́·tʸi	BD	-máꞌakə	ZS	-ꞌá·náwé (♂) -mə́·tʸi (♀)	ZD	-nâ·ya (♂) -máꞌakə (♀)

Source: Eggan (1950), Miller (1959).
Mr: Miller
*Parsons (1932)
†Kroeber (1917)
‡White Acoma

Laguna has the additional alternate-generation equations in (16), where female cross-cousins are equated with grandmother.

$$16.\ \text{FZD} = \text{♂PM}$$
$$\text{MBD} = \text{♀PM}$$

As a consequence of (16) and the $G^{+2} = G^{-2}$ equation in (14), Laguna women call their cross-cousins "grandchild." However, men call their cross-cousins "son" or "daughter," an adjacent-generation skewing equation seen below in (18).

Eggan (1950, 259) saw these alternate-generation equations as lineage-defining. However, as pointed out above, these are one of the basic equation types in tetradic theory (Allen 1989) and define exogamous units in the alliance system. The equations $G^{+2}=G^{-2}$ and $G^{+1}=G^{-1}$ define these pairs as equivalent in the cycle of alliances, and marriage between "same-generation" cross-cousins—which by the logic of the equations includes grandparents and grandchildren in that generation—is not proscribed. An aside by Parsons confirms that affinal tension is indeed implied by these equations. She wrote, "At Laguna I was told explicitly that to use the reciprocal of father's sister's daughter and mother's brother's son was tantamount to using a wife-husband term" (Parsons 1932, 384). This equation suggests patrilateral cross-cousin marriage (Whiteley, chapter 5, this volume). Even more tellingly, in Parsons 1923 (196–97) we learn that children were often "bashful" about using this term, *-baaba'a*. The term also means "grandrelative." This is entirely consistent with tetradic theory, and it is a part of Parsons's "kin" usage, not of the skewed usage associated with "clan," where we find *-k'uuya* 'FZ, FZD.'

These alternate-generation equations should be distinguished from adjacent-generation Crow-type equations that are also attested for Western Keresan, in what Parsons (1923) calls "clan" usage, as opposed to "kin" usage. The skewing equations for women of the father's matriline are shown in (17). These are

Table 6.8. Laguna (Western Keresan) Kin-Terms

	Male		Female		Male		Female	
+1	F	*-naishjiya*	M	*-naaya*	MB	*-anawe* (♂)	FZ	*-k'uuya* ~
	FB	*-naishjiya*	MZ	*-naaya*		*-miityi* (♀)		*-naaya* (♂ only)
					FZH	*-naishjiya*	MBW	*-piye ~ naaya*
0	B	*-dyumi* (♂) *-wa* (♀)	Z	*-akwi* (♂) *-a'au* (♀)				
	FBS	*-dyumi* (♂) *-waa* (♀)	FBD	*-k'uitra* (♂) *-a'au* (♀)	MBS	*-miityi* (♂) *-baaba'a* (♀)	MBD	*-m'aaka* (♂) *-dya'au* (♀)
	MZS	*-dyumi* (♂) *-waa* (♀)	MZD	*-k'uitra* (♂) *-a'au* (ws)	FZS	*-naishjiya*	FZD	*-baaba'a ~ k'uuya* (♂) *-dya'au* (♀)
−1	S	*-miityi*	D	*-m'aaka*				
	BS	*-miityi*	BD	*-m'aaka*	ZS	*-anawe* (♂) *-miityi* (♀)	ZD	*-naaya* (♂) *-m'aaka* (♀)

Source: Eggan (1950); some orthography from Lachler (2006).

identical to equations in Hopi, Arizona Tewa, and Zuni. However, they do not include a skewed term for FZH. This relative is equated with "father," not "grandfather."

$$\text{17. FZS=F (Laguna), (FZS=F) (Acoma)}$$
$$\text{(FZD=FZ)}$$

The Laguna equation for FZS in (17) has no parentheses, because Parsons (1932) records only FZS=F for Laguna. But at Acoma, the skewing equation in (17) exists alongside the Cheyenne equation in which FZS=B. The second equation has parentheses because it exists alongside FZD=Z in both Acoma and Laguna.

The Acoma situation is confusing, because the term *naaya* that appears in the Crow skewing equation FZD=FZ in (17) participates in several other equation types as well. In the meaning 'M, MZ, FZ, FBW,' it expresses generational leveling in G^{+1}. It also expresses the $G^{+1}=G^{-1}$ equation FZ=ZD. Kroeber reports that FZ at Acoma can also be called *k'uuya*, but this term figures in no equations, and simply means "senior woman of a clan" (Parsons 1932). At Laguna, *k'uuya* means 'FZ' exclusively (Miller 1959, 180), and is part of "clan" usage (Parsons 1923).

At Laguna, *naaya* means 'M, MZ.' It is used only by men in the $G^{+1}=G^{-1}$ equation ♂FZ=♂ZD. Only *k'uuya*, never *naaya*, is used in the Laguna skewing equation. Laguna *naaya* may be more usually a vocative (Parsons 1932), suggesting a possible formal (*k'uuya*) versus informal (*naaya*) distinction, reminiscent of the notion reported by Schneider and Roberts (1956) for Zuni, that Crow-skewed terms are "more respectful." And at Laguna, as at Zuni, these terms are part of an orientation to "clan." The other option for Laguna is to call FZD 'grandmother,' with the bashfulness-inducing -*baaba'a* expressing an alternate-generation equation (see [16]). For Acoma, the other option is to call FZD 'sister,' the Cheyenne equation.

The Western Keresan skewing equations for MB and MBCh are shown in (18).

$$\text{18. ♀MB=S}$$
$$\text{♂MBCh=Ch}$$

As in Arizona Tewa and Zuni, the Hopi equation ♀BCh=ChCh does not appear. The presupposition of MBCh=Ch is that MB=B, an equation found only in these languages. But MBCh=Ch is used only in men's speech, MB=S only in women's. A consequence of the equation for females is that women must use the alternate-generation grandrelative term *-baaba'a* for MBS. This situation, if correctly reported—Eggan (1950, 228) is dubious—is unique to Western Keresan.

In summary, the Western Keresan terminologies can probably be understood as a Crow system overlaid on a Cheyenne system as at Zuni, with the former used in contexts where speakers wish to highlight the unity of matrilineages. Fox's (1967) report that at Eastern Keresan Cochiti the Crow-like equations are used at weddings suggests that Crow usages may be appropriate especially when alliance is at stake.

Conclusions: Routes to, and Roles for, Crow-Type Skewing

This overview has highlighted several points. The first is that all of these languages except Hopi and Towa have alternate-generation equations alongside the adjacent-generation Crow-type skewing equations. The alternate-generation equations include $G^{+2}=G^{-2}$, $G^{+1}=G^{-1}$ (this equation variously developed, not always including all kin pairs), and, in the Keresan languages, $G^{+3}=G^{+1}$, where "great-grandparents" are "parents." Following Allen's (1989) tetradic theory of kinship, I have suggested that these encode the generational cycle of alliance in prescriptive exchange, defining the generational dimension of alliance "sections." However, none of the Puebloan groups, nor the Numic and Takic groups who have such equations, recognize sections, even when the alternate-generational equations appear alongside crossness. Alternate-generation equations, given their prediction by tetradic theory, deserve further comparative study, especially when they appear alongside skewing equations. Their presence in so many Puebloan terminological systems supports the proposal that these systems have evolved from Dravidian and Iroquois ancestral systems (Whiteley, chapter 5, this volume). The apparent relationship between Hopi terminology and systems of that type in Takic languages in California provides a historical link that also supports this evolutionary hypothesis.

The Crow skewing equations have slight differences among the languages. I have argued that the basic logical move to the Crow system in these Puebloan groups is to equate FZ with FM, with other equations being corollary to this one, and that a history that included this move can be recovered for Hopi and seen today for Arizona Tewa. However, although all of the Crow-type terminologies discussed have the equation FZS=F, which presupposes FZ=FM, no system completely follows through with the rest of the logic. In Hopi, FZ=FM has been largely lost. Only in Hopi do we find ♀BCh=ChCh (although such an equation may once have been found in Tiwa). Keresan has Crow skewing equations for FZCh and MBCh, but not for FZH. Only Towa and Western Keresan have an equation lowering MB to G^{-1}. The meanings and histories of these small differences deserve attention in a comparative project.

In Zuni and the Western Keresan pueblos Acoma and Zuni (and in the Eastern Keresan pueblo Cochiti and perhaps in others as well), we encounter two terminological options. One type, in everyday use, is a Cheyenne system, with crossness neutralized only in G°, where all kin are siblings. The second terminology, used on special occasions, has Crow skewing equations. While the contexts for the two systems have been sketched for Zuni and Cochiti, it is likely that contextual conditions are similar in the Western Keresan pueblos. The case of Fanti terminology in Africa also involves side-by-side Cheyenne and Crow, with Crow being seen by Fanti as "the more correct pattern" (Kronenfeld 2012, 157). In Hopi and Arizona Tewa, which have crossness in all generations except where interrupted by skewing, there is only one terminological system, Crow. (Of course, there are some options available to speakers, but these do not deviate from Crow logic.) In the opposite case, the Eskimo-type systems in the Tanoan pueblos where crossness is largely lost in all generations, not just in G°, there is no overlaid skewing, although historical linguistic analysis suggests that there may have been some skewing in ancient times. This apparent limitation on coexisting terminologies, which might be thought of as distinct discourses of kinship, to the Cheyenne-Crow case, is another candidate for attention in comparative study. In the Puebloan context, the apparently similar dual systems in Keresan and Zuni suggest that the "Keresan bridge" might be more accurately labeled the "Keresan-Zuni bridge."

As a final note, I agree with Whiteley (2015, 272), that "the distinction between Eastern and Western pueblos . . . is overdrawn." Dousset's (2012) insight that "horizontal skewing" in G°, as in Cheyenne and Eskimo systems, is a terminological strategy for amplifying the social and geographical range of marriage alliance, is quite similar to the conclusion that Crow skewing also opens new alliance possibilities. Whiteley (this volume) and Cruz and Ortman (2016) identify historical evidence for crossness in Tanoan terminologies, and I have suggested here that even skewing may have been present. Determining the exact circumstances that produced the shift in the east to horizontal skewing, and the times when these occurred, is a rich opportunity for collaboration among ethnologists, linguists, and archaeologists.

Notes

1. Kinship notation (see also glossary):

    M "mother"
    F "father"
    D "daughter"
    S "son"
    W "wife"
    H "husband"
    Z "sister"
    B "brother"
    P "parent"
    Ch "child"
    e "elder"
    y "younger"
    $\male$ "male's, male speaker's"
    $\female$ "female's, female speaker's"

    Examples: FFZ "father's father's sister"; FeB "father's elder brother"; yZCh "younger sister's child"; $\female$MB "female speaker's mother's brother"; $\male$PF "male speaker's parent's father."

    G^{+2} grandparents' generation
    G^{+1} parents' generation
    G^{0} Ego's generation
    G^{-1} children's generation
    G^{-2} grandchildren's generation

2. There are too many examples of similar inconsistencies between presuppositions of some equations and terminology for kin-types to note all of them in this chapter. For instance, the Hopi equation in (5) presupposes that MB=B. However, different terms are used for these two relatives.

3. Parallel cousins are the children of Ego's parents' same-sex siblings (MZCh, FBCh). In classificatory systems with "crossness," where MZ=M and FB=F, these kin are Ego's siblings. The cross-cousins are the children of Ego's parents' opposite-sex siblings (FZCh, MBCh). They are terminologically distinguished from "siblings."

4. Trautmann and Barnes (1998) state that the terms for children of cross second cousins (e.g., FFBChCh) provide a better diagnostic of a Dravidian system than

do the prescriptive equations. Gifford's (1922) Serrano consultants stated that all children of cross-cousins were called "nieces" and "nephews." In a Dravidian system, according to Trautmann and Barnes, only the children of Ego's opposite-sex cross second cousins should show this pattern, while the children of Ego's same-sex cross second cousins should be "son" and "daughter."

5.   By convention, reconstructed items (marked with a star) are not italicized.

6.   Arizona Tewa also has *kùku* "FM." This is only used if FM has cut her son's child's umbilical cord (Freire-Marreco 1914, 278).

CHAPTER SEVEN

Archaeological Expressions of Ancestral Hopi Social Organization

KELLEY HAYS-GILPIN AND DENNIS GILPIN

Introduction

Hopi oral histories describe diverse geographic, linguistic, and cultural origins for the people who came together over millennia to settle the Hopi Mesas and create the diverse settlements and ritual practices we see today as Hopi and Hopi-Tewa communities. Archaeological evidence strongly supports this account. Archaeologists conventionally organize data in a time-space matrix that classifies sites and artifacts into distinct time periods and geographic localities of varying scales. In contrast, oral traditions concern relationships among past and present groups of people and emphasize place over time. The use of traditional histories in archaeological research is complicated and problematic for many reasons (Vansina 1985). Archaeological and oral lines of evidence seldom coincide neatly and indeed are often contradictory. Yet their juxtaposition provides some interesting synergies—food for thought for both scientists and indigenous historians. Ancestral Hopi architecture and ritual paraphernalia illustrate the diverse origins of Hopi communities and their elaborate ritual calendar, and Hopi kinship and social organization clearly are structured to facilitate incorporation of outsiders.

Hopi Views

Hopis explain that "Hopi" is an amalgamation of clans that took different routes to the Hopi Mesas and contributed diverse social institutions to Hopi culture and society. For example, some clans owned ceremonies that brought rain; others were warriors who turned their skills to defense of their new communities. Because warrior societies, medicine societies, dances, kiva activities, elaborate food preparation, and feasting are impossible to parse into Western secular-versus-ritual activities, we will refer to sodality activities and community-wide ceremonial "doings" (cf. Fowles 2013; Kealiinohomoku 1989; Lomawaima 1989a, 168).

Hopi clans are matrilineal and exogamous, but as Whiteley (1998, 2002) has explained, clans are more diverse, flexible, and mutable than a simple descent model would predict. Some clans own farmland and ceremonies and some do not. Clans are not corporate units and are not residentially localized. Lineages tend to be ranked within clans. Ritual paraphernalia is passed down in lineages, and a "clan house" is the home of the primary lineage that cares for important ritual paraphernalia. Bernardini (2005a, 2012) explains that clan identities and clan migration stories have a great deal to do with the ownership, movement, and transfer of ceremonial knowledge and paraphernalia in processes of serial migration from many source areas to the Hopi Mesas over a period of many centuries. Clans are organized into phratries, groups of clans that traveled together during migrations and/or "go in" together ceremonially. Clans are related to each other in historical narratives, but equally important, they help to negotiate functional associations, symbolic connections, and ritual responsibilities that sometimes take precedence over our outside concepts of "history" as chronologically ordered events.

Clans (actually the prime lineage of the clan) own ceremonies performed by sodality members whose head priest is typically a senior member of the controlling clan. (This is in contrast to Eastern Pueblos, where sodalities are not controlled by kin groups; see Ware 2014.) Sodality membership crosscuts clans, however, because members are sponsored by ceremonial godparents from different clans, usually clans outside the child's parents' phratries. The interrelationships of kin, clan, phratry, sodality, and the overarching katsina religion (tribal sodality) tend to appeal to anthropologists as an unchanging functional structure that promotes group sodality. All these social units have histories, and these histories are complicated (Whiteley 2002; see clan migration stories in Courlander 1971; Fewkes 1898; Mindeleff 1891; Yava 1978). Exchange of sodalities among Hopi villages and other pueblos contributed to the internal diversity of Hopi villages as well as to networks of connections among Pueblos over a very broad geographic area and long span of time.

Hartman Lomawaima (1989a, 1989b) and Emory Sekaquaptewa (personal communication) emphasized that clans, ceremonies, and other aspects of Hopi life were taken in and sometimes recruited from other communities, many of whom spoke unrelated languages, but always were subject to "Hopification" (Lomawaima 1989b). To be "Hopified" is to become, or be made, compatible with Hopi values, aesthetics, and social arrangements. To become Hopified is to connect to the elaborate and flexible Hopi network of people, places, doings, and making things. All pueblos likely practiced a version of Hopification, that is, ways for migrants to assimilate into destination communities by contributing labor, marriage partners, warriors, and, for those who had them, ceremonies, while conforming to kiva language, ceremonial practices, and leadership protocols in their new homes.

One way of incorporating migrants as well as new generations into Western Pueblo communities is initiation into the katsina religion, which has probably unified villagers of diverse origins in common practices since the 1300s (Adams 1991). Katsinafication may be an important component of Hopification. Katsinas are ancestors, clouds, and rain. Hundreds of kinds of katsinas personify animals and other aspects of the natural world, deities, other tribes, warriors, and runners. Nearly all community members have roles to play as sponsors, food preparers and distributors, katsina "fathers," katsina doll carvers, and associated ritual clowns, as well as direct participants in public performances.

Clans and ceremonies are the most important social units in Hopi tellings of their social history. Whole villages sometimes moved as a group (see Whiteley 1988, 2008), and often fissioned. Orayvi, Songoopavi, Musangnuvi, and Walpi are mother villages; the others are daughter communities, formed when a village became too large for its land base or when factionalism led to residential fission. Tewa-speakers from the Galisteo Basin, and perhaps other villages, migrated to Hopi as warriors recruited to help defend Walpi from anticipated Spanish retaliation after the Pueblo Revolt of 1680, or as refugees from the Reconquest in New Mexico, depending on who is telling the story. In their new village of Hano/Tewa Village on First Mesa, they kept their Tewa language in defiance against full assimilation into the Hopi world, yet Hopi-Tewa families rapidly adopted matrilineal clans on the Hopi model and adapted their own ritual calendar to largely coincide with Hopi's (Parsons 1926).

The Tewa migration is probably just the most recent in a series of multilingual, multiethnic movements that go back at least as far as the late 1200s. Oral traditions explain that Awat'ovi was founded by the Bow Clan, but took in "people from all over" who spoke many languages and had many ceremonies. Kawàyka'a was a "Laguna" village, that is, Keresan-speaking, and the word Kawàyka'a (Kawaika) is Laguna Pueblo's Keresan name for itself (Courlander

1971, 268; Ellis 1967, 40; Hargrave 1935, 23; Hays-Gilpin and LeBlanc 2007, 124, 126–27; Stephen 1936, 578, 714; Whiteley 2002; Yava 1978).

To be Hopified is to aspire to a common set of values, not to conform to a single ideal identity. Deliberate maintenance of diversity and partition of knowledge, ceremonial responsibilities, and craft specializations are key to being Hopi. Each village has its own history and as a result its own configuration of ceremonies and clans. Dialects differ from mesa to mesa. Methods of selecting leaders differ. Basketry techniques differ. Even with a common language and recent imposition of a tribal council, Hopi villages have never united as a single community. Our main point is that Hopi diversity is deep and long-lived. The following archaeological examples illustrate Hopi's diverse origins, beginning just before dramatic large-scale population movements in the late 1200s.

Archaeological Views

Archaeological evidence demonstrates a long history of population movement and the incorporation of diverse peoples and social groups into communities (fig. 7.1). Prior to about 1400, settlement was almost continuous across what is now the US Southwest. Even so, variability in architecture, pottery, and other material culture traits signals differentiation of group identities. Population in the northern Southwest (southern Colorado Plateau and Rio Grande valley) peaked about 1300, at which time settlements began to cluster in the Hopi and Zuni areas, marking the establishment of Hopi and Zuni as recognizable and separate polities (Hill et al. 2004, 694–95; Wilcox, Gregory, and Hill 2007, 174–80). The following historical overview emphasizes architecture as evidence for social arrangements and artifacts as evidence for organized ritual practice, to reconstruct some of the events and processes of Hopification.

Post-Chaco Era, 1130–1250 or 1275 CE

Although Chacoan great houses, great kivas, or both have been identified as far west as central Black Mesa and Petrified Forest (Fowler and Stein 1992, figure 9-1), the Chaco phenomenon (Plog, chapter 11, this volume) had no obvious effect on the Hopi Mesas during its heyday. Repercussions of its reorganization in the 1100s, however, reached as far west as Flagstaff. Post-Chaco great houses dating to the 1100s and 1200s were important settlements southeast of the Hopi Mesas on the Rio Puerco of the West and in the Flagstaff area. Evidence

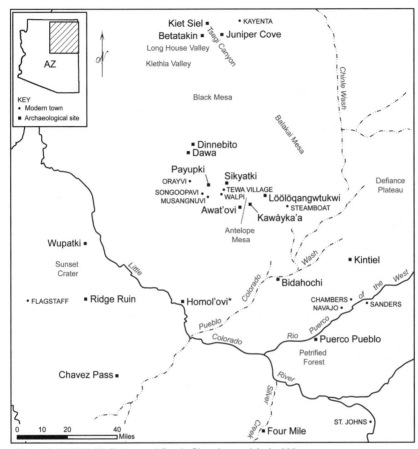

Kiet Siel ■   • KAYENTA
Betatakin ■   ■ Juniper Cove
Long House Valley
Klethla Valley

AZ

KEY
• Modern town
■ Archaeological site

Tsegi Canyon

Chinle Wash

Black Mesa

Balakai Mesa

■ Dinnebito
■ Dawa

Payupki
ORAYVI •   Sikyatki
SONGOOPAVI • • ■
MUSANGNUVI •   • TEWA VILLAGE
                • WALPI   ■ Löölöqangwtukwi
                              • STEAMBOAT
Awat'ovi ■ /   Kawàyka'a

Defiance
Plateau

Antelope
Mesa

Wupatki ■

Little

Sunset
Crater

Wash

■ Kintiel

West

Colorado

■ Bidahochi

of the

• FLAGSTAFF   ■ Ridge Ruin   ■ Homol'ovi*

CHAMBERS •
NAVAJO •   • SANDERS

Pueblo

Colorado   Rio   *Puerco*   ■ Puerco Pueblo

Petrified
Forest

Chavez Pass ■

River

Silver

Creek

0   10   20   40
▬▬▬▬▬▬▬ Miles

ST. JOHNS •

■ Four Mile

* Homol'ovi I, II, III, IV; Cottonwood Creek, Chevelon, and Jackrabbit

Figure 7.1. Map of Hopi and Hopi-ancestral sites. Commissioned by the authors.

suggests that elaborate doings in these two areas probably became part of the Hopi repertoire that was recorded by ethnographers centuries later.

Petroglyph imagery in these areas is particularly elaborate in this time period. Petrified Forest–area rock art includes images of burden baskets and women with butterfly hair whorls and dance wands, suggesting the presence of at least one women's sodality. The dance wand images resemble those used today by the Mamrawt society. Burden basket images resemble those on earlier Mimbres pottery, and actual baskets from the Kayenta, Chuska, and Chaco areas (Hays-Gilpin 2008, 250–52). Sets of painted stone and wood figurines from late Chaco and post-Chaco great houses and small houses in the

Chambers-Sanders-Navajo-St Johns area may be sodality or women's initiation paraphernalia. One set was scientifically excavated at the Puerco Bridge Site near Navajo, Arizona (Irwin 1997, 235–37). Others are in private collections or came to museums from collectors (Eaton 1991; Fane, Jacknis, and Breen 1991, 69). Most sets include explicitly female figures and babies in cradleboards, and some contain males. Other figurines represent animals and jog-toed sandals. Jog-toed sandals appear by 900 CE in the Chaco world; depictions of them as effigies, rock art, and elaborate twined sandals became important in Chaco and in the post-Chaco world, especially in rock art in southern Utah in the 1100s, but do not seem to persist into the 1200s (Bellorado, Webster, and Windes 2013). The humanlike figurines resemble later katsina figures in pottery and rock art, with semicircular heads and painted faces. Many figurine sets were accompanied by mineral pigments, crystals, fossils, and other small objects with probable ritual uses.

The Wupatki region north of Flagstaff welcomed farmers to productive conditions occasioned by deposition of an optimal mulch layer of volcanic ash after the eruption of Sunset Crater in the 1080s (Elson et al. 2011, 128). At least ten pueblos of more than twenty rooms were constructed, surrounded by over a thousand small farmsteads, field houses, and field features (Pilles 1996). Some view Wupatki Pueblo, the largest building in the area, with over 150 rooms, as a post-Chaco great house (Fowler and Stein 1992; Wilcox 2002). It has fairly elaborate masonry in some spinal rooms, and one T-shaped doorway. Pilles (1996) dates it to 1087–1213. Burchett (1990) hypothesized that the site housed twenty-six households in four localized lineages, each with its own kiva. Wupatki uniquely contains both a ballcourt and a community room that resembles an unroofed great kiva. A Flagstaff Black-on-white handle sherd or figurine fragment depicts a katsinalike face identified by Hopi consultant Ted Puhuyesva as a "storyteller" (Museum of Northern Arizona catalog number NA405.T.16.1.1).

Stone and Downum (1999) argue that as population grew, Wupatki-area farmers were unable to intensify their agricultural techniques due to lack of surface water and unpredictability of moisture from snow and rain, and thus had to invest in defense of territory for extensive dry farming. They did this by recruiting coethnics to growing communities such as Wupatki and Citadel pueblos, which were able to defend their territory and hundreds of farmsteads and fieldhouses that filled the optimal farmlands. This area appears to have been a frontier zone where distinctive Sinagua, Cohonina, and Kayenta patterns of pottery, textiles, and architecture came together. Burned and dismembered human remains have been encountered in a few sites located along the proposed frontiers between these populations. Stone and Downum (1999) attribute depopulation of the area in the early 1200s to conflict, and not to environmental conditions alone.

Ridge Ruin, just east of Flagstaff, also mixes Sinagua, Kayenta, and post-Chaco features and artifacts. It has two earthen ballcourts (ca. 1080) and a great house (ca. 1120) with at least four plazas (McGregor 1941). Most rooms are stacked basalt, but a spinal roomblock of sandstone blocks looks rather Chacoan, and Hays-Gilpin once observed a Chaco Black-on-white jar sherd on the site. A late room at Ridge Ruin contained a subfloor burial of an adult male aged thirty-five to forty, "The Magician," with one of the most complicated mortuary assemblages in the Southwest, including carved and painted swallowing sticks with hand, antelope hoof, agave leaf, and crescent-shaped finials; small shell trumpets; turquoise and shell mosaics; painted baskets; a painted wood cup; a cap of shell beads; projectile points; pigments; crystals; and numerous ornaments of shell, turquoise, argillite, jet, travertine, and other materials (McGregor 1943, Neitzel 2012). Ceramics and tree-ring dates suggest the grave dates to about 1150–1175.

McGregor (1943) reports that Hopi workmen identified the assemblage as characteristic of sodalities that were still active until recently: a warrior society—either unnamed or specifically the Momtsit—which drew its members from the Spider and Bluebird Clans. When McGregor showed Hopi consultants part of the burial assemblage, they identified other items that should also have been present in this sodality's paraphernalia—items that were in fact present when he produced the full assemblage for them to view. The Magician probably served as a leader in his community, but the burial assemblage is not necessarily evidence of great wealth; rather, the funerary assemblage could indicate that he died before passing on his ceremonial knowledge and paraphernalia to a successor, or that numerous ceremonial leaders took part in the funeral and thus renegotiated distributed power at the time of his death (O'Hara 2008). This sodality must have survived in other communities or else pueblo informants would not have retained specific knowledge of the ritual assemblage. This burial is one of our strongest links between past and present ritual-sodality practice, Hopi identity, and continuity over many centuries. Hopi commentary on the Magician indicates continuity in memory over eight hundred years and opens the way to integrate oral traditions about specific sites, regions, and clans/sodalities. Wupatki and Ridge Ruin were places where the post-Chaco world met the post-Hohokam world to contribute a dominant component of later Hopi society, including many important sodalities. The Wupatki communities also partook in some way of the Kayenta world to the north, in that a great deal of pottery was imported from Kayenta.

The Kayenta area itself did not, however, buy into Chaco or Hohokam. Until the mid-1100s, Kayenta people, like those to the north and west in the Virgin area, lived in unit pueblos. When severe drought struck at this time, people moved to better-watered areas in the Kayenta "heartland," from Navajo Mountain to Tsegi Canyon and Long House Valley. In Kayenta Period 2, 1150–1250 (Dean, Lindsay, and Robinson 1978), arroyo-cutting changed agricultural potential and settlements moved to the lower reaches of the drainages. Kayenta people maintained their basic room-cluster units, but arranged them in various ways, often around plazas that open to the southeast and courtyards. Kivas take various shapes. Pithouse villages persist in some areas. Northern Black Mesa was depopulated after 1150 (Powell 2002, figure 5.5, using Plog 1986, figure 43).

Population Reorganization, 1250/1275 to 1325 CE

In the late 1200s, much of the Four Corners region was depopulated. Out-migration was probably spurred by severe drought. Archaeologically, the late 1200s are our most significant hinge point. Village sites tend to occur in clusters with depopulated zones in between. Even though strong regional patterns in pottery emerge, architectural patterns are quite varied and different configurations of roomblocks, kivas, and plazas appear within the same settlement clusters, often as if community patterns leapfrogged over each other as extended families and larger social units moved from one place to another.

KAYENTA

From about 1250 or 1275 to 1300, people in the Kayenta heartland aggregated into large settlements, constructing villages surrounding or protected by multi-storied roomblocks (Gilpin 2001; Haas and Creamer 1993) and cliff dwellings (Dean 1969).

In the Long House Valley, habitations were relatively small until the 1250–1300 CE period, when the population aggregated into five large villages, the largest of which was Long House, with an estimated two hundred rooms (Dean,

Lindsay, and Robinson 1978). The most prominent architectural feature of Long House is a multistoried roomblock thirty meters long with walls ten feet high, situated on the top of a bench at the base of a slickrock sandstone slope, with rubble mounds clustered across the bench below it (Dean 1969, 183–86). The multistoried roomblock was built using spine- or ladder-style construction in which two long, parallel walls create a corridor that is subdivided into smaller rooms with cross walls. Sites similar to Long House are present across a vast region from Navajo Mountain to US Highway 264 and from Tonalea to Tohchinlini Mesa. The diversity in architecture on central Black Mesa during the orange ware period (Tsegi buildings, accretional pueblos, post-Chacoan buildings, Zuni-style buildings) is evidence of a multicultural amalgam (Gilpin 2001).

Dean (1969, 191–92) proposed that absence of great kivas in the Kayenta area (with the exception of Juniper Cove, which dates to the 600s) indicated that individual villages were autonomous and not organized into any intervillage system. The Long House Valley study, however, documented the intervisibility between the five large sites of the Tsegi phase in Long House Valley. This suggested some sort of intervillage organization. Haas and Creamer (1993) expanded on this observation and their own survey data from the Klethla Valley, the Kayenta Valley, and the Tsegi canyons to hypothesize that the Tsegi phase sites formed an integrated system, something like a tribe or an alliance of villages.

No katsina imagery appears in the Kayenta area that we know of, although rock art is abundant and depicts game animals, shield figures, and flute players that Hopis interpret as Flute Clan (Flute Society) migration symbols. The Sunflower Cache, a set of carved and painted wooden flowers, birds, and cones discovered in a plainware jar, has been linked to (and repatriated to) Hopi First Mesa Flute Clan (Kidder and Guernsey 1919). These were probably sodality paraphernalia, although this imagery would also be at home in the katsina world and similar items appear in central Arizona (for example, Bonita Creek) and upper Gila cave sites (Hill and Hays-Gilpin 1999).

In the Tsegi canyons, some people retreated to cliff dwellings. The largest of these were Kiet Siel, with 150 rooms, and Betatakin, with 120 rooms and three kivas. Dean (1969) classified the rooms and other architectural spaces as living rooms, granaries, storerooms, ceremonial rooms, and grinding rooms, which formed room clusters and courtyard complexes along the galleries (streets). Dean thought that Kiet Siel was founded about 1250 by families arriving independently and being joined by migrations of other families in 1272–1275 and in 1283–1286. Betatakin was founded about 1267 by the vanguard of a community who prepared the site for a substantial migration in 1275–1277 (Dean 1969, 74–75, 190).

Dean (1969, 191) proposed that the matrilocal extended household was the fundamental social unit in Kayenta social organization. Smith (1952b, 1972) summarized the problem of identifying Kayenta kivas, explaining the great variability in rooms that had been identified as kivas. Dean (1969, 29–33) summarized the situation later, stating that Kayenta kivas were so variable that a "typical" kiva could not be defined and no individual feature sufficed to identify a room as a kiva. Kivas were village facilities, representing at least one of the institutions that facilitated cooperation at the village level. In a society with high mobility, villages also needed some way to incorporate people moving in, although the variability in kivas does not indicate that all villages held similar doings.

Complicating the relationship between the Kayenta archaeological pattern and the process of becoming Hopi is strong evidence for Kayenta migration to central and even southern Arizona (Roosevelt Lake area, Point of Pines, Gila and Tonto Cliff Dwellings, Goat Hill Pueblo, and others; DiPeso 1958; Haury 1958; Lyons 2003; Woodson 1999). Many archaeologists view Salado culture as an amalgam of Kayenta and Classic Hohokam. Some think that Salado and Upper Little Colorado villages of this era might have developed the katsina religion, and brought it back to Hopi in the 1300s, thus explaining how katsinas are described as northern or local, but archaeological evidence for them is earlier in the south (Bernardini 2011).

EASTERN AREA

People to the east of the Hopi Mesas, on the Defiance Plateau, continuing west across Chinle Wash and Pueblo Colorado Wash to Balakai Mesa and the Steamboat area, continued to occupy post-Chacoan buildings, some of which grew by accretion (Gilpin 1989; Mount et al. 1993). These earlier sites all have certain architectural attributes that seem to derive from Chacoan architecture, following the Manuelito Model of post-Chacoan architectural development proposed by Fowler, Stein, and Anyon (1987; Fowler and Stein 1992), in which Chacoan great houses were superseded by post-Chacoan buildings with plazas fully enclosed by a row of rooms, which in turn were superseded by pueblos with plazas fully enclosed by roomblocks. Among the Chacoan architectural attributes are the completely enclosed plaza plan, which required planning the building as a whole, and the ladder (or spine) construction of the building. This type of construction allowed extensive planned buildings to be constructed quickly by having large construction teams build the overall outline while smaller groups finished the interior rooms. Kintiel was a planned building in the Zuni style with 650 ground-floor rooms and perhaps 1,300 rooms in total (Mindeleff 1891). All of the post-Chacoan Zuni-style buildings of the 1250/1275–1325 period have rectangular kivas. The formalized plans of post-Chacoan sites in the area east of Hopi, between Black Mesa and the Defiance Plateau, indicate directed or cooperative planning and construction at a village-wide scale. These sites represent a Western expression of a pattern centered at Zuni (Fowler et al. 1987; Kintigh 1985), but at least two examples (Löölöqangwtukwi and Kawàyka'a, see below) extended to Antelope Mesa and contributed to the architectural and social history of Hopi.

FLAGSTAFF AREA

In the Flagstaff area, settlement coalesced into five sites, four of them on Anderson Mesa. Four of these sites are massed roomblocks, but Chavez Pass Southwest is a large, square plaza-oriented site similar to the post-Chacoan and Zuni sites described above (Bernardini 2005a, figure 3.7; Upham 1982, figure 46). Architectural plans of Flagstaff villages thus represent at least two architectural traditions, one of which was derived from Chaco and linked to Zuni, reflecting a pattern of incorporating social diversity that would continue when the descendants of the Flagstaff area communities moved to Hopi.

SOUTHERN AREA

Areas that took in migrants during the late 1200s reorganization of the Colorado Plateau population include the upper Little Colorado River, the Rio Puerco of the West, Silver Creek, Homol'ovi, and central/eastern Arizona, including the Roosevelt Basin. Archaeologists have characterized this area as a frontier between Mogollon and "Anasazi" archaeological cultures due to a mix of architectural and pottery traditions as early as the 800s.

Along the Rio Puerco of the West, population began to aggregate into at least half a dozen large pueblos during the 1250/1275–1325 period. Puerco Pueblo (Burton 1990) is like a Zuni site, with rows of rooms arranged around a square plaza, but ceramics are mainly Hopi yellow ware and locally produced Winslow Orange Ware.

Homol'ovi IV, west of the Little Colorado River, was founded around 1260 as an Acropolis-style building (see below) by migrants from the Hopi Mesas, based on pottery and architecture (Adams 2002). Homol'ovi III (founded around 1290) blends Hopi and Silver Creek architectural styles and ceramics; it lasted a generation or two as an autonomous village, then was reoccupied as a seasonal farming village. Cottonwood Creek, Chevelon, and Homol'ovi I were founded around 1280, likely settled by immigrants from the Hopi Mesas. Homol'ovi I grew accretionally around a massed roomblock. One later addition included adobe roomblocks, which suggests that it absorbed immigrants from the south. Homol'ovi III initially comprised rows of large rooms and a rectangular great kiva, suggesting that immigrants from the Mogollon area joined with immigrants from the Hopi Mesas. Pottery includes both Hopi orange ware and some Tusayan and Little Colorado White Ware, together with White Mountain Red Ware, Cibola White Ware, and locally produced Winslow Orange Ware that combines features of both traditions. All the Homol'ovi sites have Hopi-style rectangular kivas, often with loom holes. Adams argues that the post-1275 rectangular kiva came from the Mogollon tradition (1989, 43).

HOPI MESAS

Many villages were established on all four of the Hopi Mesas, though we know the most about Antelope Mesa due to Peabody Museum surveys in the 1930s. The architecture is quite diverse, suggesting that migrants came from many directions. Löölöqangwtukwi (Harvard's "Lululongturque") is almost like a Zuni site: a square around a plaza.

The earliest building at Kawàyka'a, in the southwestern quarter of the site, is a large, rectangular building measuring one hundred by sixty-five meters with a completely enclosed plaza (Mindeleff 1891, plate 9), much like earlier sites to the east of the Hopi Mesas. The kivas of this early unit were in front of its highest section (Smith 1972, figure 3). Later development of Kawàyka'a was of the accretional type that has been better studied by the excavations of Awat'ovi. This pattern is consistent with an already socially cohesive group migrating and founding a new village. Later, other social groups joined them, and communities grew as new generations were born there.

Occupants of Awat'ovi's early component, the Western Mound, built a Homol'ovi III–type unit of around forty rooms with two rectangular kivas in front. Bidahochi initially comprised a roomblock high on a natural mound, thus accentuating the height and size of the village, a pattern colloquially called an Acropolis (Gilpin 1988).

Population Contraction, 1325–1400/1450 CE

From about 1325 to 1375, a period marked by the production and exchange of yellow ware pottery, population on the Hopi Mesas and in the Hopi Buttes and Homol'ovi areas grew so rapidly that only in-migration can explain it. Oral traditions concur: this is the time Hopis today identify with the "gathering of the clans." Pottery style and technology were fairly uniform, but architecture was quite varied in this time period.

HOMOL'OVI CLUSTER

Jackrabbit (1350–1375) was a small community, probably populated by people from the Hopi Mesas moving to the middle Little Colorado. Its architecture resembles the Pueblo III sites at Dawa and Dinnebito on the western edge of the Hopi Mesas, with one high-relief roomblock built on a natural promontory to create the illusion of multistoried construction and lower wings enclosing a plaza at its base. Homol'ovi II was founded at the same time, but is far larger than the other sites in the Homol'ovi cluster and organized around rectangular plazas. It was evidently settled as a planned plaza-oriented village in about 1350, and perhaps took in population from the other Homol'ovi villages as well as from the Hopi Mesas. At that time, evidence for katsina imagery appears in pottery and rock art, and Homol'ovi I and Chevelon added open rectangular plazas. Homol'ovi II has kiva murals similar to those on Antelope Mesa, and the dominant yellow ware pottery at Homol'ovi I and II has been sourced mainly to Awat'ovi (Adams 2002). Bernardini (2005a) adds oral traditions to the Homol'ovi story, interpreting these large villages as containers through which migrating clans/sodalities/suprahousehold groups passed sequentially.

Adams argues that Homol'ovi sites produced cotton and other textiles in exchange for obsidian from Government Mountain that was acquired, processed, and distributed by villages on Anderson Mesa and for yellow ware pottery from the Hopi Mesas. Water birds and turtles collected along the Little Colorado River might also have been traded from Homol'ovi to the Hopi Mesas.

The Homol'ovi area thus exhibits architectural diversity across time, with Northern architecture at Homol'ovi IV but Southern architecture at Homol'ovi I and III and Chevelon. And yet the pottery assemblages become increasingly dominated by yellow ware imported from the Hopi Mesas. By the terminal occupation of Homol'ovi II, virtually no pottery from any other source appears. Here, Hopification is most visible in ceramics, and less so in architecture.

HOPI MESAS

One of the first buildings constructed at Awat'ovi during the yellow ware period was a Homol'ovi III–type unit in the Western Mound, consisting of around forty rooms with one rectangular kiva in front, similar to and east of the unit that had been constructed in the Western Mound in the previous orange ware period. Both the orange ware unit and the yellow ware unit were constructed as "spine" or "ladder" units; later, rooms were added as needed to the front and back of these units. Thus, the initial planning and initial wall construction of each ladder unit was conducted by a social group of approximately forty people acting under the direction of some leadership structure, while the subdivision of each corridor into rooms could have been conducted by the individual households within the forty-person social group. Additional ladder units were added to create the Western Mound, which ultimately became a large, square building approximately one hundred meters on a side with a dimple (never excavated by the Awat'ovi Expedition) in the middle. The Western Mound would have looked like the main mounds at Four Mile, Homol'ovi I, and Bidahochi (Adams 2002, figure 2.6; Gilpin 1988; Plog 1981, figure 31, 49). Brew (1937, 137) describes how an L-shaped wing, thirty by fifty meters, extended north of the square mound, which corresponds to how plazas were added to Four Mile, Homol'ovi I, Chevelon, Bidahochi, and Bidahochi Southeast.

Additional expansion of Awat'ovi in the 1300s was accomplished by adding roomblocks north and east of the Western Mound surrounding newly established plazas with kivas in them, in a manner corresponding to the construction of pueblos like Homol'ovi II.

The appearance of Sikyatki Polychrome pottery around 1375 signals florescence of a katsina-centered Hopi aesthetic of colorful flowers, birds, and butterflies. Sikyatki Polychrome, together with its more common bichrome counterpart, Jeddito Black-on-yellow, is characterized by asymmetrical designs that often include depictions of life-forms. Plazas are fundamental to katsina doings. Where we have depictions of katsinas on pottery and rock art, we have plazas. Ironically, the katsina religion is credited with uniting disparate peoples into stable communities (Adams 1991, 2002), but among the Western Pueblos, this pattern did not last very long outside the Hopi Mesas, and came late to the Zuni area (1400 or a little after).

By the end of this period, 1450 at the latest, only Hopi was occupied in northern Arizona, and the Classic Hohokam had dispersed into rancheria sites, with some probably migrating to Hopi and Zuni (Teague 1993) and possibly Sonora (D. Wilcox, personal communication).

The Sikyatki Period, 1400/1450–1540 CE

Sikyatki Polychrome with Sikyatki-style designs—i.e., colorful, asymmetrical, flamboyant bird and feather motifs—appears on pottery of the Hopi Mesas sometime after 1400, on Matsaki Polychrome pottery made in the Zuni villages, on Pottery Mound Glaze Polychrome and in kiva murals at Pottery Mound, and in two murals at Awat'ovi. Katsina imagery is common on Sikyatki Polychrome and in kiva murals, as are other elaborate personages and animals. The style and iconography of many murals and some Sikyatki Polychrome resemble Rio Grande rock art, and many Hopi consultants to the Museum of Northern Arizona's Hopi Mural Project have identified the Awat'ovi and Kawàyka'a figurative murals as "Eastern Pueblo, not Hopi." Elsewhere, we have called into question the presumed Hopi origin of the Pottery Mound murals, and suggest the exchange was a two-way street (Hays-Gilpin and LeBlanc 2007; Hays-Gilpin and Gilpin 2018). Put together with oral traditions identifying Awat'ovi as a multilingual community with a great many ceremonies, Sikyatki as associated with Rio Grande components, and Kawàyka'a as a "Laguna" village, we can suggest that at least First Mesa and Antelope Mesa took in many pueblo people from further east during this era.

The initial occupation at Sikyatki, which occurred in the 1200–1275 period (when black-on-white pottery was produced), was concentrated on the "Acropolis," a high ridge (Fewkes 1898, plate 116). During the Sikyatki period, massive roomblocks were added at the base of and east of the ridge to enclose a large, deep plaza, while additional roomblocks were added to the north of the ridge, resulting in a pueblo of approximately 1,500 to 2,000 ground-floor rooms.

Spanish Colonization, 1540–1680 CE

Hopi historians disagree about whether oral traditions identify Kawàyka'a or Awat'ovi as the first village encountered by Spaniards in 1540 (Sheridan et al. 2015). Either way, Kawàyka'a was not occupied after that date, and Awat'ovi was the only pueblo on Antelope Mesa at the time of the 1629 founding of three Spanish missions at Awat'ovi, Old Songoopavi, and Orayvi on the Hopi Mesas. Archaeological evidence for Mission-period communities comes mainly from the Peabody Museum's Awat'ovi excavations (Montgomery, Smith, and Brew 1949). Oral traditions about the Mission period have recently been published, together with translations of Spanish documents (Sheridan et al. 2015). Also inhabited at this time were Old Walpi (Qötsaptuvela) on First Mesa and Old Musangnuvi on Second Mesa, where the Spaniards established *visitas* (chapels). These comprise a much smaller set of much larger villages than were present in earlier times.

Archaeological evidence for the abuses of the Spanish missionaries includes superpositioning of the Mission San Bernardo de Aguatubi over one of the largest and most elaborately painted kivas in the village (Room 788; see Smith 1952a). This was the first time that Hopis were forced to accept the hegemony of another society. There is some archaeological evidence for resistance. Mission-period San Bernardo Polychrome pottery and associated utility wares show some evidence of passive resistance to Spanish demands. The vessels are more expediently made and the clay is grittier and not well processed (Capone 1995), and painted designs are loosely rendered, with only a few overtly Spanish forms such as soup plates and candlesticks. Flowers and butterflies might covertly reference katsinas; crosses and dragonflies may be conflated (Buckley 2010). Of course, the ultimate act of resistance was Hopi participation in the Pueblo Revolt of 1680, when the Hopis destroyed the three missions and two visitas and killed all four priests assigned to the missions.

Independent Period, 1680–1846 CE

Even though the Hopis did not militarily oppose the Reconquest in 1692, only Awat'ovi agreed to accept missionaries, which led the other Hopi villages to destroy it in the winter of 1700–1701. The Pueblo Revolt and Reconquest brought waves of refugees from the Rio Grande, resulting in the founding of Payupki (Mindeleff 1891) and Tewa Village (Dozier 1966). Payupki was an isolated village on Second Mesa with a planned, enclosed plaza (Mindeleff 1891, 59–60, plate 13). Tewa Village was founded as a "guard pueblo" on First Mesa, architecturally similar to the other Hopi villages. In 1742 and 1745 the Spaniards persuaded refugees from the Rio Grande to return to the Rio Grande, and Payupki was vacated. Tewa Village, of course, remains occupied.

Archaeological evidence from the post-Revolt period is limited to the Walpi Project (Adams 1991), a Museum of Northern Arizona excavation funded by the National Park Service that was conducted in the course of stabilizing and restoring historic structures in Walpi village. Painted pottery from the 1700s, Payupki Polychrome, broadly resembles Keresan pueblo styles. Copeland (2012) suggests that this style developed in the course of pan-Pueblo alliance and broad ethnogenesis following the Pueblo Revolt. Timothy Wilcox's study of Gobernador Polychrome (2016) suggests Navajo participation in this phenomenon as well. In the 1800s, Polacca Polychrome closely resembled Zuni painted pottery. This is not a pan-Pueblo tradition, but one that is shared only between Zuni and (primarily First Mesa) Hopi; it reflects material patterns that facilitated integration of refugees and frequent mobility among pueblos throughout the region.

American Period, 1846–Present

Today the US government administers Hopi as one tribe, but perhaps the mesas should have been allowed to continue as independent polities. In spite of common language and kinship arrangements, village differences are strong. Cultural diversity persists within contemporary Hopi communities, leadership roles are still plural and often contested, sodality doings continue in the kivas, and the katsinas still arrive every year to encourage cooperation among fractious interest groups. Most important for our understanding of Hopi history is the development of Hopi archaeology and ethnohistory, conducted by and for Hopi scholars with a variety of university, museum, agency, and contractor collaborators (Kuwanwisiwma, Ferguson, and Colwell 2018)..

Braided Streams

The Hopi Mesas and the Flagstaff, Virgin, Fremont, and Kayenta areas were, for much of their history, less densely settled than the Mesa Verde and Cibola areas to the east. All of these probably contributed to what became Hopi settlements as population contracted in the twelfth through thirteenth centuries. In addition, significant influxes of migrants from east and south of the Colorado Plateau came from communities with denser populations, more hierarchical leadership, and more elaborate ceremonial arrangements. From the east, the Hopi Mesas received migrants from the post-Chaco Puebloan world. From the south came migrants from the Mogollon, Salado, and Sinagua cultures. These southern source populations and interactions are for the most part distinctive to Hopi and Zuni, and did not seem to contribute to Acoma or Eastern Pueblo communities.

Hopi connections with Zuni, Keresan, Tewa, and other Rio Grande Pueblos are historically attested since about 1600, but evidence suggests that east–west exchanges began much earlier. Ritual paraphernalia, ritual vocabulary, songs, and imagery are shared, though not identical, repertoires. Katsina imagery and, by implication, the katsina religion appear to have multiple origins in several times and places. Katsinas are portable and adaptable and transcend Pueblos with disparate languages and kinship systems.

We have examined the formation of Hopi identities over centuries, and emphasized a long history of mobile populations in the Southwest interacting with each other and forming communities and alliances. In a braided or reticulated model of ethnogenesis (in contrast to a unilinear or dendritic model), "local traditions are linked together by crosscutting ties of contact, diffusion, borrowing, and human movement. In the reticulated model, ethnic groups reorganize themselves so that each new group is rooted in several antecedent societies" (Ferguson et al. 2013, 110). We are not just using archaeology, history, and oral traditions to identify social groups, but also examining how and why those social groups formed in the contexts of demographic, social, and cultural changes. Hopification is a braided process.

CHAPTER EIGHT

A Diachronic Perspective on Household and Lineage Structure in a Western Pueblo Society

TRILOKI NATH PANDEY

Introduction

Households, matrilineal lineages and clans, and sodalities have been regarded as the primary elements of Western Pueblo social organization. This chapter addresses how these units, especially households, operate, and how these have changed in the empirical context of Zuni society over the course of a century. The Zuni social system has been extensively researched and analyzed by anthropologists since the 1870s, but anthropological understanding has often relied on reduced models of that system rather than attending to the empirical contexts of changing Zuni behavior. It is my aim in this chapter to provide a more nuanced interpretation of the ways Zuni households operate and how these have changed over time. I also address the operation of lineages, especially in relation to ritual organization.

Early American anthropology has a lot of information on the things Indians possessed but not much on how they lived and how they organized their culture and society. It was the appearance of *Kinship and Social Organization* by W. H. R. Rivers (1914) that led F. W Hodge, the editor of *American Anthropologist*, to persuade anthropologists such as A. L. Kroeber, Robert H. Lowie, and Edward Sapir to take up projects to study the social life of Southwestern Indians. In 1915, Kroeber went to Zuni, by far the largest and best-known of the modern Pueblos, and produced *Zuni Kin and Clan* (1917). Lowie went to work among the Hopi at around the same time, but his *Notes on Hopi Clans* and *Hopi Kinship* did not appear until more than a decade later (Lowie 1929a, 1929b). In his book, Rivers was critical of Kroeber's (1909) classic paper "Classificatory Systems of Relationship," which argued that kinship systems are governed more by psychological than social relationships. Lowie supported Rivers's critique (see Lowie 1915a; also Schneider 1968). However, Kroeber's *Zuni Kin and Clan*, which included extensive comparisons with other Pueblo societies, established a benchmark against which Fred Eggan's *Social Organization of the Western Pueblos* (1950; originally presented as a Ph.D. thesis in 1933) developed its structural-functionalist arguments. Eggan's attention to lineages, households, and clans as the core of Western Pueblo social forms was an exemplar of "descent theory," but did not much consider contextual variation in the economic or ritual operation of such units. This chapter is an attempt to provide a diachronic perspective on the structure and functioning of households in Zuni society.[1] It deals with the changes which have taken place in the pueblo over a century. In the process of doing that, it will try to shed some light on the role of clans and lineages in the changing political economy of the pueblo.

Zuni Households in Economic, Social, and Historical Context

From Frank Hamilton Cushing's time (1879–1884) to the present day, almost every scholar has acknowledged that certainly the household is important in Zuni, where it continues to be the basic unit in the modern pueblo social structure. Over a period of time the household's organization and activities have changed, but it remains a vital part of Zuni social and economic life. Ruth Bunzel, perhaps the best ethnographer of Zuni, considers it as an economic unit, composed of an extended family based upon matrilocal residence (also see Eggan 1950, 177). Like A. M. Shah (1974), my take on household is that it is one of the several dimensions of the family and it emphasizes the unit of day-to-day living of its family members.

For Bunzel, the household's central economic aspects are as follows:

Among the Zuni the economic ideal, now somewhat obscured by the intrusion of White traders, was the self-sufficient household within the self-sufficient tribe, with mechanisms to ensure cooperation and fluidity of wealth. Every man commanded all the major skills, every woman the major female skills. Organized trade and barter were negligible; only the feeble and widowed were forced to exchange manufactures for food. The important property distributions were not exchanges of values of different kinds but simple quantitative adjustments. For all purposes of daily living each household was completely self-sufficient. This homogeneous economy is combined with the most minute differentiation in ceremonial function, which suggests that differentiation may have some other basis than simply technical efficiency (Bunzel 1938, 372).

Bunzel goes on to describe the nature of the matrilineal/matrilocal household's operation, for example in agriculture and house-building. She outlines how the household's members come together to cooperate in joint economic activity, and the practical division of labor by gender. Bunzel also highlights the content of a household's sociality in empirical practices. Participation in work-parties is voluntary and there are no institutional means to compel individual coopera- tion. But there is a guiding ethic of mutual reliance that rests upon conscious- ness of other household members' respective needs over time. Bunzel frames this sense of mutual rights and obligations in the household to the larger con- text of pueblo-wide economic exchange and sociality in feasts that engage all households together:

The household group may include as many as twenty-five individuals occupying a single house of several rooms, using a common kitchen and drawing upon a common storehouse. Agricultural work is done jointly on fields scattered in many places and "owned" individually by male mem- bers. The stores are pooled as the collective property of the women. For any large task like planting, harvest, or house-building the men invite a miscellaneous group of blood and affinal relatives, ceremonial associ- ates, and neighbors to assist. They come if convenient, or they stay away. The men who respond work in the fields; their wives come also to help the women of the house in their work. After the day's work all are feasted and the women receive gifts of food. These combinations for mutual help are not partnerships with definite obligations. They are not permanent or even reciprocal. There is no compulsion on anyone to respond, nor is the man who refuses penalized in any way. If he systematically refuses aid he is regarded as uncooperative, but he can always get help when he needs it; for a feast with meat, a day of sociability, and the opportunity to flirt with a pretty girl make helpfulness a pleasure rather than a tedious burden. Also a man, by helping a neighbor, conserves his own stores and avails himself of the neighbor's surplus. This is the chief economic point of tribal feasts (Bunzel 1938, 353).

The matrilocal household and its day-to-day operations contrast with another primary Zuni socioeconomic unit, the sheep camp. Sheep camps, at a distance from the village, comprise only groups of related men, who cooperate in another system of mutually beneficial reciprocity and obligation:

> The herding complex that has been superimposed upon the old agricultural base has a somewhat different ideology. Sheep are individually owned by men; they are earmarked and are inherited in the male line. But this rule, like that of land tenure, may always be set aside in the interests of expediency. A group of male relatives herd their sheep together at a distance from the village, and take turns in watching them, theoretically on a strictly reciprocal basis, each man going out for a month. But the whole system of reciprocity is unbalanced by the feeling of social responsibility on the part of the old toward the young. If a boy goes to herd for his father, the whole cooperative group assumes responsibility for him, giving him presents of animals; the leader, who is also richest in sheep, gives the most, so that the young man soon has a herd of his own. Direct reciprocity between individuals obviously is not a principle of Zuni economic structure (Bunzel 1938, 353–54).

However, Bunzel noted that in the first part of the twentieth century, the dynamics of reciprocal obligation in Zuni society had begun to shift in the patricentric sheep camp as a result of recent influence by the American political economy. Moreover, this influence, especially via male land ownership and patriarchal inheritance, had begun to intrude into the "main stem" of the Zuni economy, i.e., the system of agriculture organized by matrilineal/matrilocal households:

> The Zuni system is in the process of change due to contact with Whites. The profit motive, so foreign to the aboriginal system, has been introduced into the sheep-herding. There is also a new emphasis on wealth, since only men who own sheep can get credit at the store. But up to 1929 these attitudes were confined to dealings with Whites. The profits were all made from selling to traders. Within the tribe the old attitudes and values still ruled. But there are signs of change in the frequency of litigation over inheritance of sheep. Quarrels over land are practically unknown. This conflict may be due to the fact that male ownership and inheritance, taken

over from the Whites, cut across the main stem of economic structure, the solidarity of the female line. It is also an indication of increasing interest in the acquisition and retention of property, now that they have come to realize its possibilities in relation to Whites (Bunzel 1938, 356–57).

In the above quotations, Bunzel contrasts an organization for agriculture and an organization for animal husbandry. Glimpses of this contrast can also be seen in Virgil Wyaco's autobiography *A Zuni Life* (1998) and other modern accounts. The picture gets complicated in modern times, however, by another major change in the Zuni economy: silverwork. As a craft or cottage industry, silverwork, like sheepherding, became increasingly geared to the market economy. The development of ceramics for the non-Zuni market similarly transformed many women's and men's economic activities. Even a cursory look at *Zuni: A Village of Silversmiths* (Ostler, Rodee, and Nahohai 1996) and *Dialogues with Zuni Potters* (Nahohai and Phelps 1995) confirms Bunzel's observations.

In the post–Second World War economy, silverwork became far more important. John Adair, who did fieldwork for his doctoral dissertation on Zuni veterans, noted, "The smith now had the tourist in mind when designing jewelry, and not the [fellow] Indian. Much of his silver became the Indian's idea of the trader's idea of what the white man thought was Indian design. Not only did the design of silver change, but the whole economic life of the pueblo was affected by growing demand for Zuni silver" (Adair 1944, 135). There were not more than one hundred silversmiths during the 1940s, but just two decades later when I arrived in Zuni, their number had multiplied by ten times (see Pandey 1968). During the early 1970s, over eighty non-Zuni licensed traders were buying jewelry, and, as one of my Zuni friends put it, "Teachers, preachers, doctors, nurses—everybody is buying and selling except you." The growth of this handicraft brought an economic revolution in the pueblo. The Gallup merchants even started a bank in Zuni in order to manage the new money.

These days, in addition to the potters and people making jewelry, there are many skilled artisans in Zuni making other types of crafts. There are carvers who make Kachina dolls representing the important religious figures of the Zunis. Other carvers work in stone, antler, and other materials and make fetishes— carvings of animals. Carving miniature fetishes and stringing them together into necklaces is currently popular among the Zunis. For a decade the tribe ran two outlets in Los Angeles and San Francisco to market these things. Beltweaving is a craft that was almost forgotten, but it has recently been reintroduced by a program in Zuni High School. There are also a number of excellent Zuni painters. Most of them paint subjects revolving around the spiritual heritage of their community. The celebrated art teacher Phil Hughte published *A Zuni Artist Looks at Frank Hamilton Cushing* (1994), featuring cartoons of the anthropologist as well as his adventures. It is rare to go into a Zuni household these days that does not contain at least one local painting. It was certainly not like this during the 1960s when I began my work there.

During the early 1950s, John M. Roberts and his associates studied three Zuni households and two sheep camps and reported their findings in *Zuni Daily Life* (Roberts 1956). Roberts highlighted a focal unit within the Zuni household, i.e., the "key nuclear family." Others in the overall household, Roberts found, identified their membership and their positions within it as flowing from specific links to the key family:

> The members of the households were kinsmen organized into kin groups. In each household there was a key nuclear family composed of the male head, his wife, and their children. The place of other members in a household could be stated in terms of their kin relationship to the members of the nuclear family. In other words, the key nuclear family provided a point of reference (an "Ego" family) analogous to that of "Ego" in a conventional kinship chart.
>
> Each of the households had members who did not belong to the key nuclear family and two of the households had more than one nuclear family, one was the home of a small extended family while the other housed an extended family of some size and complexity. In these extended families the parents in the key nuclear family were in the "grandparent" generation (Roberts 1956, 9).

In my publications (see Pandey 1975, 1978, 1979) I have discussed the two households that sponsored my research, which reflect the same patterns Roberts discussed. One of the households studied by both of us was somewhat marginal, but the other manages the priesthood of the South (Onawa), the third most important religious office in the pueblo.[2] It is also one of the largest families, and I believe one out of every fifteen Zuni is related to it through either blood or marriage. Its members are conscious of their status and power in the society. As I have said elsewhere, "The oldest woman member of the family . . . is universally respected" and I have never heard anything but praise for her (see

Pandey 1978). Her younger brother, the priest of the South, was one of the religious spokesmen of the pueblo until his death in 1982.

In his masterly overview of the Zuni social and political organization up to the 1970s for the Southwest volume of the *Handbook of North American Indians*, Zuni anthropologist Edmund Ladd reported additional patterns of change in Zuni matrilineal/matrilocal households. While households persisted within the overall operation of Zuni society, their economic underpinnings had begun to shift even further in interaction with the market economy and state and federal assistance programs. The cottage industry in crafts, especially silversmithing, now enabled the economic budding-off of nuclear-family units independent of the household, which could sustain themselves more quickly and easily than in earlier times:

> The mother's household is the social, religious, and economic unit. Normally, it is composed of a maternal lineage segment: an older woman, her sisters, and the married and unmarried daughters to which from time to time are added various male relatives and in-laws.
>
> In the 1970s the maternal household was still the social and religious center of the family. However, the economic base and the makeup of the household have changed. Male members who join the household bring into it well-developed skills and knowledge by which they gain immediate status. In most cases, husband and wife have skills (usually silversmithing) by which they can support their family and become independent of the household early in life — something that took years of planning and preparation under the old system. And, because heads of families gain more and better assistance from the state and federal social services, there is a tendency toward separation from the maternal household. Although young people move away from their maternal household early, they maintain strong ties with their respective households to which they return for all major social and religious occasions (Ladd 1979, 482).

During the period Ladd mentioned, I counted 110 trailer homes bought by the young couples who had suddenly made money from silversmithing and other crafts. This surely had an impact on the matrilocal pattern, as did the HUD houses built in the pueblo of Zuni and at nearby Black Rock. These days Black Rock contains as many Zuni houses as the old pueblo did when Kroeber surveyed it one hundred years ago.

We need a serious study of this development. My preliminary observations suggest that with changes in its economy—no one is farming these days—Zuni society is no longer self-sufficient. It has been sucked into the larger capitalist, market-driven economy, and is affected by the sudden shifts in that economy as well. With time, the trailer homes began to disappear; earlier this year, when I passed through Zuni, I could hardly see more than five. Almost everywhere except the central part near the Old Church, they had built new houses, and they have their own fence with a gate and a dog to ward off intruders. Gated homes have started to appear in Zuni as well. The pueblo no longer looks like what Kroeber described in his *Zuni Kin and Clan* (1917).

Lineages

Like the Hopi, the Zuni do not have a term for lineage. Lineage is certainly an analytical concept as used by Fred Eggan in his justly celebrated book *Social Organization of the Western Pueblos* (1950). In his chapter on Zuni, Eggan analyzed the clan data presented by Kroeber (1917) and concluded that "the Zuni tend to equate lineage with household, except in cases of recent expansion or budding off" (189). For him, the concept of lineage provided "a bridge between the household and the clan" (197). I must say that he was quite enamored of the concept of "bridges": he himself was a bridge-builder, between British structural-functionalism and American cultural processual anthropology.

From the Boasians—Kroeber, Benedict, and Bunzel—Eggan had learned that the Zuni clan was normally composed of several lineages, and that there was some division of function (ceremonial, economic) between them. He quotes Bunzel (1932), who wrote, "The clan as such has no social or political functions, although each individual feels his closest ties to be with members of his clan, upon whom he calls for assistance in any large enterprise, such as harvest, house building, initiations, etc." (478). Eggan found this "self-contradictory," particularly when the clan's function as an exogamous unit is considered. My own work has detailed the clan's political functions (Pandey 1977, 1994). Further, Eggan pointed out that Kroeber set "the clan and lineage in opposition rather than seeing the clan as an enlarged lineage" (Eggan 1950, 186, 211). In comparison to the Hopi, he found Zuni clans to be "definitely weaker" (198) and thought this might have been due to difference in scale and the relative sizes of the clans and the villages.

In his unpacking of Hopi clans, Peter Whiteley (1985, 1986) has drawn our attention to how Eggan's structural-functionalist depiction rests upon the same Africanist model found to be problematic by John Barnes (1962) in his celebrated critique "African Models in the New Guinea Highlands." Whiteley has given very rich ethnographic details from his fieldwork to challenge Eggan's and Mischa Titiev's views of Hopi clans as corporate economic, political, and religious groups. I am in agreement with his overall assessment.

One of the clearest developments of lineage theory, and an exemplar of its Africanist basis, was undertaken by Meyer Fortes in his study of social organization among the Ashanti of Ghana. For the Ashanti, Fortes argued, the lineage was part of their "politico-jural domain," as it regulated "their field of descent relations" (Fortes 1969, 158–62). The concept of lineage dominates his analysis of both Ashanti and Tallensi social and political life.[3] In his celebrated 1949 paper "Time and Social Structure," Fortes pointed out that over the previous thirty to forty years of his fieldwork he had noticed that social and cultural changes had affected Ashanti households. Similar observations have been made by many scholars working in different parts of the tribal world that are still organized by clans and lineages. In his masterly critique of lineage theory, Adam Kuper (1982, 92) concludes that the lineage model has "no value for anthropological analysis." While that may be so for understanding the "vital political or economic activities" he mentions, I certainly saw the value of lineage for understanding the theocratic organization in Zuni and how its various political-religious offices are distributed in the pueblo.

The confrontation between model and social reality is at the heart of social and cultural anthropology. Several studies—to cite just three, Tim Ingold's *Key Debates in Anthropology* (1996), Kuper's "Lineage Theory: A Critical Retrospect" (1982), and Susan McKinnon's "Domestic Exceptions: Evans-Pritchard and the Creation of Nuer Patrilineality and Equality" (2000)—remind us of Sir Edmund Leach's claim that "anthropological theories often tell us more about the anthropologists than about their subject matter" (1966, 46). It was Alfred Radcliffe-Brown, Eggan's model for his scholarship and his view of social anthropology "as a natural science of society," who developed the idea of "the solidarity and unity of the lineage group" in his study of the social organization of Australian tribes (see Eggan 1949; Fortes 1949; Radcliffe-Brown 1931). Radcliffe-Brown's idea became the model for Eggan's classic study *Social Organization of the Western Pueblos* (1950). In his review of that book in *American Anthropologist*, Eggan's close friend George Peter Murdock said that "the volume offers little that is new in ethnographic fact. This little is confined to the Hopi, for on the other Pueblos the author depends exclusively on materials gathered by others" (Murdock 1951, 250). As I have said in my essay on Eggan for the University of Chicago centenary volume, he first came to the Southwest in 1930 and returned in 1932 for fieldwork in Oraibi. One of his fellow fieldworkers, Edward Kennard, my colleague at the University of Pittsburgh during 1967–1969, told me, "I was working on the Hopi language, Mischa [Titiev] was studying Hopi politics and religion, and that left Fred to figure out their kinship system . . . Fred did not have to work too hard; with the help of Radcliffe-Brown, he had already figured that out. I don't know why he had to come there, in the first place" (Pandey 1991, 101). That much Eggan himself admits when he says that "the analysis of the kinship system . . . was developed in part before fieldwork was carried out among the Hopi" (Eggan 1950, 178). When Eggan came to visit me in 1965, he said that he had visited Zuni for a day en route to Hopiland while Bunzel was working there in 1938.

There are different contexts for the use of kinship and friendship terms at Zuni, particularly in the sacred domain, and these illustrate some perspectival variations in Zuni social thought deriving from a differentiation of lineages into those that hold ceremonial knowledge and those that are ceremonially "poor." While commenting on building the relationship of "ceremonial-friendship" *kihé*, I am not clear whether Eggan was aware of the secular and sacred dimensions of such relationships (1950, 187). One can find similar confusion in Cushing's (1882, 17) account of his adventures in Zuni. During the early period of my fieldwork, whenever I called a Zuni friend kihé, I noticed discomfort on his face. When I asked him why he froze when I used this term, his reply was, "I am not dead, I am still around. I am your *kuwayé*, not kihé." *Kuwayé* is the everyday term for "friend"; while *kihé*, "ceremonial brother," is used in the context of ritual sodalities, and thus by those lineages that belong to a ritual elite. In the ethnographic literature on Zuni, there is little appreciation of the diverse contextual perspectives Zuni have on their culture and society. My Zuni friends taught me that there is a difference between a "poor" man's—a commoner's— view of things and that of what John Ware calls a "ritual elite's," the different priests, *ashiwanni*, of Zuni.

Ware's excellent book *A Pueblo Social History* (2014) reinforces my view that there is a difference between a commoner's perception of the role of clans and lineages in Western Pueblos and that of a ritual elite. I have mentioned above my close association with the two households in Zuni. The first was associated with Frog clan (*tekkakwe*), one of the small clans, with few ceremonial responsibilities. The other household, associated with Badger clan (*tonaasikwe*), on the other hand, was one of the elite families, housing the fetish (*ettonne*) of the South Onawa priesthood that furnishes the fire god, who brings new fire every year. The house chief (*kiakwemosi*), the head of the priestly hierarchy, comes from the Dogwood clan (*picchikwe*), the largest clan in Zuni, with well over a thousand members. The priest of the West, the second in the priestly hierarchy, also comes from this clan. "The Elder Brother" Bow Priest, head of the powerful order of war, comes from the Eagle clan (*kiakalikwe*)—second only to the Dogwood clan as feeder to the theocratic structure of Zuni. These are three of the largest clans in Zuni and they are divided into several lineage segments. The smaller clans such as Frog, Bear, Deer, and Coyote have small lineage segments within them. In my work on Zuni theocracy, I have discussed the association between various clans, their lineage components, and different political and religious offices (see Pandey 1968, 1977, and 1994).

A future question for me concerns the relationship between these structural features—households, clans, lineages, sodalities—and the various religious and ceremonial performances that are time-consuming and require a lot of resources. Who makes investments in their performances—just ritual elites, or commoners as well? Do clans and lineages add any value, or they are just ornamental, as Kroeber opined in his *Zuni Kin and Clan*? John Ware's timely book helped me to wrangle with these questions in my own meditation on Zuni culture and society. But I shall take that up on another occasion. Here, my focus has been to deal with different socioeconomic changes that have taken place in Zuni since the 1870s, when anthropologists began visiting the pueblo.

Acknowledgments

I thank John Ware and Peter Whiteley for including me in the conversations that took place at the School for Advanced Research in Santa Fe. I found them immensely stimulating and they made me optimistic about the future of our discipline. I also want to thank all my fellow participants. I am especially indebted to Peter Whiteley for his constructive comments on my paper and to T. J. Ferguson and Barbara Mills for sharing with me their own fieldwork experiences.

Notes

1. Many institutions and individuals have supported my research in the American Southwest, spanning well over five decades. I have listed them in my various publications. The Advanced Seminar in which this volume is rooted gave the participants an opportunity to honor the memories of Fred Eggan, Edmund Ladd, and Alfonso Ortiz, whose loss I continue to mourn.

2. An anthropology student from the University of California, Berkeley, Ingrid Jordt, spent a month in Zuni and took the inventory of three households—one from Nutria, one of the four farming villages, and two from the main pueblo. She discovered that my hostess's household had goods whose market value was well over one million dollars in 1980.

3. I am deeply appreciative of the help Meyer Fortes gave me in understanding the genesis of the lineage concept. It can be glimpsed in an anecdote I wish to share with you. In July 1973, the Second Decennial Conference of the Association of Social Anthropologists of the Commonwealth was held at Oxford University where, as David Parkin put it, "the giants of British Social Anthropology"—Evans-Pritchard, Firth, Fortes, Gluckman, Leach—were sitting together for the last time under the same roof. As the conference ended, I saw Meyer Fortes escorting Evans-Pritchard to a taxi. I joined them and heard the older man shouting, "Meyer, you lie about me. I tell you, you lie about me," and Fortes responding, "E-P, let me take you home." I was startled and did not want to embarrass them. I bid my good-bye and rushed to catch my bus to Cambridge. A few days later, I saw Fortes again and he invited me to his home for a cup of tea. I was curious to know why Evans-Pritchard was so upset. Fortes told me that soon after Evans-Pritchard had returned from his Nuer fieldwork, he was wondering how to analyze his vast material. Radcliffe-Brown was in London to attend a meeting and Fortes invited him to his apartment for tea with Evans-Pritchard. It was there that R-B told E-P that he should use the concept of lineage in his analysis of the dynamics of Nuer politics. Fortes told me that "it was this that I had said and now E-P does not want to hear it." Radcliffe-Brown had introduced the concept of lineage in his *Social Organization of Australian Tribes* (1931) and Evans-Pritchard, Eggan, and Fortes, among others, followed him. As I have said, concepts are culturally constructed and they have their own history. Tim Ingold's *Key Debates in Anthropology* (1996) is very helpful in understanding the current status of various concepts used in British social anthropology (see also McKinnon 2000).

CHAPTER NINE

An Archaeological Perspective
on Zuni Social History

BARBARA J. MILLS AND T. J. FERGUSON

Elsie Clews Parsons (1940, 214) observed that there is an obvious relation between ethnology and archaeology in the Southwest, "where extant cultures are historically related to cultures under archaeological research." Differences in the scale and resolution of social units in the archaeological and ethnographic records, however, create a challenge for anthropologists interested in corre-lating archaeological and ethnographic information. People in the Southwest have always been innovative and mobile, readily adopting social institutions and practices from their neighbors. We think that cultural fluidity and creativity provide a basis for understanding social histories, especially when combined with insights from multiple anthropological subfields and Pueblo traditional histories. Here, we combine information from multiple lines of evidence to present a long-term view of Zuni social history. In short, we are interested in how Zuni society became what it is today.

Whiteley (2004, 151–55) argues that archaeologists must tack between "upstreaming" and "downstreaming" to successfully articulate changing social structures. In downstreaming, it is useful to consider deep histories to under-stand how long-term practices emerged and why they persisted. For instance, to understand the post-Chacoan Pueblo World of the twelfth century onward, it is necessary to understand the formation of—and resistance to—the Chacoan World (Lekson 2012; cf. Fowles 2012). In upstreaming, we look at how specific social structures that occur in the present-day Pueblo world are organized to create models for interpreting the past, as Ware (2014) has done.

Ethnographic understanding of Zuni social organization is derived from the work of Stevenson (1904), Kroeber (1917), Bunzel (1932), Parsons (1933), Eggan (1950), Ladd (1979), and Watts (1997) (see also Pandey, chapter 8, this volume). The population of Zuni is large compared to other pueblos—1,700 in 1915; more than 10,000 today. The basic economic unit is the matrilocal household, composed of an extended family comprising a maternal lineage augmented with husbands and male relatives, although in 1915 10 percent of households were patrilocal (Kroeber 1917, 105). Zunis are born into their mother's clan but they are "children" of their fathers' clans, introducing a bilateral element into what is otherwise a matrilineal, totemically named, exogamous clan system. There were sixteen clans in the late nineteenth century (Cushing 1896) and fourteen in the late twentieth century (Ladd 1979). The Zunis have an elaborate ritual organization that includes six kivas, twelve medicine societies, and two priesthoods (Ladd 1979).

Eggan (1950, 221) believed that the complexity of Zuni ceremonial organization stems from the consolidation of sodalities from several communities into a single system at Zuni Pueblo following the Pueblo Revolt of 1680. In this chapter we challenge that interpretation and instead show how Zuni society was the result of multiple transformative processes, many of which predate the Pueblo Revolt. We argue that much of the complexity can be attributed to a millennium of successive and successful migrations into the central or core Zuni area. We look at evidence for sodalities, which Ware (2014) has asserted first emerged in the northern Southwest between 750 and 900 CE as networks that linked residential and kinship groups. Religious architecture is used to identify the emergence, diversity, and scale of sodal organizations.

Spatially, we take (as we think most Zunis do) the present-day Zuni pueblo Halona:wa as the center place and then look at how the center relates to the greater Zuni or Cibola area (fig. 9.1) at different periods of time. Our discussion relies heavily on architecture because this structures social interaction and can therefore be used to study social change. Nonetheless, we recognize that many social institutions and practices are not readily interpreted from architecture.

Archaeological Evidence of Migration and Zuni Social Diversity

The complexity of Zuni society stems from at least eight major archaeologically documented historical transformations: (1) the pithouse-to-pueblo transition and expansion of Pueblo I period villages; (2) incorporation into the Chaco World; (3) regional reorganization in the post-Chaco era; (4) late thirteenth-century aggregation and coalescence; (5) mid- to late fourteenth-century migrations and depopulation of upland areas; (6) fifteenth-century depopulation of the interstitial areas within the Pueblo world; (7) seventeenth-century European

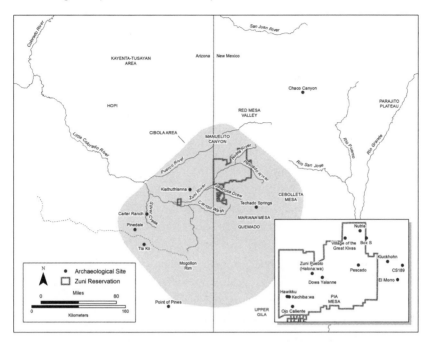

Figure 9.1. The greater Zuni or Cibola area. Created by the authors.

missionization; and (8) Pueblo Revolt–era coalescence of the contact period villages on top of Dowa Yalanne and subsequent resettlement at Halona:wa. Each of these transformations involved population movement, social negotiations, and religious changes that contributed to the complexity of Zuni social organization.

THE PITHOUSE-TO-PUEBLO TRANSITION AND EARLY ZUNI VILLAGES

Prior to about 500 CE, like families across the rest of the Southwest, Zuni families practiced a high degree of mobility, and settlements larger than a few families were rare (Herr and Young 2012). Rapid population growth after 500 CE indicates that people in the Southwest experienced a relatively late Neolithic Demographic Transition (Kohler and Reese 2014; Young and Herr 2012). Yet, even after 500 CE, sites with large numbers of pit structures may not have constituted villages. In the Zuni area, most "pit house villages" resulted from families building houses in the same location over time rather than contemporaneous occupation (Peeples, Schachner, and Huber 2012).

Ware (2014) suggests that it wasn't until aboveground structures were con-structed during the Pueblo I period "pithouse-to-pueblo transition" that year-round residence became common in southwestern Colorado and other areas of the Southwest. This is when villages first appear in the Cibola area, includ-ing settlements along the Rio Puerco, in Hardscrabble Wash, and in the Petri-fied Forest. Schachner, Gilpin, and Peeples (2012, 110) point out that the "type" site for this period is White Mound Village, which was a farmstead or hamlet housing a few families rather than a large village per se. Other settlements, such as Cottonwood Seep along the Rio Puerco, had large numbers of contempo-raneous rooms but were still apparently used seasonally. During the Pueblo I period, then, the number of structures per settlement varied, and there was a range in durations of occupation from seasonal to year-round.

Following Schachner (2001) and Wilshusen and Ortman (1999), Ware (2014) also suggests that ranked lineages developed during the pithouse-to-pueblo transition when some families built oversized pit structures (e.g., at McPhee Pueblo) and hosted feasts. Great kivas date earlier, starting in the Basketmaker III period in several areas of the Colorado Plateau. However, in the Zuni area, community architecture at this scale did not occur until after 900 CE (Peeples, Schachner, and Huber 2012, 177). There is a "dance court" or unroofed great kiva at Whitewater Village, south of the Puerco River, which dates to the late 800s to early 900s CE (Schachner, Gilpin, and Peeples 2012, 11). Iconography provides evidence for community rituals such as the Basket Dance in the late eighth and early ninth centuries in the Upper Little Colorado area (Webster et al. 2014; Young and Gilpin 2012). The lack of evidence for great kivas in the Zuni area prior to 900 CE may be sampling bias or a case of lower popu-lation sizes compared to southwestern Colorado. Herr (2001) suggested that labor was a factor in determining whether great kivas were roofed or unroofed during the following two centuries. In low-density areas we therefore expect less architectural formalization of community structures. The overall picture is one of a high degree of household autonomy, little evidence for ranked house-holds, relatively low population densities compared to other areas to the north, and population movement into and through the area. However, iconographic glimpses of communal ceremonial participation point to social networks that crosscut households.

Migration during the Pueblo I period accounts for the density and diversity of populations in Cibolan subareas, such as the Puerco River valley. Here, archi-tectural diversity for the early Pueblo period (600–900 CE) is high, as people migrated from at least three areas with varying traditions of pit structure construction: the northern San Juan, Chaco, and Kayenta-Tusayan areas (Throgmorton 2012). The Puerco Valley was a borderland between the Zuni and Hopi areas (see also Hays-Gilpin and Gilpin, this volume) and social distinctions were maintained for at least a generation or two following migration.

After 800 CE settlements included hamlets and villages. In the Upper Little Colorado area, including Zuni, the use of aboveground architecture for habitation increased during the tenth century—again, later than in the northern Southwest. This corresponds to an "explosion" in population in the Zuni area after 925 CE (Schachner, Gilpin, and Peeples 2012, 125), and increases in the size of coresidential groups. Nonetheless, most households still lived in hamlets rather than villages. The Zuni version of the unit-pueblo pattern of aboveground domestic and storage rooms with one or more subterranean pit structures in front appeared. Many houses were built on top of clusters of pit structures, suggesting a temporal/social gap between the pit structure occupation and aboveground houses in the Puerco drainage (Sant and Marek 1994). A smaller number of settlements were larger and more well-planned than surrounding sites and had smaller structures that are the Zuni version of sodality structures.

ZUNI AND THE CHACOAN WORLD

Zuni was at the edge of the Chaco World in the period 800 to 1130 CE. The Red Mesa Valley may have had more interaction with Chaco Canyon based on Chacoan procurement of Zuni Mountain timbers during early construction episodes of canyon great houses, ca. 800–1020 CE (Guiterman, Swetnam, and Dean 2015). Some San Juan Basin households moved into the Cibola area, especially during the period of major great house construction after 1020 CE. They likely followed the same social ties established during the ninth century and perhaps earlier.

Within the greater Cibola area, Chaco great houses are concentrated in the Red Mesa Valley, Puerco River, Hardscrabble Wash, and Quemado/Fence Lake areas. Only a couple of great houses are known from the present-day Zuni Indian Reservation—many more lie in a surrounding arc. The population increases that accompanied the establishment and growth of great house communities and contemporaneous non–great house communities in the Zuni area are more than can be accounted for by internal growth, and some in-migration must have taken place. Duff and Schachner (2007) specifically note that Chaco great house communities in the Quemado area were not built in areas that had been previously settled. Similarly, the Chacoan great house at Kiatuthlanna (Roberts 1931) was built near a large, earlier pit house village, but there may be a gap of a century or more between the two occupations. Chacoan-period communities in the central Zuni area from the tenth through twelfth centuries include the Village of the Great Kivas (Roberts 1932). However, there are more Chaco great houses and great kivas outside the central Zuni area than within it, including relatively dense clusters in the Puerco drainage, Red Mesa Valley to the northeast, and the Quemado area (see, e.g., Cameron and Duff 2008, Duff and Lekson 2006, Roberts 1931). These include large-scale architecture in the form of a great house surrounded by a community of dispersed roomblocks, usually (but not necessarily) with one or more great kivas.

Chacoan social organization has been much debated (see also Plog, chapter 11, this volume). For example, Ware (2014) and Fowles (2005) favor an Eastern Pueblo pattern for Chacoan social organization, including exogamous moieties (see also Whiteley 2015). Moiety organization is not known ethnographically at Zuni. We note that all pueblos have Summer and Winter dances, and there are many examples of dual plaza spaces (some including dual religious architecture) and dual roomblock organization at Zuni. Recent genetic evidence from Pueblo Bonito shows that at least one matrilineal descent group was present at that site (Kennett et al. 2017), a pattern that often goes hand in hand with matrilocal residence. We are intrigued by the evidence from the southern edge of the Chaco World (Duff and Nauman 2010), which suggests that women from below the Mogollon Rim were marrying into local Chacoan communities, a pattern that would result in at least some families practicing patrilocal residence. Chaco Canyon was related to surrounding great houses in various ways (Cameron and Duff 2008) and we should not necessarily expect a homogenous social organization throughout the Chaco World. But the extent to which matrilineal descent and matrilocal residence is present in the Pueblo world today suggests that this pattern has deep roots and that the patrilocality at the southern edge of the Cibola area was an "edge" effect, resulting from women's mobility and intermarriage from areas further south.

After 1050 CE, perhaps spurred by stream channel erosion and the adoption of drought-resistant strains of maize that facilitated farming using rainfall runoff, people in the Cibola area expanded settlements into a wider range of environmental settings. This territorial expansion was related to the development of Chacoan and post-Chacoan great houses that provided centers for community-scale organization (Fowler and Stein 1992; Kintigh, Howell, and Duff 1996). Large-scale religious structures in the form of both square and circular great kivas, the latter of which may be unroofed or roofed, were associated with these settlements (Herr 2001; Peeples 2018). In many archaeological reconstructions, these structures are considered "integrative" communal buildings (Lipe and Hegmon 1989), but recent work challenges this idea, proposing that great kivas are evidence of competitive social relationships (Dungan 2015). The varied form and long use of these kivas suggest that they were used by groups with varying social scales and structures.

In the Cibola area, circular, roofed great kivas are primarily associated with Chacoan great houses. Most of these great kivas are clustered in the Rio Puerco and Quemado areas. The low frequencies of great kivas and great houses in the central Cibola area are striking. One major exception is the Village of the Great Kivas, where two great kivas were probably used sequentially, one of them during the post-Chacoan era. In general, Chacoan great houses in the Zuni area do not conform with the more symmetrical layouts of Bonito phase sites at Chaco Canyon itself, although they are larger and more well-built than their surrounding sites.

Mills (2015) suggests that Pueblo Bonito great kivas were associated with different houses in the sense of Lévi-Strauss's (1982) house society model. Although Ware (2014) argues that early great kivas represent sodalities, which developed into moieties, we think that Chacoan great kivas and great houses are better viewed as religious structures associated with corporate bodies that transfer wealth, both "immaterial and material" (Lévi-Strauss 1982, 194). Houses in the Lévi-Straussian sense are often bilaterally organized, and in most cases are composed of individuals who contribute to the house but may not reside there permanently. Unlike the Rio Grande, there is an absence of moieties in later Zuni history, and although principles of duality are present, we see little evidence that moiety organization was part of the greater Cibola world.

Unroofed circular great kivas tend to be associated with discrete clusters of small houses rather than great houses, or they are found at post-Chacoan settlements (Peeples 2018). Early unroofed circular kivas are concentrated in the southwestern part of the Cibola area and date to the eleventh and twelfth centuries, although one may date to the tenth century. Settlements with unroofed circular great kivas are not great houses because they lack multistoried construction, core-veneer masonry, and other Chacoan architectural hallmarks. They are, however, generally larger and longer-occupied than their surrounding settlements, containing up to twelve rooms (Herr 2001). Circular great kiva sites were likely occupied by a single extended family who sponsored the construction of the ceremonial structure with labor drawn from multiple surrounding families. The great kivas would hold more people than those who lived in associated domestic structures that consisted solely of living and storage rooms (Dungan and Peeples, 2018). A few circular great kivas in the Mogollon Rim area were roofed and are associated with larger pueblos (e.g., Tla Kii in the Forestdale Valley and Carter Ranch in the Hay Hollow Valley). Importantly, some of these extend into the post-Chacoan period, evidence of the persistence of families and their ability to attract others to live with them.

CIBOLA IN THE POST-CHACOAN WORLD

The post-Chacoan reorganization of the mid-twelfth through mid-thirteenth centuries entailed people moving from the central San Juan Basin to the surrounding uplands. In the Cibola area, post-Chacoan great houses were established in tributary drainages of the Rio Puerco and Upper Little Colorado rivers, including Manuelito Canyon (Fowler and Stein 1992), Jalarosa Draw (Kintigh et al. 1996), and the Zuni River valley. Some settlements without great houses were built. Population increased in the Pescado and El Morro valleys (Kintigh, Glowacki, and Huntley 2004; Schachner 2012), Mariana Mesa, and the Hay Hollow and Silver Creek areas (see Peeples 2011, figure 3.5). Some of the people who moved to these areas came from regions other than the San Juan Basin, including northeastern Arizona.

The unroofed circular great kivas associated with post-Chacoan sites probably had different social roles than the earlier unroofed circular great kivas in the Mogollon Rim area and the roofed circular great kivas found in the Chaco World. Three unroofed great kivas, contemporaneous with post-Chacoan great houses, were built at massive nucleated communities at the Box S, Kluckhohn, and CS189 sites. In the El Morro Valley, unroofed great kivas varied in terms of size and internal organization, suggesting differences in the kinship structures organized around them. The large size of the great kivas and their open, unroofed structure made it possible for these larger communities to observe or hear ceremonies performed within them (Duff and Schachner 2007).

Further to the west and southwest, migrants from the Kayenta-Tusayan area probably joined local populations in the Silver Creek and Hay Hollow settlements. Small rectangular kivas and other ceremonial rooms, both subterranean and within roomblocks, are new to these areas and are interpreted as sodality rooms. Some settlements continued to include small kivas that were circular, D-shaped, or keyhole-shaped. The variety of kiva forms, often in the same settlements, indicates multiple sodality organizations at these sites and a layering of religious architecture rather than a replacement. The heterogeneity in religious architecture and ceramic design styles at individual settlements suggests connectivities with the Kayenta-Tusayan areas, including probable intermarriage. Social networks established between 1100 and 1275 CE appear to have been divided into two large north–south groups, with settlements in the Zuni River and Carrizo Wash drainages separated from other areas to the south and along the Upper Little Colorado River (Peeples 2018).

AGGREGATION AND COALESCENCE IN THE THIRTEENTH AND FOURTEENTH CENTURIES

Population aggregation from the mid-thirteenth through fourteenth centuries may be one of the most-studied aspects of Zuni social history. Analyses of ceramics and architectural features from these centuries suggest that there was population movement throughout the area, with networks of interaction identifiable at varying social and spatial scales (Duff 2002, Peeples 2018, Schachner 2012).

Starting in the mid-1200s CE, many large pueblos in the eastern portion of the Zuni region were constructed, entailing cooperative labor by many households. Ceramic distribution networks were reorganized, and boundaries developed between village clusters (Schachner 2012; Schachner, Huntley, and Duff 2011). Circular unroofed great kivas are present at some sites, but plazas largely replaced them as the main form of community-scale architecture. Small kiva construction is harder to track because so few of these sites have been excavated, but Schachner (2012, 144–45) suggests for the El Morro valley that there were multiple classes of kivas that might indicate intersettlement differences in ritual power.

A large number of aggregated sites were built in the southern and southwestern Zuni area during the late thirteenth and fourteenth centuries (the Early Pueblo IV period). The migrations that began in the Pueblo III period led to the depopulation of northeastern Arizona at the end of the thirteenth century. Migrants settled along the Mogollon Rim and in the Silver Creek, Upper Little Colorado, Petrified Forest, and Zuni River areas (Hill et al. 2004; Mills 1998).

The area south and west of the Zuni River shows the greatest diversity in architecture and ceramics. This suggests that co-residing groups were experimenting with different social institutions (Peeples 2011, 370–71). Regional-scale social network analyses show that settlements in this southwestern Cibola area were characterized by weak or bridging ties that linked people on the Colorado Plateau with those in the Transition Zone and areas further south (Peeples and Mills 2018). Innovations in ceramic technology spurred by the migration of skilled potters from northeastern Arizona resulted in community-scale pottery specialization and the distribution of pottery over a large area, including well below the Mogollon Rim (Mills et al. 2016).

ZUNI COMMUNITIES IN THE FIFTEENTH AND EARLY SIXTEENTH CENTURIES

Social diversity continued to grow in the fifteenth and sixteenth centuries in the Zuni area. Large plaza-oriented settlements grew by accretion rather than the highly planned and centralized construction events of earlier centuries (Kintigh 2007, Reed 1956). There was a small but culturally significant influx of population at Zuni at this time, with migration from areas to the south or west (Cushing 1896). There are no tree-ring dates after 1390 CE in the Silver Creek area (Mills, Herr, and Van Keuren 1999), and the entire southern portion of the Cibola area was depopulated. A few settlements in the Petrified Forest date into the 1400s, creating a bridge between the Zuni and Hopi areas, but migrants who left other villages would have had to find new homes. Correlations among traditional migration histories (Ferguson 2007), place name distributions (Ferguson and Hart 1985), pilgrimage routes that continue to be used to the present day, and archaeologically documented networks (Duff 2002; Mills et al. 2013) indicate that some migrants joined people living in the Zuni area.

Groups of people migrating to Zuni in the fifteenth century introduced new ceramics (Salado Polychrome) and new mortuary practices, including cremation and the intentional "killing" of associated pottery (Crown 1994; Mills 2007b; Smith, Woodbury, and Woodbury 1966). These introductions are well-documented at Hawikku and Kechiba:wa, occupied when the Spaniards arrived in the sixteenth century (Cushing 1896, 365-66; Howell 1995, 1996; Howell and Kintigh 1996; Smith, Woodbury, and Woodbury 1966). The migrations of the fifteenth century, especially from the Point of Pines and Upper Gila areas, account for the dual burial practices of cremation and inhumation, which are found in distinct cemeteries at both Hawikku and Kechiba:wa. Peeples's (2014) analysis of skeletal variation suggests substantial migration to Zuni from several areas, including east-central Arizona, Kayenta, Upper Gila, and southern Arizona. Following diverse migration pathways, the immigrants joined a population that had long resided in the Zuni area, introducing new forms of material culture, ceramic designs, and burial practices (Mills 2007b, 2008). The archaeological evidence of migrations that influenced the social and cultural development of the Zuni people in the fifteenth and sixteenth centuries is independently supported by evidence found in Zuni traditional history and linguistics (Cushing 1888, 1896; Ferguson 2007; Shaul and Hill 1998).

Rinaldo (1964) suggested that the migration of people from Mogollon sites contributed to the cultural coherence of modern Zuni. However, we view this migration as evidence for a layering of social institutions and ethnic co-residence in the late pre-Hispanic period that was not yet in the form that historic ethnographers encountered. The six or seven pueblos that were established in the lower Zuni River Valley in the fifteenth century were occupied when the Spaniards arrived in 1540. Although often talked about as a single cluster, there are eastern and western concentrations of villages that may be socially meaningful. In addition, in each concentration there are larger and smaller villages that may be analogous to Hopi's mother–daughter village relationships (Kintigh 2000).

MISSIONIZATION AND THE PUEBLO REVOLT

There was a significant decline in population after the arrival of the Spanish, and the number of permanent villages diminished. Cremation burial practices were suppressed (Kintigh 2000). Howell's (1995) analysis of pre-Mission vs. Mission period burials at Hawikku points to a decrease in the number of women with leadership positions in the seventeenth century. Based on a combination of genetic affinity, distribution of burial goods, and discrete cemetery clusters, Howell and Kintigh (1996) argued that leadership was concentrated in a few of the lineages represented at Hawikku, some of which were ascriptive positions, and that burial clusters within cemeteries represent kin groups.

During the Pueblo Revolt of 1680, the entire Zuni population moved into a single defensively located settlement on top of Dowa Yalanne, where they were joined by small groups of refugees from the Rio Grande Pueblos (Ferguson

1996, 2002; see also Preucel and Aguilar, chapter 10, this volume). The open spatial structure of the settlement on Dowa Yalanne encouraged social interaction during the initial reorganization of multiple towns into a single village with a centralized social organization. Following the Pueblo Revolt, the entire Zuni population settled in Halona:wa (Zuni Pueblo). A Catholic mission that had been constructed at the edge of the pueblo in 1629 became encircled within a plaza as roomblocks were constructed around it (Ferguson and Mills 1987).

CONSOLIDATION AT HALONA:WA

A demographic bottleneck occurred in the seventeenth century, perpetuated by epidemic diseases. An especially bad smallpox epidemic is recorded among the Pueblos in the late eighteenth century (Simmons 1979a, 193). Recurrent periods of dramatic population decline from centuries of epidemics must have been associated with significant loss of religious leaders. This would have decreased the number and diversity of religious groups and concentrated religious leadership in fewer positions. As disease epidemics made the transmission of religious leadership along ascribed lines more difficult, key ceremonial activities were probably perpetuated by individual leaders taking on multiple roles or by recruiting new leaders from other clans or lineages. Demographic change thus contributed to the complexity of Zuni ceremonial organization as documented by ethnographers.

Following the Pueblo Revolt, the Zunis began to use seasonally occupied farming villages and sheep camps in outlying areas where villages had been occupied in preceding centuries. Zuni Pueblo (Halona:wa) remained the ceremonial center of the tribe even though most of the population spent a considerable portion of their time at the outlying settlements. The plan of Zuni Pueblo in the eighteenth century was oriented around plazas where ceremonial activity occurred, and the narrow streets and limited paths of entry into the village provided an inward focus to the community. The pacification of neighboring Athapaskan tribes in the nineteenth century led to less need for defensive architecture, and architectural change was spurred by a developing market economy and improved methods of transportation. Domestic space within Zuni Pueblo increased in both the size and number of rooms occupied by families (Dohm 1990; James 1997). This led to both a more open village plan that facilitated social encounters and suburban expansion of the village (Ferguson and Mills 1987).

Social Diversity and Religious Sodalities

Religious sodalities are non-kin-based social groups with ceremonial functions. In order to answer questions about when and where they became part of Pueblo society, and the pathways of convergence and divergence in their historical relationships, we need to look at what sodalities do. At Zuni, medicine societies have a long and complex history and appear to be older than kachina (*kokko*) ceremonies. Zunis today say they had medicine societies at the time they emerged in the Grand Canyon, and that these societies perfected their ceremonies during a sojourn on the Pajarito Plateau near the Rio Grande (Octavius Seowtewa, personal communication to TJF, 2010). This suggests that sodalities have long been a part of Zuni society and were not simply adopted by Pueblo IV–period villagers from the Rio Grande Pueblos.

Ritual sodalities in the Southwest date to at least the Pueblo I period, if not earlier. These social groups were incorporated into subsequent Pueblo societies in a variety of forms. Ware (2014), for instance, argues that sodalities developed during the Pueblo I period to incorporate male members of the household returning to their natal matrilocal and matrilineal families for religious events. These related males, or "avunculate," built and used subterranean kivas in front of roomblocks, forming unit pueblos. Kivas, then, may provide material evidence for sodalities that crosscut residence and kinship. Whether they were used exclusively by men, however, is not a foregone conclusion, nor is their use for exclusively religious activities (Lekson 1988).

The earliest identifiable Cibolan small kivas are found at Pueblo II–period sites, during the 900s CE, in the Puerco River valley and on the Zuni Indian Reservation. Pueblo II–period kivas occur at Chacoan great houses and in other settlements. They have a diversity of forms, although the excavated sample is small. In non–great house settlements, kivas include small subrectangular subterranean structures with vents, deflectors, ash pits, sipapus, and niches constructed in front of roomblocks (e.g., NA 14,083 [Gratz 1977]). The Puerco Valley contains a high proportion of subterranean D-shaped kivas with eastern or southeastern benches. Some excavators simply call these pit structures, but we consider them to be kivas because they have features that distinguish them from other structures, including recesses, benches, pilasters, plastered walls, sipapus, prayer-stick holes, inset floor stones, and subfloor vaults (e.g., Sant and Marek 1994, 579). D-shaped kivas dating to the eleventh century have been identified on Pia Mesa (Varien 1990) and along Oak Wash (Howell 2000).

The Chacoan great house of Kiatuthlanna has four kivas, all blocked in by rooms; two kivas are D-shaped, and two are circular (Roberts 1931). Village of the Great Kivas, another Chacoan great house, has at least nine kivas, with circular, D-shaped, and keyhole shapes (Roberts 1932). D-shaped kivas are earthen-walled and subterranean; keyhole-shaped kivas are made of masonry and blocked in by rooms. The latter are probably later at Village of the Great Kivas, which was occupied to about 1200 CE. Nearby, along the Nutria Road, several keyhole-shaped kivas and a subrectangular kiva were excavated (Zier 1976).

Kivas were rare, however, south of the Upper Little Colorado River in the 1100s, including the Mogollon Rim. Square or rectangular kivas, most of which are subterranean or semisubterranean, first occurred in the late 1100s or 1200s in the southern and western Cibola area, including Silver Creek and Hay Hollow Valley (e.g., Martin et al. 1962; Mills, Herr, and Van Keuren 1999), Upper Little Colorado (Danson 1957; Martin and Rinaldo 1960), Mariana Mesa (Smith et al. 2009), and on the western Zuni Reservation (Dongoske and Dongoske 2014). The formal similarities of these kivas with those in the Kayenta and Tusayan areas suggest people migrated between these two areas, setting up migration streams that were followed in the late 1200s CE, when northeastern Arizona was depopulated. Rectangular kivas became larger in the 1300s CE, and flagstone floors and loom anchors more common, a pattern similar to that in the Hopi-Tusayan area. Eastern benches are common features. They co-occur with other kiva forms, especially outside the central Zuni area, with the exception of the Mariana Mesa area, where rectangular kivas were exclusively used at sites like Techado Springs (Smith et al. 2009). Evidence for a migration to this area from the broader Kayenta-Tusayan area includes a predominance of Kayenta Black-on-white and late Tsegi Orange Ware ceramic designs on locally produced Cibola White Ware (Mills 2007b). This area seems anomalous and a probable enclave. Peeples (2011, 2018) finds that material culture differences were greatest between the Mariana Mesa and other Cibolan areas and notes that this is also one of the few areas where there is unequivocal evidence of violence (see also Smith et al. 2009).

After 1400 CE, all identifiable kivas in the Cibola area are rectangular, as they are at Zuni today. The best example of a late pre-Hispanic/early historic kiva is the one excavated at Hawikku, which was found while trenching the plaza (Hodge 1939; Smith, Woodbury, and Woodbury 1966). The Hawikku kiva was used into the early historic period and Hodge suggested that its use ended sometime after the friars arrived at Zuni in 1629 (1939, 211–13). If this is the case, then that kiva would have been an example of Spanish missionary "erasure" of earlier ceremonial structures. Contemporary Zuni kivas are aboveground structures within or adjacent to roomblocks.

Feasting is an important part of ceremonies performed by sodalities, and archaeological evidence indicates feasts at Zuni increased from the late thirteenth through fifteenth centuries when the population moved into large plaza-oriented pueblos (Mills 2007a). As Potter (2000) notes, feasting is associated with ritual knowledge fundamental to authority, and the kinds and distribution of fauna at fourteenth-century Zuni villages suggest that hunting sodalities became prominent following aggregation in the late thirteenth century. Feasts in the Zuni area became large communal events that integrated communities and sets of communities within settlement clusters. But they may also have included some competitive aspects as hosts associated with prominent families and sodalities established and maintained their positions, as Dungan (2015) suggests for earlier periods.

The evidence for *kokko* (kachinas) is relatively late in the Zuni area, dating to as late as the mid-1400s. Although kachina depictions are found on Late White Mountain Red Ware in the Silver Creek and Upper Little Colorado areas in the 1300s, especially Fourmile Polychrome (Carlson 1970, Van Keuren 2011), there is only one definite kachina depiction on a Late Zuni Glaze Ware—a Pinnawa Glaze-on-white from Hawikku. Pinnawa Glaze-on-white dates to the 1300s and was largely replaced in the decorated assemblage by Matsaki Buff Ware by about 1400. Matsaki Polychrome has abundant images of kachinas on bowl interiors (and, significantly, not on jar exteriors), suggesting that secrecy was an important part of the religion. Rock art in the Zuni area also supports a late adoption of full kachina imagery (Schaafsma and Young 2007, 262).

One implication of the relative lack of depictions of kokko in Zuni iconography before 1400 CE is that the kachina religion was not fully adopted at Zuni until the late migrations of the fifteenth century. Based on the analysis of ritually retired materials in the greater Zuni area, especially after 1000 CE, and kiva form diversity, it is apparent that the kachina religion was an overlay on top of a diversity of already existing religious sodalities (Mills 2004a). Webster's (2007) analyses of perishables demonstrate that many kinds of ritual objects found at Hawikku and other Zuni sites have antecedents in both the Mogollon and Chacoan areas, including painted wooden objects, miniature bows and arrows, prayer sticks, cane tubes, and reed cigarettes. The evidence suggests an active resistance to the adoption of the kachina religion in the central Zuni area until the fifteenth century, at least two generations after it had become important to communities living in the Silver Creek, Homo'lovi, Petrified Forest, and Hopi areas.

The archaeological record includes glimpses of sodalities that are still present at Zuni Pueblo, especially after 1400 CE. The archaeological distribution of conch shell trumpets in the Southwest points to two ancient ritual networks that are historically associated with sodalities still present at Zuni: the *Tsu Wanna* (Great Shell Society) and the *Kolowisi* (Plumed Serpent) ceremonies (Mills and Ferguson 2008). Mortuary practices at Hawikku and Kechiba:wa provide other evidence of identifiable sodalities. Hodge (1966) documented two graves that his Zuni workmen identified as belonging to Bow Priests based on funerary objects, and Hodge thought another grave represented a Fire Priest. Hodge described "sacerdotal deposits" that are replete with items associated with ritual sodalities at Zuni Pueblo, including pipes, fetishes, flutes, reed cigarettes, concretions, pigments, minerals, feathers, bird bones, war clubs, projectile points, ritual offerings, medicine bags, medicine-man paraphernalia, and prayer sticks (Smith, Woodbury, and Woodbury 1966). Inalienable possessions were passed down through sodalities and the lineages associated with them, and point to inequalities that were based on ritual knowledge (Mills 2004a). Sodalities may have had male and female members, and women's roles in Zuni ceremonial life may have been more important than historic and ethnographic accounts reveal (see Howell 1996).

Leaders important in the social structure of Zuni society are associated with religious sodalities. Howell and Kintigh expect those leaders to have multiple social roles that result in rich and diverse mortuary assemblages, and they analyzed more than a thousand burials at Hawikku and the nearby village of Kechiba:wa to identify male and female leaders (Howell 1996; Howell and Kintigh 1996). Howell concluded that the relatively small number of leaders at Hawikku represent a centralized form of decision-making rather than a council form of government, and that over time European influences and Athapaskan intrusions led to more limited female participation in decision-making and a shift in male leadership roles from ritual to warfare. In comparing ceramics and mortuary practices at Hawikku and Kechiba:wa, Kintigh (2000) concluded that there were differences in social identities that might reflect ethnic differences, as well as ritual or political prominence between the two contemporaneous villages. Hawikku had much richer burials and he suggested that there may have been a mother–daughter village relationship between the two settlements. This is an important finding in understanding how the Zunis were organized in a polity during the period when they occupied multiple villages. Hawikku fits a model of concentration of power in religious offices associated with a small number of lineages. This concentration may be the result of population decline, which appears to broadly affect the Southwest starting in the fifteenth century—even prior to European contact and colonization.

Conclusions

Our understanding of Zuni social organization can be accomplished by tracing the broad outlines of its development from small social groups living in dispersed households to large communities living in nucleated and aggregated plaza-oriented pueblos. Two things stand out to us in this review. First, the Zuni sequence begins with a relatively low density of settlement compared to many areas of the Southwest but culminates in one of the most densely occupied areas by the end of the pre-Hispanic period. Unlike the northern San Juan, Pueblo I villages are rare in the Cibola area, and Chaco outlier communities seem intrusive rather than homegrown. Diversity rather than homogeneity characterizes the different subareas of the Cibola area, with evidence for different functions for "public architecture," multiple ways of constructing residential communities, and sodality participation.

Second, multiple migrations into the core Zuni area can be documented, each one bringing new social institutions and transforming existing ones. Some migration entailed small-scale shifts of people within the Zuni River and its tributaries, but other migrations involved the movement of people from other regions into the greater Zuni area, at least some of whom would have spoken different languages. Jane Hill (2007) established that Zuni is a true language isolate, not a creole nor related to Penutian, and that its status as an isolate must have started at least several thousand years ago. The Zuni area was at the periphery of Southwest population distributions during the Archaic through Pueblo I periods. Surrounding areas were more intensively used and the historical trajectory of Zuni included multiple migrations into the area, any one of which might potentially have been composed of Zuni-speakers if those in the core were not the original speakers. We do not have an archaeological basis for proposing that the Zuni core was *not* the place where Zuni was first—and still is—spoken, but consideration of the relative number and scale of migration events and their implications for language histories is warranted.

Eggan's (1950) reconstruction of Zuni's complexity as dependent on the consolidation of Zuni after the Pueblo Revolt overlooks the earlier contributions of migration to its social history. Much of this archaeological history is, of course, reliant on more recent research and reinterpretation of past excavations. In many ways, Zuni's history is much like that of Hopi, where there were many different migrations, each of which contributed to ceremonial life in the destination villages (Bernardini 2005b). Yet, there are significant contrasts between Zuni and Hopi. Rather than being a history of clans, as at Hopi, Zuni traditional histories are the histories of kiva groups, priesthoods, and medicine societies (Dongoske et al. 1997, Ferguson 2007). It is instructive to recall the order in which these groups arrived at Zuni in the narratives. For example, the medicine societies may not be the late arrivals suggested in Pueblo IV population histories, but instead the result of Western Keresan or Uto-Aztecan migration into the Kayenta-Tusayan area and then immigration to the Zuni area via the Puerco Valley, Upper Little Colorado, and Mogollon Rim. Keresan use of shrines in the Upper Little Colorado River drainage, including Zuni Salt Lake and Wenima, suggests ancient ties to this region by people now living along the Rio San José and Rio Grande (Bunzel 1932, 482; White 1943, 314; White 1962, 111). Although outside the Cibola area, many of the twelfth-century objects in the Magician's Burial are those used in medicine societies documented in the nineteenth century (such as swallowing sticks). Another thirteenth-century site on the Mogollon Rim, near Pinedale, shares a few of the same objects (McGregor 1943).

A Zuni social history must be viewed as an accumulation of social institutions, including sodalities. Contrasts between the center and peripheries of the Cibola area indicate that a diversity of people moved in, interacted with, and eventually became part of existing communities. These communities were highly variable when seen in a regional context. We think that the diversity in religious institutions documented ethnographically at Zuni Pueblo has deep roots and was augmented though multiple migrations. One of these late migrations may have been responsible for introducing the kachina religion to Zuni, which was an overlay on top of an already rich ceremonial life made up of multiple religious sodalities. The diversity of sodality organizations appears to have been a part of the formation of Pueblo period villages; it is evident at least architecturally, in the use of multiple forms of religious architecture at Chacoan and post-Chacoan great houses and later settlements dating to the thirteenth and fourteenth centuries.

The calculus of descent and residence, which even in the ethnographic present was more variable than contrasts between Eastern and Western Pueblos often acknowledge, must also take into account Zuni's internal diversity over the past two millennia. We have taken an archaeological approach, downstreaming more than upstreaming, but both perspectives are important for understanding Zuni social history. While upstreaming alerts us to the potentialities, downstreaming allows us to construct a narrative history—one that may not fit the ethnographic models—to acknowledge greater diversity and complexity.

CHAPTER TEN

From Mission to Mesa

Reconstructing Pueblo Social Networks during the Pueblo Revolt Period

ROBERT W. PREUCEL AND JOSEPH R. AGUILAR

On the morning of September 14, 1692, Governor Diego de Vargas stood in the plaza of Santa Fe and proclaimed the repossession of the kingdom of New Mexico. After the *alférez* raised the royal standard three times, he ordered the Tewa and Tano Indian inhabitants to repeat three times, "Long live the king, our lord (may God keep him), Carlos II, king of all the Spains, all this New World, and the kingdom and province of New Mexico" (Kessell and Hendricks 1992, 402).[1] Twelve years earlier, a confederation of Pueblo nations and their Indian allies had risen up in a united front and forced Governor Antonio de Otermín to flee from Santa Fe and retreat in ignominy to El Paso del Norte. The loss of New Mexico was a severe blow to the expansionist goals of the Spanish empire. For this reason, Vargas's repossession was a spectacular triumph; he had accomplished what neither of his predecessors, Governors Pedro Reneros Posada and Domingo Jironza Petríz de Cruzate, could do. Spain had reestablished her northern colony.

The status of the new colony, however, was quite precarious. Vargas's authority was restricted to Santa Fe and its immediate vicinity. Of special concern were the rebels living in their mesatop redoubts in the Keres and Jemez districts. Over the next two years, Vargas visited these villages to try to persuade the people to come down from their mesas and take up lives in their mission homes. Each time he was rebuffed in his efforts, as Pueblo leaders stalled for time. Finally, he was forced to attack them, one after another. In a letter to the viceroy of New Spain, he recounted, "I went on to the other nations of the Keres, with the goal of reducing and conquering for our holy faith and royal crown four pueblos: the Pecos; the Keres of Cochiti and San Felipe on the mesa of La Cieneguilla [de Cochiti]; the Keres of Santo Domingo, Santa Ana, and Zia on the mesa of the

Cerro Colorado; and the Jemez on the mesa of La Cañada [de Jémez]" (Kessell and Hendricks 1992, 609). Three of these four pueblos were mesa villages.

Our chapter is an examination of Pueblo Indian social networks during the Pueblo Revolt period (1680–1700). This period was the time of the largest population reorganization since the migrations from Chaco Canyon and Mesa Verde during the eleventh and twelfth centuries. During this period, numerous families and social groups fled their mission villages to take refuge with relatives and Indian allies living at the edge of the Spanish empire. In some cases, they returned to their mission homes; in others, they remained with their hosts and became active members of these communities. In many ways, these movements set the social character of the modern Pueblos. Adopting a microhistorical approach combining ethnohistorical and archaeological data, we have placed the Rio Grande mesa villages at the center of our investigation. We are particularly interested in tracing out the movements of people to and from these villages as a means of understanding mobility strategies, indigenous diplomacy, and the forging of political alliances. We also seek to humanize the Pueblo Revolt period by identifying some of the Pueblo actors and highlighting their agency and decision-making during this tumultuous time.

A Microhistorical Perspective

The Pueblo Revolt period offers a particularly appropriate context for microhistorical study. Microhistory is the intensive historical investigation of a relatively well-defined context, usually an event, a community, or even an individual person (Ginzburg and Poni 1991, 3). The goal is to focus on the micro to shed new light on the macro; for example, it typically involves questions of family structure, network relationships, religious ideology, and other aspects of the past (Orser 2007, 28). The approach is closely associated with the work of Carlo Ginzburg (1980, 1993), who used sixteenth-century Inquisition records to reveal the world of Domenico Scandella, a miller from Montereale, Italy. Ginzburg establishes links between Scandella's testimony and the texts that unconsciously influenced him and, in the process, examines the relationships between elite and popular culture. Microhistory is sometimes regarded as a method for opening up history to "peoples without history" (Wolf 1982). It typically uses a wide variety of texts and documents, working them against one another. The premise is that different kinds of documents can be used to reveal insights into different classes. For example, the biases of official documents may be confronted by texts that record the actual words of lower class witnesses (Muir 1991). A microhistory approach is gaining considerable support in historical archaeology (see Brooks et al. 2008), but has yet to be applied in Southwestern historical archaeology.

It can be argued that James Deetz introduced a microhistory sensibility to historical archaeology in the 1970s as expressed particularly by his influential book *In Small Things Forgotten* (1977). However, a microhistory perspective drawing explicitly from Ginzburg's work is a recent development. For example, Christopher DeCorse (2008) has examined African–European interactions between the fifteenth and nineteenth centuries at Elmina in coastal Ghana. He is particularly interested in examining small pieces of evidence to interpret larger social processes. Mary Beaudry (2008) has conducted "archaeological biographies" to trace the lifestyles of two New England merchants across the late eighteenth century. They allow her to link ambition and desire for social prestige to broader issues of power relations and identity formation in the early republic. Kent Lightfoot (2008) has examined women's lives at the nineteenth-century Russian Colony Ross in northern California. This allows him to contribute significantly to the broader questions of mercantilism and power dynamics in the Russian colony.

Of special interest for the microhistorical study of the Pueblo Revolt period are Diego de Vargas's journals and letters, collated, translated, and published by John Kessell's Vargas Project. Vargas maintained official records of his activities and kept regular correspondence with authorities in Mexico City. Not surprisingly, his letters pose interpretive challenges in part because they tend to present his actions in the best possible light. But even with these biases and limitations, they provide valuable insights into the actions, motivations, and events during the reconquest and resettlement period. They also identify specific Indian actors and their changing relationships with each other and the Spanish colony.

The Mesas and Their Villages

The mesas of the Northern Rio Grande district occupied during the Revolt period are physically imposing landscape features. They tend to be located in rugged or isolated regions apart from the mission villages. For example, San Ildefonso mesa is a basaltic monolith rising 550 meters above the Rio Grande river (fig. 10.1). Cochiti mesa is a potrero composed of volcanic tuff located at the southeastern edge of the Pajarito Plateau and situated 540 meters above Rio

Figure 10.1. Tunyo (San Ildefonso mesa). Photograph by Woody Aguilar.

Chiquito. Guadalupe mesa, also composed of volcanic tuff, towers some 980 meters above the confluence of the Guadalupe and Jemez rivers. These mesas all served as strong and defensible locations and afforded good visibility for tracking the movements of Spanish military forces. The Pueblo people regarded the mesas as sacred places, homes to supernatural deities that provided strength to their people. Significantly, these mesas continue to be venerated to this day (Aguilar and Preucel 2013, Liebmann 2012).

The villages newly established on these mesas constituted the core of the Revolt period settlement system (fig. 10.2). They served as important nodes for population movements between the mission pueblos situated along the Rio Grande and the ephemeral camps established high in the mountains (Barrett 2002, Liebmann et al. 2017). Over the last twenty years, considerable archaeological research has been conducted at these villages, inspired largely by Ferguson's (1996, 2002) important work at Dowa Yalanne. Preucel (2000, 2006; Preucel, Traxler, and Wilcox 2002) has mapped Kotyiti on Cochiti mesa and Wilcox (2009) has mapped Kotyiti East, the adjacent rancheria. Liebmann (2012, Liebmann and Preucel 2007) has mapped Patokwa on a low rise below Guadalupe mesa, Astialakwa on Guadalupe mesa, Boletsakwa on San Juan

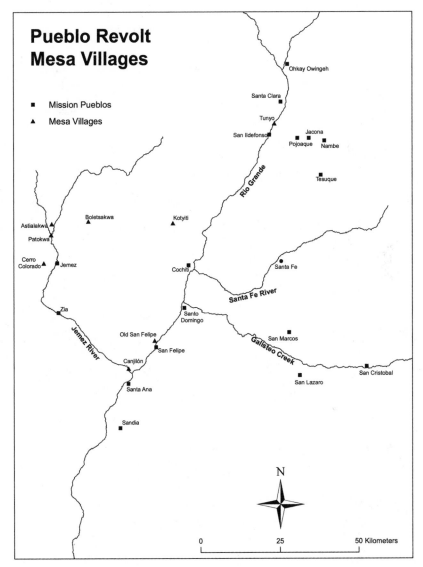

Figure 10.2. Northern Rio Grande settlement system during the Pueblo Revolt Period. Map by Rob Weiner.

Table 10.1. Rio Grande Mesa Village Room Counts, Population Estimates, and Date Ranges

Mesa Village	Total Rooms	Max Pop Estimate*	Date Range Estimate	Reference
Patokwa (LA 96)	359	598	1683?–1693	Liebmann 2012, 174
Boletsakwa (LA 136)	168	280	1683?–1694	Liebmann 2012, 174
Kotyiti (LA 295, 84)	137	228	1683?–1694	Preucel 1998, 47
Cerro Colorado (LA 2048)	167	278	1690?–1694	Liebmann 2012, 174
San Felipe (LA 2047)	64	107	1690?–1694	Lange, Riley, and Lange 1975, 69,70
Astialakwa (LA 1825)	160	266	1693–1694	Liebmann 2012, 191
Tunyo (LA 23)	?	?	1693–1694	Aguilar 2013, 35

*Maximum population estimate is calculated by dividing total room number by 0.6 people per room (following Liebmann 2012, 93).

mesa, and Cerro Colorado village on Cerro Colorado mesa. Aguilar (2013, Aguilar and Preucel 2013) is currently mapping Tunyo, the village on San Ildefonso mesa. In addition, Ferguson and Preucel (2005) and Liebmann, Ferguson, and Preucel (2005) have examined the mesa villages, including those at Hopi and Zuni, within a broader post-Revolt regional study.

These studies have documented three main construction phases (table 10.1). The first building events took place around 1683 and involved the villages of Patokwa, Boletsakwa, and Kotyiti. These villages were built at the height of the famous Pueblo revitalization movement (Preucel, Traxler, and Wilcox 2002; Liebmann 2012). The second phase occurred around 1690 and is represented by the villages of Cerro Colorado and Old San Felipe.[2] These villages appear to have been constructed in response to Posada's attack on Santa Ana in 1687 and Cruzate's destruction of Zia in 1689. The third phase took place in 1693 with the establishment of the villages of Astialakwa and Tunyo. These villages were more hastily built and functioned as immediate protection against Vargas's aggressive military campaign.

In the sections that follow, we highlight the social agency of the northern Rio Grande mesa villages using the Vargas documents. We begin with Vargas's accounts of his reconquest (1692), his inspection tour (1692), his recolonization (1693), his military campaigns against the mesa villages (1694), and his military response to the Second Pueblo Revolt (1696). Our goal is to place the movements of Pueblo social groups in historical context. We then highlight the ways in which the mesa villages mediated changing social and political relationships.

VARGAS'S RECONQUEST, 1692

When Vargas took ritual possession of New Mexico in 1692, he encountered a markedly different social landscape from the one Otermín had left behind twelve years earlier. The Pueblo people had largely dispersed. Some had taken refuge in mesa villages and mountain camps, where they were strategizing with their Navajo and Apache allies against the Spaniards. Others fled to the safety of the distant villages of Acoma, Zuni, and Hopi. Only a handful of people remained behind in their mission villages. These shifts in settlement were a dynamic strategy for survival. The decisions by Pueblo leaders, to ally with the rebels or throw in their lot with the Spaniards, evolved under changing conditions with profound consequences for the security of their people. Indeed, the Pueblo people were well aware of the Spanish crown's determination to reestablish their kingdom and some even anticipated their return. As one Pueblo informant put it, the Spaniards were destined to regain their kingdom because they were "sons of the land and had been bred in it" (Hackett and Shelby 1942, 382, cf. 235).

In planning his reconquest, Vargas's immediate goal was to conquer Cochiti Pueblo (Kessell and Hendricks 1992, 87). He wrote, "It was an established opinion that the surrender of the pueblo [of Cochiti] would be a victory of greater consequence and triumph than even that of the villa [of Santa Fe]" (382–83). This was for two reasons. Cochiti was considered the "most populous and strongest of the pueblos" (380) and thus the center of greatest resistance. Vargas was also aware that Cochiti had singlehandedly thwarted Otermín's reconquest bid in 1681 (Hackett and Shelby 1942, 75). When Dominguez de Mendoza, Otermín's lieutenant, and his men arrived at Cochiti in mid-December, they nearly

Figure 10.3. Old San Felipe Pueblo Mission church, New Mexico, 1920(?). Courtesy Palace of the Governors Photo Archives (NMHM/DCA), negative number 003405.

fell victim to a plan to have Pueblo women seduce the soldiers and render them vulnerable to a nighttime attack (Hackett and Shelby 1942, 322, 383).

On September 11 Vargas mounted a dawn raid on Cochiti. However, when he reached the pueblo, he found it abandoned. He noticed signs of recent occupation: the fields were planted in corn, melons, and squash. Vargas described the village's roomblocks and dwellings as being in "poor condition" (Kessell and Hendricks 1992, 382). He learned from some informants that the Indians had abandoned their pueblo due to their fear of the Spaniards.[3]

Vargas continued on to Santo Domingo but also found it abandoned. He described it as being "very strong and with high walls and abandoned dwellings and cuarteles" (Kessell and Hendricks 1992, 384).[4] While still at Santo Domingo, Sergeant-Major Fernando Durán y Chaves and Captain Antonio Jorge arrived and reported that the San Felipe people were living in their mesa village (Old San Felipe) (fig. 10.3).[5] They also related meeting a San Felipe man and telling him and his fellow villagers to come down and reoccupy their pueblo. The Indian replied that they wanted peace with the Spaniards and protection, since the Tewas and Tanos were making war, causing them much damage (Kessell and Hendricks 1992, 385).

VARGAS'S INSPECTION TOUR, 1692

After successfully reconquering Santa Fe in 1692, Vargas embarked on an inspection tour of the Tewa, Tiwa, Towa, Jemez, and Keres provinces, as well as those of the more distant Acoma, Zuni, and Hopi. He visited twenty-five villages, four of which were the mesa villages of Kotyiti, Cerro Colorado, Boletsakwa, and Dowa Yalanne. At each village, Vargas typically noted such details as the number of roomblocks (*cuarteles*), the names of the officials, and the number of people baptized. This information is especially valuable because it provides an indication of the relative sizes of the mesa villages during a two-month period.

Vargas arrived at Kotyiti on October 21 (Kessell and Hendricks 1992, 515). He reported climbing the mesa and finding most of the Cochiti people living there (fig. 10.4). They had set up a large cross and arches to receive him. Vargas described the village as possessing three roomblocks and another large, separate one.[6] The principal leader was "Juan" (probably El Zepe). Fray Francisco Corvera granted the villagers absolution and baptized 103 people, with Vargas serving as godfather to the captain's son. Vargas discovered that the residents

Figure 10.4. Kotyiti, an ancestral Cochiti mesa village, after the Las Conchas fire of 2011. Photograph by Robert Preucel.

were from Cochiti, as well as from San Marcos and San Felipe. He learned that they had moved up onto the mesa out of fear of the Tewas, Tanos, and Picuris.

Departing Kotyiti, Vargas arrived at Cerro Colorado on October 23 (Kessell and Hendricks 1992, 518). He was met by a group of Indians on a low mesa and then escorted up to the top. He was pleased to see that arches and crosses had been set up in the plaza and on most of the roomblocks according to his instructions.[7] Captain Antonio Malacate and his people received Vargas, carrying crosses. They then prepared a room for him to rest. Fray Corvera granted them absolution and baptized 123 people. Vargas served as godfather to Malacate's son, who was given the name Carlos, after the king. Vargas then ordered the people to return to their pueblo and they assured him that they would do so.

Vargas reached Boletsakwa on October 24 (Kessell and Hendricks 1992, 520). He reported that three hundred Indians came down to meet him, with another two hundred on the mesa. The meeting was confrontational: the warriors immediately began calling out war cries, throwing dirt in his men's eyes, and making warlike gestures. When Captain Roque de Madrid asked them to stop, they claimed they were celebrating the arrival of the Spaniards. Vargas then ascended the mesa. He was very cautious, however, and instructed his men to keep their weapons at the ready, for he had learned that the Jemez people had recently hosted a war council. Captain Sebastian met him at the arched entrance of the pueblo, holding a cross. Vargas described two plazas, one with an entrance leading into the other, garrisoned and closed, each constructed of four roomblocks.[8]

The Indians then began preparing a war dance. Fearing attack, Vargas demanded that the people come out of their houses and surrender their weapons. He then formally reclaimed and revalidated the land and the people. He had his proclamation translated into both the Towa and Keres languages, the latter for the Santo Domingo people present. Fray Corvera granted absolution and baptized 117 people. Vargas served as godfather to some of the unmarried women and widows. Vargas then went up to a second-story room to eat with the officials and war leaders. Several Apaches who had been hiding in some of the rooms revealed themselves and pledged their loyalty. He then ordered the Indians to come down from the mesa and reoccupy their pueblo and bring him some supplies. They agreed to do this the following morning.

Vargas then pressed on to Zuni, arriving at Dowa Yalanne mesa on November 11 (Kessell and Hendricks 1992, 548). He and his men climbed the mesa and were peaceably received. Vargas described the village as having three roomblocks.[9] He ordered a large cross to be set up in their plaza and requested that all of the people be brought forward for baptism. Frailes Corvera and Cristóbal Alonso Barroso granted them absolution and baptized 294 people. Again Vargas served as godfather to the child of their captain. Vargas was then taken to a second-story room where he was astonished to discover an altar with two lit tallow candles and ecclesiastical objects, including cast bronze crucifixes, a religious painting, a monstrance, chalices, candlesticks, bells, a missal, and various religious books. Vargas was overcome with emotion at the sight of these objects. They may have been preserved by a priest who was spared during the revolt. A Zuni oral history account mentions a "Father Greyrobe," a favored priest who sympathized with the Pueblo cause (Wiget 1996).

VARGAS'S RECOLONIZATION, 1693

On October 13, 1693, Vargas departed from El Paso del Norte to embark upon his recolonization expedition. As with his original entrada, he followed the Rio Grande northward, stopping at some of the same pueblos and Spanish haciendas he had visited earlier. Food and provisions were in short supply so he sought them out at several Keresan pueblos along the way. Of the villages he visited, four—Cochiti, Zia, San Felipe, and Santo Domingo—were abandoned. Only Santa Ana and four mesa villages—Old San Felipe, Kotyiti, Cerro Colorado, and Boletsakwa—were occupied.

As he neared the Keres district, Vargas was disturbed to learn that the kingdom was now in a state of unrest (Kessell, Hendricks, and Dodge 1998, 59). Lorenzo, a Zia informant, explained that all of the nations were allied with one another, and that the war captains, elders, and leaders were holding meetings in Santa Fe to plan a coordinated response to the Spaniards' return. Equally troubling was the fact that they had also requested help from the Apache. The Pueblo warriors were preparing their arrows, lances, clubs, hooks, leather jackets, and horse armor. Their plan was to surround Vargas's camp and stampede his horses. Lorenzo was afraid that his own village of Zia had joined the enemy camp.

Vargas arrived at Old San Felipe on November 13 with fifty soldiers and sixty mules and mule drivers (Kessell, Hendricks, and Dodge 1995, 401, 405, 406). He was well received. A large cross had been erected at the entrance and smaller crosses were on the houses. The plaza had been swept clean and there were benches in place, with the women congregated on the opposite side. The San

Felipe leaders explained to Vargas that they were on their mesa because they had been threatened by their enemies due to their alliance with the Spaniards. Because several Cochiti people were present, Vargas instructed them to go tell Captain Malacate to come down off Cochiti mesa and meet him.

Meanwhile, don Luis, the governor of Pecos and five men arrived and gave a report on the events that had occurred in Santa Fe over the summer. The governor related that Pedro de Tapia, Vargas's interpreter, had been spreading the story that Vargas was going to behead all the leaders, only sparing those up to fourteen years of age, when he returned (Kessell, Hendricks, and Dodge 1998, 63). Vargas realized that this rumor was the reason the Jemez leaders were wary of his pardon.

On November 22, Malacate came to meet Vargas as instructed (Kessell, Hendricks, and Dodge 1995, 425). He was accompanied by Captain Cristobal, the leader of the San Marcos contingent. They exchanged greetings and then proceeded together up the mesa. Once he reached the top, Vargas saw a large cross at the entrance of the village. The people, probably those of Cochiti and San Marcos, came out to receive him in two separate groups. Vargas then repeated what he had said the previous year: namely that he represented the king and was granting them pardon. He encouraged them to come down and reoccupy their pueblos, where they would enjoy abundant harvests. He also promised protection against the Apaches. The Kotyiti people agreed to these conditions and promised to come down. Vargas then traded with them, exchanging beef for corn and flour. Malacate's son and another boy were baptized.

Vargas arrived at Cerro Colorado on November 25 (Kessell, Hendricks, and Dodge 1995, 434). He met the Zia people on a low mesa, where they had erected a cross. They were in the midst of a war dance with more than twenty-four dancers. He greeted them and they stopped dancing. They then went up to the top of the mesa together, where he found crosses set up in the plaza and on most of the houses. Vargas made the same pronouncements as he had to the Cochiti people. He then announced that the term of Governor Cristobal had expired and required them to elect a replacement. They did so and also elected other officials and a war captain. Vargas gave them staffs and canes of office and ordered them to come down off the mesa and reoccupy their village. The Indians promised to rebuild the church they had destroyed in the revolt. Fray Francisco de Jesús baptized twenty-four children. The Indians then fed Vargas a meal in one of the first-story rooms.

Vargas continued on to Boletsakwa on November 26 (Kessell, Hendricks, and Dodge 1995, 441). After climbing the mesa, he was well received by the inhabitants, and entered the plaza. He repeated what he had told the people of Zia at Cerro Colorado. They seemed pleased at his arrival, and he bartered for provisions, receiving shelled maize and flour for beef. The community had few crops because the fields had been infested with the chokecherry worm. Even so, Vargas paid them two cattle to obligate them to provide maize to him in the future. Frailes Juan de Alpuente and Francisco de Jesús baptized some of the children, but did not have time for all one hundred seeking baptism. Then they all sat down and ate a meal.

VARGAS'S CAMPAIGNS AGAINST THE MESA VILLAGES, 1694

When Vargas returned to New Mexico in 1693, he made a point of sending a strong message to the rebels. He publicly executed seventy Pueblo captives in the Santa Fe plaza as an indication of his steadfast resolve to put down all resistance. However, this act had little effect, and the Pueblos remained fortified in their mesa villages, refusing to come down to reoccupy their mission homes. They continued raiding livestock at Santa Fe as well as at San Felipe, Santa Ana, and Zia, villages friendly with the Spaniards. Vargas was forced to embark upon a nine-month military campaign and targeted the mesa villages of Tunyo, Kotyiti, Astialakwa, and Boletsakwa as the worst offenders (Hendricks 2002).

Vargas's first move was to go north to punish the Tewa villages that had aided the Tano in the battle of Santa Fe. He found that the pueblos of Tesuque, Nambé, and San Ildefonso were all abandoned and that their people had fled to Tunyo. On January 10, 1694, he arrived at the base of the mesa and demanded that they return to their villages (Kessell, Hendricks, and Dodge 1998, 119). He freed five Nambé prisoners as a sign of his goodwill. An emissary, Nicolás, came down from the mesa to report that the people wished to come down. Vargas then gave him his sword belt as a sign of their meeting and sent him back to tell the leaders that he would wait a day for them to descend. Nicolás returned in the evening and said that the leaders insisted that Vargas, his priest, and an interpreter come up. Vargas refused and repeated his original demand that they come down the next day. The leaders, however, refused and Vargas was forced to withdraw to Santa Fe.

On March 4, Vargas returned to make an all-out attack on Tunyo (Kessell, Hendricks, and Dodge 1998, 148). He estimated that there were more than a thousand people on the mesa. He attempted to fire an artillery piece at the most densely occupied part of the mesa, but it exploded and badly injured the face of

Alonso Romero. Vargas then divided his men into two groups: one to scale the mesa from the front and the other, led by himself, to cut off possible retreat. The Indians, however, drove back the Spaniards' frontal assault, raining stones down upon them. Captain Lázaro de Mizquía was wounded, and between twelve and fifteen Indians were killed. Sensing little progress, Vargas abandoned his campaign and withdrew again to Santa Fe.

On March 8, Vargas returned to begin another siege (Kessell, Hendricks, and Dodge 1998, 156). The mesa had been fortified: the damaged ramparts had been repaired and new ones were erected. On March 11, Vargas ordered a troop of twenty men to attack via the main trail up the mesa. They failed due to an intense barrage of rocks, sling stones, and arrows. Several officers were badly wounded, and five or six Pueblo rebels were killed. Vargas then withdrew to his camp on the plain below the mesa. A day later, a party of rebels descended the mesa and attacked an outpost. They were turned back, but the entire company was placed on high alert. Vargas finally raised the siege on the nineteenth and returned to Santa Fe.

Later that spring, Vargas decided to subdue the rebels at Kotyiti (Kessell, Hendricks, and Dodge 1998, 190). He was responding to an urgent plea for assistance from the friendly villages of Santa Ana, Zia, and San Felipe. The Cochiti and their allies were a persistent problem, continually raiding Santa Fe and driving off horses, cattle, sheep, and goats. Vargas ordered Roque de Madrid to select ninety soldiers to accompany twenty militiamen, a standard-bearer, and two others on the expedition. The party left Santa Fe on April 13, reaching San Felipe on the fifteenth, where they gathered together the Indian auxiliaries.

On April 17 at two in the morning, Vargas mounted a four-pronged attack (Kessell, Hendricks, and Dodge 1998, 192).[10] One group consisted of Juan Holguín and Eusebio de Vargas with forty soldiers, accompanied by Bartolomé de Ojeda and one hundred Indian auxiliaries. They were to attack via the trail by which the people brought up their horses, cattle, and sheep. The second consisted of Roque de Madrid and his men. They were to attack up the main trail. The third comprised Adjutant Diego Varela and ten men, who were to guard the trail down to the river. A fourth group led by Vargas remained with the horses on the slope, ready to provide assistance to the others.

After furious fighting, the Cochiti people were finally overwhelmed. Vargas captured 342 noncombatants (women and children) and thirteen warriors. He ordered the latter absolved and then immediately executed. Seven warriors died in the fight; another was burned alive in his house. Seventy horses were captured and more than nine hundred sheep and goats were seized. The horses with brands and four hundred of the livestock animals were returned to their owners among the militia. Vargas gave his Indian allies the unbranded horses and clothing and other plunder. He ordered a leader and ten men to stand guard over the prisoners, who were to remain outside during the day but be incarcerated in the kiva at night.

After the battle, Ojeda petitioned Vargas to allow him to return to Zia. He was concerned that the escaped rebels might attack it while its warriors were absent. He also requested an escort of soldiers for added protection. Vargas agreed. A day later the militia requested permission to go with their livestock to San Felipe Pueblo in order to ford the Rio Grande. Vargas also granted this request. Meanwhile, a rebel fugitive arrived at the pueblo with a cross as a sign of safe conduct. He explained that he was from San Marcos Pueblo and that its people, who had their houseblock on the second plaza of Kotyiti, were very regretful and wished to come down and talk. He also said that El Zepe had ordered the execution of Governor Cristobal and his brother Zue. Vargas assured him that if his people would come down, he would pardon them and they could settle at the pueblo homes. At sunset, Luis Granillo, the lieutenant governor of Santa Fe, arrived and reported the disturbing news that the Tewa and their allies had attacked Santa Fe the previous day and laid an ambush for their pursuers.

The next day, another rebel arrived. He reiterated that the people of San Marcos wanted to come down with their wives and be pardoned. He indicated that they had already captured El Zepe and two others and that they were seeking out the rest of the leaders. Vargas ordered him to return with the captives, saying that he would pardon them all. On April 20, a war captain of San Felipe reported that he had met with some rebels and was told that they had already captured nine Indians, including El Zepe.

On the twenty-first, the Keres rebels, aided by Tewa and Tano warriors, mounted a counterattack. Because Vargas had sent some men to aid Santa Fe and others to accompany the packtrain of shelled maize, he had only twenty-six men. The warriors were divided into two groups and entered both plazas simultaneously. The Spanish were caught off guard, unarmed and without their leather jackets. The rebels killed a servant boy of Captain Mizquía and, in the confusion, Miguel Luján was accidentally wounded by one of his fellow soldiers. On the rebel side, Juan Griego, a San Juan war captain, and three others were killed. After freeing more than half of the prisoners, the Indians fled back into the mountains. Vargas then spent a tense two nights in the pueblo, fortifying it and preparing for a possible attack. On the twenty-fourth, he departed for Santa Fe, setting fire to the stored corn to prevent reoccupation.

Three months later, on July 23, Vargas mounted an attack on Astialakwa (Kessell, Hendricks, and Dodge 1998, 324). He sent Captain Eusebio de Vargas and twenty-five men up the back of the mesa. He instructed Captain Antonio Jorge and his men to attack from the south site, the main way up the mesa. Vargas remained behind on the slope with a militia captain and four soldiers. Both squadrons were heavily attacked with arrows and stones, but they succeeded in gaining the top of the mesa. Some Indians barricaded themselves in their houses, while others fled. Seven threw themselves off the mesa.[11] Fifty-five were killed in the fighting at the pueblo. Vargas captured two prisoners, a Jemez man and an Apache man, whom he first had baptized and then executed. He rounded up 361 noncombatants and 172 head of sheep and goats and some horses and descended the mesa. The next day, Vargas assigned a detail to protect the stored maize on the mesa and on the twenty-fifth he sent up between fifty and one hundred Indian women to carry it down in sacks. Over the next two days, they recovered 165 sacks of maize ears.

As Vargas's men were loading up the wagons to take the food to Santa Fe, they heard shots fired on the mesa and immediately went to investigate. They returned an hour later with a prisoner, a war captain from Santo Domingo Pueblo. He had apparently thrown himself over the edge of the mesa and, although injured, survived. Vargas deposed him and learned where the rebels had fled. The war captain reported that thirteen families had gone to Taos, others to join the Cochiti, and another few to the Navajo Apache. He also stated that there were stores of maize hidden at Boletsakwa. Vargas spared his life so that he could lead him there.

On the twenty-seventh, Vargas's men captured a Jemez scout, who revealed that some of the Jemez people were in the mountains with the Santo Domingo people, while the rest had scattered. Vargas had Fray Alpuente absolve the scout before ordering him executed. Fearing attack, Vargas took refuge in Patokwa and fortified it by closing off three of its four gateways. Over the next few days, he ordered more maize brought down from Astialakwa and used some of it to pay his Zia, Santa Ana, and San Felipe allies. On August 2, he ordered that Astialakwa be burned.

Two days later, Vargas traveled to Boletsakwa to verify the Santo Domingo war captain's claim (Kessell, Hendricks, and Dodge 1998, 339). He climbed the mesa and saw that the houses had been swept clean with nothing left behind. Vargas then asked the prisoner to show him where they had hidden the stores of maize. The war captain confessed that he did not know and that it was likely the Indians had taken everything. Vargas's Indian allies then told him that this war captain was among the worst of the rebels. He had gone to Acoma, Hopi, and Zuni to petition those pueblos to join the rebellion against the Spaniards. Vargas had one of the priests absolve the man and then ordered him shot.

Vargas returned to Tunyo to renew his siege on September 4 (Kessell, Hendricks, and Dodge 1998, 378). There were a number of skirmishes over the next several days and Antonio Jorge was wounded. On September 8, one of the rebel captains came down to convey the desire of his people to resolve things. Vargas sent a message back stating that his only intention was for them to become loyal vassals of the king and to acknowledge that they were Christians. If they would do this, he would pardon them. Vargas then climbed up to the foot of the slope to meet the governor and war captains. He greeted them as if they were children and encouraged them to come down without fear, holding up the royal standard as a means of publicly pardoning them of their crimes. The Tewa leaders expressed their pleasure and gave him gifts of buffalo, deer, and elk hides.

The next day Captain Domingo and the captains from Nambé and Cuyamungue came down from the mesa. Because their fields were dispersed and their villages were in disrepair, they explained that they wished to spend the winter on the mesa. Vargas insisted that his pardon was contingent upon the people moving back to their villages. Later in the day, the captains returned and said that they needed time to pack up their clothing, pots, *metates*, and other household goods and would come down in fifteen days. Vargas compromised and gave them eight days to complete the move.

VARGAS'S MILITARY RESPONSE TO THE SECOND PUEBLO REVOLT, 1696

On June 4, 1696, the Pueblo people joined together in what is popularly called the Second Pueblo Revolt. Once again, the areas of resistance were the Keres, Jemez, and Tewa districts. As before, Pueblo people abandoned their mission homes and established temporary camps high in the mountains or took refuge with the Hopi, Zuni, Navajo, and Apache. Three mesa villages, Kotyiti, Astialakwa, and Tunyo, were briefly reoccupied and many new mountain rancherias, including Los Pedernales and Embudo, were established.[12]

On the day of the revolt, Fray Alonso Jiménez de Cisneros wrote to Vargas saying that the entire pueblo of Cochiti had gone up to their mesa with their livestock (Espinosa 1988, 239). On June 17, Vargas learned from a Santo Domingo captive that the Cochiti people were at the pueblo on their mesa and in the arroyo farther on. He also learned that the Tewa had gone to Cochiti and insisted that the Santo Domingo people rise up with them. The people from Cochiti were led by El Zepe and Lucas Naranjo (Lobón). Those from Santo Domingo followed Cristobal.[13]

By the end of June, Vargas learned that the Tewa people had also abandoned their villages and taken refuge in the mountains. The people of San Juan and Picuris Pueblos were scattered at Embudo and in the mountains near the box canyon of the Rio Grande, the Santa Clara people were in the mountains opposite their pueblo, and the people of San Ildefonso were on their mesa and in the mountains on the other side of the river opposite their pueblo (Kessell, Hendricks, and Dodge 1998, 783). He mentions that that he was unaware as to the whereabouts of the Nambé, Pojoaque, Jacona, and Cuyamungue people.

On July 26, Vargas received a letter from Captain Chavez informing him that Acoma Indians had come to the aid of the Jemez pueblos. Worried, he instructed Captain de Lara to follow the enemy's tracks. On June 29, Captains de Lara and Fernando and their Santa Ana, San Felipe, and Zia allies went to Guadalupe mesa. The Indians came down from the mesa and began an attack. The company then withdrew to Boletsakwa on San Juan mesa and engaged in a fierce battle in which they captured an Acoma and a Jemez warrior. According to Captain de Lara, the Acoma, Zuni, Hopi, Jemez, Tewa, and Tano were planning to attack the Spaniards on Sunday, July 1, in Zia, Santa Ana, Bernalillo, and San Felipe (Kessell, Hendricks, and Dodge 1998, 796).

Vargas and his company went in search of the Tanos. Domingo, the governor of Tesuque and a Spanish ally, served as his guide. The Indian scouts reported that the Tanos were living in a rancheria in the heart of the mountains between the road that ran from Pecos to Taos and the one into the mountains to Picuris. They found the camp but it was recently abandoned, with provisions and clothing left behind. They divided these up among their Pecos allies.

On July 10, Captain Chavez sent scouts from San Felipe Pueblo to search for the rancherias of the Cochiti and Santo Domingo people. They came back to report that the tracks led into the heart of the mountains opposite their mesa village. The next day, Vargas prepared for a dawn raid. They found the enemy rancheria and the Indians fled with their women and children. Vargas's men killed six warriors and recovered some books, a missal, some silver censers, and other furnishings belonging to Fray Alonso Jiménez. They seized thirty-one captives and more than eighty head of sheep and goats. Vargas then withdrew to Cochiti Pueblo and designated it as his *plaza de armas*. He learned from an old woman captive that four men were responsible and had forced the people to leave their pueblos. These men were El Zepe, their governor; Mateguelo, his lieutenant; Lobón, the interpreter; and Salvador, the Indian sacristan. Vargas instructed her to take a message to the rebels and tell them that if they would come down he would pardon them. If they failed to do so, he would destroy their crops.

On July 14, Vargas rode out from Cochiti Pueblo in search of the enemy. He climbed the mesa to Kotyiti, but found no trace of them there. He went on to the rancheria, located near the entrance of a funnel canyon. He found it abandoned and so returned to Cochiti Pueblo. The next day he went forth again and saw enemy activity in the hills. Captain de Lara noticed his belt was missing and returned to look for it. When he mounted his horse, he was attacked by a group of Indians and successfully fought them off, killing one. Vargas's men found more than one hundred *fanegas* (Spanish bushels) of maize. With no response to his message, he decided to return to Santa Fe.

On July 21, Vargas marched north from Santa Fe to make a dawn raid on the rancheria of the Tano and the Tewa pueblos of Cuyamungue, Nambé, Pojoaque, and Jacona, located in the hills of Chimayo. The rancheria he had attacked earlier in the month had not been reoccupied. The next day, Captain Antonio de Valverde captured an Indian prisoner, Juan Domingo of Cuyamungue, who testified that the four Tewa pueblos had joined together and led them to the new rancheria. They attacked it, killing three men and an old woman and capturing eight women and children. The Jacona people had fled to the Navajo. All but six families from Pojoaque went away; those from Nambé were in the mountains except for a few who went with those from Cuyamungue to Taos.

On July 23, Vargas pushed north, seeking to attack the Santa Clara people, who were in a camp adjacent to a funnel canyon near Embudo. He went directly to the canyon and found that Lucas Naranjo and his warriors had blocked it by cutting down a tree. The Indian warriors were barricaded, hidden among the boulder fields on either side of the canyon. Vargas's men made repeated volleys and Antonio Cisneros shot Naranjo in the neck, killing him instantly. Vargas seized five women and children as captives. This military action marked the end of the second revolt.

Pueblo Indian Biographies

Scholars writing about the Pueblo Revolt period have typically focused on
Po'pay, one of the key leaders of the 1680 uprising (Beninato 1990, Ortiz 1980,
Sando and Agoyo 2005), and Lucas Naranjo, the instigator of the 1696 revolt
(Beninato 1990, Chavez 1967). However, these revolts could not have taken place
without the cooperation of governors, war captains, and caciques from across
the pueblos. Testimony given to Antonio de Otermín reveals the names of some
of the lesser-known leaders of the 1680 revolt. For example, Juan of Tesuque
related that twenty-two Tewa war captains were involved. Josephe identified the
prime movers as El Pope (Po'pay) and El Taqu from San Juan, Saca from Taos,
and Francisco (El Ollita) from San Ildefonso (Hackett and Shelby 1942, 236,
239). Here we wish to highlight three individuals: Antonio Malacate, a Zia captain; Cristobal, a San Marcos captain; and Domingo Tuguaque, a Tesuque captain. Taken together, the activities of these individuals give a fascinating glimpse
of the tensions and struggles Pueblo people faced during these difficult times.

ANTONIO MALACATE OF ZIA PUEBLO

Antonio Malacate was an influential Zia governor and war captain who helped
establish alliances across the Jemez and Keres districts. He was away on a hunting expedition when Cruzate attacked Zia Pueblo in 1689 and thus escaped the
bloody battle (Kessell, Hendricks, and Dodge 1995, 117, 145). He and his fellow
survivors built a new mesa village at Cerro Colorado in the Jemez district for
defense and shelter. He was living there when Vargas arrived on October 24,
1692, as part of his inspection tour (199). Malacate manipulated Vargas into
relieving him of his role as governor, citing health grounds, that he was "old and
sick" (201). He likely did this to hide his advocacy of the rebel cause. To allay any
suspicion, he requested that Vargas serve as godfather to his son.

In 1693, Malacate returned home to Zia to get married (Kessell, Hendricks,
and Dodge 1995, 401). But at the end of summer, he moved to Kotyiti, one of
the centers of the rebellion. There, he advocated war with the Spaniards, against
the wishes of his Zia relatives, who urged him to stay neutral (404). According
to Ojeda, he was "worshipping the things of the devil every night" in order to
kill the Spaniards (Kessell, Hendricks, and Dodge 1998, 33). Vargas learned that
Malacate was "the leader of the disturbance along with another Indian from
that pueblo [El Zepe] and one of those from the pueblo of San Marcos who is

living there" (Kessell, Hendricks, and Dodge 1995, 540). He was such a skilled negotiator that the rebel leader Luis el Picuri contacted him to secure the aid of the Jemez and Navajo Apache in a planned revolt scheduled for the end of December 1693 (67).

CRISTOBAL OF SAN MARCOS PUEBLO

Cristobal was the governor and captain of the people from San Marcos living at Kotyiti. He and his brother Zue, also a captain, became disaffected with the talk of the rebel faction. They reached out to Vargas on January 5, 1694, to warn him of a pending attack on Santa Fe by a combined force of Jemez and Cochiti warriors (Kessell, Hendricks, and Dodge 1998, 30). Cristobal reported that Malacate and El Zepe had unsuccessfully petitioned the leaders of San Felipe, Santa Ana, and Zia to join the resistance and were harassing them.

Vargas quickly took advantage of his sympathies. He enlisted Cristobal's help to test the intentions of the Cochiti people (Kessell, Hendricks, and Dodge 1998, 61). Vargas instructed him to take some beef to Kotyiti to trade for corn and other supplies. Cristobal dutifully set out with the loaded mules, but was warned off by an Indian woman coming at a dead run. She explained that she was on the way to San Felipe to warn Vargas that all the nations were coming together at the Las Bocas outpost. She explained that Kotyiti was divided into factions and that she was unsure whether they would come down and reoccupy their mission villages. Cristobal was worried for the fate of his brother and proposed to go to Kotyiti to check on the situation (Kessell, Hendricks, and Dodge 1995, 412).

When he arrived at Kotyiti, Cristobal and his brother were seized as traitors. El Zepe ordered their execution by a firing squad consisting of three Cochiti Indians and three San Marcos Indians (Kessell, Hendricks, and Dodge 1998, 200–1).

DOMINGO TUGUAQUE OF TESUQUE PUEBLO

Domingo Tuguaque, also referred to as "Domingo" or "Dominguillo," was a captain of Tesuque Pueblo who shifted allegiances in order to better protect his people (Kessell, Hendricks, and Dodge 1995, 439). At first, he was an implacable foe of the Spaniards and responsible for the "gathering of nations" (Kessell, Hendricks, and Dodge 1998, 228). According to the testimony of Agustin, a prisoner from San Lazaro Pueblo, Domingo was "the only governor of all the pueblos" and traveled among them with "his junta" of war captains at Picuris, Taos, and other pueblos (235). His influence was far-reaching among the pueblos and he "went to see everyone" to plot an ambush on the Spanish horses (232). He was the leader of the Tewa resistance movement at Tunyo in 1694 and proved to be a thorn in Vargas's side during his military campaign.

After the siege at Tunyo, Domingo became an ally of the Spaniards. Information he provided to Vargas proved crucial in suppressing an early 1696 uprising. Domingo reported to Lieutenant General Roque de Madrid that "all the people of the other pueblos had risen up and that [Madrid] should send soldiers to them before the Indians killed the priests; and that only his pueblo of Tesuque, which was under his control, remained loyal" (Kessell, Hendricks, and Dodge 1998, 727). Once a prominent rebel who led nine Tewa villages in the defense of Tunyo, Domingo was now a loyal Spanish subject. So discontented were the Tewa with his treason that they plotted to assassinate him "because he liked the things of God, the fathers, and the Spaniards" (771). With the protection of Vargas, Domingo was spared. He went on to participate in and lead several battles against the Tewa alongside Vargas and his forces in the hills and mesas of Chimayo and Santa Cruz throughout 1696.

Revolt Period Social Networks

We can begin to reconstruct aspects of the Revolt period social networks by examining the movements of people to and from the mesa villages. The unit of movement was almost never an entire village, but rather consisted of some smaller subset, commonly families, extended families (*ma:tu'in*, see Ford, chapter 2, this volume), societies, and clan groups. The general pattern is for people from one linguistic group to join with relatives of the same group and for movements to involve longer distances over time.[14]

The mesa villages are a physical manifestation of the Pueblo Revolt revitalization movement. Immediately after the revolt of 1680, Po'pay and Alonso Catiti made an inspection tour of the pueblos. They preached renouncing Spanish customs and practices and advocated living according to the "laws of the ancestors" (Liebmann and Preucel 2009, Preucel 2006). This discourse generated a series of population relocations as whole villages were vacated and people sought refuge in defensible mesa locations (fig. 10.5). In 1683, the Cochiti established Kotyiti on Cochiti mesa with San Marcos and San Felipe refugee families

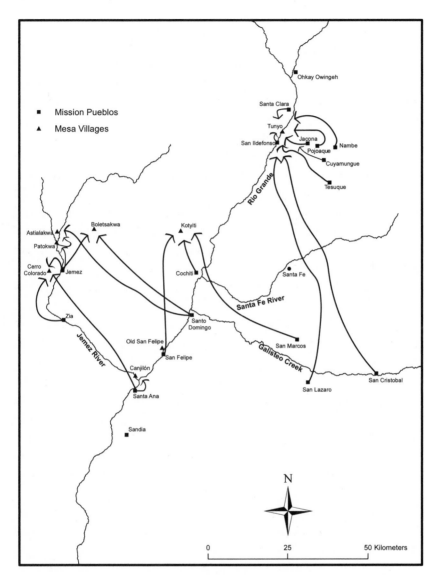

Figure 10.5. Northern Rio Grande population movements during the Revolt Period.
Map by Rob Weiner.

(Kessell, Hendricks, and Dodge 1995, 200). In the same year, Santo Domingo families moved in with their Jemez relatives at Boletsakwa on San Juan mesa (Kessell and Hendricks 1992, 522, Kessell, Hendricks and Dodge 1998, 371).

One of the striking features of the early Keres and Jemez mesa villages is the standardization in architectural design.[15] The three mesa villages, Kotyiti, Patokawa, Boletsakwa, built after 1680, share a common dual plaza plan. Two of these villages, Patokwa and Kotyiti, have kivas located within their plazas, while one, Boletsakwa, has kivas located immediately outside of the village walls. Cerro Colorado, built in 1689, has two plazas, but no kivas. This common dual plaza layout strongly indicates centralized planning and can be associated with the Turquoise and Pumpkin kiva groups by homology with the modern Pueblos. The Pueblo caciques and ritual leaders were likely seeking to rebuild the Pueblo social order and key to this process was reemphasizing the moiety principle so fundamental to Keres and Jemez social and religious life.

The double plaza pueblo architecture can also be understood as a local Keres and Jemez expression of the cultural revitalization movement (Liebmann 2012, 108). The dual plaza architecture functioned as a cosmogram, marking out the sacred places and the homes of important deities in the Pueblo pantheon. At Kotyiti, the gateways between the roomblocks likely referred to different mythological referents. For example, the gateway between the two northern roomblocks can be interpreted as the "gate to shipap," the place of emergence in Cochiti oral history (Preucel 2006, 227). In this way, village architecture would have made material the popular Revolt period discourse of "living in accordance with the laws of the ancestors" (Hackett and Shelby 1942, 248). Peoples would have consciously thought about their traditional responsibilities and shared histories as they circulated throughout the roomblocks.

Not all of the Keres people were receptive to the revitalization discourse. Notably, Santa Ana and Zia were resistant and remained secure in their mission homes. However, things changed dramatically with the Spanish reconquest attempts. In 1687, Posada attacked Santa Ana and Zia and two years later, Cruzate destroyed Zia, leveling the village (Twitchell 1914, 454). Immediately following these devastating events, the Zia established a new mesa village at Cerro Colorado, where they were joined by Santa Ana and Santo Domingo families (Kessell and Hendricks 1992, 431; Kessell, Hendricks, and Dodge 1995, 113). It seems likely that San Felipe people built their "presidio style" mesa village at this time. The architectural form implies a close allegiance to the Spaniards.

In 1693, San Ildefonso people established a village on Tunyo along with people from the six Tewa villages of Santa Clara, Nambé, Jacona, Pojoaque, Tesuque, Cuyamungue and the two Tano villages of San Cristobal, and San Lazaro (Kessell, Hendricks, and Dodge 1998, 116, 117, 232). Current research by Aguilar indicates that the village was composed of clusters of dugouts or pit dwellings, somewhat similar to the agricultural dugouts known from the Chama (Bandelier 1892, 46). This construction is consistent with the fact that the village was erected quickly. In the same year, the Jemez people withdrew from Patokwa to build Astialakwa on Guadalupe mesa in an eight month period (Liebmann 2012).[16] By this time, architecture was no longer a viable medium for the expression of cultural revitalization and the mesa settlements tended to be dispersed and informal. The village consists of 190 rooms distributed in linear roomblocks and in one or two room clusters (Liebmann 2012). There are no kivas. This organization is somewhat reminiscent of Dowa Yalanne, the Zuni mesa village, which also has both formal and informal groupings (Ferguson 1996).

The many new arrivals to the mesa villages posed constant challenges to the social order. The first of these was housing. Here physical proximity is assumed to be a rough measure of social standing; people that are allowed to live in adjacent dwellings are regarded differently than those who are required to live at a distance. Processes of spatial incorporation and spatial segregation can both be seen at Kotyiti. A large contingent of people from San Marcos Pueblo, led by Cristobal and his brother Zue, joined the village sometime before 1692. Presumably, there were very close ties between the San Marcos people and the Cochiti people since they were invited to build their own roomblock on the second plaza. Other immigrants were welcomed at Kotyiti, but were required to set up their rancheria some three hundred yards east of the plaza pueblo. This rancheria may have been established by refugees (possibly Tewa) who did not enjoy particularly close ties with the Cochiti people.

The new arrivals came with a range of political ideas. In some cases, disputes broke out and the disaffected left to seek new allies. A good example of this is the split at Patokwa that led to the founding of Boletsakwa in 1683 (Liebmann et al. 2017, 150). In this case, a dispute appears to have emerged among different Jemez leaders as they debated strategies on how best to resist the Spaniards. A splinter group allied with the Santo Domingo people moved to San Juan mesa to establish the village of Boletsakwa. Another example is the unrest at Kotyiti that led the San Felipe to leave and join their relatives at Old San Felipe (Lange et al. 1975, 69–70). The San Felipe people later joined with Zia and Santa Ana in allying with the Spaniards and even assisted Vargas as auxiliaries in his 1694 attack on Kotyiti.

Each mesa village was a cosmopolitan community with social ties to multiple Pueblo and other Indian allies. For example, after the battle at Astialakwa, thirteen families went to Taos, others to Cochiti, and another few joined the Navajo Apache (Kessell, Hendricks, and Dodge 1998, 332). Here we see Jemez and Santo Domingo families taking refuge with or returning to their relatives at nearby (Cochiti) and distant villages (Taos). Presumably some families left to follow charismatic leaders like Antonio Malacate. The social landscape was in continuous flux, with people forced to balance village identities and political affiliations.

In 1696, the Second Pueblo Revolt broke out. This time, the mesa villages no longer provided protection. The Pueblo people chose to reoccupy only three of their mesa villages: Kotyiti, Astialakwa, and Tunyo. They did not stay there long, perhaps because of their checkered histories in repelling the Spaniards. They quickly escaped into the mountains in advance of Vargas's soldiers. By November, Vargas learned that the two Jemez pueblos (Patokwa and Boletsakwa), the two Tano pueblos (San Cristobal and San Lazaro), and Santa Clara were scattered (Kessell, Hendricks, and Dodge 1998, 1102–1103). Some of the people had gone to Zuni, Hopi, and Acoma, while others took refuge with the Navajo Apaches, the Apaches of Embudo, and the sierra of Los Pedernales. Again, the strategy of fleeing to distant friends and relatives was crucial.

The political confederations uniting different Pueblo villages constantly evolved over time. Many Pueblo war captains led contingents of warriors into battle in support of allied communities. Juan Griego, of San Juan Pueblo, was one of these leaders. We know his name because he was killed in the battle at Kotyiti in 1694 (Kessell, Hendricks, and Dodge 1998, 206). Pueblo leaders worked hard to build and maintain these coalitions. According to Vargas, the unnamed Santo Domingo war captain who assisted in the Jemez cause in the battle at Astialakwa, had petitioned Acoma, Hopi, and Zuni to join the rebellion against the Spaniards (Kessell, Hendricks, and Dodge 1998, 339). Similarly, Domingo Tuguaque traveled from pueblo to pueblo with "his junta," consisting of the war captains of Picuris, Taos, and other pueblos to secure allies (Kessell, Hendricks, and Dodge 1998, 235).

Conclusions

The Pueblo Indian social networks of the Pueblo Revolt period were composed of unstable and ever-changing alliances, confederations, and unions largely precipitated by the stresses and strains of the Spanish reconquest. The northern Rio Grande mesa villages were key nodes in these networks as centers of resistance to Spanish authority that threatened the success of the newly reestablished colony. They were so important that Vargas visited them multiple times and eventually attacked them. These villages were cosmopolitan communities—home to families, extended families, and social segments from a variety of mission villages and Indian encampments. In most cases, refugees chose to join the mesa villages where they had close social ties. When further pressed due to Spanish attacks, they commonly took refuge with the Hopi, Zuni, Acoma, and Navajo, all communities located at the edges of Spanish authority. These population relocations and displacements were major factors in shaping the social fabric of contemporary Pueblo, Apache, and Navajo people.

A microhistorical perspective encourages us to think about the intimate and reciprocal interrelationships of people and place. The mesa villages were political theaters in which individual actors such as Antonio Malacate, Cristobal, and Domingo Tuguaque emerged as charismatic leaders. The Keres and Jemez mesa villages of Patokwa, Boletsakwa, Cerro Colorado, and Kotyiti served as the centers of much of the cultural revitalization discourse. Their very architectural design was a material expression of the Turquoise and Pumpkin moieties that remain central to modern Keres and Jemez identity. They thus embodied traditional principles and values of balance and harmony congruent with the revitalization mantra "living in accordance with the laws of the ancestors." However, this discourse transformed over the twelve-year Spanish interregnum and was no longer expressed in village architecture after the return of the Spaniards. The last of the mesa villages, Astialakwa and Tunyo, represent more expedient responses to the Spanish military threat.

A microhistorical approach also sheds light on aspects of Pueblo diplomacy and negotiation strategies. We see that the Pueblos often greeted Vargas with what he interpreted as a "war dance." In some cases, the warriors taunted him and threw dirt into his soldiers' eyes. When the Indians saw that the Spaniards were undaunted in their resolve, they quickly feigned allegiance and escorted Vargas to their mesatop villages. There, after witnessing the Spanish proclamations and baptisms, they provided him with a room in which to rest, prepared a shared meal, and exchanged gifts, all indicators of hospitality. When Vargas demanded that they come down off their mesas to return to their mission homes, they agreed but kept drawing out the timetable to secure time for additional reinforcements to arrive. This was particularly the case at Tunyo, where the Tewa leaders initially requested fifteen days, claiming that they needed extra time to pack up their provisions and food. These negotiations give insights into the complex and uncertain nature of different Pueblo strategies for survival.

Finally, our study provides insights into the dynamics of Pueblo alliance formation. At different times, different pueblos allied with each other or joined with the Spaniards as they sought to achieve safety and security for their families and communities (Liebmann et al. 2017). For example, at the time of the 1692 reconquest, Ojeda reported that the Zia, Santa Ana, San Felipe, Cochiti, and Santo Domingo, along with the Jemez, Taos, and Pecos, were waging continuous warfare against the Tewa pueblos and Picuris (Kessell and Hendricks 1992, 26).[17] However, these animosities may have been exaggerated, for new alliances quickly emerged. Only two years later, Cochiti, Santo Domingo, and Jemez were closely allied with the Tewa against the Spaniards just as the San Felipe, Santa Ana, and Zia threw in their lot with the Spaniards as auxiliaries. These shifting alliances are thus among the most telling indicators of Pueblo agency, which in this overall light appears as multisited, fragmentary, and subject to serial re-formation, as needs and perspectives changed in the face of reconquest and resettlement.

Acknowledgments

We thank Peter Whiteley and the members of the SAR workshop for their valuable feedback on our chapter. In particular, we would like to single out Barbara Mills, T. J. Ferguson, John Crandall, John Ware, and Dick Ford. We also want to acknowledge Matt Liebmann, Mike Wilcox, and Loa Traxler, who have been our close collaborators over the years. We also wish to thank Mike Bremer (USFS–Santa Fe National Forest), US Army Corps of Engineers–Cochiti Dam, Los Alamos National Laboratory, the Pueblo of Cochiti, and the Pueblo of San Ildefonso for their support. Robert Weiner drafted figures 10.2 and 10.5.

Notes

1. The raising of the standard was a symbolically charged, performative act. The standard was the same one used by Juan de Oñate during his colonization of New Mexico in 1598 (Kessell, Hendricks, and Dodge 1995, 373).

2. The construction date of Old San Felipe is not firmly established. Hodge, Hammond, and Rey (1945, 260) suggest that it was built between 1683 and 1692. We favor the end of this period, shortly after the attack on Zia in 1689.

3. Archaeological evidence reveals that the Cochiti people had taken refuge in a new village, known as Kotyiti (or Hanat Kotyiti, "Cochiti above"), located on Cochiti mesa (Preucel 2002, Preucel, Traxler, and Wilcox 2002).

4. Archaeological evidence indicates that the Santo Domingo people were living with their Jemez relatives at Patokwa (Turquoise moiety place) and Boletsakwa (Abalone place) (Liebmann 2012).

5. Old San Felipe (Basalt Point Pueblo) was mapped by Adolph Bandelier and contains fifty-eight rooms (Lange et al. 1975, 69–70). The church in the northeast corner dates to 1694 (Kubler 1973, 106).

6. The village may have been under construction, for Preucel (2002, 76) has mapped it as having six roomblocks with 137 ground-floor rooms.

7. Liebmann (2012, 170) has identified 167 ground-floor rooms at Cerro Colorado.

8. This accords well with the archaeological data. Liebmann (2012, 105) has reported 168 ground-floor rooms.

9. Ferguson (1996, 51) has mapped the village and recorded two L-shaped roomblocks, one containing at least 123 ground-floor rooms and the other 148 rooms, and numerous isolated room clusters.

10. Cochiti oral history reveals that Vargas captured a Cochiti man who had been living at Jemez Pueblo and tortured him into revealing the locations of the trails to the top of the mesa (Benedict 1931, 186).

11. According to Jemez Pueblo oral history, some of the warriors jumped over the cliff edge and survived the fall (Sando 1982, 120). An image of the likeness of San Diego then appeared on the cliff face.

12. Neither Los Pedernales nor Embudo have yet been identified archaeologically (Preucel and Fowles 2015).

13. Lobón is another name for Lucas Naranjo, the leader of the Second Pueblo Revolt of 1696 (see Kessell, Hendricks, and Dodge 1998, 906).

14. There are notable exceptions to this rule. The Vargas journals reveal that

between 1692 and 1696 Pueblo people of different language groups congregated at Hopi, Zuni, and Acoma and joined with the Navajo and Apache.

15. The Keres and Jemez share a number of cultural similarities. Acknowledging the obvious language differences, Charles Lange (personal communication, 1996) held that in many ways, Jemez could be considered a Keresan pueblo.

16. On November 10, 1693, Vargas discovered that the Jemez had learned of his coming from the Apache and "had begun to move their provisions from their pueblo on the mesa [Patokwa] up into the monte [Astialakwa]" (Kessell, Hendricks, and Dodge 1995, 404).

17. The reasons for this warfare are unclear, but they may be related to Popé's imperious behavior following the revolt. Fray Sylvestre Velez de Escalante wrote, "The Queres, Taos, and Pecos fought against the Tehuas and Tanos, and these deposed Popé for the despotism and severity with which he compelled obedience and for the large tribute which, in his frequent visitations, he compelled them to pay him" (cited in Twitchell 1914, 276).

CHAPTER ELEVEN

Dimensions and Dynamics of Pre-Hispanic Pueblo Organization and Authority

The Chaco Canyon Conundrum

STEPHEN PLOG

Significant transformation occurred among Pueblo societies of the northern Southwest during the ninth century. Research in southwestern Colorado, for example, has shown frequent shifting of people from one area to another, leading to notable population increases in some areas and decreases in others. In addition, some unusually large agricultural villages emerged during this era in both southeastern Utah and southwestern Colorado, contrasting with the more typical small settlements in which most people resided. By roughly 880 CE, however, these large sites became uninhabited and population levels in both southeastern Utah and southwestern Colorado dropped significantly.

While these processes were unfolding to the north, Chaco Canyon in northwestern New Mexico (fig. 11.1) emerged as a key region characterized by multiple large pueblos, now referred to as great houses, constructed in association with population increase and other notable changes such as the evolution of important new short- and long-distance trade networks. Over the next three centuries—ca. 800 to 1130 CE—Chaco became arguably the most important area in the Pueblo Southwest, influencing a remarkably broad swath of the region. Understanding Chaco is thus central to an understanding of the evolution of pre-Hispanic Pueblo society.

The archaeological exploration of Chaco Canyon began more than 150 years ago. Throughout this era, scholars have posed innumerable questions and offered multiple answers: descriptive, chronological, and explanatory. My focus is on proposed models of Chaco sociopolitical organization, including the possible occurrence of lineages, moieties, sodalities, and house groups, as well as the question of whether Chacoan society was hierarchical.

In my evaluation, I take the perspective of Ware (2014, 130; see also Whiteley

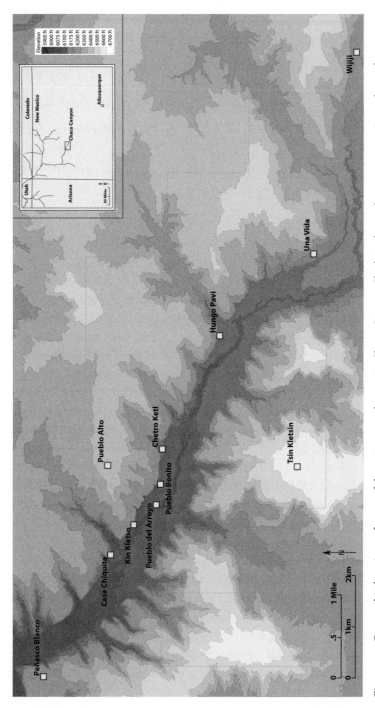

Figure 11.1. Geographic locations of some of the major great houses in Chaco Canyon. Shading shows elevation ranges. Inset shows the location of Chaco Canyon in the American Southwest. Created by Ed Triplett; from Plog and Heitman 2010.

2004, 2015) that Chaco must "be understood in historical context or not at all," but I will argue that we need to reconceptualize that history. As an initial, central component of my evaluation, I propose a revised chronology that, if correct, has significant implications for our understanding of sociopolitical organization and change.

The Foundation: Traditional Chaco Culture History

Explanations of the history of Chaco Canyon vary widely (Sebastian 2006), but at the core of this diversity is a widely accepted chronology (e.g., Lekson 2006a, 2008; Kantner 2004; Mathien 2005; Nelson 2006; Ware 2014), whose key components are:

- Chacoan people constructed the earliest great houses in the mid- to late ninth century CE;
- the source of the great house concept, and perhaps the people who built them, was migrants to Chaco from southwestern Colorado (e.g., Windes and Van Dyke 2012, 72);
- after initial construction at a few early great houses, a marked drop in building activity occurred through much of the tenth and early eleventh centuries (Lekson 1984);
- beginning about 1030–1040 CE, Chaco Canyon and the surrounding region were transformed by:

  1. an unprecedented period of major construction, including an expansion of early great houses and establishment of multiple new canyon great houses;
  2. construction of scores of outlying great houses throughout much of the Four Corners region;
  3. creation of roads;
  4. construction of a complex irrigation system;
  5. establishment of two intramural mortuary crypts within Pueblo Bonito, one in the northern section of the pueblo and one in the west (fig. 11.2);
  6. procurement of materials (e.g., copper bells, macaws, cacao, shells) from Mesoamerica; and
  7. production of unusual quantities of turquoise and shell ornaments.

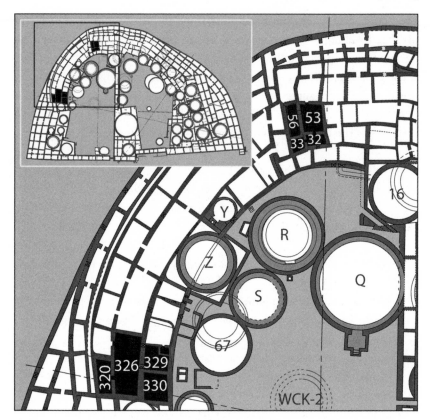

Figure 11.2. Plan view of Pueblo Bonito highlighting the locations of the two major burial crypts. Created by Ed Triplett; from Plog and Heitman 2010.

This hypothesized transformation between 1030–1040 and 1130 CE is commonly referred to as the Chaco phenomenon, the Chaco florescence, or Chaco's "Golden Century" (e.g., Judge 2004, 1, 2; Mathien 2005, 128).

Problems with the Outline

THE PUEBLO BONITO BIAS

There are several problems with this temporal model. The first plagues virtually all attempts to address questions about Chaco great houses: the only one we know well is Pueblo Bonito. Almost every room in Bonito has been excavated and it thus has been the focus of considerable analysis and discussion.

Unfortunately, this bias is largely unavoidable. Hewett's (e.g., 1936) excavations of nearby Chetro Ketl—a pueblo comparable in size to Bonito—left the worst field records for any major excavation project in the canyon. The only other excavated great houses to compare with Pueblo Bonito are Pueblo Alto and Pueblo del Arroyo. Only about a dozen pueblo rooms were excavated at Pueblo Alto, so contextual information is limited. Judd (1959) uncovered more rooms and kivas at Pueblo del Arroyo, but he neither published detailed artifactual and contextual information nor found the rich deposits that have stimulated so much study of Pueblo Bonito.

DENDROCHRONOLOGY

Chacoans inhabited Pueblo Bonito for over three hundred years. Because of excellent wood preservation and recent efforts to date visible construction wood (e.g., Windes and Ford 1996), Chaco research is blessed by tree-ring dates orders of magnitude higher than other regions of the Southwest, reinforcing the common assumption that the chronology of the canyon is well-known. Wilcox's (1999, 12) conclusion that "based as it is on tree-ring dating, the Chaco chronology is less prone to fundamental disputes" is one many Chaco scholars would endorse.

Dendrochronology is a superb aid in dating construction and renovation. However, tree-ring dates are not without problems, as they may provide limited insight when dating materials from complex cultural deposits that accumulated in rooms utilized for centuries, as occurred at Pueblo Bonito. Also, many first-floor rooms at Pueblo Bonito are deeply buried (Judd 1964, 26) and thus ceiling beams and lintels from those rooms were rarely accessible when recent tree-ring samples were extracted. The great depth of these early rooms was demonstrated when the National Park Service allowed me to enter a locked gate and descend stairs into an intact first-story room, 3b, immediately west of Room 33 (discussed below). The floor of Room 3b is several feet below the current ground surface of Bonito. Afterward, I realized that the still-visible door between what I had thought were first-story Rooms 32 and 33 is actually the door between the second-floor rooms just above them, 52 and 58. This is a common mistake—so common that the tree-ring dates from the lintel in that doorway are incorrectly assigned to Rooms 32 and 33.[1] Dendrochronology thus provides limited information on construction dates of the earliest rooms of Pueblo Bonito, particularly in the complex northern cluster.

AMS ^{14}C DATES

Chaco archaeologists have largely eschewed radiocarbon dating because such dates once had large error ranges. The introduction of Accelerator Mass Spectrometry (AMS) radiocarbon dating, however, provided greater precision. The method is thus increasingly being used to date organic material—bone, basketry, and textiles—from Chaco (Plog and Heitman 2010; Watson 2012; Watson et al. 2015; Kennett et al. 2017).

These recent AMS samples are transforming our understanding of key aspects of the standard chronology. First, eleven burials in a frequently discussed context, Room 33 in the northern mortuary cluster, have been dated (Kennett et al. 2017). These dates demonstrate that the two stratigraphically lowest burials in Room 33, Burials 14 and 13, took place no later than the beginning of the ninth century. Nine other burials produced AMS dates ranging from the mid-800s to the early 1100s (Kennett et al. 2017). The mortuary crypt thus was not a post–1030 CE phenomenon, but began much earlier, with interments continuing for 300 to 350 years. Particularly significant, contrary to the foundational chronology, the richest burials anywhere in the canyon, the aforementioned numbers 13 and 14, predate 1030 CE by approximately two hundred years (fig. 11.3). AMS dates for the western mortuary cluster have not yet been published, but they also span a lengthy period. Any discussion of organization and authority in Chaco Canyon must take this long-term use of these unusual crypts into account.

A second study using AMS dated the skeletons of fourteen scarlet macaws (*Ara macao*) recovered from three rooms, also in the northern section—a significant portion of the thirty-five known scarlet macaws recovered from canyon excavations (Watson et al. 2015). Scholars have typically concluded that these colorful birds, native to southern Mexico and Central America, were first brought to Chaco after 1030 CE (e.g., Kantner 2010, 277; Mathien 2005, 271–72; Neitzel 2003b; Nelson 2006; Toll 2006, 128; Ware 2014, 105). The AMS dates, however, demonstrated that six of the macaws died in the canyon between 890 and 970 CE. A second set of six macaw dates fall between the end of the tenth century and approximately 1030 CE. Thus, Chacoans acquired twelve of fourteen dated macaws before the Chaco florescence.

Also of note, the earliest macaws date to a period of diminished great house construction, a period during which, it has been suggested, little of importance occurred in Chaco (Kantner 2010, 274). These AMS dates thus highlight the problem noted earlier of overreliance on tree-ring dating to provide insights into social dynamics in pueblos occupied for centuries.

TURQUOISE

Although direct dating of turquoise is not possible, given the AMS dates just discussed, it now appears the acquisition of turquoise was largely a pre–1030 CE phenomenon. A large proportion of the tens of thousands of pieces of turquoise recovered from Pueblo Bonito is from Room 33 (>85 percent, more than fifty thousand pieces) (Neitzel 2003a, 111). Although fewer than two thousand pieces were deposited in room corners, around twenty thousand were associated with early Burials 13 and 14 (Pepper 1909, 1920; Plog and Heitman 2010). The room with the second highest amount (around four thousand pieces) is Room 53 (Neitzel 2003a, 110), northeast of Room 33 and part of the northern mortuary cluster (fig. 11.2). Neitzel (2003a, 111, figure 9.5) also shows that the most frequent occurrences of turquoise occur in the rooms at Bonito constructed using the earliest Chacoan masonry type.

Other evidence indicates that an ornament industry emerged in Chaco quite early (Windes and Van Dyke 2012, 85). Windes has observed that "during the A.D. 900s and early 1000s in Chaco Canyon, participation in turquoise jewelry manufacture was almost universal, or nearly so" at small house sites (1992, 162; see also Judge 1989, 235; Mathien 2001). High frequencies of turquoise ornaments with Burials 13 and 14, however, demonstrate that the procurement of turquoise began even earlier, in the early ninth century. The earlier presence of turquoise (and shell) ornaments in Basketmaker sites in Canyon de Chelly west of Chaco is thus intriguing and consistent with the Chaco evidence (Morris 1925).[2]

Frequencies of turquoise from late great houses also contrast markedly with Pueblo Bonito. Judd (1959, 125) states that at post–1030 CE Pueblo del Arroyo, "turquoise was conspicuously lacking." His catalog records and note-cards from del Arroyo indicate a total of fewer than two hundred ornaments or turquoise fragments.[3] Similarly, Mathien (1987, 383, table 6.1) lists only 278 pieces of turquoise from Pueblo Alto despite extensive excavations in the trash mound. Fewer than 1,500 turquoise chips, beads, or pendants were recovered from Chetro Ketl, based on available records.[4] Also noteworthy: the remarkable necklaces recovered from sealed niches in a Chetro Ketl great kiva were made of stone and shell; only a handful of turquoise beads or pendants were associated.

A significant proportion of turquoise found in the canyon thus dates to the pre–1030 CE period, with more limited amounts found after 1030 CE. This contradicts the foundational chronology that has regarded turquoise as post–1030 CE (Judge 1989) largely because of the common belief, now known to be incorrect, that turquoise-rich Burials 13 and 14 in Room 33 were interred after 1030–1050 CE (e.g., Kantner 2010, 78; Lekson 2006b, 30; Neitzel 2003b, 145; Toll 2006, 128; Van Dyke 2008, 122; Windes 2003, 32).

A Revised Chronology (Based Heavily on Pueblo Bonito)

As emphasized in the introduction, I concur with Ware (2014) and Whiteley (2004, 2015) that a temporal perspective is necessary to understand Pueblo history, but I also suggest we need to reconceptualize Chacoan history in many ways. Pueblo Bonito and a few other great houses were constructed no later than 800–850 CE and possibly were established even earlier.[5] Judd also found at least two earlier pithouses underneath Pueblo Bonito, and multiple pithouses, now buried by several feet of alluvium on the canyon floor, have been exposed by the erosion of the sidewalls of Chaco Wash (e.g., Judd 1924, 1964, 21, 22; Wills et al. 2012). Soil aggradation on the canyon floor in the eighth and ninth centuries, along with the exposure of multiple buried pithouses, suggests that the canyon was likely inhabited and farmed extensively in the 700s CE. In addition, there are a few stratigraphically lower foundation walls under the northern room cluster (e.g., Room 56 [Pepper 1920, 217]) that indicate possible earlier construction of masonry rooms under Bonito. There was thus an established population in the canyon prior to the construction of the great houses. This conclusion is supported by recent isotope analysis (Price et al. 2017) that suggests Pueblo Bonito was constructed by local residents, evidence that is inconsistent with the common hypothesis that migrants from southwestern Colorado were the founding group(s) that constructed the initial great houses.

I believe that some, perhaps all, of the northern rooms were the first to be built at Pueblo Bonito, as Judd (1964, 58) initially suggested. (Many construction sequences have been proposed, e.g., Vivian 1990, 160; Lekson 1984, 114; Windes 2003, 20.) The northern rooms are irregular in shape and variable in size. They thus depart from the more patterned construction of larger rooms that characterizes the rest of Pueblo Bonito. The earliest AMS dates we have obtained from Bonito, some of which predate 800 CE, are also on materials from the northern room cluster. I thus concur with Judd (1964, 58): "If a nucleus is to be found anywhere . . . it lies among the cluster of relatively small, crowded structures at the top of the crescent" shape of Bonito. No later than 852 CE, however, Chacoans constructed the initial eastern and western wings off the initial nucleus (Windes and Ford 1996). Although some have suggested that the eastern wing was smaller than the western, Judd (1964, 86) notes that as many as thirty early eastern rooms were razed during later construction events. Finally, Burials 13 and 14 in Room 33 demonstrate that the acquisition of significant amounts of turquoise and shell had begun no later than the early ninth century. In fact, if any materials symbolized ninth-century Pueblo Bonito, they may have been turquoise and shell.

Although a marked decrease in great house construction occurred beginning about 920–940 CE and continued through the end of the century (Lekson 1984), other types of important behavior continued or were initiated. In particular, by the early tenth century the inhabitants of Pueblo Bonito began to acquire scarlet macaws, demonstrating the establishment of long-distance procurement networks to the south. By contrast, no other Southwest region, excluding the Hohokam, appears to have acquired macaws prior to the early eleventh century (Watson et al. 2015). Shell was also rarely to infrequently found outside of Chaco and in amounts an order of magnitude below Chaco's. Interments in the northern burial crypt also continued during this period, although with fewer exotic grave goods (Plog and Heitman 2010; Kennett et al. 2017).

About 1030 CE a transformation again occurred in Chaco and the Four Corners region, primarily a marked increase in great house construction (fig. 11.2; Watson et al. 2015). These changes have been well-described elsewhere and I will focus on only a few dimensions. Across much of the Colorado Plateau, this was a period of rapid population increase. Although striking differences occur between the size of settlements in Chaco and most surrounding areas, the rate of increase in construction activity in the canyon is strongly correlated with rates of population growth elsewhere on the Colorado Plateau (Plog 2007, 112; Wills 2000, 38). This was likely a prosperous period for Pueblo people because of a favorable climate that allowed increases in agricultural productivity. Many believe that it was after 1030 CE that most Chacoan-style great houses (i.e., outliers) began to be constructed over much of the Four Corners region and roads and berms became common features on the Chacoan landscape.

Chaco had become a central node for a broad swath of the Pueblo Southwest by 1030 CE, likely having a significant impact on ritual and cosmology over a large area, but a more limited impact than some scholars have postulated on sociopolitical relations. Trade and acquisition networks for different materials and the spatial extent of sociopolitical and ritual relations were not geographically isomorphic. I thus agree with studies that have concluded that there was no Chaco "system" (Kantner 2003; Vivian 1996) and I have significant doubts (see Plog and Watson 2012; Wills 2001) that Chaco was a major pilgrimage center or a locus of "grand and glorious gatherings" (Van Dyke 2008, 198). It would not be surprising, however, if smaller groups of people visited the canyon regularly to learn new rituals, obtain ritual paraphernalia, and perhaps participate in rite-of-passage ceremonies at key points in their lives.

Chaco Social History

Surprisingly few in-depth discussions of Chaco sociopolitical organization exist *relative to* the vast literature on the canyon, but many have offered at least brief comments. There is a remarkable range of interpretations and lack of consensus, and few references to specific forms of organization (Sebastian 2006). Brief allusions to social units such as lineages and clans are common, but typically not supported with evidence.

The interpretations proposed are so diverse that it is impossible to outline them all, much less evaluate them. Evaluation is also difficult because of the chronological problems noted earlier. In the following sections, I will thus address two topics: (1) some fundamental issues that are key to how we approach reconstructing and explaining Chaco social history, and (2) the nature of the social and political units that may have been central to Chacoan society.

FUNDAMENTAL ISSUES

Two basic issues affect discussions of Chaco social history: the degree of cultural continuity between past and present and whether the great houses were primarily or exclusively ceremonial centers with few inhabitants (Bernardini 1999; Windes 1984, 1987) or contained a significant residential population. As Mills (2002, 76) has suggested, "Population size is an important linchpin to arguments for the complexity of Chaco social and political organization." I consider this issue first.

The Population of Chaco Great Houses

I reject proposals that most great houses had a small number of inhabitants. The evidence used to support that interpretation is questionable for two reasons. Both Windes's and Bernardini's analyses, the former based on the number of documented hearths as an index of households and the latter on the identification of residential suites as suggested by connections between rooms (doorways or roof hatches), rely heavily on first-floor architecture at Bonito or a small sample of excavated rooms at Pueblo Alto. At Bonito, both Windes and Bernardini suggest a larger early population that decreased markedly through time. Windes (1984, 83) proposes a maximum population of one hundred people, Bernardini (1999, 449) no more than seventy.

These conclusions are not surprising given the estimation methods employed. Early Bonito was largely a single story and thus room-floors and features, as well as lateral connections between rooms, were preserved and documented by excavations. In subsequent periods when multistory architecture became typical, evidence of either hearths or room connectivity was unlikely to have been found given (a) the collapse of most roofs/upper floors, the specific places where connections between rooms or the presence of hearths were most likely in multistory pueblos (Bustard 2003, 92; Mills 2002, 76) and (b) the coarse excavation methods—removal by pick and shovel—employed by Pepper and Judd when clearing collapsed upper-story rubble from lower-floor rooms.

Judd's discussion of Bonito architecture (1964, 86, 100, 128, 194, *passim*) also repeatedly emphasizes the extent to which building episodes at Bonito destroyed prior construction: "Demolition, reconstruction, and replacement are everywhere evident" (100). The result is that a significant proportion of the rooms built at Bonito were demolished during subsequent building episodes. Such frequent demolition and renovation makes estimates of population through time difficult.

At Pueblo Alto, a single-story great house where Windes (1987, 391) has estimated a resident population of twenty-five to fifty people, the primary issue is the small number of rooms excavated, approximately a dozen. Even accepting his conservative conclusion that only two were habitation units (385), when we take sampling error into account, the resulting 95 percent confidence interval ranges from a low of three estimated habitation units to a high of forty-three (Plog and Watson 2012, 463). We thus have no firm basis to conclude that the resident population of Pueblo Alto was as small as Windes proposes.

I expect that Chaco great houses served multiple functions and that activities within them were diverse. Some portions of Bonito were unquestionably ceremonial in nature, some served as mortuary crypts, and some as storage for sacred materials and food; some may have been specialized production spaces, and the latest rooms may have been built largely as display behavior. Nevertheless, I suggest there is enough evidence in the form of hearths and hatchways in the limited number of preserved upper-floor rooms, upper-story walls covered with soot from the frequent use of hearths, and the contents of rooms to suggest a higher residential population at Pueblo Bonito (perhaps two hundred to four hundred people) during most of the occupation of the great house.

Although Bonito has sometimes been described as having many empty rooms, Neitzel's (2003a, 124) study of artifact frequencies and distributions "should lay to rest the notion that with the exception of a few highly prolific burial and storage rooms, Pueblo Bonito was an empty site artifactually." As we entered room-by-room artifact information into the Chaco Research Archive (http://www.chacoarchive.org), we reached the same conclusion. A study by Heitman (2016) based on data from the archive, for example, has shown that minimally a thousand pieces of ground stone were recovered at Bonito, a finding inconsistent with a small residential population. Finally, I suggest that Crown's (2016) study of the Bonito mounds also supports a more substantial population at Pueblo Bonito, as she found that ceramic discard rates in the mounds "suggest an overall pattern of primarily normal domestic trash" (231) that is equivalent to discard rates at other sites throughout the canyon (234). Crown concludes that "the accumulation of material relative to other sites in the canyon indicates that the inhabitants of Pueblo Bonito included many households discarding trash at a regular rate during the life of the mounds" (237).

Architectural, feature, and artifactual data thus suggest that the population estimates of Windes and Bernardini are too low. Nevertheless, we lack the analyses needed to provide more reliable estimates, particularly ones that assess population change through time. To achieve that goal, intensive room-by-room studies examining multiple lines of evidence are needed.

Continuity and Analogy/Homology

Although no one doubts that some historic Pueblo peoples descend from the people of Chaco Canyon, some scholars question the degree of continuity between past and present and thus whether Pueblo ethnography is relevant to

Chaco. Wills (2000, 21), for example, states, "It seems paradoxical that archaeologists should find in Chacoan great houses evidence for a ritual organization indistinct from modern Pueblos. For one thing, there are no ethnographic examples of communal production in Pueblo communities involving large and protracted labor organization." Lekson (2006b) also rejects a historical perspective, though for a different reason: "Pueblos did not *develop from* Chaco; rather, they represent a *reaction against* Chaco. . . . The remarkable shifts in Pueblo architecture, settlement, iconography, and society around 1300, when sites begin to look like modern pueblos, represent Pueblo peoples' conscious, deliberate reaction to and rejection of Chaco, distancing themselves from that bad experience" (29, emphases in original).

My own views fall between those expressed by Wills and Lekson. I reject the latter's notion that Pueblo history after 1300 CE was a reaction against an alleged "bad experience" in Chaco. Certainly, Pueblo history changed dramatically due to multiple waves of depopulation over the northern Southwest between 1110 and 1450 CE, but those changes can be observed across most of the Pueblo world, not just in the Chacoan region. Puebloan peoples everywhere were exploring new and varied organizational solutions to the challenges they faced.

Nevertheless, despite the discontinuities that Wills rightly emphasizes and that need to be accounted for, archaeological evidence also reveals significant continuity between past and present not only in characteristics such as subsistence and aspects of pueblo architecture, but also in core components of Pueblo symbolism, ritual, and cosmology (e.g., Heitman 2015; Plog 2012; Plog and Heitman 2010; Whiteley 2015). The National Park Service has found no shortage of Pueblo groups whose oral histories emphasize their ancestral ties to Chaco. There was a connection between past and present; the question is how tangled that path may have been.

I thus concur with those (Ware 2014; Whiteley 2004, 2015) who conclude that knowledge of Pueblo ethnographies is critical to understanding Chaco and the prehistoric Pueblo Southwest, that we should view Chaco from a historical perspective, and that historic Pueblo societies provide homologies as opposed to analogies. As Eggan (1991, 107) succinctly stated, "not to use ethnographic evidence is to cut oneself off from a major source of information." I further agree with Ware (2014) that, in particular, archaeologists must become more familiar with Eastern Pueblo ethnographies in order to escape the overly common application of Hopi models to Chaco (Heitman and Plog 2005), the frequent belief among archaeologists that the Pueblos are egalitarian, and the too-common separation of ritual and political power by archaeologists as well as some ethnographers (Whiteley 1987, 696–97).

I have no objection, however, to cross-cultural analogies drawn from any area of the world. What matters most, from my perspective, is not the source of a model or interpretation, but whether we find archaeological information that supports or rejects that model. Models drawn from Pueblo history must never be neglected, but they must also be evaluated against the archaeological record in order to avoid simply imposing the ethnographic present on the past. Disparities between Chaco and historic-era Pueblos noted by Wills, for example, suggest that aspects of Chaco social history have no subsequent parallel among the historic Pueblos, East or West. The density of Chaco great houses was never again duplicated, nor was their remarkable architecture. Similarly, there are dimensions of Chaco mortuary behavior that depart from what we know about similar historic practices (Plog 2012). We thus must become better informed about the historic Pueblos, particularly the diversity among them that Ware has presented so effectively, but we should also be cautious and always seek archaeological data that allow us to evaluate the extent to which Pueblo ethnography helps model Chaco social history.

DIMENSIONS OF CHACO SOCIAL ORGANIZATION

Descent and Residence

Most discussions of Chaco have either assumed or, in a few cases, argued based on analysis of data that the initial "unit pueblos" or "Prudden units" were matrilineal, based on logic similar to that outlined decades ago by Steward (1937). Most have also suggested that the early, but much larger, pueblos of southwestern Colorado and Chaco were matrilocal and matrilineal (e.g., Peregrine 2001; Ware 2014, 111–12, 114). Chaco great houses are also often hypothesized to have been composed of matrilineal descent groups (e.g., Peregrine 2001; Ware 2014, 122, 125).

Initial efforts to provide empirical support for the nature of descent in Chaco have been based on indirect methods. A 2017 study, however, that examined the mitochondrial and nuclear DNA of nine of the burials in Room 33, including the two earliest ones with the rich assemblages of grave goods, demonstrates that those individuals had the same mitochondrial DNA and thus were members of the same matriline (Kennett et al. 2017). Nuclear DNA of a smaller number of individuals revealed even closer ties, with possible mother–daughter and grandmother–grandson relationships between two different burial pairs. The nine burials were interred over at least three centuries, demonstrating that the matrilineage was maintained throughout the occupation of Pueblo Bonito, a remarkably long time period. It is thus clear that matrilineages were a key component of Chacoan organization. Moreover, the association of the Room 33 matriline with such substantial amounts of turquoise and shell and in close proximity to other rooms with a macaw aviary and large caches—found in no other Chaco settlement in or outside the canyon—of ~250 to 300 wooden ceremonial staffs and ~115 cylindrical vessels used for the consumption of a beverage based on cacao, strongly suggests it was an elite matriline with substantial control over life in Bonito for three centuries. This evidence supports earlier hypotheses (Plog and Heitman 2010; Watson et al. 2015) that Chaco was a hierarchical society.

Dualism and Moieties

Fox (1967, 31–32, emphasis in original) was perhaps the first to suggest explicitly that Chacoan society had a dualistic dimension: "The Anasazi peoples practised irrigation and built huge communal houses. Chaco towns have two large *Kivas*. It is not impossible that a moiety system was some sort of response to these conditions." He later added, assuming a tie between the Keres and Chaco, that Chaco had "quite extensive, even if primitive, irrigation works. If, as Wittfogel and Goldfrank suggest, communal activity and hydraulic economy are conducive to a moiety system, then the preexisting system may have been reinforced in these conditions" (189–90).

Subsequent scholars (Fritz 1978, 1987; Heitman and Plog 2005; Vivian 1970, 1990; Van Dyke 2004; Whiteley 2015) have also highlighted dualism in canyon architecture and settlement distributions. Fritz, for example, identifies symmetrical patterns in the distributions of the internal features of great kivas (primarily Casa Rinconada) and the architectural patterns of Pueblo Bonito and Chetro Ketl, including the distribution of paired great and small kivas at Pueblo Bonito (1987, 320–23). Fritz further notes that an axis defined by the location of Casa Rinconada and the midpoint between Pueblo Bonito and Chetro Ketl divides the canyon, with a roughly equal number of great houses in each half (323–24; see also Van Dyke 2004). He then speculates that "there may be a one-to-one correspondence between social units repeated in the great kiva, great house, and canyon" and, more specifically, hypothesizes that within great houses these may have been moieties, with similar "groups . . . symbolically located in either half of the valley and great kiva" (324).

The hypothesis of moieties as a key organizational dimension of Chaco has also been proposed by Vivian (1970, 1990). Although he offered this hypothesis as one to be tested, he also highlighted a few known aspects of Pueblo Bonito consistent with a dual division such as the eastern and western "wings" extending off of the original northern core of Bonito (also present at many other Chaco great houses), the presence of one or two great kivas at some great houses, and two discrete burial areas in Pueblo Bonito (1970, 80–81).

Heitman and Plog (2005) also state (cf. Vivian 1970) that the dual mortuary crypts in Bonito may suggest emergent dualism or moiety organization materialized through the burial of important ancestors. This proposition is consistent with different frequencies of materials found in the crypts, with turquoise and shell being orders of magnitude more abundant in the northern mortuary cluster than the west. Flutes occur exclusively in the northern burial cluster, whereas bifurcate baskets and ceramic representations of those baskets are found only in the western cluster. On the other hand, the much larger number of individuals interred in the western cluster is less consistent with a moiety organization, where one would expect similar numbers of individuals to be interred in each crypt. It is possible that the moieties were not equal, but one was ranked higher than the other, with membership in the higher-ranking group more restrictive. However, I would now suggest that the disparity is significant enough to raise questions about interpreting the two discrete burial areas as the product of moieties.

More recently, Whiteley (2015) has highlighted other dimensions of dualism in Chaco and historic pueblos, noting that dualism is particularly evident in some of the later great houses such as Wijiji and Hungo Pavi, which have two great (or very large) kivas along with few or, in the case of Wijiji, no smaller kivas. This pattern contrasts markedly with Pueblo Bonito, where there are multiple small kivas in addition to one or two contemporary great kivas, as well as a row of rooms separating the plaza into eastern and western halves. Whiteley (2015, 273) proposes a new and promising way of interpreting such variation in the canyon, noting that Native American architecture "typically incorporates conscious symbolic projections of social structural forms" and that much Chaco architecture reflects deliberate alignments. He further emphasizes that "*kinship* provided the 'idiom' and structures for social organization and social reproduction in all societies prior to (and in many cases after) the development of full-fledged social stratification. Structurally, some key kinship system types represent markedly dual and plural forms, and the latter especially seem to occupy a cusp of sociopolitical complexity" (280). To oversimplify a complex argument, Whiteley ties this dual-plural complex to Iroquois and Crow-Omaha kinship systems and suggests that "the formation of new colonies" (as represented, for example, by Wijiji[6]) "could successfully deploy oscillating dual-plural modalities to maintain and extend social networks" (299). This accounts for temporal dynamics in Chaco in a manner not possible with simple structural-functional classifications.

I should emphasize that aspects of dualism occur in all Pueblo groups, East and West, as well as many other Amerindian groups (Whiteley 2015); thus, evidence for dualism alone cannot necessarily be regarded as evidence for the existence of moieties. Nevertheless, there seems to be more evidence of dualism in Chaco than in most regions of the Southwest prior to 1130 CE.

Sodalities

Ware (2014) has suggested that the "germs" or "roots" of sodalities emerged in the Eastern Pueblo region during the eighth century. He equates the emergence of sodalities with the appearance of kivas in the eighth and ninth centuries and suggests they initially offered a place for the dispersed avunculate of matrilineal groups to "meet and fulfill their lineage responsibilities away from the prying eyes of their sisters' resident husbands" (94). The change from kin-based ceremonial-political organization to a focus on sodalities is then hypothesized to have "coincided with the early development of 'lineage kivas' during the 700s and 800s" and "is best understood in terms of the dynamics of multidescent matrilineal communities and the emergence of male interest groups centered on the ritual avunculate" (93).

In Chaco, Ware (2014, 122; see also 131) suggests that the ninth- and early tenth-century system of "descent group ranking . . . validated by communal ritual" broke down in the early to mid-1000s as great houses became largely ritual rather than domestic structures. Ware then argues that "changes after AD 1040 mark the incipient crystallization of Eastern-Pueblo-style, sodality-based organizations on the plateau. That is, Chaco Canyon shifted from closed, kin-based leadership to open, sodality-based leadership once the existing sodalities managed to detach themselves from the kinship system" (122–23). Ware further suggests this argument "is strengthened by burials with ceremonial staffs, shell trumpets, bear paws, and cloth-wrapped cactus stalks at Pueblo Bonito" (123).

Given the size of some great houses and the frequency of kivas in Chaco, the proposal that sodalities may have been present is certainly plausible, perhaps even more so in light of Whiteley's (2015) emphasis on the pluralism at Bonito in contrast to some other great houses. We should ask, however, about empirical evidence. First, the revised chronology for Chaco (above) is inconsistent with Ware's argument. The acquisition of macaws and likely cacao, for example, did not begin in the Classic Bonito phase as he suggests (Ware 2014, 126), but much earlier. An architectural transformation certainly occurred in Chaco around 1030 CE, but many of the other once-accepted Classic Bonito characteristics, whether macaws or turquoise, began much earlier.

Second, the new DNA evidence demonstrates that matrilineages likely remained significant throughout the history of Bonito. Sodalities may have coexisted with the matrilineages and had important roles, but the DNA data do not support the hypothesis of a *shift* from "closed, kin-based leadership to open, sodality-based leadership" as Ware (2014, 122–23) proposes. The coexistence and importance of both sodalities and important kin groups is possible, however. At Hopi, for example, sodality membership crosscuts kin groups, but ownership of kivas, key ritual knowledge, and ritual paraphernalia are often controlled by the elite lineages of clans.

Third, some of Ware's statements about associations of artifacts with particular burials are inaccurate. A shell trumpet was found with only one burial (Burial 14 in Room 33). Wooden staffs may have accompanied some burials,[7] but the bulk of these staffs were cached in the northwest corner of Room 32, with a handful in the ceiling of Room 33. There were no bear claws in association with burials and the one cloth-wrapped cactus stalk was found in Room 32, not in direct association with the one partial individual found in the room. Mortuary goods were dominated by turquoise and shell ornaments in the richest burials, while primarily ceramic vessels or baskets accompanied most other interments.

Beyond the materials that Ware postulated to be associated with sodalities, but that do not support his proposal, we must ask what other types of evidence would support the hypothesized emergence of sodalities. This is admittedly a difficult question to answer given the many types of Pueblo sodalities, but it is one that must be addressed in order to test Ware's hypothesis. If, for example, medicine societies, which are among the most powerful sodalities in the historic Eastern Pueblos, emerged in Chaco, we might expect to find bones or claws from animals such as bears, badgers, or mountain lions; fetishes of them made from stone; or representations of them in ceramics in multiple kivas or special masonry rooms (Stirling 1942; White 1930).

The virtually complete excavation of Pueblo Bonito, along with the excellent preservation of material, makes the site a good case study. A search of the Chaco Research Archive database, however, demonstrates that the objects listed above are rare at Bonito.[8] Faunal remains from bears are the most common item with skeletal elements, including foot bones in two instances, found in as many as eight masonry rooms and the Bonito mounds. No stone or ceramic images of bears are reported in fieldnotes or catalogs. The primary concentration of bear remains, notably all parts of the paw or foot, was in Great Kiva Q (at least some and perhaps all found enclosed within the north wall) (Judd 1954, 323), where Judd found seventy-six proximal phalanges, four claws, four metatarsals, eight metacarpals, "26 disunited digital extremities," and twenty-seven sesamoid bones (like those found in paws) from black bears (*Euarctos americanus*). Skeletal elements from bear paws were thus remarkably abundant in Kiva Q, but bear bones were present in only small numbers elsewhere in the pueblo. No tree-ring dates are available for Kiva Q, unfortunately. Judd characterizes it as having third-style masonry, suggesting it was constructed post–1030 CE. Windes (2003, 21) regards it as having been constructed in the 1040s.

Claws of the mountain lion were also found in the north wall of Kiva Q (Judd 1954, 323). In addition, a single claw from a possible cat was excavated in one masonry room of Bonito. No stone fetishes of cats were documented. Badger remains, including one skull and half of a lower jaw, were recovered in five masonry rooms and a single badger effigy handle (ceramic) was found in one kiva. No stone fetishes of badgers were identified. Thus, animals that are often important to medicine societies are rare and do not suggest comparable types of activities at Pueblo Bonito. In addition, parts of such animals have been known to be associated with kin groups as well as sodalities (Peter Whiteley, personal communication).

It is also worth noting that the remarkable cache of wooden ritual objects found at Chetro Ketl, the next-largest great house in Chaco Canyon, contained primarily images of birds or flowers; bears, mountains lions, badgers, and other animals were not represented (Vivian, Dodgen, and Hartmann 1978). Furthermore, birds (possibly ducks), frogs, and tadpoles were by far the most commonly represented animals in the ornaments (and pottery, in the case of birds) from Pueblo Bonito (Pepper 1920; Plog 2012). The common iconography of the great houses thus rarely included the most potent animals associated with Pueblo medicine societies. Such iconography could be an indication of a different type of sodality from medicine societies known historically, but could also be associated with important matrilineages, and so do not provide the type of unambiguous test that is desirable. We thus have no clear-cut evidence to support the hypothesis that sodality leadership replaced kin-group leadership at Chaco. Nevertheless, I should emphasize that there has been remarkably little study of specific aspects of Chaco ritual, especially of variation among kiva architecture and material contents.

Authority and Hierarchy

With respect to sociopolitical inequality, viewpoints run the gamut, from Chaco as egalitarian, corporate, and consensual, and primarily a ritual center (e.g., Renfrew 2001; Van Dyke 2008) to Chaco as a centralized hierarchy with "lords" or "kings" (Lekson 2006c, 2008). Perhaps most common are statements (e.g., Toll 2006, 138) that there is little evidence of status differences or hierarchy except for a short period after 1040–1050 CE. The latter qualification typically refers to two burials in Room 33 of Pueblo Bonito containing elaborate grave goods, including exceptional amounts of turquoise and shell, and the earlier belief that they postdated 1030–1040 CE (fig. 11.3).

I suggest that the hypothesis of a short, but late period of hierarchy was the consensus view in the late twentieth and early twenty-first century. Nonetheless, since the mid-1970s, a small but increasing number of archaeologists have proposed that Chacoan society was hierarchical in nature or had some type of institutionalized leadership over a long period (e.g., Akins 2001, 2003; Grebinger 1973; Heitman 2015; Plog and Heitman 2010; Schelberg 1992; 2006; Watson 2012; Watson et al. 2015). Some arguments for hierarchy have emphasized either the variation in the size of great houses or the dichotomy between great and small houses, but the crux of much of the debate has primarily involved different interpretations of the mortuary remains from Room 33 in Pueblo Bonito, along with dating of the acquisition of macaws and large amounts of turquoise and shell. Akins (2001, 2003) and Sebastian (1992) are among the few who have suggested that the interments occurred over several centuries. As emphasized earlier, however, most Chaco scholars assumed that all the burials postdated

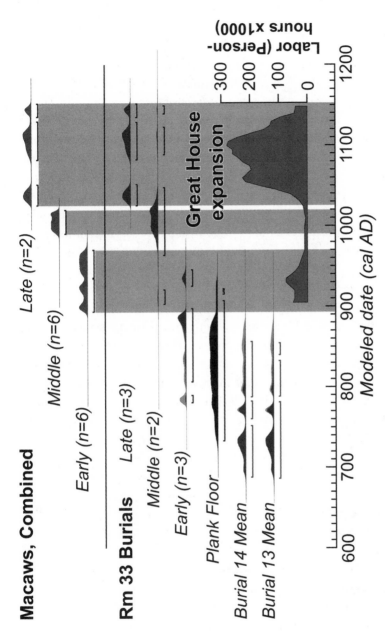

Figure 11.3. Modeled distributions of AMS ¹⁴C dates on Pueblo Bonito macaws (Watson et al. 2015) as well as human burial dates from Room 33 (Plog and Heitman 2010) relative to total construction effort in Chaco Canyon (Lekson 1984). Macaws and above-floor burials were grouped and combined in Oxcal based on ¹⁴C ages, and stratigraphic data from Room 33 were incorporated. Created by Thomas Harper; from Watson et al. 2015.

1030–1040 CE and that the abundance of turquoise and shell with Burials 13 and 14 and the macaws found elsewhere in Bonito had not been acquired or produced in large amounts until after the major increase in building activity at 1030–1040 CE. Most also concluded that all the individuals buried in the northern and western crypts had been interred after that date.

Recent AMS dating confirms that the burials occurred over a long period, beginning in the northern cluster by the late eighth or early ninth century and somewhat later in the western cluster, and continuing into the late tenth or early eleventh century (Plog and Heitman 2010; Kennett et al. 2017). We also now know that macaws (Watson et al. 2015), shell, and turquoise were acquired in large amounts prior to 1040 CE. Two recent analyses of Room 33 and nearby structures in the early, northern section of Bonito have suggested it was symbolically and ritually significant, perhaps representing a microcosm of Pueblo cosmology (Plog and Heitman 2010) and the "axis mundi" of the Chacoan world (Ashmore 2007).

Burials 13 and 14 in Room 33, both interred by the early ninth century beneath a floor of carefully shaped wooden planks—perhaps symbolizing an underworld-upperworld division—were accompanied by large amounts of ceremonially important material. Although these goods have been regarded as primarily religious, leading to the inference that any power they indexed was ritual, many have noted that in Pueblo ethnography, "the control of ritual goes hand in hand with the control of prime farmland" (Ware 2014, 110). Ritual power can thus not be separated from economic or political power.

There may be an emerging consensus that Chaco was more hierarchical than suggested by most models proposed in the 1980s through the early 2000s. House theory as originally proposed by Lévi-Strauss (1982) and elaborated by others (e.g., Helms 1998; McKinnon 1991) has played an important role in the new interpretations of both the mortuary and settlement data. (See Heitman and Plog 2005; Heitman 2015; Mills 2015; Plog and Heitman 2010; and Whiteley 2015 for more in-depth discussions of house theory.)

Using house theory, some (Heitman and Plog 2005; Plog and Heitman 2010) have proposed that the northern mortuary crypt and nearby rooms in the early northern core of Pueblo Bonito may demonstrate the control of ritual paraphernalia and knowledge by the highest-ranking house group at Bonito given the material remains from these rooms described earlier. As noted above, Great Kiva Q is also very close to these rooms. Given the DNA evidence, any elite Chaco house group would have a matrilineal core. One advantage of house theory, however, is that it also allows for the inclusion of affines and recruited non-kin, as demonstrated by many ethnographic examples.

Plog and Heitman (2010) also proposed that the two individuals buried beneath the wooden floor in the crypt were among the original founders of Pueblo Bonito and thus controlled the prime farmland at the intersection of Chaco Wash and South Gap. Subsequently, the highest-ranking descendants of these founders may have led the house group for periods of time and been buried after death in Room 33, above the wood floor, over a three-hundred-year period. The AMS radiocarbon dates are consistent with such a pattern of periodic interments (Kennett et al. 2017). An elite northern house group thus may have controlled Bonito throughout most of the occupation of the great house.

Conclusions

We are entering an exciting new period in the study of Chaco Canyon. New analytical methods in combination with alternative theoretical approaches and a reemphasis on social organization, kinship, and social history have led to a transformation in our knowledge of Chaco cultural history and ways of understanding that history. There remains no consensus among Chaco scholars, but I believe we are not only asking exciting questions from new perspectives, but also seeking the empirical evidence needed to evaluate alternative answers to those questions. My hope is that the present summary will continue to be elaborated upon and revised within the next decade after more new studies are conducted—theoretical, historical, and empirical.

Notes

1. These dates are available at: http://www.chacoarchive.org/cra/chaco-resources /tree-ring-database/.

2. The ornaments from Canyon de Chelly include turquoise mosaics (Morris 1925) of the sort also present with Burial 14.

3. The total is from a Chaco Research Archive database query (http://www .chacoarchive.org/cra/query-the-database/), January 27, 2016, of Pueblo del Arroyo artifacts, searching for "minerals" as material type and "turquoise" as a material subtype. Artifact entries for each room are based on catalog records and, frequently, uncataloged materials mentioned in Judd's notecards for each room.

4. Chaco Research Archive database query, January 27, 2016.

5. There was, however, no "piling up" of great houses "in downtown Chaco" in the ninth century (Ware 2014, 117), when groups from southwestern Colorado may have migrated south to Chaco. Pueblo Bonito was the *only* great house in downtown Chaco in the ninth and early tenth centuries.

6. Many scholars believe Wijiji may never have been occupied because of minimal artifact deposition at the site. Nevertheless, the construction of Wijiji appears to have been complete, so that we can identify the number of rooms and kivas. Even if never occupied, the architectural pattern at Wijiji is still consistent with Whiteley's hypothesis.

7. There are many broken ceremonial staffs in Room 33, but Pepper's notes and publications do not record any associated directly with burials. Nevertheless, given the significant disturbance caused by the continual interment of individuals in such a small room, we cannot rule out the possibility that some of the wooden staffs were once associated with the burials.

8. Chaco Research Archive database query, January 27, 2016.

CHAPTER TWELVE

Afterword

Reimagining Archaeology as Anthropology

JOHN A. WARE

In the nearly half-century (forty-six years, to be exact) that elapsed between the SAR seminar that resulted in *New Perspectives on the Pueblos* (Ortiz 1972) and the one that gave birth to the present volume, Pueblo research has gone through a transformation. In *New Perspectives*, eleven chapters dealt with various aspects of Pueblo ethnography and only one was devoted to precolonial history—and that chapter apparently grew, as something of an afterthought, out of debates surrounding Richard Ford's contributed paper on "Immigration, Irrigation, and Warfare" (Eggan 1972, 289–90). By contrast, the current volume deals overwhelmingly with archaeological and historical subjects. Why the shift in emphasis?

In the years since Ortiz's "New Perspectives" seminar in 1969, ethnographic research on the Pueblos has come to a virtual standstill. Since the 1980s Pueblo ethnographers have focused mostly on ethnohistorical data or their research has been explicitly collaborative in nature, dealing with land claims, water rights, and other tribal interests (Brandt 2002). Meanwhile, Pueblo archaeological research has grown exponentially, thanks in part to historic-preservation laws enacted in the second half of the last century that provided funds for thousands of archaeological research projects in the northern Southwest. As archaeology assumed the lead in research, a chasm opened up between Pueblo ethnography and archaeology. Each year there are fewer ethnographers conducting research in the Pueblo Southwest and archaeologists have increasingly turned away from the ethnographic data corpus as they probe deeper into the details of precolonial Pueblo history. One of the goals of the 2015 SAR "Puebloan Societies" Advanced Seminar was to bridge this chasm by bringing ethnographers and archaeologists together to discuss issues of mutual interest and concern.

My task in this chapter is to review and synthesize a few of the central themes that emerged during our discussions in Santa Fe. Embedded within the thematic discussions are comments on individual chapters. I should be clear at the outset that this review is deeply biased. I agree wholeheartedly with our session organizer and volume editor, Peter Whiteley, who has argued for years that a serious dialogue between Southwestern archaeology and ethnology has been neglected for far too long, "to the analytical impoverishment of both disciplines" (e.g., Whiteley 2004). Pueblo archaeology's interest in the Pueblo ethnographies has waxed and waned as ethnographic analogy has come into and out of fashion, but as Whiteley points out (chapter 1), the ethnographic Pueblos are more than simple analogs for the Pueblo past. The ethnographic Pueblos are the principal descendants of precolonial Pueblo populations, so a strong case can be made that Pueblo *homology* and the direct historical approach should be privileged over simple analogy. Because Pueblo ethnographies represent the outcomes of trajectories of change that often began in deep history, knowing the ethnographic "destination" allows archaeologists to trace those trajectories to their historical roots in the past, and in the process gain a much deeper understanding of Pueblo prehistory. This is especially useful for reconstructing past practices and institutions that left behind few unambiguous material remains, such as social organization and religion, two of the most important themes to come out of our Santa Fe discussions.

Needless to say, historical perspectives are equally valuable to the comparative ethnographer. Lacking diachronic data from the past, ethnographers often resort to functional explanations of ethnographic variation. But, of course, historical contingencies profoundly shape all historical outcomes, so a detailed knowledge of cultural history is essential if we are to achieve one of the iconic goals of anthropology, the explanation of cultural differences and similarities.

I begin this review with a discussion of kinship, one of the principal themes of the SAR discussions. From there I move on to Pueblo ritual and religion, and conclude with a look at the multiethnic character of Pueblo communities and its implications for understanding the history of Pueblo migrations and social integration. Many more themes emerged during the seminar in Santa Fe, so my discussion is hardly comprehensive. The following themes impressed me as especially important for ongoing research on the Pueblos, but the choice of themes also reflects my particular interest in Pueblo social organization and social history. Throughout the chapter, when I refer to "contemporary" Pueblos I am referencing mainly the Pueblo ethnographies that were compiled during the first half of the twentieth century.

Kinship

Kinship studies, in decline in social anthropology since the 1970s, are a virtual nonsubject in archaeology. So why, in a volume dominated by archaeological chapters, did kinship emerge as an important theme? Perhaps the ever-hopeful proddings of our colleague Peter Whiteley have found their mark at last! Or perhaps archaeologists are finally willing to acknowledge that kinship is the principal idiom of social and political relations in nonstate societies, so if we are to truly understand social practices in deep history, we need to become more fluent in kinship theory. This is not to deny that inferences about prehistoric kinship systems are fraught with interpretive challenges. They most certainly are. However, data on precolonial architecture—the material containers of kin-based groups—along with settlement and community patterns and the historical insights of Pueblo homology, may help us turn possibilities into probabilities. And as the chapters by Whiteley (5) and Hill (6) demonstrate, analyses of contemporary kinship terminologies also provide valuable insights into past kinship practices, as do analyses of prehistoric genomic data (Kennett et al. 2017). For those who have not encountered a kinship diagram since their undergraduate days, some historical background may be helpful.

Mid-twentieth-century kinship studies were framed by discipline-wide debates over the relative importance of descent versus marriage in the shaping of kinship systems. In the first half of the century many scholars of kinship took their theoretical lead from British anthropologists, whose work in Africa convinced them that the stable functioning of nonstate societies required corporate kin groups based on an ideology of unilineal descent. Such groups have unambiguous social boundaries and continuity through time and can therefore act as corporations to control both people and heritable property in societies that lack formal political institutions. Much of the early work among the Southwestern Pueblos was influenced by descent theorists such as A. R. Radcliffe-Brown, who taught a generation of American anthropologists at the University of Chicago in the 1930s. The influence of British structural-functionalism helps explain why there was such a strong emphasis in early studies on lineages and clans among the Western Pueblos and the "lapse" of such organizations in the east (e.g., Eggan 1950).

The principal challenge to descent theory came out of the fertile mind of French anthropologist Claude Lévi-Strauss (1949), who argued that marriage alliance, not descent, formed the irreducible atom of human kinship systems.

The incest taboo is generally considered to be a negative prohibition, but Lévi-Strauss showed that when the taboo was combined with reciprocal gift exchange, it had the positive effect of creating the most basic of all kinship equations. The exchange of women between groups of men was nothing less, Lévi-Strauss argued, than our species' transition from nature to culture. Robin Fox was the first anthropologist to bring alliance theory to the Pueblo Southwest when he challenged Eggan's "Keresan bridge" hypothesis. Fox argued that Keresan moieties were not the result of the breakdown of an ancient lineage system, as Eggan had proposed, but the remnants of a reciprocal alliance system involving two exogamous patrimoieties (1967). More recently, Peter Whiteley (e.g., 2008, 2012) has applied alliance theory to archetypal Hopi descent groups and found strong evidence of marriage preferences linking Hopi clans and clan-sets in repetitive alliance patterns that had escaped the notice of earlier investigators. And in this book, Whiteley amplifies Fox's hypothesis to argue that elementary alliance systems probably underlie *all* Pueblo kinship systems.

Four chapters in this volume deal with various aspects of Pueblo kinship systems. Dick Ford describes and discusses the Tewa *ma:tu'in*, the traditional ambilocal extended family that is so central to Rio Grande Tewa kinship and community structure (and is decidedly not a "clan"); Triloki Pandey addresses the effects of twentieth-century market economy forces on traditional Zuni household structure, and he also reflects on the relevance of lineage theory to understanding Zuni social organization; and the two chapters by Peter Whiteley and Jane Hill infer characteristics of precolonial Pueblo kinship systems on the basis of contemporary Pueblo kinship terminologies. The last two papers, in particular, are potentially transformative and therefore merit special comment. Whiteley's analysis especially provides a new perspective on the evolution of Pueblo kinship systems, so most of my comments will focus there.

Whiteley begins by contrasting the two dominant theories of East–West Pueblo social divergence. Fred Eggan's (1950) descent-based model argued that the shift from classificatory lineage-based kinship systems of the Western Pueblos to the descriptive bilateral systems of the Eastern Pueblos was the result of destabilizing migrations off the plateau and Spanish acculturation effects. According to Eggan, Eastern Pueblo moieties arose as a simple organizational solution among Pueblo migrants whose lineage and clan systems had lapsed. Alfonso Ortiz (1969) challenged Eggan's hypothesis, arguing that the dual divisions of the Tewa—and by inference the other Tanoan Pueblos—were part of the ritual organization, as opposed to the kinship system, and likely had deep roots in the Pueblo past, since they were so central to contemporary Tewa social organization. In this volume, Whiteley uses alliance theory and data from surviving Pueblo kin-terminologies to construct an alternative hypothesis for east–west divergence.

Whiteley calls our attention to the strong correlation seen worldwide between *crossness*, the terminological distinction between cross and parallel relatives,[1] and exogamous moieties, the dual community and tribal divisions that govern restricted marriage exchange in so many nonstate societies. Exogamous moieties are common in Dravidian kinship systems (Trautmann 1981), where prescriptive cross-cousin marriage is encoded in the kin-terminology, and moieties remain common in Iroquois systems where crossness is preserved in the terminology but marriage to a cross-relative is no longer specified directly by the terminology (however, marriage with a classificatory cross-cousin may still be the norm). Whiteley is able to document terminological traces of crossness in all Tanoan-speaking groups—even the most thoroughly bilateral Northern Tiwa—and on this basis he advances two compelling hypotheses: first, that a Dravidian/Iroquois elementary kinship structure underlies all Pueblos, West as well as East, and second, that the nonexogamous ritual moieties of the Rio Grande Pueblos likely grew out of exogamous moieties. (Fox [1967], of course, made a similar case for the Rio Grande Keres.) Whiteley's arguments challenge several iconic assumptions about Western and Eastern Pueblo differences. Against expectation, for example, he finds deep dualist structures in Hopi kinship in the form of marriage alliances between paired clan-sets, and these marriage patterns converge with various ritual dualities at Hopi to further diminish the distinctions typically drawn between the Eastern and Western Pueblos. He concludes that Western Pueblo Crow terminologies may be an overlay on a Dravidian/Iroquois base that exhibits both elementary (dual) and semicomplex (plural) alliance strategies.

One of the more intriguing of Whiteley's proposals comes from his detailed study of the kin-terminology of the Western Tewa village of Hano, whose crossness and vertical *skewing*[2] terms conform closely to Hopi Crow kin-terminologies. Owing mostly to Dozier's work at Hano in the 1950s, the majority view for many years has been that Hopi and Hano kinship systems converged as a result of extensive intermarriage between the two groups. However, some early investigators, including Barbara Freire-Marreco and Alfred Kroeber, believed that seventeenth-century Arizona Tewa terminologies were closer to an ancestral Iroquois/Crow root and that the Rio Grande Tewa shifted more recently toward a descriptive bilateral terminology under acculturative influence from the Spanish. Whiteley comes down firmly on the side of these earlier investigators. Let me comment first on his Hopi-Tewa "flyover" theory (an obvious play on Eggan's Keresan bridge), and then address his ideas about exogamous and ritual moieties.

I agree with Whiteley (and Eggan and many others) that Euroamerican acculturation, including Spanish-Pueblo intermarriage and the imposition of Roman Catholic marriage restrictions, likely influenced the descriptive bilateral shift among the Rio Grande Tewa, although, as Whiteley acknowledges, the lack of a comparable shift among the Rio Grande Keresans remains troubling and requires further study. Whiteley argues that Hano is closer to its Ancestral Tewa classificatory kin-terminology because it was beyond direct Spanish influence following Tewa migrations to Hopi in the 1690s CE. Needless to say, this presumes that all Tewa-speakers on the Rio Grande were still at least partly enmeshed in Iroquois and perhaps Crow (see Hill, this volume) classificatory alliance patterns through the end of the seventeenth century, so most of the bilateral-descriptive shift in the east evolved fully in the roughly three hundred years separating the Spanish conquest and the first anthropological descriptions of the Tewa in the early twentieth century. That endogamous communities would go through such a profound shift in just a dozen or so generations seems unlikely to me, although there are complicating facts that should be mentioned in Whiteley's favor. First, historic-period population losses on the Rio Grande may have favored exogamous marriages to prevent Pueblo communities from disappearing entirely. If many of these marriages were with local Hispanos, the descriptive bilateral shift would no doubt have been accelerated. Second, Eggan (1937a) argued for a very rapid, two-to-three-generation, descriptive bilateral shift among the matrilineal Choctaw of the Southeast. If that shift happened as quickly as Eggan claimed, my concerns about the rapidity of such a shift on the Rio Grande may be unwarranted.

The principal alternative to Whiteley's hypothesis is that the Tewa bilateral shift began much earlier and that intermarriage and acculturation encouraged the historic convergence of Arizona Tewa and Hopi kinship systems. Whiteley demurs, arguing that despite extensive intermarriage with the Hopi of First Mesa, Arizona Tewa kinship would not have "gone backward" from a descriptive to a classificatory system, citing Nick Allen's (2004) tetradic model that has clear directional implications. (Iroquois crossness without prescribed cross-cousin marriage was almost certainly preceded by Dravidian crossness *with* prescriptive marriage; Crow-Omaha crossness and skewing is almost certainly a later overlay on Iroquois crossness.) According to Whiteley, "in light of Allen's argument for evolutionary irreversibility, a hypothesis that Hano-Tewas preserved crossness, and perhaps also skewing, from their premigration Rio Grande ancestors seems worth investigating. And if that proves out, the full-fledged bilateralism and descriptivism of Eastern Tewa kin-terms likely postdates the Pueblo Revolt" (chapter 5, this volume). Elsewhere, Whiteley (2015) has argued for the reversibility of Crow-Omaha plural and Iroquois dual systems, and in fact, he suggests that Crow-Omaha is often an optative overlay on a basic Iroquois dual system. However, in Allen's model the shift from a descriptive to a classificatory system would likely pose a much greater challenge because it involves a major conceptual shift, from lineal-collateral to cross-parallel distinctions.[3]

Of course, if Dozier, Ortiz, and others are right that Tewa bilateralism has roots deeper than three hundred years, we are challenged to explain why the bilateral shift occurred in the first place. As one alternative, I have argued that the bilateral shift among Tanoans happened in part because of the rise of sodality-based polities in the east that undermined the residential base of unilineal groups (Ware 2014, 129). That is, as the land base and ceremonial status of corporate descent groups were usurped by emergent priesthoods, beginning perhaps as early as the eleventh century in Chaco, descent groups that lacked residential support were gradually eroded and eventually declined. The result would have been bilateral kindreds lacking discrete membership and continuity through time, precisely what we see in all Rio Grande Tanoan pueblos today (see Murdock 1949, 208–9). There is, in fact, some empirical archaeological support for this hypothesis. The unit pueblo, which some believe housed a localized descent group (e.g., Steward 1955), persisted up until the depopulation of the plateau in the late thirteenth century. But as migrants swelled the population of the Rio Grande in the 1300s–1400s, unit pueblos disappeared and were replaced by plaza-oriented pueblos, most with ladder-style roomblocks indicative of a coordinated communal labor force under central direction. Historically, of course, that central direction came from the priests and their appointed surrogates.

Whatever the case, it seems to me that Whiteley's model doesn't need Western Tewa kinship conservatism to make the point that most if not all Tanoan kinship systems retain elements of an antecedent classificatory system. In my judgment, that insight remains the critical contribution of this important paper.

Regarding Whiteley's hypothesis that Eastern Pueblo ritual moieties ultimately derive from exogamous moieties, I am intrigued but remain uncon-
vinced. (I am also not convinced by the moiety amalgamation models[4] that
seem to be in vogue among my archaeological colleagues on the Rio Grande,
despite the fact that amalgamation is woven into most Pueblo origin narratives,
e.g., Fowles 2005; Ortman, chapter 3, this volume.) Theories must align with
facts, and the fact is that all Eastern Pueblo ritual moieties are tribal sodalities
(Driver 1969, 345) that do not align with marriage systems and most articulate
with descent only through a *patrivirilateral*[5] recruitment principle. (In all Rio
Grande Pueblos with the exception of Santa Ana, individuals are assigned and
initiated into moieties, not born into them.) And all Eastern Pueblo moieties
are directed by exclusive priesthoods and routinely establish chapters across linguistic boundaries, so they *behave* more like sodalities than elements of kinship
systems. For example, Jemez adopted Keresan ritual moieties (Turquoise and
Pumpkin) in their entirety from their Keresan neighbors, and the distribution
of Keresan moieties looks like a diffusion gradient from the Northern Tewa
(Ware 2014, 64).[6] The institutions that have been misnamed "moieties" among
the Eastern Pueblos are actually dual tribal sodalities that function in a fashion
similar to the Katsina cults of the West: both systems require a minimal level
of ritual participation by all community members (which explains why Katsina
and ritual moiety initiations occur during adolescence, when tribal-wide ritual
participation can be more easily enforced).

But what about ultimate origins? Did Eastern Pueblo dual tribal sodalities
originate in Dravidian and Iroquois dualism, which Whiteley has shown underlies all Pueblo kinship systems, or are they, as Ortiz argued, part of the ritual
system that never articulated with the kinship system? At least two independent lines of archaeological evidence tend to support Ortiz's case. First is the
association between Eastern Pueblo tribal sodalities and oversized communal
kivas. Communal or "great" kivas first appear on the eastern plateau during
Basketmaker III times (circa 500–700 CE) and they continue, with inevitable
structural modifications, up to the present in the Rio Grande, where they are
invariably associated with ritual moieties. That is, wherever ritual moieties are
found, they are *always* associated with large communal kivas, and vice versa.
Much more work on prehistoric great kivas needs to be done before we can
conclude that this observed structural-functional correlation is over 1,500 years
old, but the strong contemporary association is certainly suggestive of deep
roots.

Second, despite the terminological evidence that Dravidian-Iroquois dualities underlie all Pueblo kinship systems, the strongest archaeological evidence
of dual community structures appears relatively late in Ancestral Pueblo culture
history. Hints of dual organizations in the form of dyadic architectural patterns
appear toward the close of Chaco in the late eleventh and early twelfth centuries, but the strongest patterns are found in the central Mesa Verde region
in the twelfth and thirteenth centuries, where most communities larger than a
few households are divided in two by a wall, street, drainage, or other structural
feature (Lipe and Ortman 2000; Nordby 1999).[7] With few exceptions, Basketmaker through early Pueblo communities were strongly segmented, consisting
of clusters of multiple habitation units and associated pithouse-kivas suggestive
of semicomplex alliance strategies (and Pueblo homology strongly favors Iroquois and Crow as the dominant alliance equations). Given the irreversibility of
Allen's tetradic model, if Eastern Pueblo ritual moieties ultimately sprang from
Dravidian-Iroquois dual alliance structures, we might reasonably expect dual
community patterns appearing early, to be replaced some time later by plural
alliance forms as communities became larger and marriage systems began to
open up the field of potential alliance possibilities. But in fact, the observed
archaeological pattern is just the opposite. The implication is that the Ancestral
Pueblos made the shift to semicomplex alliance strategies very early during the
Neolithic transition on the plateau, and that much later evidence of dual organizations emerged in the ritual rather than the kinship sphere.

There are important caveats in all this. Today on the Rio Grande, architecture and community structure are unreliable indicators of the relative importance of ritual moieties in the social and political life of individual communities.
Nowhere are dual organizations more pivotal than among the Rio Grande
Tewa, and yet most Tewa communities lack the obvious dual kiva structures
of the Eastern Keresan villages and the strong dyadic community divisions of
the Northern Tiwa (Dozier 1961, 107). We should be careful, therefore, not to
ascribe too much significance to precolonial dyadic architectural patterns. We
should also note that if Crow is an optative overlay on an Iroquois dual alliance
pattern, the two patterns may coincide throughout the Pueblos' long social history, just as they coincide today on Second Mesa at Hopi (see discussion in
Whiteley 2015).

Jane Hill's chapter (6) may be difficult for archaeologists to appreciate
because it combines historical linguistics with kin-terminology—two subjects
given short shrift and sometimes omitted entirely from archaeologists' formal

training. This is unfortunate, because Hill's analysis provides a number of important insights that should be of special interest to historians and archaeologists. One such insight is that Hopi shares eight of fifteen core consanguineal kinship terms with Takic, a Uto-Aztecan subfamily from southern California, and only two with the Numic languages of the Great Basin. Because Steward and Eggan used the Great Basin Shoshone as the primary model for their reconstruction of proto-Hopi social organization, Hill's findings suggest that it is perhaps time to revisit some of those assumptions. Second, her analysis of vertical and horizontal skewing equations among the Pueblos helps us to understand how endogamous pueblos developed alliance equations that accommodated large population aggregates and perhaps also enabled the assimilation of migrants by opening up the field of potential affines. Hill also provides linguistic evidence of ancient Tanoan skewing equations, in support of Whiteley's Tewa "flyover" hypothesis: that "there are historical linguistic hints that Crow skewing may have a deep Tanoan history. These hints challenge the claim by Eggan (1950, 153) and Dozier (1955, 248) that skewing in Arizona Tewa derives entirely from contact with Hopi."

Finally, Hill agrees with Whiteley that, given traces of crossness and skewing in Tanoan kin-terminologies, the distinction between Eastern and Western Pueblo kinship systems is probably overdrawn. Hill and Whiteley convince me on this point, and their analyses suggest the need for new studies that will help to resolve some of the historical questions raised. I would simply add that, in my judgment, Western and Eastern Pueblos are divided primarily on ritual-political as opposed to kinship grounds.

One final note on Hill, Whiteley, and alliance vs. descent. It is reasonably clear, I think, that for most of human history kinship was primarily about marriage alliance — men exchanging sisters for wives and various complex permutations thereof (some equations so complex and inscrutable that anthropologists still puzzle over their internal logic). However, an important overlay was added during the Neolithic, when kinship was used to create landholding and resource- and people-controlling corporations. In the words of Eric Wolf (1982, 91), "The circle of kinship was drawn tightly around the resource base by means of stringent definitions of group membership." As anthropologists long ago pointed out, this "tightening of the circle" was often accomplished by adopting an ideology of unilineal descent, but we now know that corporate kin groups can also be formed on cognatic principles by simply specifying an apical ancestor and a rule of bilateral descent from the designated individual. We also know, thanks mostly to the work of Peter Whiteley at Hopi, that alliance strategies continue to play an important role in semicomplex social relations long after kin-based corporate groups emerge (just as they do in marriages among the various royal households of Europe and the wealthy classes of modern industrial democracies—read a sample of *New York Times* marriage announcements if you harbor doubts about the latter). It is perhaps time to put the descent-versus-alliance debate to rest once and for all so that we may better appreciate how both help to structure the most important social relationships in nonstate societies.

In the final kinship chapter, Loki Pandey's analysis moves us "downstream" to the twentieth century to examine a number of important changes in household and community organization at Zuni as the pueblo was drawn inexorably into the US market economy. Except for the occasional kitchen garden and ceremonial corn field, the traditional self-sufficient agricultural base of the Zuni economy had lapsed by the early twentieth century, to be replaced by wage work and other engagements with the larger market economy. In particular, Pandey shows how sheep herding and the silver jewelry industry combined to challenge the primacy of Zuni's traditional matrilocal extended-family household. Sheep herding is a cooperative male activity that has introduced patrilineal inheritance practices among the historically matrilineal Zuni, while silversmithing has contributed to the breakup of extended matrilocal households as economically self-sufficient nuclear families bud off to occupy single-family houses with fences, gates, and barking dogs—a transition that began with trailer homes after World War II, to be succeeded by single-family HUD housing units in the 1960s and '70s. Most ethnographies are snapshots of a year or two in the life of a community, but Pandey's longitudinal study captures the inherent dynamism of Zuni social organization.

In the second part of his chapter, Pandey explores whether concepts such as "lineage" and "clan" are socially relevant for the Western Pueblos. His answer is a qualified "yes." Contrary to recent studies that question the validity of lineage theory (e.g., Kuper 1982), Pandey tells us that the importance of lineage at Zuni depends almost entirely on whom one asks. For members of a ritually prominent household whose status is based on its control of important communal ceremonies, lineage membership and descent-reckoning are vital. Keeping track of descent is much less important for commoner households, presumably because they have much less at stake in the reckoning. This observation confirms my impression that Pueblo kinship and ritual are so deeply entangled that it is nearly always difficult to explain one without the other.

Religion

Kinship is important, but it's not everything, and in many pueblos, especially on the Rio Grande, it isn't the most important thing. In the growth of complex agrarian societies, religion was one of the most powerful of all social regulators. Not only was it effective at encouraging individuals to direct their behavior toward cooperative rather than competitive ends, but religion was also a powerful instrument of political control. Through the use of supernatural sanctions that are rarely questioned, religion can operate on a scale unimaginable in other authority regimes. The ethnographic pueblos are a well-documented case in point.

All pueblos are organized from top to bottom on theocratic principles. Distinctions are made between the ceremonially rich and ceremonially poor, and the ceremonially rich are traditionally organized in secret ritual sodalities that are staffed by men usually without regard to kinship or co-residence.[8] (Women's sodalities were present in all pueblos as well but they usually played a subordinate role in community governance to the men's associations.) Pueblo sodalities are responsible for rain and weather control, the curing of illness and control of witchcraft, success in hunting and warfare, social conformity through the instruments of clowning, ridicule, and burlesque, and the initiation of the community's youth via tribal rites of passage. The priesthoods are also responsible for appointing or at least ratifying the appointment of all religious and secular leaders. Most band and tribal societies embrace an egalitarian ethos (Boehm 1999), and the Pueblos are no exception. The only people who are routinely permitted to transcend the egalitarian ethos are priests (or their surrogates) who control sacred knowledge considered beneficial to the entire community — individuals who have the power that comes with knowledge to intervene with the spirits and the gods to ensure rainfall, fertility, protection from witches and other enemies, and so on.

There is little consensus on when Pueblo ritual associations first emerged. Some argue that sodalities evolved for the first time in the late prehistoric aggregation period (ca. 1300–1500 CE) in order to regulate irrigation systems and the political affairs of large population aggregates (e.g., Dozier 1970; Adams 1991). There is, however, material evidence of sodality ritual much earlier (e.g., McGregor 1943; Vivian, Dodgen, and Hartmann 1978), and architecture normally associated with sodalities makes its appearance as early as Basketmaker III (ca. 600 CE) and is widespread by the early Pueblo period. I have argued that the earliest sodalities on the plateau were probably tribal sodalities associated with great kivas (the likely precursors of ritual moieties). Some time later, the germ of restricted sodalities emerged in the first year-round sedentary farming communities that would help shape the ritual-political organization of all Ancestral Pueblo communities by, among other things, validating the social, political, and economic status of community founders (Ware 2014).

Kinship works primarily at the local level, but there is always the need to form regional relationships enabling extralocal action, especially on an unpredictable and unforgiving landscape like the southern Colorado Plateau. In the long continuum of Pueblo social history, religion formed the main content of those relationships, and ritual sodalities were its principal instruments. Virtually all Eastern Pueblo sodalities have chapters in multiple pueblos, even across language boundaries. Because of their pan-Pueblo character, if a chapter of a sodality should die out in a particular pueblo, the sodality can be reconstituted by sending initiates to another pueblo where the sodality is intact. According to Alfonso Ortiz (1994, 304–5), the Tewa word for this process translates roughly to "reinvigorating the vine." Ortiz went on to claim that pan-Pueblo sodalities were the most important instruments of Pueblo cultural survival, now and in the distant past.

Cross-culturally, sodalities tend to thrive in multiethnic and multilinguistic contexts, where interethnic relationships need to be continually negotiated and potential conflicts mediated. One of the better examples comes from the Great Plains of North America, where the introduction of the horse in the eighteenth century CE inspired the short-lived Plains equestrian bison-hunting cultures. Pan-tribal sodalities arose in virtually all of the Plains tribes, where they organized hunting and war parties, supervised camp relocations and rituals, and directed other communal activities. Because the same age-graded sodalities crossed ethnic and linguistic boundaries, Plains ritual associations also helped to negotiate boundaries and mediate conflicts among linguistically diverse peoples (e.g., Lowie 1954). Corn horticulture was the Southwest analog of the Plains horse, encouraging culturally diverse tribal groups to converge on a common socioeconomic adaptation on the Colorado Plateau and around its periphery in the early centuries of the Common Era. Once they emerged, Pueblo sodalities no doubt persisted and spread in part because they helped to negotiate relationships among linguistically diverse farming groups. Sodalities and their rituals were exchanged among plateau farmers just as they were among Plains hunters. Eventually, Pueblo secret societies crosscut local communities and crossed language boundaries to form a broad set of regional interactions based on ritual that, among other things, helped to address the inherent risks associated with small isolated farming populations.

Two chapters in the current volume touch on Pueblo ritual sodalities and their archaeological recognition. Steve Plog's chapter (11) reviews the material data from Pueblo Bonito in Chaco Canyon and concludes that there is little direct evidence of ritual sodalities comparable to those that proliferated among the Pueblos in the late precolonial period. Singling out my ideas about the likely role of ritual sodalities in Chaco (Ware 2014), Plog makes the important point that hypotheses about practices and institutions in deep prehistory, even when they are derived from Pueblo homology, must always be tested against material archaeological data. I couldn't agree more, but in this case there are important caveats. The problem with direct evidence of ritual sodalities is that most of their rituals and associated paraphernalia are cloaked in secrecy, *especially within their own communities*, so sodality members routinely curate sacred objects or decommission and destroy them when they reach the end of their effective-use life. As a result, it is reasonable to expect the material record of ritual sodalities to be very thin. Exceptions occur when a ritual and its associated sodality lapse without trained replacements to carry on the traditions, as perhaps happened in the twelfth century at the Ridge Ruin east of Flagstaff where the "Magician Burial" was recovered (McGregor 1943; see description in Hays-Gilpin and Gilpin, chapter 7, this volume); or when sites or site components were abandoned precipitously and ritual materials were left *in situ*, which happened at San Lazaro Pueblo south of Santa Fe when residents abandoned a fifteenth-century roomblock so quickly that they left everything behind, including multiple rooms with ritual objects on floors and leaning against walls (Ware and Blinman 2000). These are rare events that probably represent the tip of the sodality iceberg, reminding us that absence of evidence should not necessarily be construed as evidence of absence.

Despite the paucity of direct evidence in the form of altar pieces (Plog specifically mentions bear effigies) and other sacred paraphernalia, the circumstantial evidence of ritual sodalities in Chaco and other Ancestral Pueblo communities is nevertheless compelling (see discussion in Ware 2014, 122–26). Ritual sodalities, though highly variable in form and function, are present in all pueblos from every Pueblo language group, suggesting deep historical roots. The close contemporary association between kivas and secret male societies is also suggestive of sodality roots that stretch back at least to the early Pueblo period, when the first "lineage kivas" appear (and perhaps to Basketmaker times, when great kivas come onstage). Moreover, genomic evidence from the northern burial crypt at Pueblo Bonito, where two male members of a high-rank matri-line were buried with vast quantities of turquoise and shell next to a room filled with wooden staffs, ceramic cylinder vessels, and other ritual objects, aligns perfectly with my avunculate sodality hypothesis (Ware 2014, 92–97). With the ritual avunculate in place, there is a clear path to avunculate-based Western Pueblo "embedded" sodalities, a pattern most strongly expressed at Hopi and Zuni but with traces persisting at Acoma, as well as Jemez and the downstream Jemez River Keresan villages (Dozier 1961, 106).

Our challenge, of course, is to explain when and where the independent sodalities of the Rio Grande Pueblos first emerged. I have argued that, at some point, avunculate-based sodalities detached from matrilineages to become the independent sodality-based authority structures that govern all Eastern Pueblos today. Sodality detachment might have happened at any time from the early Pueblo period to the arrival of the Spanish, but the profound changes that occurred during the second half of the eleventh and early twelfth centuries encourage me to think that the rupture first occurred during the Classic Bonito phase, when hundreds of outlier great houses and accompanying roads, earthworks, and shrines were constructed throughout the San Juan Basin and beyond. If, as Plog suggests (Kennett et al. 2017, 2), Chaco was governed by kin-based "Hopi-like" organizations throughout its 330-year history, the expansion of Chacoan influence in the second half of the eleventh century becomes highly problematic. Consider that the avunculate-embedded sodalities of the Hopis and Zunis show little inclination to project their influence beyond their respective language communities, whereas the independent sodalities of the Rio Grande Pueblos have established sodality chapters throughout the Pueblo world with little apparent regard for linguistic or other cultural boundaries. Consequently, when Chaco "goes nuts" in the second half of the eleventh century to form the nexus of a ritual emulation network that encompasses an area of the southern Colorado Plateau the size of New England, the behavior looks decidedly more eastern than western. I realize that this and other homology-based arguments may not impress scholars who believe that the Chaco conundrum will eventually be explained by focusing an increasingly powerful microscope on Pueblo Bonito, but I remain convinced that Chaco will be explained in historical context or not at all.

Scott Ortman's contribution to this volume (chapter 3) focuses on the evolution of Rio Grande Tewa ritual sodalities and other social institutions. Building on his case for Mesa Verde Tewa origins presented in his award-winning book *Winds from the North* (2012), Ortman argues that many contemporary Tewa sodalities have roots that stretch back to the Tewa ancestral homeland in Mesa Verde; others appear to have grown out of the merging of cultural traditions, when Mesa Verde refugees combined with resident Tanoan-speakers in the northern Rio Grande; still others may have emerged en route from the northern San Juan to the northern Rio Grande. Although I am deeply impressed by the many interdisciplinary analyses that Ortman brings to his work in *Winds*, I nevertheless disagree with some of his more expansive conclusions, including his arguments for a proto-Tiwa-Tewa homeland in the central Mesa Verde and his hypothesis of a massive coordinated migration of Mesa Verdeans to the northern Rio Grande. Needless to say, these disagreements color my reactions to his present work, but this is not the place to present those critiques. I will focus instead on the logic of his sodality arguments, which link Tewa oral traditions and Mesa Verde archaeology. I have space in this chapter to address only one of Ortman's hypotheses, but others deserve the same comparative treatment.

Ortman notes that Tewa informants told early ethnographers that the *K'ósa*, one of two Tewa clown societies, was part of the original Tewa migration from the north. Ortman acknowledges that there is no obvious evidence of black-and-white-striped *K'ósa* clowns in the northern San Juan,[9] but he speculates that since the K'ósa are invariably present in communal plaza ceremonies in contemporary Tewa villages, perhaps they arose when central plazas appeared at Yucca House, Yellowjacket, Goodman Point, and a few other mid-1200s Mesa Verde sites. According to Ortman (chapter 3), "Such features appear to date no earlier than the middle 1200s, coincident with a transformation of great kivas from roofed to unroofed forms . . . Perhaps the K'ósa society was adopted as these new public ceremonial spaces developed."

Perhaps, but Ortman might have pointed out that striped-clown sodalities are present under several names (K'ósa among the Tewa, *Koshare* among the Keres, Black-eyes among the Tiwa, *Koyala* among the Western Tewa and Hopi) at all Rio Grande pueblos as well as Jemez, Acoma, Laguna, and as far west as the Arizona Tewa and Hopi. Jorgensen (1980, 240), Ortiz (1994, 298–99), and others have suggested that both Tewa clown groups (K'ósa and *Kwirena*) originated with the Rio Grande Keresans.[10] In fact, Tewa anthropologist Edward Dozier (1970, 171) suggested that Tewa K'ósa and Kwirena are cognates of

Keresan Koshare and Kurena and were likely borrowed by the Tewa along with the Katsina cult, which the Keresan clowns manage and direct, in the late pre-colonial period. Consistent with this hypothesis, Keresan clowns have much broader and more complex roles in Keresan than in neighboring Tanoan communities, affirming Dozier's observation that borrowed sodalities tend to shed many of the ancillary functions they serve in their communities of origin (175–76). Additional support comes from the relative rank of Keresan clown sodalities, which share the apex of the Keresan sodality hierarchy with the closely related medicine societies. Parsons (1939, 132) insisted that Keresan medicine and clown societies were different aspects of the same ritual association, and the dual membership patterns of Keres medicine-clown sodalities bear her out. Among the Rio Grande Keresans, for example, medicine men almost invariably hold dual membership in their associated clown association. As just one prominent example, the head priest of the highest-ranking Flint medicine society is also the head priest of the Koshare clown society as well as the village cacique (Lange 1959).

Despite Ortman's disclaimer that his chapter is not a comparative analysis of Tewa social institutions, some of the arguments he constructs and the conclusions he reaches about those institutions *require* comparative analysis because of the essential pan-Pueblo character of Pueblo ritual institutions. Ultimately, oral histories can help guide us in reconstructing the convoluted histories of Pueblo ritual sodalities, but only if we compare and contrast the oral histories with the histories of sodality exchanges across *all* pueblos.

Identity and Ethnicity

For me, one of the most important "takeaways" from the SAR seminar was the extent to which most if not all pueblos, east and west, have multiethnic roots stretching back to at least the late precolonial period and probably earlier. Hays-Gilpin and Gilpin (chapter 7) point out that the well-known Tewa migration to Hopi in the late seventeenth century was simply the most recent in a long series of multiethnic/linguistic migrations that go back to at least the 1200s CE. Throughout the Tusayan region room counts doubled during the late fourteenth and early fifteenth centuries (Clark et al., forthcoming), a period that Hopi oral tradition describes as the "gathering of the clans." Population on the Hopi Mesas and along the Little Colorado south of Hopi grew so rapidly that only large-scale in-migration could account for the growth. Most of what we know about late precolonial Hopi archaeology comes from the Peabody Museum's surveys and excavations on Antelope Mesa, and according to Hays-Gilpin and Gilpin, all the villages on Antelope Mesa had diverse origins and were populated by people who spoke not just Hopi but also Keresan, Zunian, and perhaps other languages. That pattern continued during the early historic period. After the Spanish Reconquest the Hopis allowed Tewa, Jemez, Sandia, and other refugees from the Rio Grande to settle among them (Reed 1952).

Zuni multiethnicity is also supported by both ethnohistorical and archaeological data. According to Mills and Ferguson (chapter 9), a significant number of human remains from Hawikku and Kechiba:wa Pueblos consisted of cremations in association with Salado Polychrome, and morphological studies of Zuni skeletal populations (Peeples 2014) document migrations to Zuni not just from southern Arizona but from the Upper Gila, east central Arizona, and the Kayenta region. These and other movements are documented in Zuni oral traditions, which identify, among other places, the Grand Canyon of northern Arizona and the Pajarito Plateau in northern New Mexico as important sources of founding populations.

Moving to the Rio Grande, Severin Fowles (chapter 4) points out that nearly half of M. C. Stevenson's Taos informants in the early twentieth century self-identified as descendants of Jicarilla Apache, and that many Utes and a complement of Santo Domingo Keresans had also assimilated at Taos. Beyond Taos, we know from historical documents that a substantial number of Tanos from Galisteo Pueblo were assimilated into Santo Domingo following a smallpox epidemic that swept the Galisteo Basin in 1793 (Simmons 1979a, 187). Isleta provided sanctuary for a large number of Laguna migrants in the late nineteenth century, motivated, apparently, by the desire to obtain Laguna Katsina ceremonialism that had lapsed at Isleta (Parsons 1928). Jemez assimilated migrants from Pecos Pueblo in the early nineteenth century, who may or may not have been native Towa-speakers. And this is hardly an exhaustive list of this understudied phenomenon, so graduate students should take note!

I suspect that Pueblo assimilation processes have deep roots in the Pueblo past and are ultimately related to the uncertainties associated with farming on the Colorado Plateau, where annual moisture deficits combine with a short frost-free growing season to make farming a risky venture even in good years. As a result of such uncertainties, most Ancestral Pueblo communities were occupied for no more than a generation or two before the community packed up and moved or simply dissolved and dispersed, so migrants were probably never in short supply. Against this historical backdrop, we need better theory to explain assimilation processes and their effects. Whiteley and Hill (this volume) have shown how all Pueblos, east and west, employed various forms of kin-terminological skewing to open up their marriage alliance systems, permitting larger intermarrying populations to coalesce and no doubt facilitating the assimilation of migrants. And we have seen how pan-tribal sodalities may have served as social bridges to help mediate language and culture differences in multiethnic communities. These bridges would have been especially important in endogamous matrilocal-matrilineal communities where intercommunity marriage alliances were likely precluded (Levy 1994). The matrilineal Iroquois of the Northeast and the matrilineal Creeks of the Southeast used political confederacies to build regional alliances. The matrilineal Pueblos of the Southwest employed pan-tribal sodalities for the same purpose. Ritual affiliations would have been a convenient and highly flexible way to incorporate migrants into existing communities. If immediate kin ties could not be established, perhaps ritual moiety affiliation, or membership in a ritual society, or knowledge of a certain ceremony would have facilitated the assimilation process.

Hays-Gilpin and Gilpin (chapter 7) call the Hopi assimilation process *Hopification*: "To be 'Hopified' is to become, or be made, compatible with Hopi values, aesthetics, and social arrangements. To become Hopified is to connect to the elaborate and flexible Hopi network of people, places, doings, and making things." Other pueblos require similar levels of conscious assimilation. Zunis are a mix of linguistically diverse people but all contemporary Zunis speak the same Zunian language and adhere, at least outwardly, to Zuni cultural beliefs and practices. Taos incorporated large numbers of Apaches, Utes, and, no doubt, other Plains and Pueblo peoples, but despite their diverse origins all Taos citizens speak the same language, attend the same kiva ceremonies, and identify as Taoseños. There are historical examples of cultural enclaves among the Pueblos. The Western Tewa on First Mesa at Hopi were allowed to establish an enclave village in order to serve as an advance guard against Spanish incursions from the east, and Laguna migrants to Isleta in the late nineteenth century were permitted to retain their Laguna identity as long as they shared their katsinas with their Isleta hosts. But these appear to be exceptions to the general rule that immigrants are expected to assimilate fully into the host community by learning the host language, adhering to the host's authority structure and ritual cycle, and sharing any rituals that complement the host's ceremonial suite (e.g., Kroskrity 1998). Needless to say, the advantages of migrant assimilation accrue to both migrants and hosts. Migrants find a new home and the host community gains an expanded marriage, labor, and warrior pool, as well as the potential to gain new and powerful ceremonies that strengthen the hand of the local ritual elites.

The implications of Pueblo assimilation processes are profound but until now, I think, mostly underappreciated. For example, the ability to assimilate Pueblo immigrants of all stripes and complexions may help to explain how multiethnic communities coalesced around skilled military leaders during the early historic period to facilitate collective action against a common European enemy (Preucel and Aguilar, chapter 10). Historical assimilation processes also allow us to accept the bulk of Scott Ortman's interdisciplinary analyses in *Winds from the North* without necessarily embracing his Mesa Verde Tiwa-Tewa homeland hypothesis and a Tewa culture hero (*P'oseyemu*) given agency in a massive coordinated migration for which there is virtually no archaeological evidence. We have just begun to scratch the surface of this important subject, and this volume takes a giant leap forward.

Notes

1. Crossness is the terminological differentiation of all relatives as either cross or parallel. For example, parallel cousins are the children of same-sex siblings; cross-cousins are the children of different-sex siblings.

2. Skewing is the merging of kin-terminologies down a unilineal descent line. For example, in Crow skewing, father's mother, sisters, sisters' daughters, sisters' daughters' daughters, and so on are all referred to by the same kin-term. Omaha skewing is the mirror patrilineal image of the Crow-matrilineal pattern.

3. In the descriptive Eskimo terminologies of the Rio Grande Tanoans, lineal kin (e.g., F, M, D) are distinguished from collateral kin (e.g., MB, FZ). In classificatory systems (e.g., Dravidian, Iroquois, Crow-Omaha) kinship terminologies merge lineal and collateral kin (e.g., FB=F, MZ=M).

4. Many Eastern Pueblo origin narratives claim that moieties formed when two very different groups amalgamated to form a single community. For example, Tewas talk about an eastern group of hunters coalescing with a western group of farmer-gatherers to form a single community that preserved the original groups as Winter (hunter) and Summer (farming-gathering) moieties.

5. "Patrivirilateral" is a term coined by Robin Fox (1967) to describe ritual moiety recruitment rules. Children are normally initiated into the ritual moiety of their

father (patri), and wives who belong to the moiety opposite their husband normally reinitiate into the ritual moiety of their husband (viri).

6.   Coincidentally, these arguments have convinced Robin Fox (personal communication, 2012), who preceded Whiteley in arguing that the ritual moieties of the Keresans were formerly exogamous (Fox 1967, 1972).

7.   Evidence of dualism clearly antedates the Chacoan Bonito Phase, but dualism is a theme that runs through all of Pueblo history and likely has very deep roots on the Colorado Plateau. The dual community structures that appear at a number of early Pueblo communities (McPhee Village and Old Bonito are two prominent examples) could well be the remnants of true exogamous moieties representing the original intermarrying community founders. Significantly, exogamous moieties are much more common under matrilineal than alternative descent ideologies (Murdock 1949, 215).

8.   In the Western and some intermediate pueblos, ceremonies are typically owned by matrilineal descent groups that provide the head priest for the sodality that performs the ceremony, and the office of head priest routinely passes down within the avunculate (i.e., from mother's brother to sister's son).

9.   According to Polly Schaafsma (personal communication, 2015), there are no known graphic depictions of striped clowns on the Colorado Plateau. The earliest depictions date to the late precolonial period in the Rio Grande Valley.

10. The Keresan origin view is not quite unanimous. Parsons (1939, 1090) believed that striped clowns might have originated among the Tewa.

As the volume periodically discusses kinship issues (especially in chapters 1, 2, 3, 4, 5, 6, and 12) that may be unfamiliar to some readers, a glossary is provided below. Kinship notation has been standardized for the volume. Regarding linguistic matters, it has not been possible, nor is it desirable (for faithful rendering of earlier texts), to establish a uniform orthography. Some chapters include variant orthographies for the same language (notably Tewa, in chapters, 2, 3, 5, and 6), but correspondences should be readily identifiable, with a little patience!

Kinship Notation

B: brother
Ch: child
D: daughter
E: spouse
F: father
H: husband
M: mother
P: parent
S: son
W: wife
Z: sister
e: elder, for example, FeB=father's elder brother
y: younger, for example, MyZ=mother's younger sister
♂: male's, male speaker's, for example, ♂ZS=a male's sister's son
♀: female's, female speaker's

All of these symbols may be combined in possessive strings: e.g., "MBW" means "mother's brother's wife"; "♀FZD" means a "woman's father's sister's daughter," etc.

G^{+2}: grandparents' generation
G^{+1}: parents' generation
G^{0}: Ego's generation

G^{-1}: children's generation

G^{-2}: grandchildren's generation

affines: Kin by marriage; in-laws.

agnates: Relatives linked via a line of males only (*see also* patrilineal descent).

alliance/marriage alliance: Institutional ties between groups linked by
    marriage(s); *see also* elementary, complex, and semicomplex structures.

alliance theory: Approach to kinship developed by Claude Lévi-Strauss
    (especially 1949, 1969) that concentrates on marriage exchange as the
    principal engine of a social system in small-scale societies. Alliance
    theory's "elementary" and "semicomplex" structures repositioned
    interpretations of Iroquois, Dravidian, and Crow-Omaha kin-
    terminologies especially.

ambilocal residence: Postmarital residence with either the husband's or wife's
    family.

bifurcate-merging: Type of kin-terminology in which F and FB are
    "merged"—called by the same term—and both are distinguished from MB,
    who is called by a different term (reflecting "bifurcation" between "parallel"
    and "cross" kin); M and MZ are similarly merged, and distinguished from
    FZ. Primarily used for Iroquois and Dravidian systems, secondarily for
    Crow and Omaha. "Bifurcate-merging" is Lowie's equivalent to Morgan's
    "Classificatory" and Murdock's "Iroquois" (which includes "Dravidian"
    [Godelier et al. 1998, 9]).

bilateral kindred: Group based on ties through both F and M, and lacking
    a rule of unilineal descent. Relationships are typically reckoned "Ego-
    centrically," as opposed to "socio-centrically."

bilocal residence: Postmarital residence options include both husband's and
    wife's families; *see also* ambilocal residence.

Cheyenne: Type of kinship terminology in which crossness is recognized in
    above and below generations but not in one's own.

clan: (evolved in anthropological usage over time, but by the mid-twentieth
    century) A unilineal descent group larger than a lineage, and comprising
    several such lineages.

clan-set (a.k.a. *phratry*): A group of clans defined by a sense (usually not
    demonstrable) of common unilineal descent; the operative exogamic
    group in a semicomplex structure (e.g., Hopi).

classificatory systems: Kinship terminologies merging lineal kin (e.g., F, M)
   with collateral kin (e.g., FB, MZ).
cognatic kin: Kin linked to Ego via M and F with no distinction made between
   male or female links.
collateral kin: Kin linked to Ego outside a direct line of descent (e.g., FB, FMB,
   MMZ, BD, ZS, etc.).
complex structure: A system of kinship whose only rules for marriage are
   negative, i.e., proscribing marriage within a narrow circle of consanguines.
consanguines: Kin by "blood," i.e., descendants of a common ancestor.
cross-cousins: MBCh, FZCh.
cross-kin: Kin to Ego via an opposite-sex link to a collateral relative (e.g.,
   FZCh, MBCh, FFZS, MMBD).
crossness: Differentiation of all relatives as either cross or parallel (via
   bifurcate-merging terminology). The two basic types of crossness are
   Iroquois and Dravidian.
cross-parallel neutralization: A rule or practice eliminating terminological
   differentiation of cross and parallel kin, typically in one generation, e.g.,
   in Ego's generation in a Cheyenne system.
Crow: A terminological type characterized by "lineal equations" that skew
   identifications of kin through generations down a matrilineal descent line
   (e.g., FZ=FM=FZD=FZDD, F=FMB=FZS=FZSS). Mirror opposite of an
   Omaha system.
descent groups: Social action groups comprised by a common principle of
   descent, typically unilineal, i.e., patrilineal or matrilineal.
descent theory, a.k.a. *lineage theory*: Associated with the "British school" of
   A. R. Radcliffe-Brown and his students (M. Fortes, E. E. Evans-Pritchard,
   et al.); identified unilineal descent groups as the primary social form in
   small-scale societies and stated that these comprised jural corporations
   for land-owning and other purposes. In North American anthropology,
   especially associated with Fred Eggan (Radcliffe-Brown's student at the
   University of Chicago).
descriptive systems: Kinship terminologies that distinguish lineal kin (e.g.,
   F, M) from collateral kin (e.g., FB, MZ). Morgan's category "descriptive"—
   as opposed to classificatory—is applied principally to Eskimo and
   Sudanese terminologies.
Dravidian: A terminological type characterized by crossness, which equates

cross-kin with affines (MB=FZH, ♂MBD=♂FZD=♂W, etc.) typically
associated with a rule of prescriptive cross-cousin marriage.

dual organization: A system that divides society into two exchanging halves;
typically involves exogamous kinship moieties and cross-cousin marriage
(coordinate with Dravidian or Iroquois kin-terminology). Rio Grande
pueblo dual organization exceptionally comprises politico-ritual units
arranged on patrilines that do not govern marriage.

Ego: I, the center of a kinship diagram, especially for a bilateral kindred.

Ego-centric: Specification of kinship relationships relative to a particular
person, an Ego. As regards kinship systems, typically associated with
cognatic groups and contrasted with socio-centric, which are typically
coordinate with classificatory systems.

elementary structure: A system of kinship with rules that prescribe marriage
with a specific category of relative, e.g., typically, a cross-cousin.

endogamy: Marriage inside a social unit (e.g., a village).

equation: *See* kin-type equation.

Eskimo: A terminological type characterized by distinctions of lineal kin (e.g.,
F, M) from collateral kin (e.g., FB, MZ), and lacking crossness. Globally a
widespread type, typical of contemporary North American and European
societies.

exogamy: Marriage outside a social unit (e.g., a clan or a kinship moiety).

generational moieties: Groupings that link all relatives of alternate generations
for certain purposes, distinguishing them from those of the intermediate
generations. Thus one's parents' generation belongs to the same moiety as
one's children's, and one's own generation is in the same moiety as one's
grandparents and grandchildren. *See also* sections.

Hawaiian (generational): A terminological type characterized by distinctions
only of gender and generation, lacking both crossness and lineality (e.g.,
F=MB=FB, M=MZ=FZ, MBCh=MZCh=FBCh=FZCh, ZCh=BCh=Ch,
etc.).

Hawaiianization: Elimination of a distinction of cross vs. parallel relatives,
typically for one generation; also known as cross-parallel neutralization.

house societies (sociétés à maison): Societies in which significant social groups
are not based on a distinctive kinship rule, but include relatives by descent
or affinity or often both; following the model of European noble "houses."
Lévi-Strauss coined the term to describe Northwest Coast cultures such as
Kwakwaka'wakw and Salish, which lack a principle of unilineal descent.

Iroquois: A terminological type characterized by crossness (e.g., F=FB≠MB, M=MZ≠FZ) that allows marriage with cross-kin, but does not prescribe it, and makes no terminological equations between cross-kin and affines (so, unlike Dravidian, MB≠FZH, ♂MBD≠♂W, etc.).

kin: Generally speaking, one's relatives, but specifically used also to distinguish consanguines (so-called blood relatives) from affines, i.e., relatives by marriage.

kindred: *See* bilateral kindred.

kin-term: The term used in a particular language to refer to one relative or a group of relatives (e.g., "cousin," in English).

kin-type: The specific type of relative referred to by a kin-term. For example, FZ (father's sister), MB (mother's brother), MFF (mother's father's father).

kin-type equation: How a kin-term groups (equates) certain kin-types insofar as it refers to all of them. For example, Hopi kin-term *kya* (colloquially, "aunt") refers to the kin-types FZ, FZD, and FZDD and others. The "meaning" of *kya* thus involves an equation: FZ=FZD=FZDD. Such equations specifically contrast with kin-type distinctions. So, unlike English "aunt," Hopi *kya* cannot refer to MZ, a distinction that may be expressed as: FZ=FZD=FZDD≠MZ.

lineage: Used variously by different authorities, but by convention primarily an abbreviation for "unilineal descent group," i.e., a social unit comprising relatives via matrilineal or patrilineal links; a segment within a unilineal "clan." Contrasts with bilateral kindred.

lineal kin: Kin linked to Ego through a direct line of descent (e.g., F, FF, M, MM, DS, DDS, SDS, etc.).

matrilateral kin: Relatives on the mother's side (in a society with primarily patrilineal descent, or in a bilateral system).

matrilineal descent: A rule that key relatives are traced through a line of women (e.g., M–MM–MMM). May be the basis for corporate groups— matrilineal descent groups.

matrilocal residence: Postmarital residence with or near the wife's parents.

moieties: A division of society into two halves, often though not always composed by a rule of descent. *See also* dual organization.

neolocal residence: Postmarital residence separate from the natal households of both husband and wife.

neutralization: *See* cross-parallel neutralization.

nibling: Nephew or niece.

Omaha: A terminological type characterized by "lineal equations" that skew
identifications of kin through generations down a patrilineal descent line
(e.g., MF=MB=MBS, MZ=MBD=MBSD). Mirror opposite of a Crow
system.

parallel kin: Kin to Ego via same-sex links to a collateral relative (e.g., FBCh,
MZCh, FFBCh, MMZDCh).

patrilateral kin: Relatives on the father's side (in a society with primarily
matrilineal descent, or in a bilateral system).

patrilineal descent: A rule that relatives are traced through a line of men (e.g.,
F–FF–FFF). May be the basis for corporate groups — patrilineal descent
groups.

patrilocal: Postmarital residence with or near the husband's parents.

phratry: *See* clan-set.

prescriptive: Used of kinship systems with a rule that marriage must be with
a specific category of relative, e.g., a cross-cousin.

sections: Exogamous elements within moieties; section systems may coincide
with "generation moieties" that group kin of alternate generations,
distinguishing them from intermediate generations (especially pertinent
for Tanoan kin-terminology). Used primarily for aboriginal Australian
kinship systems.

semicomplex structure: A system of kinship combining elementary (positive)
and complex (negative) marriage rules. Marriage is not prescribed with a
specific category of relative, but in these small-scale societies, a substantial
proportion of potential mates are off limits (as classificatory consanguines).
The effect is an almost positive rule, allowing marriage within a limited
remaining class. Prohibitions shift with each generation, depending on
the specific alliance created by the parents' marriage. Semicomplex rules
"disperse" marriage alliances in plural rather than dual fashion, among a
broader set of kin groups than in an elementary system.

skewing: The merging of kin down a unilineal descent line, producing lineal
generational equations (e.g., FZ=FZD=FZDD), as in terminologies of
Crow or Omaha type.

socio-centric: Specification of kinship relationships relative to a particular
group (e.g., one's clan, as related to other clans), and its place within
the society as a whole, rather than from the perspective of individual
relationships. As regards kinship systems, typically associated with

unilineal descent groups, and contrasted with ego-centric, the type associated with bilateral kindreds.

Sudanese: A terminological type that distinguishes lineal kin (e.g., F, M) from collateral kin (e.g., FB, MZ), and assigns each kinship position its own separate term, with no classificatory merging of categories (so F≠MB≠FB, M≠MZ≠FZ, MBD≠MZD≠FBD≠FZD, etc.).

unilineal descent: A rule that relatives are traced through a same-sex line, either of men (e.g., F–FF–FFF), patrilineal, or of women (e.g., M–MM–MMM), matrilineal. May be the basis for corporate groups known as unilineal descent groups or lineages.

Abbreviations

ARBAE. Annual Report of the Bureau of American Ethnology. Washington, DC: Government Printing Office.

BAEB. Bureau of American Ethnology Bulletin. Washington, DC: Government Printing Office.

PICA. Proceedings of the International Congress of Americanists.

PNAS. Proceedings of the National Academy of Sciences.

UCPAAE. University of California Publications in American Archaeology and Ethnology. Berkeley: University of California Press.

Aberle, D. F. 1970. Comments. In Longacre 1970, 214–23.

Adair, J. J. 1944. *The Navajo and Pueblo Silversmiths*. Norman: University of Oklahoma Press.

Adams, E. C. 1989. "Changing Form and Function in Western Pueblo Ceremonial Architecture from AD 1000 to AD 1500." In Lipe and Hegmon 1989, 155–60.

———. 1991. *The Origin and Development of the Pueblo Katsina Cult*. Tucson: University of Arizona Press.

———. 2002. *Homolʻovi: An Ancient Pueblo Settlement Cluster*. Tucson: University of Arizona Press.

Adams, K. R., and V. E. Bowyer. 2002. "Sustainable Landscape: Thirteenth-Century Food and Fuel Use in the Sand Canyon Locality." In *Seeking the Center Place: Archaeology and Ancient Communities in the Mesa Verde Region*, edited by M. D. Varien and R. H. Wilshusen, 123–42. Salt Lake City: University of Utah Press.

Adler, M. A., and R. H. Wilshusen. 1990. "Large-Scale Integrative Facilities in Tribal Societies: Cross-Cultural and Southwestern US Examples." *World Archaeology* 22: 133–45.

Aguilar, J. R. 2013. "Researching the Pueblo Revolt of 1680." *Expedition* 55: 34–35.

Aguilar, J. R., and R. W. Preucel. 2013. "Sacred Mesas: Pueblo Time, Space, and History in the Aftermath of the Pueblo Revolt of 1680." In *The Death of Prehistory*, edited by P. Schmidt and S. A. Mrozowski, 267–89. New York: Oxford University Press.

Akins, N. J. 2001. "Chaco Canyon Mortuary Practices: Archaeological Correlates of Complexity." In *Ancient Burial Practices in the American Southwest*, edited by

D. R. Mitchell and J. L. Brunson-Hadley, 167–90. Albuquerque: University of New Mexico Press.

———. 2003. "The Burials of Pueblo Bonito." In *Pueblo Bonito: Center of the Pueblo World*, edited by J. E. Neitzel, 94–126. Washington, DC: Smithsonian Institution Press.

Allen, N. J. 1989. "The Evolution of Kinship Terminologies." *Lingua* 77: 173–85.

———. 2004. "Tetradic Theory: An Approach to Kinship." In *Kinship and Family: An Anthropological Reader*, edited by R. Parkin and L. Stone, 221–35. Oxford, UK: Blackwell.

———. 2012. "Tetradic Theory and Omaha Systems." In Trautmann and Whiteley 2012c, 51–66. Tucson: University of Arizona Press.

Anderson, B. 1983. *Imagined Communities: Reflections on the Origin and Spread of Nationalism*. New York: Verso.

Anthony, D. W. 1990. "Migration in Archaeology: The Baby and the Bathwater." *American Anthropologist* 92, no. 4: 895–914.

Arakawa, F., C. Nicholson, and J. Rasic. 2013. "The Consequences of Social Processes: Aggregate Populations, Projectile Point Accumulation, and Subsistence Patterns in the American Southwest." *American Antiquity* 78, no. 1: 147–65.

Arakawa, F., S. G. Ortman, A. I. Duff, and M. S. Shackley. 2011. "Obsidian Evidence of Interaction and Migration from the Mesa Verde Region, Southwest Colorado." *American Antiquity* 76, no. 4: 773–95.

Ashmore, W. 2007. "Building Social History at Pueblo Bonito: Footnotes to a Biography of Place." In *The Architecture of Chaco Canyon, New Mexico*, edited by S. H. Lekson, 179–98. Salt Lake City: University of Utah Press.

Bandelier, A. F. 1890. *Final Report of Investigations among the Indians of the Southwestern United States, Carried on Mainly in the Years from 1880 to 1885*. Papers of the Archaeological Institute of America, American Series III, pt. I. Cambridge, MA: J. Wilson and Son.

———. 1929–1930. "Documentary History of the Rio Grande Pueblos, New Mexico." Part 1: 1536 to 1542. *New Mexico Historical Review* 4, no. 4: 302–34; 5, no. 1: 38–66; 5, no. 2: 154–85; Part 2: 1542 to 1581. 5, no. 3: 240–62; Part 3: 1581 to 1584. 5, no. 4: 330–85.

Bannon, J. F. 1955. *The Mission Frontier in Sonora, 1621–1687*. New York: U.S. Catholic Hist. Society.

———. 1964. *Bolton and the Spanish Borderlands*. Norman: University of Oklahoma Press.

———. 1974. *The Spanish Borderlands Frontier, 1513–1821*. Albuquerque: University of New Mexico Press.

Barnes, J. A. 1962. "African Models in the New Guinea Highlands." *Man* 62: 5–9.

———. 1971. *Three Styles in the Study of Kinship*. London: Tavistock.

Barrett, E. M. 1997. *The Geography of Rio Grande Pueblos, Revealed by Spanish Explorers, 1540–1598*. Latin American Institute Research Paper Series 30. Albuquerque: University of New Mexico Press.

———. 2002. *Conquest and Catastrophe: Changing Rio Grande Pueblo Settlement Patterns in the Sixteenth and Seventeenth Centuries*. Albuquerque: University of New Mexico Press.

Basso, K. H. 1996. *Wisdom Sits in Places: Landscape and Language among the Western Apache*. Albuquerque: University of New Mexico Press.

Beaudry, M. C. 2008. "'Above Vulgar Economy': The Intersection of Historical Archaeology and Microhistory in Writing Archaeological Biographies of Two New England Merchants." In Brooks, DeCorse, and Walton 2008, 173–98.

Beck, R. A., Jr., ed. 2007. *The Durable House: House Society Models in Archaeology*. Center for Archaeological Investigation Occasional Paper 35. Carbondale: Southern Illinois University Press.

Beekman, C. S., and A. F. Christenson. 2003. "Controlling for Doubt and Uncertainty through Multiple Lines of Evidence: A New Look at the Mesoamerican Nahua Migrations." *Journal of Archaeological Method and Theory* 10, no. 2: 111–64.

Bellorado, B., L. Webster, and T. Windes. 2013. "Footsteps of Identity: The Contexts of Pueblo III Sandal Imagery in the Northern Southwest." Paper, Society for American Archaeology annual meeting, Honolulu.

Benedict, R. 1931. *Tales of the Cochiti Indians*. BAEB 98. Washington, DC: Government Printing Office.

———. 1934. *Patterns of Culture*. Boston: Houghton Mifflin.

Beninato, S. 1990. "Popé, Pose-yemu, and Naranjo: A New Look at Leadership in the Pueblo Revolt of 1680." *New Mexico Historical Review* 65: 419–35.

Bereznak, C. 1995. "The Pueblo Region as a Linguistic Area: Diffusion among the Indigenous Languages of the Southwest United States." Ph.D. diss., Louisiana State University.

Bernardini, W. 1999. "Reassessing the Scale of Social Action at Pueblo Bonito, Chaco Canyon, New Mexico." *Kiva* 64: 447–70.

———. 2000. "Kiln Firing Groups: Inter-Household Economic Collaboration and Social Organization in the Northern American Southwest." *American Antiquity* 65, no. 2: 365–77.

———. 2005a. *Hopi Oral Tradition and the Archaeology of Identity*. Tucson: University of Arizona Press.

———. 2005b. "Reconsidering Spatial and Temporal Aspects of Cultural Identity: A Case Study from the American Southwest." *American Antiquity* 70, no. 1: 31–54.

———. 2011. "North, South, and Center: An Outline of Hopi Ethnogenesis." In Glowacki and Van Keuren 2011, 196–220.

———. 2012. "Hopi Clan Traditions and the Pedigree of Ceremonial Objects." In *Enduring Motives: The Archaeology of Tradition and Religion in North America*, edited by L. Sundstrom and W. DeBoer, 172–84. Tuscaloosa: University of Alabama Press.

Bernhart, R., and S. G. Ortman. 2014. "New Evidence of Tewa-Style Moiety Organization in the Mesa Verde Region, Colorado." In *Astronomy and Ceremony in the Prehistoric Southwest, Revisited: Collaborations in Cultural Astronomy*, edited by G. E. Munson, T. W. Bostwick, and T. Hull, 87–100. Albuquerque: Maxwell Museum of Anthropology, University of New Mexico.

Black, M. E. 1984. "Maidens and Mothers: An Analysis of Hopi Corn Metaphors." *Ethnology* 23: 279–88.

Bloom, L. B. 1937. "Bourke on the Southwest, XI." *New Mexico Historical Review* 12, no. 1: 41–77.

Boehm, C. 1999. *Hierarchy in the Forest: The Evolution of Egalitarian Behavior*. Cambridge, MA: Harvard University Press.

Bolton, H. E. 1916. *Spanish Exploration in the Southwest, 1542–1706*. New York: Charles Scribner's Sons.

———. 1921. *The Spanish Borderlands: A Chronicle of Old Florida and the Southwest*. Albuquerque: University of New Mexico Press.

Boyer, J. L., J. L. Moore, S. A. Lakatos, N. J. Akins, C. D. Wilson, and E. Blinman. 2010. "Remodeling Immigration: A Northern Rio Grande Perspective on Depopulation, Migration, and Donation-Side Models." In Kohler, Varien, and Wright 2013, 285–323.

Brandt, E. 2002. "The Climate for Ethnographic/Ethnohistoric Research in the Southwest." In *Traditions, Transitions, and Technologies: Themes in Southwestern Archaeology*, edited by S. H. Schlanger, 113–26. Boulder: University Press of Colorado.

Brew, J. O. 1937. "The First Two Seasons at Awatovi." *American Antiquity* 3, no. 2: 122–37.

Brooks, J. F., C. R. N. DeCorse, and J. Walton, eds. 2008. *Small Worlds: Method, Meaning and Narrative in Microhistory*. Santa Fe, NM: School of American Research Press.

Buckley, R. 2010. "Change and Cultural Stability: The Material Expression of Passive Resistance at Two Hopi Communities." MA thesis, Northern Arizona University.

Bunzel, R. L. 1932. "Introduction to Zuni Ceremonialism." *ARBAE*, 1929–1930, 47: 467–544.

———. 1938. "The Economic Organization of Primitive Peoples." In *General Anthropology*, edited by F. Boas, 327–408. New York: D. C. Heath.

Burchett, T. W. 1990. "Household Organization at Wupatki Pueblo." MA thesis, Northern Arizona University.

Burton, J. F. 1990 *Archeological Investigations at Puerco Ruin, Petrified Forest National Park, Arizona*. Publications in Anthropology 54. Tucson, AZ: National Park Service.

Bustard, W. 2003. "When a House Is Not a Home." In Neitzel 2003c, 80–93.

Cameron, C. M. 2009. *Chaco and After in the Northern San Juan: Excavations at the Bluff Great House*. Tucson: University of Arizona Press.

Cameron, C. M., and A. I. Duff. 2008. "History and Process in Village Formation: Context and Contrasts from the Northern Southwest." *American Antiquity* 73, no. 1: 29–57.

Capone, P. W. 1995. "Mission Pueblo Ceramic Analyses: Implications for Protohistoric Interaction Networks and Cultural Dynamics." Ph.D. diss., Harvard University.

Carlson, R. 1970. *White Mountain Redware: A Pottery Tradition of East-Central Arizona and Western New Mexico*. Anthropological Papers of the University of Arizona 19. Tucson: University of Arizona Press.

Carsten, J., and S. Hugh-Jones, eds. 1995. *About the House: Lévi-Strauss and Beyond*. New York: Cambridge University Press.

Carter, W. B. 2009. *Indian Alliances and the Spanish in the Southwest, 750–1750*. Norman: University of Oklahoma Press.

Chavez, Fr. A. 1967. "Pohé-yemo's Representative and the Pueblo Revolt of 1680." *New Mexico Historical Review* 17: 85–126.

Clark, J., J. Birch, M. Hegmon, S. Ortman, J. Dean, et al. Forthcoming. "The Kayenta Diaspora and Tewa Ethnogenesis: Two Pathways to Coalescence." *Journal of Anthropological Archaeology*.

Coffey, G. L. 2010. "Landscape and Social Scale at Goodman Point, Hovenweep National Monument, Colorado." *Kiva* 76, no. 1: 55–82.

Cole, S. 2012. "Violence in the Central Mesa Verde Region." In *Emergence and Collapse of Early Villages: Models of Central Mesa Verde Archaeology*, edited by T. A. Kohler and M. D. Varien, 197–218. Berkeley: University of California Press.

Copeland, K. E. 2012. "Payupki Polychrome and Ethnogenesis in Post–Pueblo Revolt Hopi Society." MA thesis, Northern Arizona University.

Cordell, L. S., and M. E. McBrinn. 2012. *Archaeology of the Southwest*. 3rd ed. Walnut Creek, CA: Left Coast Press.

Courlander, H. 1971. *The Fourth World of the Hopis: The Epic Story of the Hopi Indians as Preserved in Their Legends and Traditions*. New York: Crown.

Creamer, W. 1993. *The Architecture of Arroyo Hondo Pueblo, New Mexico*. Arroyo Hondo Archaeological Series 7. Santa Fe, NM: School of American Research Press.

Crown, P. L. 1994. *Ceramics and Ideology: Salado Polychrome Pottery*. Albuquerque: University of New Mexico Press.

———. 2016. "Summary and Conclusions: Production, Exchange, Consumption and Discard at Pueblo Bonito." In *The Pueblo Bonito Mounds of Chaco Canyon*, edited by P. L. Crown, 213–37. Albuquerque: University of New Mexico Press.

Crown, P. L., J. Gu, W. J. Hurst, T. J. Ward, A. D. Bravenec, et al. 2015. "Ritual Drinks in the Pre-Hispanic US Southwest and Mexican Northwest." *PNAS* 112, no. 37: 11436–42.

Crum, B., and J. Dayley. 1993. *Western Shoshoni Grammar*. Occasional Papers and Monographs in Cultural Anthropology and Linguistics 1. Boise, ID: Boise State University.

Cruz, P., and S. G. Ortman. 2016. "The Implications of Kiowa-Tanoan Kin Terms for Pueblo Social Organization." Paper, 15th Biennial Southwest Symposium, Tucson.

Currie, A. 2016. "Ethnographic Analogy, the Comparative Method, and Archaeological Special Pleading." *Studies in the History and Philosophy of Science, Part A* 55: 84–94.

Curtis, E. S. 1926. *The North American Indian*. Vol. 17: *The Tewa*. Norwood, MA: Plimpton.

Cushing, F. H. 1882 (1967). *My Adventures in Zuni*. Palmer Lake, CO: Filter Press.

———. 1888. "Preliminary Notes on the Origin, Working Hypothesis and Preliminary Researches of the Hemenway Southwestern Archaeological Expedition." *PICA* 7: 151–94.

———. 1896. "Outlines of Zuni Creation Myths." *ARBAE*, 1891–1892, 13: 321–447.

Danson, E. B. 1957. *An Archaeological Survey of West Central New Mexico and East Central Arizona*. Papers of the Peabody Museum of American Archaeology and Ethnology 44. Cambridge, MA: Harvard University Press.

Dean, J. S. 1969. *Chronological Analysis of Tsegi Phase Sites in Northeastern Arizona.* Papers of the Laboratory of Tree-Ring Research 3. Tucson: University of Arizona Press.

Dean, J. S., A. J. Lindsay Jr., and W. J. Robinson. 1978. "Prehistoric Settlement in the Long House Valley, Northeastern Arizona." In *Investigations of the Southwestern Anthropological Research Group: Proceedings of the 1976 Conference,* edited by R. C. Euler and G. J. Gumerman, 25–44. Flagstaff: Museum of Northern Arizona.

de Angulo, J. 1925. "Taos Kinship Terminology." *American Anthropologist* 27, no. 3: 482–83.

DeCorse, C. R. N. 2008. "Varied Pasts: History, Oral Tradition, and Archaeology on the Mina Coast." In Brooks, DeCorse, and Walton 2008, 77–93.

Deetz, J. 1977. *In Small Things Forgotten: The Archaeology of Early American Life.* New York: Doubleday.

Dick, H. W., D. Wolfman, C. Schaafsma, and M. A. Adler. 1999. "Prehistoric and Early Historic Architecture and Ceramics at Picuris." In *Picuris Pueblo through Time: Eight Centuries of Change at a Northern Rio Grande Pueblo,* edited by M. A. Adler and H. W. Dick, 43–100. Dallas, TX: William P. Clements Center for Southwest Studies, Southern Methodist University.

Di Peso, C. C. 1958. *The Reeve Ruin of Southeastern Arizona: A Study of a Prehistoric Western Pueblo Migration into the Middle San Pedro Valley.* Dragoon, AZ: Amerind Foundation.

Dohm, K. 1990. "Effect of Population Nucleation on House Size for Pueblos in the American Southwest." *Journal of Anthropological Archaeology* 9: 201–39.

Dongoske, K., and C. Dongoske. 2014. *Archaeological Data Recovery and Analysis for Four Archaeological Sites Located within the New Zuni Airport, Zuni Indian Reservation, New Mexico.* ZCRE Report 1215. Pueblo of Zuni, NM: Zuni Cultural Resources Enterprise.

Dongoske, K. E., M. Yeatts, R. Anyon, and T. J. Ferguson, 1997. "Archaeological Cultures and Cultural Affiliation: Hopi and Zuni Perspectives in the American Southwest." *American Antiquity* 62, no. 4: 600–608.

Dougherty, J. D. 1980. *Refugee Pueblos on the Santa Fe National Forest.* Cultural Resources Report 2. Santa Fe, NM: USDA Forest Service, Santa Fe National Forest.

Dousset, L. 2011. "Understanding Human Relations (Kinship Systems)." In *The Oxford Handbook of Linguistic Fieldwork,* edited by N. Thieberger, 209–34. New York: Oxford University Press.

———. 2012. "'Horizontal' and 'Vertical' Skewing: Similar Objectives, Two Solutions?" In Trautmann and Whiteley 2012c, 261–77.

Doyel, D. E., ed. 1992. *Anasazi Regional Organization and the Chaco System.* Anthropological Papers 5. Albuquerque, NM: Maxwell Museum of Anthropology.

Dozier, E. P. 1954. *The Hopi-Tewa of Arizona.* UCPAAE 44, no. 3.

———. 1955. "Kinship and Linguistic Change among the Arizona Tewa." *IJAL* 21, no. 3: 242–57.

———. 1961. "Rio Grande Pueblos." In *Perspectives in American Indian Culture Change,* edited by E. Spicer, 94–186. Chicago: University of Chicago Press.

———. 1966. *Hano: A Tewa Indian Community in Arizona.* New York: Holt, Rinehart and Winston.

———. 1970. *The Pueblo Indians of North America.* New York: Holt, Rinehart and Winston.

Driver, H. E. 1969. *Indians of North America.* 2nd ed. Chicago: University of Chicago Press.

Driver, H. E., and W. C. Massey. 1957. "Comparative Studies of North American Indians." *Transactions of the American Philosophical Society,* n.s., 47, no. 2: 165–456.

Duff, A. I. 1998. "The Process of Migration in the Late Prehistoric Southwest." In Spielmann 1998, 31–52.

———. 2002. *Western Pueblo Identities, Regional Interaction, Migration, and Transformation.* Tucson: University of Arizona Press.

Duff, A. I., and S. H. Lekson. 2006. "Notes from the South." In Lekson 2006a, 315–37.

Duff, A. I., and M. Nauman. 2010. "Engendering the Landscape: Resource Acquisition, Artifact Manufacture, and Household Organization in a Chacoan Great House Community." In *Engendering Households in the Prehistoric Southwest,* edited by B. J. Roth, 12–33. Tucson: University of Arizona Press.

Duff, A. I., and G. Schachner. 2007. "Becoming Central: Organizational Transformations in the Emergence of Zuni." In *Hinterlands and Regional Dynamics in the Ancient Southwest,* edited by A. P. Sullivan III and J. M. Bayman, 185–200. Tucson: University of Arizona Press.

Dumont, L. 1953. "The Dravidian Kinship Terminology as an Expression of Marriage." *Man* 53: 34–39.

Dungan, K. A. 2015. "Religious Architecture and Borderland Histories: Great Kivas in the Prehispanic Southwest, 1000 to 1400 CE." Ph.D. diss., University of Arizona.

Dungan, K. A., and M. Peeples. 2018. "Public Architecture as Performance Space in the Prehispanic Central Southwest." *Journal of Anthropological Archaeology* 50: 12–26.

Dutton, B. 1964. "Las Madres in the Light of Anasazi Migrations." *American Antiquity* 29: 449–54.

Duwe, S. 2011. "The Prehispanic Tewa World: Space, Time, and Becoming in the Pueblo Southwest." Ph.D. diss., U. Arizona.

Duwe, S. G., and K. F. Anschuetz. 2013. "Ecological Uncertainty and Organizational Flexibility on the Prehispanic Tewa Landscape: Notes from the Northern Frontier." In *From Mountain Top to Valley Bottom: Understanding Past Land Use in the Northern Rio Grande Valley, New Mexico*, edited by B. J. Vierra, 95–112. Salt Lake City: University of Utah Press.

Dyen, I., and D. F. Aberle. 1974. *Lexical Reconstruction: The Case of the Proto-Athapaskan Kinship System*. New York: Cambridge University Press.

Eaton, L. 1991. "The Heart of the Region: The Anthropology Collections of the Museum of Northern Arizona." *American Indian Art* 16, no. 3: 46–53.

Echo-Hawk, R. C. 2000. "Ancient History in the New World: Integrating Oral Traditions and the Archaeological Record in Deep Time." *American Antiquity* 65, no. 2: 267–90.

Edelman, S. A. 1979. "San Ildefonso Pueblo." In Ortiz 1979, 308–16.

Eggan, F. R. 1937a. "Historical Changes in the Choctaw Kinship System." *American Anthropologist* 39, no. 1: 34–52.

———. 1937b. *Social Anthropology of North American Tribes*. Chicago: University of Chicago Press.

———. 1949. "The Hopi and the Lineage Principle." In *Social Structure: Studies Presented to A. R. Radcliffe-Brown*, edited by M. Fortes, 121–44. Oxford, UK: Clarendon Press.

———. 1950. *Social Organization of the Western Pueblos*. Chicago: University of Chicago Press.

———. 1964. "Alliance and Descent in Western Pueblo Society." In *Process and Pattern in Culture: Essays in Honor of Julian H. Steward*, edited by R. A. Manners, 175–84. New Brunswick, NJ: Aldine.

———. 1972. "Summary." In Ortiz 1972a, 287–305.

———. 1979. "Pueblos: Introduction." In Ortiz 1979, 224–35.

———. 1991. Review of *The Sociopolitical Structure of Prehistoric Southwestern Societies*, by S. Upham, K. G. Lightfoot, and R. A. Jewett. *Ethnohistory* 38: 106–8.

Eiselt, B. S. 2012. *Becoming White Clay: A History of Archaeology of Jicarilla Apache Enclavement*. Salt Lake City: University of Utah Press.

Eiselt, B. S., and R. I. Ford. 2007. "Sangre de Cristo Micaceous Clays: Geochemical Indices for Source and Raw Material Distribution, Past and Present." *Kiva* 73, no. 2: 219–38.

Elliott, M. L. 1982, *Large Pueblo Sites near Jemez Springs, New Mexico*. Cultural Resources Report 3. Santa Fe, NM: USDA Forest Service, Santa Fe National Forest.

Ellis, F. H. 1951. "Patterns of Aggression and the War Cult in Southwestern Pueblos." *Southwestern Journal of Anthropology* 7, no. 2: 177–201.

———. 1964. *A Reconstruction of the Basic Jemez Pattern of Social Organization, with Comparisons to Other Tanoan Social Structures*. Publications in Anthropology 11. Albuquerque: University of New Mexico Press.

———. 1967. "Where Did the Pueblo People Come From?" *El Palacio* 74, no. 3: 35–43.

Elson, M. D., M. H. Ort, P. R. Sheppard, T. L. Samples, K. C. Anderson, et al. 2011. "Sunset Crater Volcano." In *Sunset Crater Archaeology: The History of a Volcanic Landscape: Prehistoric Settlement in the Shadow of the Volcano*, edited by M. D. Elson, 103–29. Anthropological Papers 37. Tucson, AZ: Center for Desert Archaeology.

Ensor, B. E. 2013. *The Archaeology of Kinship: Advancing Interpretation and Contributions to Theory*. Tucson: University of Arizona Press.

Espinosa, J. M. 1940. *First Expedition of Vargas into New Mexico, 1692*. Albuquerque: University of New Mexico Press.

———. 1942. *Crusaders of the Rio Grande: The Story of Don Diego de Vargas and the Reconquest and Refounding of New Mexico*. Chicago: Institute of Jesuit History.

———. 1988. *The Pueblo Indian Revolt of 1696 and the Franciscan Missions in New Mexico: Letters of the Missionaries and Related Documents*. Norman: University of Oklahoma Press.

Fane, D., I. Jacknis, and L. M. Breen. 1991. *Objects of Myth and Memory: American Indian Art at the Brooklyn Museum*. New York: Brooklyn Museum.

Ferguson, T. J. 1996. *Historic Zuni Architecture and Society: An Archaeological Application of Space Syntax*. Anthropological Papers of the University of Arizona 60. Tucson: University of Arizona Press.

———. 2002. "Dowa Yalanne: Architecture of Zuni Resistance and Social Change during the Pueblo Revolt." In Preucel 2002, 32–44.

———. 2007. "Zuni Traditional History and Cultural Geography." In Gregory and Wilcox 2007, 377–403. Tucson: University of Arizona Press.

Ferguson, T. J., and E. R. Hart. 1985. *A Zuni Atlas*. Norman: University of Oklahoma Press.

Ferguson, T. J., L. J. Kuwanwisiwma, M. Loma'omvaya, P. Lyons, G. Schachner, and L. Webster. 2013. "*Yep Hisat Hoopoq'yaqam Yeesiwa* (Hopi Ancestors Were Once Here): Repatriation Research Documenting Hopi Cultural Affiliation with the Ancient Hohokam of Southern Arizona." In *Global Ancestors: Understanding the Shared Humanity of Our Ancestors*, edited by M. Clegg, R. Redfern, J. Bekvalac, and H. Bonney, 104–33. London: Oxbow.

Ferguson, T. J., and B. J. Mills. 1987. "Settlement and Growth of Zuni Pueblo: An Architectural History." *Kiva* 52: 243–66.

Ferguson, T. J., and R. W. Preucel. 2005. "Signs of the Ancestors: An Archaeology of the Mesa Villages of the Pueblo Revolt." In *Structure and Meaning in Human Settlement*, edited by T. Atkin and J. Rykwert, 185–207. Philadelphia: University of Pennsylvania Museum of Archaeology and Anthropology.

Fewkes, J. W. 1894. "The Kinship of a Tanoan-Speaking Community in Tusayan." *American Anthropologist* (o.s.) 7, no. 2: 162–67.

———. 1898. "Archaeological Expedition to Northern Arizona in 1895." *ARBAE*, 1895–1896, 17, no. 2: 519–744.

———. 1899. "The Winter Solstice Altars at Hano Pueblo." *American Anthropologist* 1, no. 2: 251–76.

———. 1900. "Tusayan Migration Traditions." *ARBAE*, 1897–1898, 19, no. 2: 573–634.

———. 1906. "Hopi Shrines near the East Mesa, Arizona." *American Anthropologist* 8, no. 2: 346–75.

Flint, R., and S. Flint. 2005. *Documents of the Coronado Expedition, 1539–1541: They Were Not Familiar with His Majesty nor Did They Wish to Be His Subjects*. Dallas: Southern Methodist University Press.

Ford, R. I. 1977. "The Technology of Irrigation in a New Mexico Pueblo." In *Material Culture: Styles, Organization, and Dynamics of Technology*, edited by H. Lechtman and R. S. Merrill, 139–54. St. Paul, MN: West.

———. 1983. "Inter-Indian Exchange in the Southwest." In Ortiz 1983, 711–22.

Ford, R. I., A. H. Schroeder, and S. L. Peckham. 1972. "Three Perspectives on Puebloan Prehistory." In Ortiz 1972a, 19–39.

Ford, R. I., and R. Swentzell. 2015. "Pre-Contact Agriculture in Northern New Mexico." In *Traditional Arid Lands Agriculture: Understanding the Past for the Future*, edited by S. E. Ingram and R. C. Hunt, 330–57. Tucson: University of Arizona Press.

Fortes, M. 1949. "Time and Social Structure: An Ashanti Case Study." In *Social Structure: Studies Presented to A. R. Radcliffe-Brown*, edited by M. Fortes, 54–84. Oxford, UK: Clarendon.

———. 1969. *Kinship and the Social Order*. London: Routledge and Kegan Paul.

Fowler, A. P., and J. R. Stein. 1992. "The Anasazi Great House in Space, Time, and Paradigm." In Doyel 1992, 101–22.

Fowler, A. P., J. R. Stein, and R. Anyon. 1987. *An Archaeological Reconnaissance of West-Central New Mexico: The Anasazi Monuments Project.* Santa Fe: Historical Preservation Division, New Mexico Office of Cultural Affairs.

Fowles, S. M. 2004. "The Making of Made People: The Prehistoric Evolution of Hierocracy Among the Northern Tiwa of New Mexico." Ph.D. diss., University of Michigan.

———. 2005. "Historical Contingency and the Prehistoric Foundations of Moiety Organization among the Eastern Pueblos." *Journal of Anthropological Research* 61, no. 1: 25–52.

———. 2009. "The Enshrined Pueblo: Villagescape and Cosmos in the Northern Rio Grande." *American Antiquity* 74, no. 4: 448–66.

———. 2012. "The Pueblo Village in an Age of Reformation, AD 1300–1600." In Pauketat 2012, 620–30.

———. 2013. *An Archaeology of Doings: Secularism and the Study of Pueblo Religion.* Santa Fe, NM: School for Advanced Research Press.

Fox, R. 1967. *The Keresan Bridge: A Problem in Pueblo Ethnology.* New York: Humanities Press.

———. 1972. "Some Unsolved Problems of Pueblo Social Organization." In Ortiz 1972a, 71–85.

———. 1994. "The Evolution of Kinship Systems and the Crow-Omaha Question." In *The Challenge of Anthropology: Old Encounters and New Excursions,* by R. Fox, 215–45. New Brunswick, NJ: Transaction.

Freeman, J. D. 1961. "On the Concept of the Kindred." *Journal of the Royal Anthropological Institute* 91, no. 2: 192–220.

Freire-Marreco, B. 1914. "Tewa Kinship Terms from the Pueblo of Hano, Arizona." *American Anthropologist* 16, no. 2: 269–87.

———. 1915. "A Note on Kinship Terms Compounded with the Postfix 'E in the Hano Dialect of Tewa." *American Anthropologist* 17, no. 1: 198–202.

Fritz, J. 1978. "Paleopsychology Today: Ideational Systems and Human Adaptation in Prehistory." In *Social Archaeology: Beyond Subsistence and Dating,* edited by M. J. Berman, C. L. Redman, E. V. Curtain, W. T. Langhorn, N. M. Versaggi, et al., 37–59. New York: Academic Press.

———. 1987. "Chaco Canyon and Vijayanagra: Proposing Spatial Meaning in Two Societies." In *Mirror and Metaphor: Material and Social Constructions of Reality,* edited by D. W. Ingersoll and G. Bronitsky, 313–48. Lanham, MD: University Press of America.

Gatschet, A. S. 1876. *Zwölf Sprachen aus dem Südwesten Nordamerikas.* Weimar: H. Böhlau.

Gifford, E. W. 1922. *California Kinship Terminologies.* UCPAAE 18. Berkeley: University of California Press.

Gilmore, K. P., and S. Larmore. 2012. "Looking for Lovitt in All the Wrong Places: Migration Models and the Athapaskan Diaspora as Viewed from Eastern Colorado." In *From the Land of Ever Winter to the American Southwest: Athapaskan Migrations, Mobility, and Ethnogenesis,* edited by D. J. Seymour, 37–77. Salt Lake City: University of Utah Press.

Gilpin, D. A. 1988. "The 1987 Navajo Nation Investigations at Bidahochi Pueblo, a Fourteenth-Century Site in the Hopi Buttes, Navajo County, Arizona." Paper, 1988 Pecos Conference, Cortez, CO.

———. 1989. "Great Houses and Pueblos of Northeastern Arizona." Paper, 1989 Pecos Conference, Bandelier National Monument, NM.

———. 2001. "Boundaries of Tsegi Phase Architecture in Northeastern Arizona." In *The Archaeology of Ancient Tactical Sites,* edited by J. R. Welch and T. W. Bostwick, 7–19. Arizona Archaeologist 32. Phoenix: Arizona Archaeological Society.

Ginzburg, C. 1980. *The Cheese and the Worms: The Cosmos of a Sixteenth-Century Miller.* Translated by J. Tedeschi and A. C. Tedeschi. London: Routledge and Kegan Paul.

———. 1993. "Microhistory: Two or Three Things That I Know About It." Translated by J. Tedeschi and A. C. Tedeschi. *Critical Inquiry* 20, no. 1: 10–35.

Ginzburg, C., and C. Poni. 1991. "The Name and the Game: Unequal Exchange and the Historiographic Marketplace." In *Microhistory and the Lost Peoples of Europe,* edited by E. Muir and G. Ruggiero, 1–10. Baltimore, MD: Johns Hopkins University Press.

Glowacki, D. M. 2010. "The Social and Cultural Contexts of the Thirteenth-Century Migrations from the Mesa Verde Region." In Kohler, Varien, and Wright 2013, 200–221.

———. 2011. "The Role of Religion in the Depopulation of the Central Mesa Verde Region." In Glowacki and Van Keuren 2011, 66–83.

———. 2015. *Living and Leaving: A Social History of Regional Depopulation in Thirteenth-Century Mesa Verde.* Tucson: University of Arizona Press.

Glowacki, D. M., and S. G. Ortman. 2012. "Characterizing Community-Center (Village) Formation in the VEP Study Area, A.D. 600–1280." In *Emergence and Collapse of Early Villages: Models of Central Mesa Verde Archaeology,* edited by T. A. Kohler and M. D. Varien, 219–46. Berkeley: University of California Press.

Glowacki, D. M., and S. Van Keuren, eds. 2011. *Religious Transformation in the Late Pre-Hispanic Pueblo World.* Tucson: University of Arizona Press.

Godelier, M. 2011. *The Metamorphoses of Kinship,* translated by Nora Scott. New York: Verso.

Godelier, M., T. R. Trautmann, and F. E. Tjon Sie Fat. 1998a. "Introduction." In Godelier, Trautmann, and Tjon Sie Fat 1998b, 1–26.

——, eds. 1998b. *Transformations of Kinship.* Washington, DC: Smithsonian Institution Press.

González-Ruibal, A. 2007. "House Societies vs. Kinship-Based Societies: An Archaeological Case from Iron Age Europe." *Journal of Anthropological Archaeology* 25: 144–73.

Gould, S. H. 2000. *A New System for the Formal Analysis of Kinship.* Lanham, MD: University Press of America.

Gratz, K. E. 1977. *Archaeological Excavations along Route Z4 near Zuni.* MNA Research Paper 7. Flagstaff: Museum of Northern Arizona.

Grebinger, P. 1973. "Prehistoric Social Organization in Chaco Canyon, New Mexico: An Alternative Reconstruction." *Kiva* 19: 3–23.

Gregory, D. A., and D. R. Wilcox, eds. 2007. *Zuni Origins: Toward a New Synthesis of Southwestern Archaeology.* Tucson: University of Arizona Press.

Guiterman, C. H., T. W. Swetnam, and J. S. Dean. 2015. "Eleventh-Century Shift in Timber Procurement Areas for the Great Houses of Chaco Canyon." *PNAS.* DOI: 10.1073/pnas.1514272113.

Gunnerson, J. H. 1969. "Apache Archaeology in Northeastern New Mexico." *American Antiquity* 34, no. 1: 23–39.

Gutiérrez, R. A. 1991. *When Jesus Came, the Corn Mothers Went Away: Marriage, Sexuality, and Power in New Mexico, 1500–1846.* Stanford, CA: Stanford University Press.

Haas, J., and W. Creamer. 1993. *Stress and Warfare among the Kayenta Anasazi of the Thirteenth Century A.D.* Fieldiana: Anthropology, n.s., 21. Publication 1450. Chicago: Field Museum.

Habicht-Mauche, J. A. 1993. *The Pottery from Arroyo Hondo Pueblo, New Mexico: Tribalization and Trade in the Northern Rio Grande.* Arroyo Hondo Archaeological Series 8. Santa Fe, NM: School of American Research Press.

Hackett, C. W., ed., and C. C. Shelby, trans. 1942. *Revolt of the Pueblo Indians of New Mexico, and Otermín's Attempted Reconquest, 1680–1682.* 2 vols. Albuquerque: University of New Mexico Press.

Hage, P., B. Milicic, M. Mixco, and M. J. P. Nichols. 2004. "The Proto-Numic Kinship System." *Journal of Anthropological Research* 60: 359–77.

Hargrave, L. L. 1935. "The Jeddito Valley and the First Pueblo Towns in Arizona Visited by Europeans." *Museum Notes* 8, no. 4: 21. Flagstaff: Museum of Northern Arizona.

Harrington, J. P. 1912. "Tewa Relationship Terms." *American Anthropologist* 14, no. 3: 472–98.

———. 1916. "The Ethnogeography of the Tewa Indians." *ARBAE*, 1907–1908, 29: 29–618.

Harris, M. 1968. *The Rise of Anthropological Theory: A History of Theories of Culture.* New York: Crowell.

Haury, E. W. 1958. "Evidence at Point of Pines for a Prehistoric Migration from Northern Arizona." In *Migrations in New World Culture History*, edited by R. H. Thompson, 1–6. University of Arizona Bulletin 29, no. 2. Tucson: University of Arizona Press.

Hawley, F. 1937. "Pueblo Social Organization as a Lead to Pueblo History." *American Anthropologist* 39, no. 3: 504–22.

———. 1950. "Keresan Patterns of Kinship and Social Organization." *American Anthropologist* 52, no. 4: 499–512.

Hays-Gilpin, K. A., and D. A. Gilpin. 2018. "Becoming Hopi: Exploring Hopi Ethnogenesis through Architecture, Pottery, and Cultural Knowledge." In *Footprints of Hopi History: Hopihiniwtiput Kukveni'at*, edited by L. J. Kuwanwisiwma and T. J. Ferguson 123–40. Tucson: University of Arizona Press.

Hays-Gilpin, K. A., D. A. Gilpin, S. L. Eckert, J. A. Ware, D. A. Phillips Jr., et al. Forthcoming. "There and Back Again." In *Interaction and Connectivity in the Greater Southwest*, edited by K. Harry and B. Roth. Boulder: University Press of Colorado.

Hays-Gilpin, K. A., and S. LeBlanc. 2007. "Sikyatki Style in Regional Context." In *New Perspectives on Pottery Mound Pueblo*, edited by P. Schaafsma, 109–36. Albuquerque: University of New Mexico Press.

Hegmon, M., S. G. Ortman, and J. L. Mobley-Tanaka. 1999. "Women, Men, and the Organization of Space." In *Women and Men in the Prehispanic Southwest: Labor, Power, and Prestige*, edited by P. L. Crown, 43–90. Santa Fe, NM: School of American Research Press.

Heitman, C. C. 2015. "The House of Our Ancestors: New Research on the Prehistory of Chaco Canyon, New Mexico, A.D. 800–1200." In Heitman and Plog 2015, 215–38.

———. 2016. "'A Mother for All the People': Feminist Science and Chacoan Archaeology." *American Antiquity* 81: 471–89.

Heitman, C. C., and S. Plog. 2005. "Kinship and the Dynamics of the House: Rediscovering Dualism in the Pueblo Past." In *A Catalyst for Ideas: Anthropological Archaeology and the Legacy of Douglas W. Schwartz*, edited by V. Scarborough, 69–100. Santa Fe, NM: School of American Research Press.

———, eds. 2015. *Chaco Revisited: New Research on the Prehistory of Chaco Canyon, New Mexico*. Tucson: University of Arizona Press.

Helms, M. W. 1998. *Access to Origins: Affines, Ancestors, and Aristocrats*. Austin: University of Texas Press.

Hendricks, R. 2002. "Pueblo-Spanish Warfare in Seventeenth-Century New Mexico: The Battles of Black Mesa, Kotyiti, and Astialakwa." In Preucel 2002, 180–97.

Héritier, F. 1981. *L'exercice de la parenté*. Paris: Gallimard, Le Seuil.

Herr, S. A. 2001. *Beyond Chaco: Great Kiva Communities on the Mogollon Rim Frontier*. Anthropological Papers of the University of Arizona 66. Tucson: University of Arizona Press.

Herr, S. A., and L. C. Young. 2012. "Introduction to Southwestern Pithouse Communities." In Young and Herr 2012, 1–13.

Hewett, E. L. 1906. *Antiquities of the Jemez Plateau, New Mexico*. BAEB 32.

———. 1936. *The Chaco Canyon and Its Monuments*. Albuquerque: University of New Mexico Press.

Hieb, L. A. 1972. "Meaning and Mismeaning: Toward an Understanding of the Ritual Clown." In Ortiz 1972a, 163–96.

Hill, J. B. 2007. "The Zuni Language in Southwestern Areal Context." In Gregory and Wilcox 2007, 22–38.

Hill, J. B., J. J. Clark, W. H. Doelle, and P. D. Lyons. 2004. "Prehistoric Demography in the Southwest: Migration, Coalescence, and Hohokam Population Decline." *American Antiquity* 69, no. 4: 689–716.

Hill, J. H., and K. Hays-Gilpin. 1999. "The Flower World in Material Culture: An Iconographic Complex in the Southwest and Mesoamerica." *Journal of Anthropological Research* 55: 1–37.

Hill, K. C. 2011. "Serrano Dictionary." MS. Private collection.

Hill, W. W. 1982. *An Ethnography of Santa Clara Pueblo, New Mexico*. Albuquerque: University of New Mexico Press.

Hodge, F. W. 1896. "Pueblo Indian Clans." *American Anthropologist* o.s. 9, no. 10: 345–52.

———. 1912. "Taos." In *Handbook of American Indians North of Mexico*, edited by F. W. Hodge, 688–91. BAEB 30, no. 2.

———. 1939. "A Square Kiva near Hawikuh." In *So Live the Works of Men: Seventieth Anniversary Edition Honoring Edgar Lee Hewett*, edited by D. D. Brand and F. E. Harvey, 195–214. Albuquerque: University of New Mexico Press.

———. 1966. "Ceremonial Deposits in the Hawikuh Cemetery." In *The Excavation of Hawikuh by Frederick Webb Hodge: Report of the Hendricks-Hodge Expedition, 1917–1923*, edited by W. Smith, R. B. Woodbury, and N. F. S. Woodbury, 279–93. New York: Museum of the American Indian.

Hodge, F. W., G. P. Hammond, and A. Rey. 1945. *Fray Alonso de Benavides' Revised Memorial of 1634*. Albuquerque: University of New Mexico Press.

Hopi Dictionary Project. 1998. *Hopi Dictionary/Hopìikwa Lavàytutuveni: A Hopi-English Dictionary of the Third Mesa Dialect with an English–Hopi Finder List and a Sketch of Hopi Grammar*. Tucson: University of Arizona Press.

Howell, T. L. 1995. "Tracking Zuni Gender and Leadership Roles across the Contact Period." *Journal of Anthropological Research* 51, no. 2: 125–47.

———. 1996. "Identifying Leaders at Hawikku." *Kiva* 62, no. 1: 61–82.

———. 2000. *The Archaeology and Ethnohistory of Oak Wash, Zuni Indian Reservation, New Mexico*. ZCRE Report 664. Pueblo of Zuni, NM: Zuni Cultural Resource Enterprise.

Howell, T. L., and K. W. Kintigh. 1996. "Archaeological Identification of Kin Groups Using Mortuary and Biological Data: An Example from the American Southwest." *American Antiquity* 61, no. 3: 537–54.

Hughte, P. 1994. *A Zuni Artist Looks at Frank Hamilton Cushing*. Zuni, NM: Pueblo of Zuni Arts and Crafts.

Ingold, T., ed. 1996. *Key Debates in Anthropology*. London: Routledge.

Irwin, D. C. 1997. "Nonflaked Lithics." In *The Rio Puerco Bridge and Road N2007 Realignment Project*, by D. C. Irwin, 221–46. Research Papers 2. Dolores, CO: La Plata Archaeological Consultants.

Ives, J. W. 1998. "Developmental Processes in the Pre-Contact History of Athapaskan, Algonquian, and Numic Kin Systems." In Godelier, Trautmann, and Tjon Sie Fat 1998b, 94–139.

James, S. R. 1997. "Change and Continuity in Western Pueblo Households during the Historic Period in the American Southwest." *World Archaeology* 28, no. 3: 429–56.

Jeançon, J. A. 1923. *Excavations in the Chama Valley, New Mexico*. BAEB 81.

———. 1925. "Primitive Coloradoans." *Colorado Magazine* 2, no. 1: 35–40.

Jones, D., and B. Milicic, eds. 2011. *Kinship, Language and Prehistory: Per Hage and the Renaissance in Kinship Studies*. Salt Lake City: University of Utah Press.

Jones, O. L., Jr. 1966. *Pueblo Warriors and Spanish Conquest.* Norman: University of Oklahoma Press.

Jorgensen, J. 1980. *Western Indians: Comparative Environments, Languages, and Cultures of 172 Western American Indian Tribes.* San Francisco: Freeman.

Josephy, A. 1993. *The Patriot Chiefs.* New York: Penguin.

Joyce, R. A., and S. D. Gillespie, eds. 2000. *Beyond Kinship: Social and Material Reproduction in House Societies.* Philadelphia: University of Pennsylvania Press.

Judd, N. M. 1924. "Two Chaco Canyon Pithouses." *Annual Report of the Smithsonian Institution 1922*: 399–413.

———. 1959. *Pueblo del Arroyo, Chaco Canyon, New Mexico.* Smithsonian Miscellaneous Collections 138, no. 1. Washington, DC: Smithsonian Institution.

———. 1964. *The Architecture of Pueblo Bonito.* Smithsonian Miscellaneous Collections 147, no. 1. Washington, DC: Smithsonian Institution.

Judge, W. J. 1989. "Chaco Canyon–San Juan Basin." In *Dynamics of Southwest Prehistory*, edited by L. S. Cordell and G. J. Gumerman, 209–61. Washington, DC: Smithsonian Institution Press.

———. 2004. "Chaco's Golden Century." In *In Search of Chaco*, edited by D. G. Noble, 1–6. Santa Fe: School of American Research Press.

Kalb, D., and H. Tak, eds. 2005. *Critical Junctures: Anthropology and History beyond the Cultural Turn.* New York: Berghahn.

Kantner, J. 2003. "Rethinking Chaco as a System." *Kiva* 69: 207–27.

———. 2004. *Ancient Puebloan Southwest.* New York: Cambridge University Press.

———. 2010. "Identifying the Pathways to Permanent Leadership." In *The Evolution of Leadership: Transitions in Decision Making from Small-Scale to Middle-Range Societies*, edited by K. V. Vaughn, J. E. Eerkens, and J. Kantner, 249–81. Santa Fe, NM: School for Advanced Research Press.

Kealiinohomoku, J. W. 1989. "The Hopi Katsina Dance Event 'Doings.'" In *Seasons of the Kachina*, edited by L. J. Bean, 51–44. Hayward, CA: Ballena.

Kennett, D. J., S. Plog, R. J. George, B. J. Culleton, A. S. Watson, et al. 2017. "Archaeogenomic Evidence Reveals Prehistoric Matrilineal Dynasty." *Nature Communications.* DOI: 10.1038/ncomms14115.

Kessell, J. L. 2008. *Pueblos, Spaniards, and the Kingdom of New Mexico.* Norman: University of Oklahoma Press.

Kessell, J. L., and R. Hendricks, eds. 1992. *By Force of Arms: The Journals of Don Diego de Vargas, New Mexico, 1691–1693.* Albuquerque: University of New Mexico Press.

Kessell, J. L., R. Hendricks, and M. Dodge, eds. 1995. *To the Royal Crown Restored: The Journals of Don Diego de Vargas, New Mexico, 1692–1694.* Albuquerque: University of New Mexico Press.

———. 1998. *Blood on the Boulders: The Journals of Don Diego de Vargas, New Mexico, 1694–1697.* 2 vols. Albuquerque: University of New Mexico Press.

Kidder, A. V. 1924. *An Introduction to the Study of Southwestern Archaeology with a Preliminary Account of the Excavations at Pecos.* New Haven, CT: Yale University Press.

Kidder, A. V., and S. J. Guernsey. 1919. *Archaeological Explorations in Northeastern Arizona.* BAEB 8.

Kintigh, K. W. 1985. *Settlement, Subsistence, and Society in Late Zuni Prehistory.* Anthropological Papers of the University of Arizona 44. Tucson: University of Arizona Press.

———. 1994. "Chaco Community Architecture, and Cibolan Aggregation." In *The Ancient Southwestern Community: Models and Methods for the Study of Prehistoric Social Organization,* edited by W. H. Wills and R. D. Leonard, 131–40. Albuquerque: University of New Mexico Press.

———. 2000. "Political Organization of the Protohistoric Cities of Cibola." In *Alternative Leadership Strategies in the Prehispanic Southwest,* edited by B. J. Mills, 95–116. Tucson: University of Arizona Press.

———. 2007. "Late Prehistoric and Protohistoric Settlement Systems in the Zuni Area." In Gregory and Wilcox 2007, 361–76.

Kintigh, K. W., D. M. Glowacki, and D. L. Huntley. 2004. "Long-Term Settlement History and the Emergence of Towns in the Zuni Area." *American Antiquity* 69, no. 3: 432–56.

Kintigh, K. W., T. L. Howell, and A. I. Duff. 1996. "Post-Chacoan Social Integration at the Hinkson Site, New Mexico." *Kiva* 61, no. 3: 257–74.

Knaut, A. L. 1995. *The Pueblo Revolt: Conquest and Resistance in Seventeenth-Century New Mexico.* Norman: University of Oklahoma Press.

Kohler, T. A., and K. M. Reese. 2014. "Long and Spatially Variable Neolithic Demographic Transition in the North American Southwest." *PNAS* 111, no. 28: 10101–6.

Kohler, T. A., and M. J. Root. 2004. "The Late Coalition and Earliest Classic on the Pajarito Plateau (A.D. 1250–1375)." In *Archaeology of Bandelier National Monument: Village Formation on the Pajarito Plateau, New Mexico,* edited by T. A. Kohler, 173–214. Albuquerque: University of New Mexico Press.

Kohler, T. A., M. D. Varien, and A. Wright, eds. 2013. *Leaving Mesa Verde: Peril and Change in the Thirteenth-Century Southwest.* Tucson: University of Arizona Press.

Kroeber, A. L. 1909. "Classificatory Systems of Relationship." *Journal of the Royal Anthropological Institute* 39: 77–84.

———. 1917. *Zuni Kin and Clan*. Anthropological Papers of the American Museum of Natural History 18, no. 2. New York: American Museum of Natural History.

Kronenfeld, D. B. 2012. "Crow- (and Omaha-) Type Kinship Terminology: The Fanti Case." In Trautmann and Whiteley 2012c, 153–72.

Kroskrity, P. 1998. "Arizona Tewa Kiva Speech as a Manifestation of a Dominant Language Ideology." In *Language Ideologies: Practice and Theory*, edited by B. Schieffelin, K. Woolard, and P. Kroskrity, 103–22. New York: Oxford University Press.

Kryukov, M. V. 1998. "The Synchro-Diachronic Method and the Multidirectionality of Kinship Transformations." In Godelier, Trautmann, and Tjon Sie Fat 1998b, 294–313.

Kubler, G. 1940. *The Religious Architecture of New Mexico in the Colonial Period and since the American Occupation*. Colorado Springs, CO: The Taylor Museum.

———. 1973. *The Religious Architecture of New Mexico in the Colonial Period and since the American Occupation*. 4th ed. Albuquerque: University of New Mexico Press.

Kuckelman, K. A. 2000. "Architecture." In *The Archaeology of Castle Rock Pueblo: A Thirteenth-Century Village in Southwestern Colorado*, edited by K. A. Kuckelman. Cortez, CO: Crow Canyon Archaeological Center. https://www.crowcanyon.org/ResearchReports/CastleRock/.

———. 2002. "Thirteenth-Century Warfare in the Central Mesa Verde Region." In *Seeking the Center Place: Archaeology and Ancient Communities in the Mesa Verde Region*, edited by M. D. Varien and R. H. Wilshusen, 233–53. Salt Lake City: University of Utah Press.

———. 2010. "The Depopulation of Sand Canyon Pueblo, A Large Ancestral Pueblo Village in Southwestern Colorado." *American Antiquity* 75, no. 3: 497–526.

Kuckelman, K. A., R. R. Lightfoot, and D. L. Martin. 2000. "Changing Patterns of Violence in the Northern San Juan Region." *Kiva* 66: 147–65.

———. 2002. "The Bioarchaeology and Taphonomy of Violence at Castle Rock and Sand Canyon Pueblos, Southwestern Colorado." *American Antiquity* 67, no. 3: 486–513.

Kuckelman, K. A., and D. L. Martin. 2007. "Human Skeletal Remains." In *The Archaeology of Sand Canyon Pueblo: Intensive Excavations at a Late-Thirteenth-Century Village in Southwestern Colorado*, edited by K. A. Kuckelman. Cortez, CO: Crow Canyon Archaeological Center. https://www.crowcanyon.org/ResearchReports/SandCanyon/.

Kuper, A. 1982. "Lineage Theory: A Critical Retrospect." *Annual Review of Anthropology* 11: 71–95.

Kurath, G. P., and A. Garcia. 1970. *Music and Dance of the Tewa Pueblos.* Research Records 8. Santa Fe: Museum of New Mexico Press.

Kuwanwisiwma, L. J. 2002. "*Hopit navotiat,* Hopi Knowledge of History: Hopi Presence on Black Mesa." In *Prehistoric Culture Change on the Colorado Plateau: Ten Thousand Years on Black Mesa,* edited by S. Powell and F. E. Smiley, 161–63. Tucson: University of Arizona Press.

Kuwanwisiwma, L. J., T. J. Ferguson, and C. Colwell, eds. 2018. *Footprints of Hopi History: Hopihiniwtiput Kukveni'at.* Tucson: University of Arizona Press.

Lachler, J. 2006. "A Grammar of Laguna Keres." Ph.D. diss., University of New Mexico.

Ladd, E. J. 1979. "Zuni Social and Political Organization." In Ortiz 1979, 482–91.

Lakatos, S. A. 2007. "Cultural Continuity and the Development of Integrative Architecture in the Northern Rio Grande Valley of New Mexico, A.D. 600–1200." *Kiva* 73, no. 1: 31–66.

Lange, C. H. 1959. *Cochiti: A New Mexico Pueblo, Past and Present.* Austin: University of Texas Press.

———, ed. 1982. *An Ethnography of Santa Clara Pueblo, New Mexico,* by W. W. Hill. Albuquerque: University of New Mexico Press.

Lange, C. H., and C. L. Riley, eds. 1966. *The Southwestern Journals of Adolph F. Bandelier, 1880–1882.* Albuquerque: University of New Mexico Press.

Lange, C. H., C. L. Riley, and E. M. Lange, eds. 1975. *The Southwestern Journals of Adolph F. Bandelier, 1885–1888.* Albuquerque: University of New Mexico Press.

Laski, V. 1959. *Seeking Life.* Philadelphia, PA: American Folklore Society.

Leach, E. R. 1966. "Virgin Birth." *Proceedings of the Royal Anthropological Institute* 1966: 39–49.

Lechner, J. 1989. "El concepto de 'policía' y su presencia en la obra de los primeros historiadores de Indias." *Revista de Indias* 41, nos. 165–66: 395–409.

Lekson, S. H. 1984. *Great Pueblo Architecture of Chaco Canyon.* Publications in Archaeology 18B, Chaco Canyon Series. Santa Fe, NM: National Park Service.

———. 1988. "The Idea of the Kiva in Anasazi Archaeology." *Kiva* 53, no. 3: 213–34.

———, ed. 2006a. *The Archaeology of Chaco Canyon: An Eleventh-Century Regional Center.* Santa Fe, NM: School of American Research Press.

———. 2006b. "Chaco Matters: An Introduction." In Lekson 2006a, 3–44.

————. 2006c. "Lords of the Great House: Pueblo Bonito as Palace." In *Palaces and Power in the Americas*, edited by J. J. Christie and P. J. Sarro, 99–114. Austin: University of Texas Press.

————. 2008. *A History of the Ancient Southwest*. Santa Fe, NM: School for Advanced Research Press.

————. 2012. "Chaco's Hinterlands." In Pauketat 2012, 597–607.

Lévi-Strauss, C. 1949. *Les structures élémentaires de la parenté*. Paris: Presses Universitaires de France.

————. 1966. "The Future of Kinship Studies." *Proceedings of the Royal Anthropological Institute* 1965: 13–21.

————. 1969. *The Elementary Structures of Kinship*. Rev. ed. translated by R. Needham, J. H. Bell, and J. R. von Sturmer. London: Eyre and Spottiswoode.

————. 1982. *The Way of the Masks*. Translated by S. Modelski. Seattle: University of Washington Press.

Levy, J. E. 1992. *Orayvi Revisited: Social Stratification in an Egalitarian Society*. Santa Fe, NM: School of American Research Press.

————. 1994. "Ethnographic Analogs: Strategies for Reconstructing Archaeological Cultures." In *Understanding Complexity in the Prehistoric Southwest*, edited by G. Gumerman and M. Gell-Mann, 233–44. Santa Fe Institute Studies in the Sciences of Complexity 16. Reading, MA: Addison-Wesley.

Liebmann, M. 2012. *Revolt: An Archaeological History of Pueblo Resistance and Revitalization in 17th-Century New Mexico*. Tucson: University of Arizona Press.

Liebmann, M., T. J. Ferguson, and R. W. Preucel. 2005. "Pueblo Settlement, Architecture, and Social Change in the Pueblo Revolt Era, A.D. 1680–1696." *Journal of Field Archaeology* 30: 1–16.

Liebmann, M., and R. W. Preucel. 2007. "The Archaeology of the Pueblo Revolt and the Formation of the Modern Pueblo World." *Kiva* 73: 197–219.

Liebmann, M., R. W. Preucel, and J. Aguilar. 2017. "The Pueblo World Transformed: Alliances, Factionalism, and Animosities in the Northern Rio Grande, 1680–1700." In *New Mexico and the Pimeria Alta: The Colonial Period in the American Southwest*, edited by J. G. Douglass and W. M. Graves, 143–56. Boulder: University Press of Colorado.

Lightfoot, K. G. 2008. "Oral Traditions and Material Things: Constructing Histories of Native People in Colonial Settings." In Brooks, DeCorse, and Walton 2008, 289–324.

Lipe, W. D. 1989. "Social Scale of Mesa Verde Anasazi Kivas." In Lipe and Hegmon 1989, 53–71.

———. 1995. "The Depopulation of the Northern San Juan: Conditions in the Turbulent 1200s." *Journal of Anthropological Archaeology* 14, no. 2: 143–69.

———. 2006. "Notes from the North." In Lekson 2006a, 261–314.

———. 2010. "Lost in Transit: The Central Mesa Verde Archaeological Complex." In Kohler, Varien, and Wright 2013, 262–84.

Lipe, W. D., and M. Hegmon, eds. 1989. *The Architecture of Social Integration in Prehistoric Pueblos.* Occasional Papers, no. 1. Cortez, CO: Crow Canyon Archaeological Center.

Lipe, W. D., and S. G. Ortman. 2000. "Spatial Patterning in Northern San Juan Villages, A.D. 1050–1300." *Kiva* 66, no. 1: 91–122.

Lomawaima, H. H. 1989a. "Commentary." In *Seasons of the Kachina*, edited by L. J. Bean, 165–71. Hayward, CA: Ballena.

———. 1989b. "Hopification: A Strategy for Cultural Preservation." In *Columbian Consequences: Archaeological and Historical Perspectives on the Spanish Borderlands West*, vol. 1, edited by D. H. Thomas, 93–99. Washington, DC: Smithsonian Institution Press.

Longacre, W. A., ed. 1970. *Reconstructing Prehistoric Pueblo Societies.* Albuquerque: University of New Mexico Press.

Lounsbury, F. G. 1965. "Another View of the Trobriand Kinship Categories." *American Anthropologist* 67, no. 5, pt. 2: 142–85.

Lowie, R. H. 1915a. "Exogamy and the Classificatory Systems of Relationship." *American Anthropologist* 17, no. 2: 223–39.

———. 1915b. "Oral Tradition and History." *American Anthropologist* 17, no. 3: 597–99.

———. 1917. "Oral Tradition and History." *Journal of American Folklore* 30, no. 116: 161–67.

———. 1923. "A Note on Kiowa Kinship Terms and Usages." *American Anthropologist* 25, no. 2: 279–81.

———. 1929a. *Notes on Hopi Clans.* Anthropological Papers of the American Museum of Natural History 30, part 6. New York: American Museum of Natural History.

———. 1929b. *Hopi Kinship.* Anthropological Papers of the American Museum of Natural History 30, part 7. New York: American Museum of Natural History

———. 1954. *Indians of the Plains.* New York: McGraw-Hill.

Lyons, P. D. 2003. *Ancestral Hopi Migrations.* Anthropological Papers of the University of Arizona 68. Tucson: University of Arizona Press.

Martin, P. S., and J. B. Rinaldo. 1960. *Table Rock Pueblo, Arizona.* Fieldiana: Anthropology 51, no. 2. Chicago: Chicago Natural History Museum.

Martin, P. S., J. B. Rinaldo, W. A. Longacre, C. Cronin, L. G. Freeman, and J. Schoen-wetter. 1962. *Chapters in the Prehistory of Eastern Arizona, I*. Fieldiana: Anthropology 53. Chicago: Chicago Natural History Museum.

Martínez, M. E. 2000. "Space, Order, and Group Identities in a Spanish Colonial Town: Puebla de los Angeles." In *The Collective and the Public in Latin America: Cultural Identities and Political Order*, edited by L. Roniger and T. Herzog, 13–36. Portland, OR: Sussex Academic Press.

Mathien, F. J. 1987. "Ornaments and Minerals from Pueblo Alto." In *Investigations at the Pueblo Alto Complex, Chaco Canyon, New Mexico, 1975–1979*. Vol. III: *Artifactual and Biological Analyses*, edited by F. J. Mathien and T. C. Windes, 381–428. Publications in Archaeology 18F, Chaco Canyon Series. Santa Fe, NM: National Park Service.

———. 2001. "The Organization of Turquoise Production and Consumption by the Prehistoric Chacoans." *American Antiquity* 66: 103–18.

———. 2005. *Culture and Ecology of Chaco Canyon and the San Juan Basin*. Publications in Archaeology 18H, Chaco Canyon Series. Santa Fe, NM: National Park Service.

Maybury-Lewis, D., and U. Almagor, eds. 1989. *The Attraction of Opposites: Thought and Society in the Dualistic Mode*. Ann Arbor: University of Michigan Press.

McConvell, P. 2001. "Language Shift and Language Spread among Hunter-Gatherers." In *Hunter-Gatherers: An Interdisciplinary Perspective*, edited by C. Panter-Brick, R. H. Layton, and P. Rowley-Conwy, 143–69. Cambridge, UK: Cambridge University Press.

———. 2012. "Omaha Skewing in Australia: Overlays, Dynamics, and Change." In Trautmann and Whiteley 2012c, 243–60.

McGregor, J. C. 1941. *Winona and Ridge Ruin, Part I: Architecture and Material Culture*. Museum of Northern Arizona Bulletin 18. Flagstaff: Museum of Northern Arizona.

———. 1943. "Burial of an Early American Magician." *Proceedings of the American Philosophical Society* 86, no. 2: 270–98.

McKinley, R. 1971. "Why Do Crow and Omaha Kinship Terminologies Exist? A Sociology of Knowledge Interpretation." *Man*, n.s., 6, no. 3: 408–26.

McKinnon, S. 1991. *From a Shattered Sun: Hierarchy, Gender, and Alliance in the Tanimbar Islands*. Madison: University of Wisconsin Press.

———. 2000. "Domestic Exceptions: Evans-Pritchard and the Creation of Nuer Patrilineality and Equality." *Cultural Anthropology* 15, no. 1: 35–83.

Mera, H. P. 1935. *Ceramic Clues to the Prehistory of North Central New Mexico*. Laboratory of Anthropology Technical Series Bulletin 8. Santa Fe: Laboratory of Anthropology, Museum of New Mexico.

Miller, W. R. 1959. "Some Notes on Acoma Kinship Terminology." *Southwestern Journal of Anthropology* 15: 179–84.

Miller, W. R., and I. Davis. 1963. "Proto-Keresan Phonology." *IJAL* 29: 310–30.

Mills, B. J. 1998. "Migration and Pueblo IV Community Reorganization in the Silver Creek Area, East-Central Arizona." In Spielmann 1998, 65–80.

———. 2002. "Recent Research on Chaco: Changing Views on Economy, Ritual, and Society." *Journal of Archaeological Research* 10, no. 1: 65–117.

———. 2004a. "The Establishment and Defeat of Hierarchy: Inalienable Possessions and the History of Collective Prestige Structures in the Pueblo Southwest." *American Anthropologist* 106, no. 2: 238–51.

———, ed. 2004b. *Identity, Feasting, and the Archaeology of the Greater Southwest.* Boulder: University Press of Colorado.

———. 2007a. "Performing the Feast: Visual Display and Suprahousehold Commensalism in the Puebloan Southwest." *American Antiquity* 72, no. 2: 210–39.

———. 2007b. "A Regional Perspective on Ceramics and Zuni Identity, A.D. 200–1630." In Gregory and Wilcox 2007, 210–38.

———. 2008. "How the Pueblos Became Global: Colonial Appropriations, Resistance, and Diversity in the North American Southwest." *Archaeologies* 4, no. 2: 218–32.

———. 2012. "The Archaeology of the Greater Southwest: Migration, Inequality, and Religious Transformations." In Pauketat 2012, 547–60.

———. 2015. "Unpacking the House: Ritual Practice and Social Networks at Chaco." In Heitman and Plog 2015, 249–71.

Mills, B. J., J. J. Clark, and M. A. Peeples. 2016. "Migration, Skill, and the Transformation of Social Networks in the Pre-Hispanic Southwest." *Economic Anthropology* 3, no. 2: 203–15.

Mills, B. J., J. J. Clark, M. A. Peeples, W. R. Haas, J. M. Roberts, et al. 2013. "Transformation of Social Networks in the Late Pre-Hispanic US Southwest." *PNAS* 110, no. 15: 5785–90.

Mills, B. J., and T. J. Ferguson. 2008. "Animate Objects: Shell Trumpets and Ritual Networks in the Greater Southwest." *Journal of Archaeological Method and Theory* 15, no. 4: 338–61.

Mills, B. J., S. A. Herr, and S. Van Keuren, eds. 1999. *Living on the Edge of the Rim: Excavations and Analysis of the Silver Creek Archaeological Research Project, 1993–1998.* Arizona State Museum Archaeology Series. Tucson: Arizona State Museum.

Mindeleff, C. 1900. "Localization of Tusayan Clans." *ARBAE*, 1897–1898, 19, no. 2: 635–53.

Mindeleff, V. 1891. "A Study of Pueblo Architecture, Tusayan and Cibola." *ARBAE*, 1886–1887, 8: 3–228.

Mobley-Tanaka, J. L. 1997. "Gender and Ritual Space during the Pithouse to Pueblo Transition: Subterranean Mealing Rooms in the North American Southwest." *American Antiquity* 62: 437–48.

Montgomery, R. G., W. Smith, and J. O. Brew. 1949. *Franciscan Awatovi*. Papers of the Peabody Museum of American Archaeology and Ethnology 36. Cambridge, MA: Peabody Museum.

Mooney, J. 1898a. "Calendar History of the Kiowa Indians." *ARBAE*, 1895–1896, 17: 129–445.

———. 1898b. "The Jicarilla Genesis." *American Anthropologist* o.s. 11, no. 7: 197–209.

Morgan, L. H. 1871. *Systems of Consanguinity and Affinity of the Human Family*. Washington, DC: Smithsonian Institution.

Morris, E. H. 1925. "Exploring in the Canyon of Death." *National Geographic* 48 (September): 263–300.

Mount, J. E., S. J. Olsen, J. W. Olsen, G. A. Teague, and B. D. Treadwell. 1993. *Wide Reed Ruin, Hubbell Trading Post National Historic Site*. Prof. Papers 51. Santa Fe, NM: Southwest Cultural Resources Center, National Park Service.

Muir, E. 1991. "Introduction: Observing Trifles." In *Microhistory and the Lost Peoples of Europe*, edited by E. Muir and G. Ruggiero, translated by Eren Branch, vii–xxviii. Baltimore, MD: Johns Hopkins University Press.

Muir, R. J. 1999. "Zooarchaeology of Sand Canyon Pueblo, Colorado." Ph.D. diss., Simon Fraser University.

Murdock, G. P. 1949. *Social Structure*. New York: Macmillan.

———. 1951. Review of *Social Organization of the Western Pueblos* by F. Eggan. *American Anthropologist* 53: 250–51.

Nadel, S. F. 1947. *The Nuba: An Anthropological Study of the Hill Tribes in Kordofan*. New York: Oxford University Press.

Nagata, S. n.d. "Crow-Omaha Kinship Types and *Sociétés à Maison*." Ms. Private collection.

Nahohai, M., and E. Phelps. 1995. *Dialogues with Zuni Potters*. Zuni, NM: Zuni A:shiwi Publishing.

Naranjo, T. 1995. "Thoughts on Migration by Santa Clara Pueblo." *Journal of Anthropological Archaeology* 14, no. 2: 247–50.

———. 2006. "We Came from the South, We Came from the North: Some Tewa Origin Stories." In *The Mesa Verde World*, edited by D. G. Noble, 49–57. Santa Fe, NM: School of American Research Press.

———. 2008. "Life as Movement: A Tewa View of Community and Identity." In *The Social Construction of Communities: Agency, Structure and Identity in the Prehispanic Southwest*, edited by M. D. Varien and J. M. Potter, 251–62. Lanham, MD: Altamira.

Naranjo, T., and R. Swentzell. 1989. "Healing Spaces in the Tewa Pueblo World." *American Indian Culture and Research Journal* 13, no. 3–4: 257–65.

Neitzel, J. E. 2003a. "Artifact Distributions at Pueblo Bonito." In Neitzel 2003c, 107–26.

———. 2003b. "The Organization, Function, and Population of Pueblo Bonito." In Neitzel 2003c, 143–49.

———, ed. 2003c. *Pueblo Bonito: Center of the Pueblo World*. Washington, DC: Smithsonian Institution Press.

———. 2012. "The Magician: An Ancestral Hopi Leader." In *The Bioarchaeology of Individuals*, edited by A. L. W. Stodder and A. M. Palkovich, 11–25. Gainesville: University Press of Florida.

Nelson, B. A. 2006. "Mesoamerican Objects and Symbols in Chaco." In Lekson 2006a, 339–71.

Newman, S. 1965. *Zuni Grammar*. UNM Publications in Anthropology 14. Albuquerque: University of New Mexico Press.

Nordby, L. V. 1999. "Introduction." In *Mesa Verde Ancient Architecture,* by J. W. Fewkes, vi–x. Albuquerque: Awanyu.

O'Hara, M. 2008. "The Magician of Ridge Ruin: An Interpretation of the Social, Political, and Ritual Roles Represented." Paper, Society for American Archaeology annual meeting, Vancouver, BC.

Opler, E. M. 1994 [1938]. *Myths and Tales of the Jicarilla Apache Indians*. New York: Dover.

Orser, C. E., Jr. 2007. "The Global and the Local in Modern-World Archaeology." In *Constructing Post-Medieval Archaeology in Italy: A New Agenda*, edited by S. Gelichi and M. Librenti, 25–33. Florence: Edizioni all'Insegna de Giglio.

Ortiz, A. 1969. *The Tewa World: Space, Time, Being, and Becoming in a Pueblo Society*. Chicago: University of Chicago Press.

———, ed. 1972a. *New Perspectives on the Pueblos*. Albuquerque: University of New Mexico Press.

———. 1972b. "Ritual Drama and the Pueblo World View." In Ortiz 1972a, 135–61.

———, ed. 1979. *Handbook of North American Indians*. Vol 9: *Southwest*. Washington, DC: Smithsonian Institution.

———. 1980. "Popay's Leadership: A Pueblo Perspective." *El Palacio* 86: 18–22.

————, ed. 1983. *Handbook of North American Indians.* Vol 10: *Southwest.* Washington, DC: Smithsonian Institution.

————. 1994. "The Dynamics of Pueblo Cultural Survival." In *North American Indian Anthropology: Essays on Society and Culture,* edited by R. J. DeMallie and A. Ortiz, 296–306. Norman: University of Oklahoma Press.

————. n.d. "A Sacred Symbol through the Ages." Ms. Private collection.

Ortman, S. G. 1998. "Corn Grinding and Community Organization in the Pueblo Southwest, A.D. 1150–1550." In Spielmann 1998, 165–92.

————. 2008a. "Action, Place and Space in the Castle Rock Community." In *The Social Construction of Communities: Agency, Structure and Identity in the Prehispanic Southwest,* edited by M. D. Varien and J. M. Potter, 125–54. Lanham, MD: Altamira.

————. 2008b. "Architectural Metaphor and Chacoan Influence in the Northern San Juan." In *Archaeology without Borders: Contact, Commerce, and Change in the U.S. Southwest and Northwestern Mexico,* edited by L. Webster and M. McBrinn, 227–55. Proceedings of the 2004 Southwest Symposium. Boulder: University Press of Colorado.

————. 2011. "Bowls to Gardens: A History of Tewa Community Metaphors." In Glowacki and Van Keuren 2011, 84–108.

————. 2012. *Winds from the North: Tewa Origins and Historical Anthropology.* Salt Lake City: University of Utah Press.

Ostler, J., M. E. Rodee, and M. Nahohai. 1996. *Zuni: A Village of Silversmiths.* Zuni, NM: A:shiwi Publishing.

Pandey, T. N. 1968. "Tribal Council Elections in a Southwestern Pueblo." *Ethnology* 7: 71–85.

————. 1975. "'India Man' among American Indians." In *Encounter and Experience: Personal Accounts of Fieldwork,* edited by A. Béteille and T. N. Madan, 194–213. Honolulu: University of Hawai'i Press.

————. 1977. "Images of Power in a Southwestern Pueblo." In *The Anthropology of Power: Ethnographic Studies from Asia, Oceania, and the New World,* edited by R. D. Fogelson and R. N. Adams, 195–215. New York: Academic Press.

————. 1978. "Flora Zuni (Zuni, 1897–1983)." In *American Indian Intellectuals of the Nineteenth and Early Twentieth Centuries,* edited by M. Liberty, 245–55. New York: West Publishing.

————. 1979. "The Anthropologist-Informant Relationship." In *The Fieldworker and the Field,* edited by M. N. Srinivas, A. M. Shah, and E. A. Ramaswamy, 246–65. New York: Oxford University Press.

————. 1991. "Fred Eggan." In *Remembering the University of Chicago: Teachers,*

Scientists, and Scholars, edited by E. Shils, 97–109. Chicago: University of Chicago Press.

———. 1994. "Patterns of Leadership in Western Pueblo Society." In *North American Indian Anthropology: Essays on Society and Culture*, edited by R. J. DeMallie and A. Ortiz, 328–39. Norman: University of Oklahoma Press.

Parsons, E. C. 1923. *Laguna Genealogies*. Anthropological Papers of the American Museum of Natural History 19, part 5. New York: American Museum of Natural History.

———. 1924. "Tewa Kin, Clan, and Moiety." *American Anthropologist* 26, no. 3: 333–39.

———. 1925. *The Pueblo of Jemez*. New Haven, CT: Yale University Press.

———. 1926. "The Ceremonial Calendar of the Tewa of Arizona." *American Anthropologist* 28, no. 1: 209–29.

———. 1928. "The Laguna Migration to Isleta." *American Anthropologist* 30, no. 4: 602–3.

———. 1929. *The Social Organization of the Tewa of New Mexico*. Memoirs of the American Anthropological Association 36. Menasha, WI: American Anthropological Association.

———. 1932. "The Kinship Nomenclature of the Pueblo Indians." *American Anthropologist* 34, no. 3: 377–89.

———. 1933. *Hopi and Zuni Ceremonialism*. Memoirs of the American Anthropological Association 39. Menasha, WI: American Anthropological Association.

———. 1936. *Taos Pueblo*. Menasha, WI: George Banta.

———. 1939. *Pueblo Indian Religion*. 2 vols. Chicago: University of Chicago Press.

———. 1940. "Relations between Ethnology and Archaeology in the Southwest." *American Antiquity* 5, no. 3: 214–20.

———. 1994 [1926]. *Tewa Tales*. Tucson: University of Arizona Press.

Pauketat, T. R., ed. *The Oxford Handbook of North American Archaeology*. Oxford, UK: Oxford University Press.

Peckham, S. L. 1996. "The South House at Puye Reexamined." In *La Jornada: Papers in Honor of William F. Turney*, edited by M. S. Duran and D. T. Kirkpatrick, 153–69. Archaeological Society of New Mexico Papers 2. Albuquerque: Archaeological Society of New Mexico.

Peeples, M. A. 2011. "Identity and Social Transformation in the Prehispanic Cibola World: A.D. 1150–1325." Ph.D. diss., Arizona State University.

———. 2014. "Population History of the Zuni Region across the Protohistoric Transition: Migration, Gene Flow, and Social Transformation." In *Building*

Transnational Archaeologies, edited by E. C. Villapando and R. H. McGuire, 93–109. Arizona State Museum Archaeology Series 209. Tucson: Arizona State Museum, University of Arizona.

———. 2018. *Connected Communities: Networks, Identity, and Social Change in the Ancient Cibola World.* Tucson: University of Arizona Press.

Peeples, M. A., and B. J. Mills. 2018. "Frontiers of Marginality and Mediation in the U.S. Southwest: A Social Networks Perspective." In *Life beyond Boundaries: Constructing Identity in Edge Regions of the North American Southwest*, edited by K. Harry and S. A. Herr. Boulder: University Press of Colorado.

Peeples, M. A., G. Schachner, and E. K. Huber. 2012. "The Zuni Region across the First Millennium A.D." In Young and Herr 2012, 166–80.

Pepper, G. H. 1909. "The Exploration of a Burial-Room in Pueblo Bonito, New Mexico." In *Putnam Anniversary Volume: Anthropological Essays Presented to Frederic Ward Putnam*, edited by F. Boas, 196–252. New York: Stechert.

———. 1920. *Pueblo Bonito*. Anthropological Papers of the American Museum of Natural History 27. New York: American Museum of Natural History.

Peregrine, P. N. 2001. "Matrilocality, Corporate Strategy, and the Organization of Production in the Chacoan World." *American Antiquity* 66, no. 1: 36–46.

Pilles, P. J., Jr. 1996. "The Pueblo III Period along the Mogollon Rim: The Honanki, Elden, and Turkey Hill Phases of the Sinagua." In *The Prehistoric Pueblo World, A.D. 1150–1350*, edited by M. A. Adler, 59–72. Tucson: University of Arizona Press.

Plog, F. 1981. *Cultural Resources Overview, Little Colorado Area, Arizona.* Phoenix, AZ: USDA Forest Service, Southwestern Region.

Plog, S. 1986. "Understanding Cultural Change in the Northern Southwest." In *Spatial Organization and Exchange: Archaeological Survey on Northern Black Mesa*, edited by S. Plog, 224–55. Carbondale: Southern Illinois University Press.

———. 1997. *Ancient Peoples of the American Southwest.* London: Thames and Hudson.

———. 2012. "Ritual and Cosmology in the Chaco Era." In Glowacki and Van Keuren 2011, 50–65.

Plog, S., and C. C. Heitman. 2010. "Hierarchy and Social Inequality in the American Southwest A.D. 800–1200." *PNAS* 107: 19619–26.

Plog, S., and A. S. Watson. 2012. "The Chaco Pilgrimage Model: Evaluating the Evidence from Pueblo Alto." *American Antiquity* 77: 449–77.

Potter, J. M. 1997. "Communal Ritual and Faunal Remains: An Example from the Dolores Anasazi." *Journal of Field Archaeology* 24, no. 3: 353–64.

————. 2000. "Pots, Parties, and Politics: Communal Feasting in the American Southwest." *American Antiquity* 65: 471–92.

Powell, S. 2002. "The Puebloan Florescence and Dispersion: Dinnebito and Beyond, A.D. 800–1150." In *Prehistoric Culture Change on the Colorado Plateau: Ten Thousand Years on Black Mesa*, edited by S. Powell and F. E. Smiley, 79–117. Tucson: University of Arizona Press.

Preucel, R. W. 1998. *The Kotyiti Research Project: Report of the 1986 Field Season*. Report submitted to the Pueblo de Cochiti and the USDA Forest Service, Southwestern District, Santa Fe, NM.

————. 2000. "Living on the Mesa: Hanat Kotyiti, a Post-Revolt Cochiti Community in the Northern Rio Grande." *Expedition* 42: 8–17.

————, ed. 2002. *Archaeologies of the Pueblo Revolt: Identity, Meaning, and Renewal in the Pueblo World*. Albuquerque: University of New Mexico Press.

————. 2006. *Archaeological Semiotics*. Oxford, UK: Blackwell.

Preucel, R. W., and S. M. Fowles. 2015. "In Search of Embudo." *Contexts: Annual Report of the Haffenreffer Museum of Anthropology* 40: 12.

Preucel, R. W., L. P. Traxler, and M. V. Wilcox. 2002. "'Now the God of the Spaniards is Dead': Ethnogenesis and Community Formation in the Aftermath of the Pueblo Revolt of 1680." In *Traditions, Transitions, and Technologies: Themes in Southwestern Archaeology*, edited by S. H. Schlanger, 71–93. Boulder: University Press of Colorado.

Price, T. D., S. Plog, S. A. LeBlanc, and J. Krigbaum. 2017. "Great House Origins and Population Stability at Pueblo Bonito 2017." *Journal of Archaeological Sciences: Reports* 11: 261–73.

Radcliffe-Brown, A. R. 1931. *The Social Organization of Australian Tribes*. London: Macmillan.

————. 1952. *Structure and Function in Primitive Society: Essays and Addresses*. Glencoe, IL: Free Press.

Read, D. W. 2001. "Formal Analysis of Kinship Terminologies and Its Relationship to What Constitutes Kinship." *Anthropological Theory* 1, no. 2: 239–67.

Read, D. W., and F. El Guindi, eds. 2016. "Back to Kinship II." *Structure and Dynamics* 9, no. 2.

Reed, E. K. 1952. "The Tewa Indians of the Hopi Country." *Plateau* 25, no. 1: 11–18.

————. 1956. "Types of Village-Plan Layouts in the Southwest." In *Prehistoric Settlement Patterns in the New World*, edited by G. R. Willey, 11–17. Chicago: Viking Fund.

Renfrew, C. 2001. "Production and Consumption in a Sacred Economy: The Material Correlates of High Devotional Expression at Chaco Canyon." *American Antiquity* 66: 14–25.

Rinaldo, J. B. 1964. "Notes on the Origins of Historic Zuni Culture." *Kiva* 29: 86–98.

Rivers, W. H. R. 1914. *Kinship and Social Organisation*. London: Constable.

Roberts, F. H. H., Jr. 1931. *The Ruins at Kiatuthlanna, Eastern Arizona*. BAEB 100.

———. 1932. *The Village of the Great Kivas on the Zuñi Reservation, New Mexico*. BAEB 111.

Roberts, J. M. 1956. *Zuni Daily Life*. Monog. 1, Notebook 3. Lincoln: University of Nebraska Laboratory of Anthropology.

Ruscavage-Barz, S., and E. Bagwell. 2006. "Gathering Spaces and Bounded Places: The Religious Significance of Plaza-Oriented Communities in the Northern Rio Grande, New Mexico." In *Religion in the Prehispanic Southwest*, edited by C. VanPool, T. L. VanPool, and D. A. Phillips Jr., 81–101. Lanham, MD: Altamira.

Sahlins, M. D. 2013. *What Kinship Is—and Is Not*. Chicago: University of Chicago Press.

Sando, J. 1979. "Jemez Pueblo." In Ortiz 1979, 418–29.

———. 1982. *Nee Hemish: A History of Jemez Pueblo*. Santa Fe, NM: Clear Light.

Sando, J., and H. Agoyo. 2005. *Po'pay: Leader of the First American Revolution*. Santa Fe, NM: Clear Light.

Sant, M. B., and M. Marek. 1994. *Excavations at Early Pueblo Sites in the Puerco River Valley, Arizona: The N-2007 Project*. Zuni Pueblo, NM: Zuni Archaeology Program.

Schaafsma, P., ed. 1991. *Kachinas in the Pueblo World*. Albuquerque: University of New Mexico Press.

Schaafsma, P., and M. J. Young. 2007. "Rock Art of the Zuni Region: Cultural-Historical Implications." In Gregory and Wilcox 2007, 210–38.

Schachner, G. 2001. "Ritual Control and Transformation in Middle-Range Societies: An Example from the American Southwest." *Journal of Anthropological Archaeology* 20: 168–94.

———. 2012. *Population Circulation and the Transformation of Ancient Zuni Communities*. Tucson: University of Arizona Press.

Schachner, G., D. A. Gilpin, and M. A. Peeples. 2012. "Alternative Trajectories during the Early Pueblo Period in the Little Colorado Drainage and Beyond." In Wilhusen, Schachner, and Allison 2012, 101–26.

Schachner, G., D. L. Huntley, and A. I. Duff. 2011. "Changes in Regional Organization and Mobility in the Zuni Region of the American Southwest during the

Pueblo III and IV Periods: Insights from INAA studies." *Journal of Archaeological Sciences* 38: 2261–73.

Schelberg, J. D. 1992. "Hierarchical Organization as a Short-Term Buffering Strategy." In Doyel 1992, 59–71.

Schmidt, P. R. 2006. *Historical Archaeology in Africa: Representation, Social Memory, and Oral Traditions*. Lanham, MD: Altamira.

Schneider, D. M. 1968. "Rivers and Kroeber in the Study of Kinship." In *Kinship and Social Organization*, by W. H. R. Rivers, 7–16. New York: Humanities Press.

———. 1984. *A Critique of the Study of Kinship*. Ann Arbor: University of Michigan Press.

Schneider, D. M., and J. M. Roberts. 1956. *Zuni Kin Terms*. Monograph 1, Notebook 3. Lincoln: University of Nebraska Laboratory of Anthropology.

Schroeder, A. H. 1979. "Pueblos Abandoned in Historic Times." In Ortiz 1979, 236–54.

Sebastian, L. W. 1992. *The Chaco Anasazi: Sociopolitical Evolution in the Prehistoric Southwest*. New York: Cambridge University Press.

———. 2006. "The Chaco Synthesis." In Lekson 2006a, 393–422.

Service, E. R. 1962. *Primitive Social Organization: An Evolutionary Perspective*. New York: Random House.

Shah, A. M. 1974. *The Household Dimension of the Family in India*. Berkeley: University of California Press.

Shaul, D. L. 2014. *A Prehistory of Western North America: The Impact of Uto-Aztecan Languages*. Albuquerque: University of New Mexico Press.

Shaul, D. L., and J. H. Hill. 1998. "Tepimans, Yumans, and Other Hohokam." *American Antiquity* 63, no. 3: 375–96.

Sheridan, T. E., S. B. Koyiyumptewa, A. Daughters, D. S. Brenneman, T. J. Ferguson, et al. 2015. *Moquis and Kastiilam: Hopis, Spaniards, and the Trauma of History*. Vol. 1: *1540–1679*. Tucson: University of Arizona Press.

Simmons, M. 1979a. "History of Pueblo-Spanish Relations to 1821." In Ortiz 1979, 178–93.

———. 1979b. "History of the Pueblos since 1821." In Ortiz 1979, 206–23.

Smith, J. E., Jr., L. Robertson, A. Tawater, B. Jameson, and G. Osburn. 2009. *Techado Spring Pueblo, West-Central New Mexico*. Special Publication 3. N.p.: LER and Sons.

Smith, W. 1952a. *Kiva Mural Decorations at Awatovi and Kawaika-a, with a Survey of Other Wall Paintings in the Pueblo Southwest*. Papers of the Peabody Museum of American Archaeology and Ethnology 37. Cambridge, MA: Peabody Museum.

———. 1952b. "When Is a Kiva?" In *Excavations in Big Hawk Valley, Wupatki National Monument, Arizona*, by W. Smith, 154–65. MNA Bulletin 24. Flagstaff: Museum of Northern Arizona.

———. 1972. *Prehistoric Kivas of Antelope Mesa, Northeastern Arizona*. Papers of the Peabody Museum of American Archaeology and Ethnology 39, no. 1. Cambridge, MA: Peabody Museum.

Smith, W., R. B. Woodbury, and N. F. S. Woodbury. 1966. *The Excavation of Hawikuh by Frederick Webb Hodge: Report of the Hendricks-Hodge Expedition, 1917–1923.* Contributions from the Museum of the American Indian, Heye Foundation, 20. New York: Museum of the American Indian.

Snead, J. E., and R. W. Preucel. 1999. "The Ideology of Settlement: Ancestral Keres Landscapes in the Northern Rio Grande." In *Archaeologies of Landscape: Contemporary Perspectives*, edited by W. Ashmore and A. B. Knapp, 169–97. Oxford, UK: Blackwell.

Spielmann, K. A. 1983. "Late Prehistoric Exchange between the Southwest and Southern Plains." *Plains Anthropologist* 28, no. 102, pt. 1: 257–72.

———, ed. 1998. *Migration and Reorganization: The Pueblo IV Period in the American Southwest*. Anthropology Research Papers 51. Tempe: Arizona State University.

Spinden, H. J. n.d. [1913]. "Tewa Field Notes, 1913." New York: Anthropology Archives, American Museum of Natural History.

———. 1933. *Songs of the Tewa*. New York: Exposition of Indian Tribal Arts.

Sprott, R. W. 1992. "Jemez Syntax." Ph.D. diss, University of Chicago.

Spuhler, J. N. 1980. "The Hopi-Tewa System of Mating on First Mesa, Arizona: Some Biological, Linguistic, and Cultural Aspects." In *The Versatility of Kinship: Essays Presented to Harry W. Basehart*, edited by L. S. Cordell and S. Beckerman, 63–104. New York: Academic Press.

Stephen, A. M. 1936, *Hopi Journal of Alexander M. Stephen*, edited by E. C. Parsons. 2 vols. New York: Columbia University Press.

Stevenson, M. C. 1904. "The Zuni Indians, Their Mythology, Esoteric Fraternities, and Ceremonies." *ARBAE*, 1901–1902, 23: 3–634.

———. 1906–1910. "Notes on the Pueblo of Taos, 1906, 1910." MS 4842, Nat. Anth. Archives. Washington, DC: Smithsonian Institution.

Steward, J. 1937. "Ecological Aspects of Southwestern Society." *Anthropos* 32: 87–104.

———. 1955. "Lineage to Clan: Ecological Aspects of Southwestern Society." In *Theory of Culture Change: The Methodology of Multilinear Evolution*, by J. Steward, 151–72. Urbana: University of Illinois Press.

Stirling, M. 1942. *Origin Myth of Acoma and Other Records*. BAEB 135.

Stone, G. D., and C. E. Downum. 1999. "Non-Boserupian Ecology and Agricultural Risk: Ethnic Polities and Land Control in the Arid Southwest." *American Anthropologist* 101, no. 1: 113–28.

Strong, W. D. 1927. "An Analysis of Southwestern Society." *American Anthropologist* 29: 1–61.

———. 1929. *Aboriginal Society in Southern California.* UCPAAE, 26.

Stubbs, B. D. 2011. *Uto-Aztecan: A Comparative Vocabulary.* Flower Mound, TX: Shumway Family Hist. Services.

Sutton, L. 2014. "Kiowa-Tanoan: A Synchronic and Diachronic Study." Ph.D. diss., University of New Mexico.

Swentzell, R. 2001. "Remembering Tewa Houses and Spaces." *Native Peoples* 3, no. 2: 6–12.

———. 2006. "Conflicting Landscape Values: The Santa Clara Pueblo and Day School." In *Canyon Gardens, The Ancient Pueblo Landscapes of the American Southwest,* edited by V. B. Price and B. H. Morrow, 125–32. Albuquerque: University of New Mexico Press.

Szijártó, I. 2013. "Introduction: Against Simple Truths." In *What Is Microhistory?: Theory and Practice,* edited by S. G. Magnússon and I. Szijártó, 1–11. London: Routledge.

Teague, L. S. 1993. "Prehistory and the Traditions of the O'Odham and Hopi." *Kiva* 58: 435–54.

Throgmorton, K. J. 2012. "Pit House Architecture in the Puerco Valley, AD 600–900: Form, Function, and Identity." M.A. thesis, University of Colorado.

Till, J. D., and S. G. Ortman. 2007. "Artifacts." In *The Archaeology of Sand Canyon Pueblo: Intensive Excavations at a Late-Thirteenth-Century Village in Southwestern Colorado,* edited by K. A. Kuckelman. Cortez, CO: Crow Canyon Archaeological Center. https://www.crowcanyon.org/ResearchReports/SandCanyon/.

Titiev, M. 1938. "The Problem of Cross-Cousin Marriage among the Hopi." *American Anthropologist* 40, no. 1: 105–11.

———. 1944. *Old Oraibi: A Study of the Hopi Indians of Third Mesa.* Papers of the Peabody Museum of American Archaeology and Ethnology 22, no. 1. Cambridge, MA: Peabody Museum.

Toll, H. W. 2006. "Organization of Production." In Lekson 2006a, 117–51.

Trager, G. L. 1935–1937. Unpublished fieldnotes from Taos Pueblo. George Trager Papers, MS.M.005, Spec. Coll., UCI Libraries, University of California, Irvine.

———. 1943. "The Kinship and Status Terms of the Tiwa Languages." *American Anthropologist* 45, no. 4: 557–71.

Trautmann, T. R. 1981. *Dravidian Kinship*. New York: Cambridge University Press.

Trautmann, T. R., and R. H. Barnes. 1998. "'Dravidian,' 'Iroquois,' and 'Crow-Omaha' in North American Perspective." In Godelier, Trautmann, and Tjon Sie Fat 1998b, 27–58.

Trautmann, T. R., and P. M. Whiteley. 2012a. "A Classic Problem." In Trautmann and Whiteley 2012c, 1–27.

———. 2012b. "Crow-Omaha, in Thickness and in Thin." In Trautmann and Whiteley 2012c, 281–97.

———, eds. 2012c. *Crow-Omaha: New Light on a Classic Problem of Kinship Analysis*. Tucson: University of Arizona Press.

Twitchell, R. E. 1914. *The Spanish Archives of New Mexico*. 2 vols. Cedar Rapids, IA: Torch Press.

Ubelaker, D. H. 2006. "Population Size, Contact to Nadir." In *Handbook of North American Indians*. Vol. 3: *Environment, Origins, and Population*, edited by D. H. Ubelaker, 694–701. Washington, DC: Smithsonian Institution.

Upham, S. 1982. *Polities and Power: An Economic and Political History of the Western Pueblo*. New York: Academic Press.

Van Dyke, R. M. 2004. "Memory, Meaning, and Masonry: The Late Bonito Chacoan Landscape." *American Antiquity* 69: 413–31.

———. 2008. *The Chaco Experience: Landscape and Ideology at the Center Place*. Santa Fe, NM: School for Advanced Research Press.

Van Keuren, S. 2011. "The Materiality of Religious Belief in East-Central Arizona." In Glowacki and Van Keuren 2011, 175–95.

Vansina, J. 1961. *Oral Tradition: A Study in Historical Methodology*. London: Routledge and Kegan Paul.

———. 1985. *Oral Tradition as History*. Madison: University of Wisconsin Press.

Varien, M. D. 1990. *Excavations at Three Prehistoric Sites along Pia Mesa Road, Zuni Indian Reservation, McKinley County, New Mexico*. Zuni Archaeology Program Report 233, Research Series 4. Zuni Pueblo, NM: Zuni Archaeology Program.

———. 1999. "Regional Context: Architecture, Settlement Patterns, and Abandonment." In *The Sand Canyon Archaeological Project: Site Testing*, edited by M. D. Varien, ch. 21. Cortez, CO: Crow Canyon Archaeological Center. https://www.crowcanyon.org/ResearchReports/SiteTesting/.

———. 2010. "The Depopulation of the Northern San Juan Region: A Historical Perspective." In Kohler, Varien, and Wright 2013, 1–33.

Vierra, B. J., and R. I. Ford. 2007. "Foragers and Farmers in the Northern Rio Grande Valley, New Mexico." *Kiva* 73, no. 2: 117–30.

Viveiros de Castro, E. B. 1998. "Dravidian and Related Kinship Systems." In Godelier, Trautmann, and Tjon Sie Fat 1998b, 332–85.

Vivian, R. G. 1970. "An Inquiry into Prehistoric Social Organization in Chaco Canyon, New Mexico." In Longacre 1970, 59–83.

———. 1990. *The Chacoan Prehistory of the San Juan Basin*. New York: Academic Press.

———. 1996. "'Chaco' as a Regional System." In *Interpreting Southwestern Diversity: Underlying Principles and Overarching Patterns*, edited by P. R. Fish and J. J. Reid, 45–53. Anthropological Research Papers 48. Tempe: Arizona State University.

Vivian, R. G., D. N. Dodgen, and G. H. Hartmann. 1978. *Wooden Ritual Artifacts from Chaco Canyon New Mexico: The Chetro Ketl Collection*. Anthropological Papers of the University of Arizona 32. Tucson: University of Arizona Press.

Walton, J., J. F. Brooks, and C. R. N. DeCorse. 2008. "Introduction." In Brooks, DeCorse, and Walton 2008, 3–12.

Ware, J. A. 2014. *A Pueblo Social History: Kinship, Sodality, and Community in the Northern Southwest*. Santa Fe, NM: School for Advanced Research Press.

Ware, J. A., and E. Blinman. 2000. "Cultural Collapse and Reorganization: The Origin and Spread of Pueblo Ritual Sodalities." In *The Archaeology of Regional Interaction: Religion, Warfare, and Exchange across the American Southwest*, edited by M. Hegmon, 381–409. Boulder: University Press of Colorado.

Watson, A. S. 2012. "Craft, Subsistence, and Political Change: An Archaeological Investigation of Power and Economy in Prehistoric Chaco Canyon, New Mexico, 850 to 1200 CE." Ph.D. diss., University of Virginia.

Watson, A. S., S. Plog, B. J. Culleton, P. A. Gilman, S. A. LeBlanc, et al. 2015. "Early Procurement of Scarlet Macaws and the Emergence of Social Complexity in Chaco Canyon, NM." *PNAS* 112: 8238–43.

Watts, L. 1997. "Zuni Family Ties and Household-Group Values: A Revisionist Cultural Model of Zuni Social Organization." *Journal of Anthropological Research* 53, no. 1: 17–29.

Weber, D. J., ed. 1999. *What Caused the Pueblo Revolt of 1680?* Boston: Bedford/ St. Martin's.

Webster, L. D. 2007. "Mogollon and Zuni Perishable Traditions and the Question of Zuni Origins." In Gregory and Wilcox 2007, 270–317.

Webster, L. D., L. S. Cordell, K. Hays-Gilpin, and E. A. Jolie. 2014. "In Praise of Collections Research: Basketmaker Roots of Chacoan Ritual Practices." In *Archaeology in the Great Basin and Southwest: Papers in Honor of Don D. Fowler*, edited by N. J. Parezo and J. C. Janetski, 322–35. Salt Lake City: University of Utah Press.

Wendorf, F., and E. K. Reed. 1955. "An Alternative Reconstruction of Northern Rio Grande Prehistory." *El Palacio* 62, no. 5–6: 131–73.

White, L. A. 1930. "A Comparative Study of Keresan Medicine Societies." *PICA* 23: 604–19.

———. 1942. *The Pueblo of Santa Ana, New Mexico*. Memoirs of the American Anthropological Association 60. Menasha, WI: American Anthropological Association.

———. 1943. *New Material from Acoma*. BAEB 136.

———. 1962. *The Pueblo of Sia, New Mexico*. BAEB 184.

Whiteley, P. M. 1985. "Unpacking Hopi 'Clans': Another Vintage Model out of Africa?" *Journal of Anthropological Research* 41, no. 4: 359–74.

———. 1986. "Unpacking Hopi 'Clans' II: Further Questions about Hopi Descent Groups." *Journal of Anthropological Research* 42, no. 1: 69–79.

———. 1987. "The Interpretation of Politics: A Hopi Conundrum." *Man* n.s. 22: 696–714.

———. 1988. *Deliberate Acts: Changing Hopi Culture through the Oraibi Split*. Tucson: University of Arizona Press.

———. 1998. *Rethinking Hopi Ethnography*. Washington, DC: Smithsonian Institution Press.

———. 2002. "Re-Imagining Awat'ovi." In Preucel 2002, 147–66.

———. 2004a. "Social Formations in the Pueblo IV Southwest: An Ethnological View." In *The Protohistoric Pueblo World: A.D. 1275–1600*, edited by E. C. Adams and A. I. Duff, 144–55. Tucson: University of Arizona Press.

———. 2004b. "Why Anthropology Needs More History." *Journal of Anthropological Research* 4: 487–514.

———. 2008. *The Orayvi Split: A Hopi Transformation*. Anthropological Papers of the American Museum of Natural History 87. New York: American Museum of Natural History.

———. 2012. "Crow-Omaha Kinship in North America: A Puebloan Perspective." In Trautmann and Whiteley 2012c, 83–108.

———. 2015. "Chacoan Kinship." In Heitman and Plog 2015, 272–304.

———. 2016. "Dualism and Pluralism in Pueblo Kinship and Ritual Systems." *Structure and Dynamics* 9, no. 2: 252–72.

Whiteley, P. M., and D. H. Snow. 2015. "Pueblo *-tiwa* Names: Hybrid Transmission in the *Sprachbund*." *Journal of the Southwest* 57, no. 4: 525–82.

Whitley, C. B. 2009. "Body Language: An Integrative Approach to the Bioarchaeology and Mortuary Practices of the Taos Valley." Ph.D. diss., Southern Methodist University.

Wiget, A. 1996. "Father Juan Greyrobe: Reconstructing Tradition Histories, and the Reliability and Validity of Uncorroborated Oral Tradition." *Ethnohistory* 43, no. 1: 459–82.

Wilcox, D. R. 1999. "A Peregrine View of Macroregional Systems in the American Southwest, A.D. 750–1250." In *Great Towns and Regional Polities in the American Southwest and Southeast*, edited by J. E. Neitzel, 115–42. Albuquerque: University of New Mexico Press.

———. 2002. "The Wupatki Nexus: Chaco-Hohokam-Chumash Connectivity, AD 1150–1225." In *The Archaeology of Contact: Processes and Consequences*, edited by K. Lesick, B. Kulle, C. Cluney, and M. Peuramaki-Brown, 218–34. Calgary: Archaeological Association, University of Calgary.

Wilcox, D. R., D. A. Gregory, and J. B. Hill. 2007. "Zuni in the Puebloan and Southwestern Worlds." In Gregory and Wilcox 2007, 165–209.

Wilcox, M. V. 2009. *The Pueblo Revolt and the Mythology of Conquest: An Indigenous Archaeology*. Berkeley: University of California Press.

Wilcox, T. 2016. "Gobernador Polychrome Pottery as Part of a Post–Pueblo Revolt Community of Practice." Paper, 15th Biennial Southwestern Symposium, Tucson.

Wills, W. H. 2000. "Political Leadership and the Construction of Chacoan Great Houses, A.D. 1020–1140." In *Alternative Leadership Strategies in the Prehispanic Southwest*, edited by B. J. Mills, 19–44. Tucson: University of Arizona Press.

———. 2001. "Ritual and Mound Formation during the Bonito Phase in Chaco Canyon." *American Antiquity* 66: 433–51.

Wills, W. H., F. S. Worman, W. Dorschow, and H. Richards-Rissetto. 2012. "Shabik'eschee Village in Chaco Canyon: Beyond the Archetype." *American Antiquity* 77: 326–50.

Wilshusen, R. H., and S. G. Ortman. 1999. "Rethinking the Pueblo I Period in the San Juan Drainage: Aggregation, Migration, and Cultural Diversity." *Kiva* 64: 369–99.

Wilshusen, R. H., S. G. Ortman, and A. Phillips. 2012. "Processions, Leaders, and Gathering Places: Changes in Early Pueblo Community Organization as Seen in Architecture, Rock Art, and Language." In Wilhusen, Schachner, and Allison 2012, 198–218.

Wilshusen, R. H., G. Schachner, and J. R. Allison, eds. 2012. *Crucible of Pueblos: The Early Pueblo Period in the Northern Southwest.* Monograph 71. Los Angeles: Cotsen Institute of Archaeology Press.

Wilson, C. D. 2013. "The Gradual Development of Systems of Pottery Production and Distribution across Northern Rio Grande Landscapes." In *From Mountain Top to Valley Bottom: Understanding Past Land Use in the Northern Rio Grande Valley, New Mexico*, edited by B. J. Vierra, 161–97. Salt Lake City: University of Utah Press.

Windes, T. C. 1984. "A New Look at Population in Chaco Canyon." In *Recent Research on Chaco Prehistory*, edited by W. J. Judge and J. D. Schelberg, 75–87. Repts. Chaco Ctr. 8. Albuquerque, NM: National Park Service.

———. 1987. *Investigations at the Pueblo Alto Complex, Chaco Canyon*, vol. I. Publications in Archaeology 18F, Chaco Canyon Series. Santa Fe, NM: National Park Service.

———. 1992. "Blue Notes: The Chacoan Turquoise Industry in the San Juan Basin." In Doyel 1992, 159–68.

———. 2003. "This Old House: Construction and Abandonment at Pueblo Bonito." In Neitzel 2003c, 14–32.

Windes, T. C., and D. Ford. 1996. "The Chaco Wood Project: The Chronometric Reappraisal of Pueblo Bonito." *American Antiquity* 61, no. 2: 295–310.

Windes, T. C., and P. J. McKenna. 2006. "The Kivas of Tsama (LA 908)." In *Southwestern Interludes: Papers in Honor of Charlotte J. and Theodore R. Frisbie*, edited by R. N. Wiseman, T. C. O'Laughlin, and C. T. Snow, 233–53. Archaeological Society of New Mexico Papers 32. Albuquerque: Archaeological Society of New Mexico.

Windes, T. C., and R. M. Van Dyke. 2012. "Pueblo I Settlement in the Greater Chaco Basin." In Wilhusen, Schachner, and Allison 2012, 72–100.

Winship, G. P. 1896. "The Coronado Expedition, 1540–1542." *ARBAE*, 1892–1893, 14, no. 1: 329–613.

Winter, J. 1988. *Stone Circles, Ancient Forts, and Other Antiquities of the Dry Cimarron Valley: A Study of the Cimarron Seco Indians.* Santa Fe: New Mexico Historic Preservation Program.

Wittfogel, K. A., and E. S. Goldfrank. 1943. "Some Aspects of Pueblo Mythology and Society." *Journal of American Folklore* 56: 17–30.

Wolf, E. R. 1982. *Europe and the People without History*. Berkeley: University of California Press.

Woodson, M. K. 1999. "Migrations in Late Anasazi Prehistory: The Evidence from the Goat Hill Site." *Kiva* 65, no. 1: 63–84.

Woosley, A. I., and B. Olinger. 1990. "Ethnicity and Production of Micaceous Ware in the Taos Valley." In *Clues to the Past: Papers in Honor of William M. Sundt*, edited by M. S. Duran and D. T. Kirkpatrick, 351–73. Archaeological Society of New Mexico Papers 16. Albuquerque: Archaeological Society of New Mexico.

Wyaco, V. 1998. *A Zuni Life: A Pueblo Indian in Two Worlds*. Albuquerque: University of New Mexico Press.

Yava, A. 1978. *Big Falling Snow: A Tewa-Hopi Indian's Life and Times and the History and Traditions of His People*. Albuquerque: University of New Mexico Press.

Yoffee, N. 2001. "The Chaco 'Rituality' Revisited." In *Chaco Society and Polity: Papers from the 1999 Conference*, edited by L. S. Cordell, W. J. Judge, and J. Piper, 63–78. New Mexico Archaeological Council Special Publication 4. Albuquerque: New Mexico Archaeological Council.

Young, L. C., and D. A. Gilpin. 2012. "Before Chaco: Pithouse Communities on the Southern Colorado Plateau (AD 200–850)." In Young and Herr 2012, 155–67.

Young, L. C., and S. A. Herr, eds. 2012. *Southwestern Pithouse Communities, AD 200–900*. Tucson: University of Arizona Press.

Yumitani, Y. 1998. "A Phonology and Morphology of Jemez Towa." Ph.D. diss., University of Kansas.

Zier, C. J. 1976. *Excavations near Zuni, New Mexico: 1973*. MNA Research Paper 2. Flagstaff: Museum of Northern Arizona.

JOSEPH R. AGUILAR
Department of Anthropology, University of Pennsylvania

T. J. FERGUSON
Department of Anthropology, University of Arizona

RICHARD I. FORD
Museum of Anthropological Archaeology, University of Michigan

SEVERIN M. FOWLES
Department of Anthropology, Barnard College, Columbia University

DENNIS GILPIN
PaleoWest Archaeology

KELLEY HAYS-GILPIN
Department of Anthropology, Northern Arizona University, and Museum of
    Northern Arizona

JANE H. HILL
Departments of Anthropology and Linguistics, University of Arizona

BARBARA J. MILLS
Departments of Anthropology and American Indian Studies, University of
    Arizona, and Arizona State Museum

SCOTT G. ORTMAN
Department of Anthropology, University of Colorado, Boulder

TRILOKI NATH PANDEY
Department of Anthropology, University of California, Santa Cruz

STEPHEN PLOG
Department of Anthropology, University of Virginia

ROBERT W. PREUCEL
Department of Anthropology, Brown University, and Haffenreffer Museum of
    Anthropology

JOHN A. WARE
The Amerind Foundation

PETER M. WHITELEY
Division of Anthropology, American Museum of Natural History

Page numbers in italic text indicate illustrations.

Aberle, David, 16

Accelerator Mass Spectrometry (AMS) radiocarbon dating, 242–43, 244, 258

Acoma, 4, 148, *150*, 154, 224; alternate-generation equations for, 149; skewing for, 152

adjacent-generation equations, 136, 150, 153; Western Keresan and, 151

agriculture, 13, 21, 41, 44, 57, 79, 94, 278; in Archaic period, 42–43; in Basketmaker periods, 43; in Developmental period, 86; Hopi and, 28; in Kayenta Period 2, 164; MV Tewa and, 66, *67*; Zuni households and, 177, 178, 182, 192–93

Allen, N. J., 121; tetradic model of, 12, 114, *116*, 119, 136, 153, 266, 269

alliance structures. *See* marriage systems

alliance theory, 16, 18, 135, 265; Fox on, 264; Hopi and, 46–47, 264; of Lévi-Strauss, 22, 114; for Zuni kin-terms, 148

alternate-generation equations, 139, 144, 147, 153; Acoma and, 149; in Crow type skewing, 136; Laguna and, 149, 150, *150*, 152; Takic languages and, 138; Western Keresan, 149, *149*, 150–51

ambilocal households, 110, 264; Tewa having, 27, 103

AMS. *See* Accelerator Mass Spectrometry

Ancestral Pueblos, 25, 273, 278–79; in Basketmaker III, 44; ethnological homologies with, 7; semicomplex systems and, 269

Apaches, 8, 100; Jicarilla, *5*, 90, *91*, 93, 95, 278; language, 90, 99; Mescalero, 4, *5*; Pueblo Revolt and, 213, 216–18, 222, 227, 232; Taos and, 10, 90, 92–96, 99; Western, 4, *108*

Archaic period, *43*; agriculture in, 42–43; Kiowa-Tanoan in, 42–43; sodality shaman groups in, 43

Arizona Tewa: Crow type of skewing, 133–34, *134*, 136, *136*, 143, 148, 154; kin-terminologies for, 265–66

Athapaskan groups, 198; of Taos, 92–96

avunculate, 199, 275; sodalities, 275

Bandelier, Adolph, 28–30, 35, 41

Basketmaker III period: Ancestral Pueblos in, 44; great kivas in, 106, 268; sodalities in, 44, 272; tribal sodality in, 44

Basketmaker periods, 1, 4, 8; agriculture in, 43; in Rio Grande, 43–44

Big Earring Kiva, 79–80

bilateralism: descent and, 18; of Tano, 20, 267; Tewa, 9, 25, 27, 48, 267; Zuni clans and, 188

bilateral kinship: of Tano, 20, 267; of Tewa, 9, 25, 27, 48, 267. *See also* Eskimo-bilateral kinship; ma:tu'in

Bourke, John G., 28–29, 35

Braudel, Fernand, 6

Bunzel, Ruth, 176–79, 182, 184, 187

Cabeza de Vaca, Alvar Nuñez, 3

Castañeda, Pedro de, 3–4, 7; on Pueblo culture-area, 6

Chaco, 6, 7–8, 9, 204–5, 208; authority and hierarchy of, 256, 258–59; culture history of, 239–40; dualism, 252–53, 269, 281n7; Hopi and, 249–50; kinship of, 252–54, 256; kivas of, 15; Lévi-Straussian house model of, 15;

Chaco (*continued*)
  matrilineal descent of, 15, 250–51, 254,
  258; moieties of, 15, 251–53; population of, 247–48; post-Chaco era, 13, 92,
  160–64, *161*, 166–67, 187; residence of,
  250–51; social history of, 246; sodalities of, 253–56, 274; Taos and, 92, 97,
  99; trade networks in, 15; Ware on, 253,
  254. *See also* Zuni and Chaco World
Chaco Canyon, 237, *238*, 239; AMS dates
  of, 242–43, 244, 258; burials in, 242,
  243, 245, 250–51, 254, 256, 258–59;
  continuity in, 248–50; dendrochronology of, 241; Pueblo Alto in, 241, 243,
  247; Pueblo Bonito in, *240*, 240–41,
  243, 244, 247, 248, 252, 255, *257*, 258,
  274–75; Pueblo del Arroyo in, 241,
  243; revised chronology of, 244–46;
  ritual and ceremony in, 245–46, 248,
  249–50, 255, 256; turquoise in, 243–44
Chaco florescence. *See* Chaco
  phenomenon
Chaco phenomenon, 14, 106, 240, 242;
  Hopi and, 160
Chaco system, 15, 246
Cheyenne type terminology: equations
  for Zuni kin-terms, 146, 148; for Western Keresan kin-terminology, 135, 149,
  152, 153
clan, 27, 146, 270; bilateralism and Zuni
  clans and, 188; identity, 158; Murdock
  on, 27; patriclans and, 137–38; skewing and orientation of, 148; Summer
  and Winter moieties and matrilineal,
  104–5; Taos peoples and, 83. *See also*
  Hopi clans; Tewa clans
Classic Period (Rio Grande), 60, *61*
classificatory kinship system, 103, 127,
  131; Crow as, 20, 110; Hano as, 120;
  Hopi as, 110; Iroquois as, 20, 110,
  112–13; Omaha and Hawaiian type
  kinship as, 110; Tano and, 267
clown society. *See* K'ósa

Coalition Period (Rio Grande): Taos in,
  97; Tewa in, 52, 60, *61*
Cochiti, 154, *215*, 218, 234, 235n10; inspection tour at, 215–16; reconquest at,
  213–14; Second Pueblo Revolt and,
  223–25; social networks of, 228, 230;
  Vargas battle with, 220–21
colonialism. *See* Spanish colonization
Colorado Plateau, 89, 160, 167, 174, 190,
  196, 245, 273, 275, 278, 281n7
Comanches, 4, 5, 8, 90, 95, *108*
complex marriage systems, 116; for
  Eskimo type kinship, 20–21; Tewa
  having, 103
Coronado, Francisco Vázquez de, 4, 6
Coronado Expedition, 3, 4
Cristobal (of San Marcos), 226, 227
cross-cousins, 117–18, 129, 131, 136; in
  Crow type skewing, 135; in Iroquois
  type kinship, 19; for Laguna, 150; marriage, 118; and moieties, 21; in Tewa
  kin-terms, 124, 126–27; in Western
  Keresan kin-terminology, 150, 151
crossness, 11, 117, 136, 265, 280n1; in
  Crow type kinship, 19, 266–67; equations for, 113, 121; in Hano kin-terms,
  122–23, 124–26; in Hopi kin-terms,
  138; in Iroquois type kinship, 19,
  112–14, 119–20, 126–27, 131, 266–67;
  marriage and, 113; Parsons on, 121; in
  Tanoan languages, 154; of Taos, 121;
  in Tewa kin-terms, 122–23, 128, *128*,
  129, 130–31; Towa and, 144; unilineal
  descent and, 119; in Zuni kin-terms,
  146
Crow-Omaha kinship systems, 113, 127,
  130, 253, 267, 280n3
Crow type kinship, 104, 107, *111*, 112, 130;
  as classificatory, 20, 110; crossness in,
  19, 266–67; of Hano, 11; Hopi and, 12;
  matrilineal descent in, 11, 12, 19, 20, 21,
  103, 110, 114, 122, 127, 133; matrilocal
  residence in, 20, 103, 110; NUA and,

136; Pueblo social organization and, 133; semicomplex systems and, 20–21, 103, 117, 148. *See also* skewing, Crow type

Curtis, Edward S., 29, 34, 35, 64, 93

dendritic models, 86, 87, 100
descent, 11, 19, 27–28, 267, 270; bilateral, 18; Tewa, 130. *See also* kindreds; matrilineal descent groups; patrilineal descent; unilineal descent group
descent theory, 49n1, 263; Eggan on, 16, 18, 21–22, 176, 264; house society model compared to, 18; problems with, 21–22; Ware and, 22; Whiteley on, 28
descriptive kinship system, 103, 114; Eskimo type kinship as, 20, 110; kin-terminologies in, 120; kin-terms in, 110–11; Sudanese type kinship as, 110; Tewa moieties and, 21
Developmental Period (Rio Grande), 96–97
directional scouts (Tewa). *See* Towa é
Dozier, Edward, 16, 34, 109, 120, 121–22, 126
Dravidian type kinship, 137, 138, 153, 155n4, 265, 269
Dry Food people (seh t'a), 26–27, 67
dualism: Chaco, 252–53, 269, 281n7; Dravidian-Iroquois, 269; of Hopi and, 11–12, 106–7, 265; in Iroquois type kinship, 131, 269; kinship, 119; Northern Tiwa language and, 79, 94; Rio Grande Tewa and, 269; ritual, 118–19; Taos and, 75, 77, 78, 79; of Tewa, 11–12, 88. *See also* moieties

Eastern Pueblo, 5, 48, 117; All Souls Eve in, 38–39; Iberian irrigation in, 45; moieties of, 11, 22, 92, 264, 280n4; ritual for, 270; ritual moieties in, *107*, 107–8, 268; ritual sodalities in, 103–4;

social organization of, *109*; sodalities in, 11; Spanish regime and, 8; tribal sodalities of, 268; Western Pueblo and, 47
Eggan, Frederick Russell, 17, 109, 266; alliance model and, 16; on descent theory, 16, 18, 21–22, 176, 264; on skewing, 135; *Social Organization of the Western Pueblos*, 104; on Tewa social organization, 104–5
elementary systems: Iroquois type kinship as, 20–21; symmetric prescriptive, 116–17
Ellis, Florence Hawley, 7, 17, 129
equations: adjacent-generation, 136, 150, 151, 153; Cheyenne type in Zuni kin-terms, 146, 148; for crossness, 113, 121; for kin-terminology, 111–13, 121–29, 132nn8–9. *See also* adjacent-generation equations; alternate-generation equations; skewing, Crow type; skewing, Zuni; Western Keresan kin-terminology
Eskimo-bilateral kinship, 20, 21, 110; Spanish colonization and, 11; Taos kinship and, 84; of Tewa, 11, 103, 107
Eskimo type kinship, 11, 19, *111*, 112, 135, 279n3; complex systems and, 20–21; as descriptive, 20, 110; as kindreds, 20; of Northern Tiwa, 107; skewing and, 154; in Tanoan pueblos, 154
ethnicity, 15; identity and, 202–3; migrant assimilation and, 279–80; sodalities and, 273; Taos and, 96, 278; Zuni, 278. *See also* migration
ethnogenesis, 173; of Hopi, 12–13, 174; of Taos, 10; of Tewa, 52, 71, 72
ethnographic analogy, 7, 17, 262
ethnological homologies, 7, 8
exogamy, 138; Hopi clans and, 158; Iroquois moieties and, 11; Lévi-Strauss on, 116; marriage systems and, 266; moieties and, 11, 21, 117, 118, 129, 265;

exogamy (*continued*)
    moieties of Iroquois elementary systems and, 21; Tewa marriage systems and, 36; Tewa moieties, 71
extended household (Tewa). *See* ma:tu'in

Ford, Richard, 9–10, 261
Fox, Robin, 48, 118, 127; alliance theory and, 264; on Keresan kinship, 16

Gatschet, Albert S., 28
great houses: Chacoan, 15, 166, 191–93, 200, 204–5; in post-Chaco era, 162; of Zuni, 191–93, 200, 204–5. *See also* Chaco Canyon
great kivas: in Basketmaker III period, 106, 268; labor and, 190, 194; in Zuni and Chaco World, 193–94

Hano: classificatory kinship system of, 120; Crow kinship of, 11; Hopi and, 121, 265; Tewa at, 108
Hano kin-terms, 108–9, *122, 123, 124, 125,* 131; crossness in, 122–23, 124–26; skewing in, 121, 123, 124–25, 127
Harrington, John Peabody, 29, 34, 35, 55, 64, 108–9, 120, 121, 125, 126–28, 131
Hawaiian type kinship, 19, *111,* 112; as classificatory, 110
Hill, Jane, 12, 270, 279
Hill, W. W., 37
historical linguistics, 133–56
Hodge, Frederick W., 36; Tewa clan table of, 28, *29–33*
Hohokam, 164, 166, 171
homology, 1, 7, 262, 263; in Tewa social history, 51
Homol'ovi cluster, 169–70
Hopi, 5, 8, 122, 183–84; agriculture of, 28; alliance theory and, 46–47, 264; Chaco and, 249–50; Chaco phenomenon and, 160; community ritual of, 26; convergence model and,

88; Crow kinship of, 12; as Crow-matrilineal, 11; diversity of, 160, 174; as dry farmers, 4, 162; dualism of, 11–12, 106–7, 265; ethnogenesis of, 12–13, 174; Hano and, 121, 265; identity, 160, 163, 174; Iroquois kinship and, 11–12; katsina ceremonialism and, 159, 166, 170–71, 174; kinship, 266; kinship as classificatory, 110; kivas of, 26, 162, 164, 173; marriage of, 11, 117, 118, 130; matrilineal descent groups of, 11, 14, 23, 25, 26, 138; matrilocal residence of, 27; migration of, 88–89, 277–78; oral histories, 157, 159, 163–64, 169, 171, 172; in post-Chaco era, 160–64, *161,* 174; Pueblo Revolt and, 172–73; ritual sodalities of, 103; as semicomplex, 117, 118, 135, 271; Tewa kinship and, 9, 11, 48, 103, 143, 159; as Uto-Aztecan, 4, 12; Ware on social structure of, 106; Zuni and, 204. *See also* Kayenta
Hopi archaeology, 157–74; in American Period, 173; Eastern area for, 166–67; Flagstaff area and, 167; Homol'ovi cluster and, 169–70; Hopi Mesas and, 168–69, 170–71, 174; in Independent Period, 172–73; Kayenta and, 164–66; in Sikyatki Period, 171–72; Southern Area for, 167–68; Spanish colonization and, 172
Hopi clans, 157; as exogamous, 158; katsina religion and, 159; matrilineal lineages in, 26, 158; patrilateral ties of, 28; sodalities and, 158; structural-functionalist analysis of, 182–83; as totemic, 26, 27
Hopification, 12, 158–59, 158–60, 174, 279
Hopi kin-terminology, *115,* 265
Hopi kin-terms, 20, *142;* crossness in, 138; Crow type skewing in, *133,* 133–34, *134,* 138, 143, 148, 153–54; exogamous

matrilineal descent lines in, 138; as PUA, 137, 139, 143

Hopi language, 4, 12, 142–43; NUA and, 136; Numic language and, 137; Takic systems and, 137, 153

Hopi Mesas, 168–69, 170–71, 174

Hopi sodalities, 163, 164; clans and, 158; ritual, 103

horizontal skewing, 135, 154–55, 270; in Numic language, 136–37; Zuni, 148

households, 175; ambilocal, 27, 103, 110, 264; MV extended family, 69, 72; patrilocal households in Iroquois type kinship, 19–20; Tewa bilateral, 9, 25, 27, 48, 267. *See also* Hopi archaeology; matrilocal households; Tewa households; Zuni households

house society model: descent theory compared to, 18; of Lévi-Strauss, 9–10, 46; Tewa and, 47

house theory, 258

Hunt Chief, of Tewa, 54, 57–58

identity, 42–43, 209, 232, 233; clan, 158; ethnicity and, 202–3; Hopi, 160, 163, 174; Laguna, 279; Taos, 85, 94; Tewa, 51

inheritance, 23, 92, 178–79, 271; Taos, 83; Tewa, 27

institutionalized violence, 9

Iroquois elementary systems, 20; exogamous moieties and, 21

Iroquois type kinship, *111*, 130, 153; as classificatory, 20, 110, 112–13; cross-cousins in; crossness in, 19, 112–14, 119–20, 126–27, 131, 266–67; dualism in, 131, 269; elementary systems of, 20–21; exogamous moieties in, 11; Hopi and, 11–12; matrilineal, 19–20; matrilocal and patrilocal households in, 19–20; parallel cousins in, 19; patrilineal descent and, 19–20; in Tanoan kin-terms, 72; of Tewa, 11–12; unilineal descent in, 19–20

irrigation, 4; ditch diversion irrigation, 44; Iberian irrigation, 45; as moiety origin, 44, 45

Isleta, 86, 107, *124*, 127, 278, 279

Jemez, 5, 12, 45, 46, 107, *108*, 122, 124, 143–44, 236n15, 268; matrilocal residence and, 20; ma:tu'in and, 36; migrants and, 278; Pueblo Revolt and, 216, 218, 222–24, 226, 227, 230–33, 235n11

kachina religion. *See* katsina ceremonialism

katsina ceremonialism, 14, 268, 277; Hopi and, 159, 166, 170–71, 174; Picuris and, 100; Taos and, 75, 99–100; in Zuni religious sodalities, 201–2

Kayenta, 161; absence of katsina imagery, 165; agriculture and, 164; kivas, 166; matrilocal extended households and, 166; Tsegi canyon, 165–66; village, 164–65

Keresan, 4, 8, 14, 34, 86, 217, 230; Crow type skewing for, 154; Eastern Keresan kin-terminologies, 149, 153; kinship, 16; kin-terminologies, 107, 129, 130, 148; matrilocal residence for, 20; moieties, 21, 118; ritual moieties, 268; ritual structures of, 107; sodalities, 277; Spanish influence and, 130. *See also* Western Keresan kin-terminology

Keresan bridge, 108, *108*, 117, 130, 154, 264

Keresan language, 90; Laguna and, 159–60

Kewa (Santo Domingo), 5, 90, 91, 129, 206, 207, 214, 216, 217, 222, 224, 229, 230, 231, 232, 234, 235n4, 278

kindreds, 47, 49n3; Eskimo type kinship and, 20; ma:tu'in and, 35

kin groups: ma:tu'in and, 48–49; MV unilineal, 72; Taos, 81; Taos corporate, 81–82; Taos kivas and, 80 kinship, 1–2, 12, 103, 109–10, 262, 264, 273; bilateral, 9, 20, 25, 27, 48, 267; of Chaco, 252–54, 256; dualism, 119; history of studies in, 263; Hopi, 266; Keresan, 16; key principles of, 18–22; Neolithic period and, 270; of Rio Grande Tanoan, 104; ritual organization and, 15; ritual sodalities and, 16–17, 21; tetradic model of, 114, *116*; of Tewa, 9, 10, 11; Ware on, 16–17, 80. *See also* kin-terms, in classificatory kinship systems; Crow type kinship; descent; descriptive kinship system; Eskimo type kinship; Iroquois type kinship; kin-terminology; marriage systems; postmarital residence; Taos kinship

kinship theory, 11, 21, 103

kin-terminology, 11, 110, *111*, 117, 269–70; for Arizona Tewa, 265–66; descriptive, 120; in descriptive kinship system, 120; Eastern Keresan, 149, 153; equations for, 111–13, 121–29, 132nn8–9; Hopi, *115*, 265; Keresan, 107, 129, 130, 148; Kiowa, 129; Numic, 136–37; of Rio Grande, 12, 127, 131; of Tiwa, 121, 127, 130; types of, 19. *See also* Crow type kinship; Dravidian type kinship; Eskimo type kinship; Hawaiian type kinship; Iroquois type kinship; Omaha type kinship; Sudanese type kinship; Tewa kin-terminologies; Western Keresan kin-terminology

kin-terms, 11, 109; in classificatory kinship systems, 110; in descriptive kinship system, 110–11; Iroquois type kinship in Tanoan, 72; linguistic perspective on, 12; ma:tu'in and, 35–36; mother in, 20; Serrano, 138, *140–41*; Spanish, 127; Taos, 84, 85, *85*; of Towa, 144, *144*; Zuni, *146*. *See also* crossness; Hano kin-terms; skewing; Tewa kin-terms

Kiowa kin-terminology, 129

Kiowa-Tanoan family, 87, 129, 145; in Archaic period, 42–43; PKT in, 143, *145*; Tiwa and Towa in, 4

kiva groups, 78, 101n3, 107, 204. *See also* Squash; Turquoise

kivas, 44, 274–75; of Chaco, 15; of Hopi, 26, 162, 164, 173; Kayenta, 166; of ma:tu'in, 41; in mesatop refuge villages, 14; at Rio Grande mesas, 230; ritual moieties, 268; Tewa, 68, 269; of Tewa in MV, 66–67. *See also* Taos kiva; Zuni kivas

K'ósa (clown society), 54, 55, *64*, 276–77; MV and, 63–64

labor, 6, 45, 195, 249, 267; gender and, 177; great kivas and, 190, 194; ma:tu'in and, 35, 40

Laguna, 4, 151, *151*; alternate-generation equations for, 149, 150, *150*, 152; cross-cousins and, 150; identity, 279; Keresan language of, 159–60

language, 22; Apache, 90, 99; Keresan, 90, 159–60; Kiowa-Tanoan family, 4, 42, 87, 129, 143, 145, *145*; MV and Tewa, 51–52; Northern Tiwa as, 8–9, 75, 76–77, 79, 86, 90, 94, 99; NUA as, 136, 139; Numic, 136–37, 153; PKT as, 143, *145*; PUA, 137, 139, 143; Takic, 137–38, 153; Tanoan, 143–44, 154; Tewa and, 71, 90, 159; Tiwa, 76, 86, 144, 145; Tiwa language of Picuris, 76, 86; Uto-Aztecan, 4, 87; of Zuni, 203–4. *See also* Hopi language; kin-terminology; kin-terms; Kiowa-Tanoan family; Taos language; Towa

Lévi-Strauss, Claude, 16, 18, 263; alliance theory of, 22, 114; Chaco house model of, 15; on exogamy, *116*; house societies model of, 9–10, 46; incest taboo and, 264; marriage taxonomy of, 20

lineages, 28; Ashanti and, 183; ritual elite

and, 184–85; Western Pueblo and, 271; Zuni, 182–85, 186n3, 190, 271. *See also* unilineal descent group
Lowie, Robert, 7

Made people (pa:t'owa), 26–27, 54, 103
Malacate, Antonio, 226–27
marriage systems, 19, 132n7, 270, 279; cross-cousin, 118; crossness and, 113; elementary systems, 20–21, 116–17; exogamous, 266; for Hopi, 11, 117, 118, 130; house society model and, 18; intermarriage, 266; of Taos, 86. *See also* semicomplex system; Tewa marriage systems
matrilineal descent groups, 104, 279; of Chaco, 15, 250–51, 254, 258; in Crow type kinship, 11, 12, 19, 20, 21, 103, 110, 114, 122, 133; of Hopi, 11, 14, 23, 25, 26, 138; Iroquois type kinship and, 19–20; skewing and, 124; Tewa moieties and, 71; Towa and, 143–44; Western Keresan kin-terminology and, 153; Western Pueblos and, 9, 22; Zuni households as, 13, 147, 181, 192; Zuni kin-terms and, 147
matrilineal villages, 44
matrilocal households: Basketmaker III period and, 44; in Crow type kinship, 20, 103, 110; of Hopi, 27; Iroquois type kinship and, 19–20; for Jemez, 20; Kayenta, extended, 166; for Keresan, 20; in Western Pueblo, 20; of Zuni, 13, 176, 178, 181, 188, 192, 271
ma:tu'in (Tewa extended household), 25, 26, 47, 119, 264; All Souls Eve for, 38–39; calendrical rituals for, 38; death for, 38, 40; family rituals and shrines for, 39–40; Jemez and, 36; kindreds and, 35; kin groups and, 48–49; kin-terms and, 35–36; kivas for, 41; labor and, 35, 40; land distribution system for, 40; leadership in, 37; names of,

36; rites of passage for, 37–38; ritual moieties of, 9; sodality membership for, 39; summer field house of, 41–42; Tewa clans compared to, 35
medicine societies, 254–55; Zuni religious sodalities, 199, 204
mesatop refuge villages, 14
Mesa Verde (MV), 208, 269; Taos and, 99
Mesa Verde (MV), Tewa at, 10, 71, 72, 276, 280; agricultural production in, 66, 67; Ancestral Tewa and, 52, 55; archaeology and, 58, 60; contemporary Tewa society and, 69; K'ósa and, 63–64; language and, 51–52; migration and, 57; scouting activity and, 63; sodalities of, 66; war in, 65. *See also* Tewa social institutions, in oral tradition
Mesa Verde (MV), Tewa houses: bilocalization of house groups for, 60; extended-family households in, 69, 72; kivas in, 66–67; unilineal kin groups in, 72; unit pueblos in, 66–67, 71, 72, 73n6
mesa villages. *See* Mesatop refuge villages
microhistory, 208–9, 233
migration: assimilation and, 279–80; of Hopi, 88–89, 277–78; Jemez and, 278; of Taos, 88–89; of Tewa, 41–42, 159, 277; Tewa MV, 57; of Zuni, 188, 190, 191, 195–97, 203–4
Mission period (seventeenth-century), 7–8
mission villages, 14
moieties, 14; of Chaco, 15, 251–53; Eastern Pueblo, 11, 22, 92, 264, 280n4; exogamous, 11, 21, 117, 118, 129, 265; Iroquois kinship and exogamous, 11; irrigation and, 44, 45; Keresan, 21, 118; kinship, 116; kinship moieties, 116, 126, 131; origin of, 44, 45; patrimoieties,

moieties (*continued*)
107; on Rio Grande, 11; of Taos, 10,
77, *78*; Turquoise, 21; Ware on, 21; in
Western Pueblos, 11; Zuni, 192. *See
also* ritual sodalities; sodalities; Tewa
moieties; tribal sodality
Morgan, Lewis Henry, 18
Murdock, George Peter, 27
MV. *See* Mesa Verde

NAGPRA. *See* Native American Graves
Protection and Repatriation Act
Nambé, 48, 225
Native American Graves Protection and
Repatriation Act (NAGPRA), 23, 53
Navajo, 4, 5, 8, 90, *108*, 173, 213, 222, 223,
225, 227, 232, 233, 235–36n14
neolocal residence, 110
networks. *See* social networks
Nizza, Marcos de, 3
non-Pueblo Native peoples, 4, 5
Northern Tiwa language, 8–9, 76–77, 95;
dualism and, 79, 94; Eskimo termi-
nologies and, 107; skewing and, 127; of
Taos, 75, 86, 90, 99
Northern Uto-Aztecan (NUA) language,
136, 139
Numic language, 153; Hopi and, 137;
horizontal skewing in, 136–37

Ohkay Owingeh (San Juan pueblo), 28,
29, 34–35, 37, 40, 41, 42, 53, *124*, 126,
127, 129, 221, 224, 226, 232
Okhąngep'o:kwinge (Sandy Lake Place),
53, 55, 56
Omaha type kinship, 19, *111*, 112; as
classificatory, 110; patrilineal descent
and, 110, 114, 127; as patrilocal, 110; as
semi-complex system, 117; skewing in,
113, 114, 127
Oñate, Juan de, 45, 235n1
oral traditions, 7, 10, 277; of Hopi, 157,
159, 163–64, 169, 171, 172; Pueblo origin

narratives in, 53. *See also* Taos oral traditions; Tewa origin narratives; Tewa
social institutions, in oral tradition
Orayvi, 117–19
Ortiz, Alfonso, 25, 35, 48, 264; on Tewa
social organization, 105; *The Tewa
World*, 104
Ortman, Scott, 10, 45, 190, 275–77, 280
outside chiefs (Tewa). *See* Towa é
owingeh (Tewa community), 26–27

parallel cousins, 135, 155n3, 265; in Iroquois type kinship, 19
Parsons, Elsie Clews, 34, 125–26, 151,
187; on crossness, 121; on Taos, 75–76,
81–82, 83, 93
pa:t'owa. *See* Made people
patriclans, 137–38
patrilineal descent: Iroquois type kinship
and, 19–20; for Keresan moieties, 21;
Omaha type kinship and, 110, 114, 127;
Taos kinship and, 10, 83, 84, 99; of
Tewa moieties, 21, 35, 58
patrilocal: Iroquois type kinship and,
19–20; Omaha type kinship and, 110;
Zuni households as, 13
patrimoieties, 107
patrivirilateral, 280n5
Pecos, 5, *108*, 207, 218, 224, 234, 278
phylogenetic trees, 23. *See also* dendritic
models
Picuris, 76, 86, 95; katsina ceremonialism and, 100
Piro, 8
PKT. *See* Proto-Kiowa-Tanoan
pluralism, 106
Pojoaque, 41, 48, 225
post-Chaco era, 13, 92, 166–67, 187;
conflict in, 162–63; great houses in,
162; Hopi in, 160–64, *161*, 174; Zuni in,
194–95, 204–5
postmarital residence, 19. *See also*
ambilocal households; avunculate;

matrilocal households; neolocal residence; patrilocal pre-Hispanic Pueblo. *See* Chaco Canyon

Proto-Kiowa-Tanoan (PKT), 143, *145*

Proto-Uto-Aztecan (PUA), 137, 139, 143

Puebloan commonality, 4, 5

Pueblo Bonito, *240*, 240–41

Pueblo I period, 6; Zuni in, 14, 190–91; Zuni religious sodalities in, 199; Zuni villages in, 190

Pueblo II period, 199

Pueblo Revolt, 7–8, 236n17; Apache and, 213, 216–18, 222, 227, 232; Cristobal and, 226, 227; Hopi and, 172–73; Jemez and, 216, 218, 222–24, 226, 227, 230–33, 235n11; Malacate and, 226–27; Mesa-top refuge villages after, 14; micro-history and, 208–9, 233; population reorganization in, 208; ritual sodalities in, 14; Second, 223–25; social networks in, 228, 229, 230–34; Tano in, 214, 221; Taos and, 76; Tewa and, 26, 41, 208, 214, 219, 221, 226; Tuguaque and, 227–28; Zuni and, 188, 189, 197–98. *See also* Rio Grande mesa pueblos

Pueblos: contemporary, 262; Coronado Expedition and, 3, 4; discovery of, 3–5; Galisteo Basin, 60, 159, 278; historical anthropological argument for, 16–19; Hopification of, 12, 158–60; oral traditions of, 53; problematic period for, 7–8. *See also* Eastern Pueblo; Rio Grande Valley; Western Pueblo

A Pueblo Social History (Ware), 7

Pumpkin moiety/kiva. *See* Squash

Radcliffe-Brown, Alfred, 16, 49n1, 183, 184, 186n3, 263

Red Person (Taos), 93

religion, 15, 104, 272; for Zuni, 180–81, 185, 204. *See also* katsina ceremonialism

residence. *See* postmarital residence

Ridge Ruin, 163

Rio Grande mesa pueblos, 208–10, *211*, *212*, *214*, *229*; baptisms at, 215, 216, 217, 222, 233; campaigns against, 219–23; construction phases for, 212–13; fortification of, 220; inspection tour of, 215–17, 226; kivas at, 230; recolonization and, 217–19; reconquest and, 213–14, 234; Second Pueblo Revolt and, 223–25, 232; social networks of, 228, 229, 230–34

Rio Grande pueblos: Basketmaker period in, 43–44; kin-terminologies of, 12, 127, 131; moieties and, 11; ritual moieties and, 11, 21, 269; sodalities of, 275; Tano, 104, 117; Tewa, 10, 11, 28; tribal sodalities and, 21; unit pueblo of, 267; Ware on social organization of, 72. *See also* Eskimo type kinship; Keresan; Tano

Rio Grande Tewa, 10, 11, 20, 21, 25, 26, 28, 51, 57, 60, 65, 67–68, 70, 72, 103, 104, 105, 108, 109, 118, 119, 120, 121, 265–66; dualism and, 269. *See also* Tewa kin-terminologies; Tewa kin-terms

Rio Grande Valley, 4, 43–44, 86, 88, 94, 160, 281n9

ritual, 117; in Chaco Canyon, 245–46, 248, 249–50, 255, 256; dualism and, 118–19; for Eastern and Western Pueblos, 270; for Eastern Pueblo, 270; elite, 184–85; Hopi and, 26; Tewa and, 105, 264–65

ritual moieties, 9, 117, 131; in Eastern Pueblos, 107–8, *107*, 268; Keresan, 268; kivas, 268; of ma:tu'in, 9; on Rio Grande, 11, 21, 269; for Tano, 23; of Tewa, 45–46, 105–6

ritual organization, 104; kinship and, 15

ritual sodalities, 107; in Eastern Pueblos, 103–4; of Hopi, 103; kinship and, 16–17, 21; Pueblo Revolt and, 14; secrecy of, 274; of Tewa, 10, 26, 103, 276; of Zuni, 13, 14, 184, 199

Romero, Venturo, 80

Sandia, *5*, 86, *124*, 127, 278
Sandy Lake Place. *See*
  Okhąngep'o:kwinge
San Felipe, 129, 207, *212*, 214, 217–21, 224,
  227, 230–32, 234, 235n2, 235n5
San Ildefonso, *5*, 29, 34, 41, 119, 209, *210*,
  212, 219, 224, 226, 229, 231, 234
San Juan (Basin, drainage), *5*, 42–45, 57,
  65, 71, 72, 99, 104, 191, 194, 203, 275,
  276
San Juan (pueblo). *See* Ohkay Owingeh
Santa Ana, 129, 212–13, 217, 219, 220, 224,
  227, 229, 230, 232, 234, 268
Santa Clara, *5*, 34, 35, 37, 41, 53, 55, 71,
  109, 120, 128, 224, 225, 229, 231, 232
Santo Domingo. *See* Kewa
SAR Advanced Seminar "Puebloan
  Societies: New Perspectives across the
  Subfields," 6, 15, 261
SAR seminar "New Perspectives on the
  Pueblos," 7, 261
SAR seminar "Reconstructing Prehis-
  toric Pueblo Societies," 6
Scandella, Domenico, 208
Schneider, David M., 16, 146
Second Pueblo Revolt, 232; Cochiti and,
  223–25; Tewa and, 224; Vargas and,
  223–25
seh t'a (Dry Food people), 26–27, 67
semicomplex system: Ancestral Pueblos
  and, 269; bilateral cross-cousins as,
  135; for Crow type kinship, 20–21,
  103, 117, 148; Hopi as, 117, 118, 135, 271;
  Omaha type kinship as, 117; prescriptive and proscriptive rules for, 117
Serrano, 138, *140–41*
Sikyatki Period, 171–72
Sip'ophene (Tewa preemergence home),
  53, 55, 56
skewing, 12, 119, 130, 133, 279, 280n1; for
  Acoma, 152; clan orientation and, 148;

Eggan on, 135; Eskimo type kinship
  and, 154; in Hano kin-terms, 121, 123,
  124–25, 127; lineal, 11; matrilineal, 124;
  Northern Tiwa and, 127; in Omaha
  type kinship, 113, 114, 127; Taos kinship
  and, 84; of Tewa kin-terms, 126, 128,
  128, *265*; unilineal descent and, 119;
  for Western Keresan kin-terminology,
  149, 151–53, 154. *See also* horizontal skewing; skewing, Zuni; vertical
  skewing
skewing, Crow type, 12, 19, 108, 113, 114,
  121, 122, 127; alternate-generation
  equations in, 136; of Arizona Tewa,
  133–34, *134*, 136, *136*, 143, 148, 154;
  cross-cousins and, 135; Hopi and, *133*,
  133–34, *134*, 143, 148, 153–54; Keresan, 154; as overlay, 134–35; Tanoan
  languages and, 143–44; in Tiwa
  language, 144; Towa and, 143, 144,
  154; vertical, 135; for Western Keresan
  kin-terminology, 149, 151–53, 154;
  Zuni, 134–35, 145–46, 147, 152. *See
  also* adjacent-generation equations
skewing, Zuni: Cheyenne type equations
  in, 146; Crow type skewing in, 134–35,
  145–46, 147; horizontal, 148
social networks: alliance formation of,
  234; of Cochiti, 228, 230; in Pueblo
  Revolt period, 228, *229*, 230–34
social organization, 51, 72, 107–9; Crow
  type kinship and, 133; Early Pueblo, 58,
  59; Keresan bridge and, *108*; Taos, 77,
  81–83, 99; Tewa, 51, 52, 56, 57, 104–5; of
  Western and Eastern Pueblo, *109*; of
  Western Pueblo, 106, *109*. *See also* kiva
  groups; Tewa social organization
*Social Organization of the Western
  Pueblos* (Eggan), 104
sodalities, 281n8; Archaic period and
  shaman, 43; avunculate, 275; in Basketmaker III period, 44, 272; of Chaco,
  253–56, 274; in Eastern and Western

Pueblo, 11; ethnicity and, 273; Hopi, 103, 158, 163, 164; Hopi clans and, 158; Keresan, 277; of Rio Grande, 275; Zuni plural, 23. *See also* ritual sodalities; Tewa sodalities; tribal sodality

Spanish colonization, 6, 14, 120, 131; assimilation in, 8; Eskimo-bilateral kin-terminologies and, 11; Hopi archaeology and, 172; Keresan kin-terminologies and influence of, 130; kin-terms and, 127; Rio Grande mesas and recolonization, 217–19; Taos and, 76, 90, 95; Tewa kin-terminologies and, 121, 130; Zuni and missionization, 197. *See also* Pueblo Revolt; Vargas, Diego de

Spinden, Herbert J., 29

Squash (Pumpkin) moiety/kiva, 21, 233

Stevenson, Matilda Coxe, 10; on Taos, 76–77, 82, 83–84, 89–90, *91*, 92, 100nn2–3

Steward, Julian, 250, 270

structural-functionalist analysis, 13, 176, 263, 268; of Hopi clans, 182–83

Sudanese type kinship, 19, *111*, 112; as descriptive, 110

Summer moiety (Tewa), 21, 27, 36, 103, 107, 118; matrilineal clan system of, 104–5; Summer Chief in oral traditions, 54–55, 58

Summer people (Taos), 88, 92, 94, 100

Swentzell, Rina, 47

T'aitöna, 86, 96, *97*

Takic languages: alternate-generation equations in, 138; Hopi and, 137, 153; Serrano kin-terms in, 138

Tano, 8, 14, 42, 207; bilateralism of, 20, 267; classificatory system and, 267; kin-terms of, 72; in Pueblo Revolt, 214, 221; Rio Grande, 104, 117; ritual moieties for, 23; ritual structures for, 107. *See also* Taos

Tanoan languages: crossness in, 154; Towa as, 143–44

Taos, 73n3, 279; ancestral, 75, 85; Apaches and, 10, 90, 92–96, 99; Chaco and, 92, 97, 99; clans, 83; in Coalition Period, 97; colonialism and, 76, 90, 95; convergence model for, 88–89; corporate kin groups of, 81–82; crossness of, 121; dendritic models of, 86, 87, 100; in Developmental Period, 96–97; dualism at, 75, 77, 78, 79; ethnicity of, 96, 278; ethnogenetic network model of, 10; houses as unit pueblo, 95; identity, 85, 94; inheritance, 83; katsina ceremonialism for, 75, 99–100; marriage of, 86; migration histories of, 88–89; MV and, 99; Parsons on, 75–76, 81–82, 83, 93; pottery, 95, 97, *97*, *98*; Pueblo Revolt and, 76; Stevenson on, 76–77, 82, 83–84, 89–90, *91*, 92, 100–101nn2–3; T'aitöna and, 86, 96, 97; Tiwa contrast with, 77–78

Taos kinship, 101n4; bilateral Eskimo system of, 84; kivas and, 85–86; as patrilineal, 10, 83, 84, 99; skewing of, 84

Taos kin-terms, 84, 85, *85*

Taos kiva, 77; Big Earring Kiva, 79–80; kin groups and, 80; kinship and, 85–86; membership of, 79, 82–83

Taos language: ancestral, 89, 90, 92; Apache language of, 90, 99; Northern Tiwa, 75, 86, 90, 99

Taos moieties, 10, 77, *78*

Taos oral traditions, 10, 89, 90, 92–93, 94

Taos people groups, 80, 89, *91*; Athapaskan groups and, 92–96; ceremonial duties of, 81; clans compared to, 83; patrilineal inheritance of, 83; as Red Willow People, 100; Summer and Winter People as, 88, 92, 94, 100

Taos social organization, 99; kivas in, 77; ritual societies in, 81–83

Tesuque, 5, 48, 224, 226. *See also* Tuguaque, Domingo

tetradic model, 12, 114, *116*, 119, 136, 153, 266, 269

tetradic theory, 150–51

Tewa, 4, 8–9, 231, 234; allegiance order for, 36; Ancestral, 51, 52, 55–56, 66; Arizona, 133–34, *134*, 136, *136*, 143, 148, 154, 265–66; bilateralism, 9, 25, 27, 48, 267; ceremonial sodalities of, 26; in Classic Period, 60, *61*; in Coalition Period, 52, 60, *61*; defensive pueblos of, 40–41; descent, 130; dualism of, 11–12, 88; Eggan on social organization of, 104–5; Eskimo-bilateral kinship of, 11, 103, 107; ethnogenesis of, 52, 71, 72; flyover, 108, 130, 266, 270; at Hano, 108; homology in social history of, 51; Hopi kinship with, 9, 11, 48, 103, 143, 159; identity, 51; inheritance, 27; Iroquois kinship and, 11–12; kinship groups of, 9, 10, 11; language groups of, 71, 90, 159; migrations of, 41–42, 159, 277; Ortiz on social organization of, 105; proto-Tiwa-Tewa society, 87; in Pueblo Revolt, 26, 41, 208, 214, 219, 221, 226; Rio Grande, 10, 11, 20, 21, 25, 26, 28, 51, 57, 60, 65, 67–68, 70, 72, 103, 104, 105, 108, 109, 118, 119, 120, 121, 265–66; rituality of, 105, 264–65; ritual moieties of, 45–46, 105–6; Second Pueblo Revolt and, 224; Sip'ophene of, 53, 55, 56; trade of, 36; traditional ceremonies of, 55–56. *See also* ma:tu'in; Tewa sodalities

Tewa clans: anthropologist pioneering studies on, 26–29, 34–35; Hodge's table of, 28, *29–33*; as matrilineal, 35, 109; ma:tu'in compared to, 35; unilineal descent groups and, 9, 35, 72; Ware on, 48

Tewa households, 26, *69*; ambilocal households for, 27, 103; early, 67–68; house society model for, 47; kiva as, 269; nuclear family in, 69, 72; San Juan Pattern unit pueblo houses, 71; village kivas and, 68. *See also* Mesa Verde (MV), Tewa houses

Tewa kin-terminologies, 105, 107, 109, 119–20; Spanish influence in, 121, 130

Tewa kin-terms, 71, 108, 119–20, *122*, *123*, *124*, *125*; cross-cousins in, 124, 126–27; crossness in, 122–23, 128, *128*, 129, 130–31; Eastern, 121; skewing for Arizona, 133–34, *134*, 136, *136*, 143, 148, 154; skewing of, 126, 128, *128*, 265

Tewa marriage systems, 38; adoption rituals in, 36; as complex, 103; as exogamous, 36

Tewa moieties, 26, 72, 75; archaeology for, 58, 59; descriptive system for, 21; matrilineal exogamous, 71; origin of, 45–46; patrilineal descent for, 21, 35, 58; ritual, 45–46, 105–6; Summer moiety as, 21, 27, 36, 54–55, 58, 103, 104–5, 107, 118; Ware on, 73n4; Winter moiety as, 21, 27, 36, 54, 56–57, 58, 103, 104–5, 107, 118

Tewa origin narratives, 10, 52; ethnogenesis in, 71; Okhą̄gep'o:kwinge in, 53, 55, 56; Sip'ophene in, 53, 55, 56; spiritual significance of, 56

Tewa social institutions, in oral tradition, *59*, 66, 71; directional scouts in, 60, *61*, *62*, 62–63; Hunt Chief in, 54, 57–58; K'ósa in, 54, 55, 63–64, *64*, 276–77; Scalp Societies, 54, 64–65; Summer Chief in, 54–55, 58; Winter Chief in, 54, 58; Women's Societies, 54, 64–65

Tewa social organization, 51, 52, 56, 57, 104–5; ancestral, 71. *See also* Mesa Verde (MV), Tewa at; Mesa Verde (MV), Tewa houses

Tewa sodalities, 39, 48; Dry Food people as, 26–27, 67; Made people as, 26–27, 54, 103; MV and ancestral, 66; outside chiefs as, 26–27, 62; ritual sodalities, 10, 26, 103, 276; tribal, 105–6; Ware on, 65, 72, 105–6

Tewa villages: community in, 26–27; sodalities in, 26

The Tewa World (Ortiz), 104

Tiwa, 8; kin-terminologies of, 121, 127, 130; in Kiowa-Tanoan family, 4; proto-Tiwa-Tewa society, 87; Taos contrast with, 77–78. *See also* Northern Tiwa language

Tiwa language, 145; Crow skewing in, 144; Picuris and, 76, 86; proto-Tiwa and, 86

Tompiro, 8

Towa, 4, 8; crossness for, 144; Crow type skewing of, 143, 144, 154; kin-terms of, 144, *144*; matrilineal descent of, 143–44

Towa é (outside chiefs, directional scouts), 26–27, 60, *61*, 62–63

Trager, George, 10, 84, 101n4

tribal sodality, 273; in Basketmaker III period, 44; of Eastern Pueblos, 268; katsina ceremonialism as, 14; Rio Grande, 21; of Tewa, 105–6

Tuguaque, Domingo, 227–28

Turquoise: in Chaco Canyon, 243–44; moiety/kiva, 21, 230, 233

unilineal descent group, 18, 47; crossness and, 119; in Iroquois type kinship, 19–20; MV Tewa houses and, 72; skewing and, 119; Tewa clans and, 9, 35, 72. *See also* clan; matrilineal descent groups

Utes, 4, 278, 279

Uto-Aztecan: Hopi as, 4, 12; language, 4, 87; NUA and, 136, 139; PUA and, 137, 139, 143; Yumans and, 5

Vargas, Diego de, 14, 227–28; campaigns against Rio Grande mesas by, 219–23; Cochiti battle with, 220–21; inspection tour of, 215–17, 226; letters of, 209; New Mexico repossession by, 207; recolonization by, 217–19; reconquest of, 213–14, 234; Second Pueblo Revolt and, 223–25

vertical skewing, 135, 270

Vivian, Gwinn, 16

Ware, John, 9, 14, 15, 44, 131, 237, 239; on Chaco, 253, 254; descent theory for, 22; on Hopi social structure, 106; on kinship, 16–17, 80; on moiety pattern, 21; *A Pueblo Social History*, 7, 185; Rio Grande social organization for, 72; on sodalities of Tewa, 65, 72, 105–6; on Tewa clans, 48; Tewa moieties and, 73n4; on Tewa ritual moieties, 105–6

Waterflow Panel, *59*

Western Keresan kin-terminology, 130, *150, 152*; adjacent-generation equations and, 151; alternate-generation equations in, 149, *149*, 150–51; Cheyenne-type system for, 135, 149, 152, 153; cross-cousins in, 150, 151; Crow skewing for, 135–36, 149, 151–53; loan for Zuni kin-terms, 148; matrilineal descent groups and, 153; skewing for, 149, 151–53, 154; tetradic theory and, 150–51. *See also* Acoma; Laguna

Western Pueblo, 5, 117; Eastern Pueblo and, 47; lineage and, 271; matrilineal descent groups in, 9, 22; matrilocal residence in, 20; moieties in, 11; ritual for, 270; social organization of, 106, *109*; sodalities in, 11. *See also* Crow type kinship

White, Leslie, 17, 129

Whiteley, Peter, 28, 46, 75, 182–83, 268

Winter moiety (Tewa), 21, 27, 36, 56–57, 103, 107, 118; matrilineal clan system and, 104–5; Winter Chief in oral traditions, 54, 58

Winter People (Taos), 88, 92, 94, 100

Yavapais, 4
Yumans, 5

Zia, 4, 5, 129, 207, 212, 217–19, 220, 221, 222, 224, 226, 227, 229, 230, 232, 234, 235n2. *See also* Malacate, Antonio
Zuni, 4–5, 8, 160, 175, 279; agriculture, 177, 178, 182, 192–93; archaeology of, 187–207; bilateral clans, 188; Crow type skewing for, 134–35, 145–46, 147, 152; ethnicity, 278; in fifteenth and sixteenth centuries, 196–97; friendship terms of, 184; Hopi and, 204; inspection tour of, 216–17; language of, 203–4; lineages, 182–85, 186n3, 190, 271; migrations of, 188, 190, 191, 195–97, 203–4; missionization of, 197; moieties, 192; pit house villages of, 189; plural sodalities of, 23; population, 187–88, 189, 195; in post-Chaco era, 194–95, 204–5; in Pueblo I, 14, 190–91; Pueblo Revolt and, 188, 189, 197–98; religion and ceremony, 180–81, 185, 204; Spanish colonization and, 197; in thirteenth and fourteenth centuries, 195–96; transformation periods for, 188–89, *189*; unit-pueblo of, 191
Zuni and Chaco World: agriculture in, 192–93; great houses of, 191–93, 200, 204–5; great kivas in, 193–94; moieties of, 192
Zuni economy, 176–77, 188, 271; artisans in, 179–81; sheep camps and, 178, 180, 198; silverwork in, 179
Zuni households, 175, 184–85; agriculture and, 177, 178, 182, 192–93; great houses as, 191–93, 200, 204–5; as matrilineal, 13, 147, 181, 192; as matrilocal, 13, 176, 178, 181, 188, 192, 271; nuclear family in, 180, 203; as patrilocal, 13
Zuni kin-terms, *146*; alliance theory and, 148; Cheyenne type equations in, 146, 148; crossness in, 146; Crow-type skewing in, 134–35, 145–46, 147, 152; Keresan kin-terminology loan for, 148; matriline in, 147; role designating in, 146. *See also* skewing, Zuni
Zuni kivas, 195, 200–201; great kivas, 190, 194; in Pueblo II period, 199
Zuni religious sodalities, 188, 191; feasting for, 201; at Hawikku, 200–201, 202–3; katsina ceremonialism and, 201–2; leaders of, 202–3; medicine societies, 199, 204; Pueblo I period and, 199; ritual networks in, 202; ritual sodalities and, 13, 14, 184, 199
Zuni villages: pit house villages as, 189; in Pueblo I period, 190